D1641002

LIBRARY OF NEW TESTAMENT STUDIES

553

Formerly Journal for the Study of the New Testament Supplement Series

Editor
Chris Keith

Editorial Board
Dale C. Allison, John M.G. Barclay, Lynn H. Cohick, R. Alan Culpepper,
Craig A. Evans, Robert Fowler, Simon J. Gathercole,
John S. Kloppenborg, Michael Labahn, Love L. Sechrest, Robert Wall,
Steve Walton, Catrin H. Williams

THE FATE OF THE JERUSALEM TEMPLE IN LUKE–ACTS

An Intertextual Approach to Jesus' Laments Over Jerusalem and Stephen's Speech

Steve Smith

Bloomsbury T&T Clark
An imprint of Bloomsbury Publishing Plc

B L O O M S B U R Y
LONDON · OXFORD · NEW YORK · NEW DELHI · SYDNEY

Bloomsbury T&T Clark

An imprint of Bloomsbury Publishing Plc

Imprint previously known as T&T Clark

50 Bedford Square	1385 Broadway
London	New York
WC1B 3DP	NY 10018
UK	USA

www.bloomsbury.com

BLOOMSBURY, T&T CLARK and the Diana logo are trademarks of Bloomsbury Publishing Plc

First published 2017

© Steve Smith, 2017

Steve Smith has asserted his right under the Copyright, Designs and Patents Act, 1988, to be identified as Author of this work.

All rights reserved. No part of this publication may be reproduced or transmitted in any form or by any means, electronic or mechanical, including photocopying, recording, or any information storage or retrieval system, without prior permission in writing from the publishers.

No responsibility for loss caused to any individual or organization acting on or refraining from action as a result of the material in this publication can be accepted by Bloomsbury or the author.

British Library Cataloguing-in-Publication Data
A catalogue record for this book is available from the British Library.

ISBN: HB: 978-0-5676-6646-8
ePDF: 978-0-5676-6647-5

Library of Congress Cataloging-in-Publication Data
A catalog record for this book is available from the Library of Congress.

Series: Library of New Testament Studies, volume 553

Typeset by Forthcoming Publications (www.forthpub.com)
Printed and bound in Great Britain

Copyright Acknowledgements

'New Revised Standard Version Bible, copyright 1989, Division of Christian Education of the National Council of the Churches of Christ in the United States of America. Used by permission. All rights reserved.'

Septuaginta, edited by Alfred Rahlfs, Second Revised Edition, edited by Robert Hanhart, © 2006 Deutsche Bibelgesellschaft, Stuttgart. Used by permission.

Nestle-Aland, Novum Testamentum Graece, 28th Revised Edition, edited by Barbara and Kurt Aland, Johannes Karavidopoulos, Carlo M. Martini, and Bruce M. Metzger in cooperation with the Institute for New Testament Textual Research, Münster/Westphalia, © 2012 Deutsche Bibelgesellschaft, Stuttgart. Used by permission.

Unless otherwise indicated, quotations are taken from A New English Translation of the Septuagint, ©2007 by the International Organization for Septuagint and Cognate Studies, Inc. Used by permission of Oxford University Press. All rights reserved.

New Revised Standard Version Bible, copyright 1989, Division of Christian Education of the National Council of the Churches of Christ in the United States of America. Used by permission. All rights reserved.

Contents

Acknowledgments	ix
Notes on Texts	xi
Abbreviations	xiii

Chapter 1
INTRODUCTION — 1
- The Focus of the Study — 2
- Luke's View of Jerusalem and the Temple — 6
- Plan for This Study — 8

Chapter 2
THE OLD TESTAMENT IN LUKE–ACTS — 9
- Luke–Acts and the Septuagint — 9
- Jewish Exegesis — 11
- The Fulfilment of Prophecy in Quotation and Typology — 12
- Allusion and Intertextuality — 14
- The Interaction of Scripture and the Narrative — 17
- Rhetoric — 23
- Summary — 25
- Old Testament Allusions in This Study — 26

Chapter 3
LUKE 13.31-35:
THE REJECTED PROPHET AND SAVIOUR — 35
- Jesus a Rejected Prophet — 36
- A Prophetic Evocation of Restoration or Exile — 38
- The Identification of Jesus as Saviour — 48
- Conclusion — 53

Chapter 4
LUKE 19.29-46:
THE REJECTED MESSIAH AND THE TEMPLE — 55
- The Non-Triumphal Entry (Luke 19.29-40) — 55
- The Lament (Luke 19.41-44) — 59
- The Action in the Temple (Luke 19.45-46) — 68
- Conclusion — 79

Chapter 5
LUKE 21.20-28:
THE SON OF MAN AND JERUSALEM — 81
- The Fate of the City: Luke 21.20-24 — 82
- Cosmic Disturbances: Luke 21.25-28 — 93
- Conclusion — 118

Chapter 6
LUKE 23.26-31, 44-45:
THE DEATH OF THE SAVIOUR AND THE FATE OF THE CITY — 119
- Jesus as the Rejected Saviour — 119
- The Fall of Jerusalem — 124
- The Temple Veil (Luke 23.44-45) — 131
- Conclusion — 138

Chapter 7
ACTS 7:
STEPHEN AND THE TEMPLE — 140
- The Narrative Setting — 143
- Quotations in Acts 6–7 — 147
- Allusions and the History of Israel — 154
- Reading the History of Israel — 163
- The Interpretation of the Speech — 171
- Conclusion — 188

Chapter 8
CONCLUSION — 190
- Jesus the Prophet and Saviour — 190
- The Fate of the Temple — 192
- General Observations — 192

Bibliography — 195
Index of References — 217
Index of Authors — 231

Acknowledgments

I wish to express particular gratitude to my Ph.D. supervisor, Professor Steve Moyise: our discussions were always stimulating, and his insightful comments and critical judgement were invaluable in helping me to shape this project. I am also grateful to the regular members of the Annual Seminar on the use of the Old Testament in the New Testament, from whom I have learned so much; I am especially appreciative for feedback on my papers presented there.

I wish to thank Professor Steve Walton, who encouraged me in the early stages of my journey into New Testament studies; he encouraged my enthusiasm for Luke–Acts, and gave helpful guidance for this study. I am also thankful to Professor Gene Green who gave me his time to discuss relevance theory, and to Dr Peter Doble for his critique of my thesis at examination.

Locating research material can be a challenge in itself, and I wish to express my thanks to Jane Rackstraw who was particularly helpful in locating numerous monographs and articles. I also wish to thank Roger Forster for his example, support and encouragement throughout my research.

Finally, my greatest thanks are to my wonderful wife, Suman. Without her support and help I could never have completed this project; throughout my theological education she has provided for the family, and enabled me to have time for research. I am so very grateful for the sacrifices she has made.

Notes on Texts

Unless otherwise stated, all English New Testament quotations are taken from NRSV, and English Old Testament quotations are taken from NETS. Quotations from the Greek New Testament are from NA^{28}, and LXX quotations from *Septuaginta*, edited by Alfred Rahlfs.

Abbreviations

AB	Anchor Bible
ABRL	Anchor Bible Reference Library
ACNT	Augsburg commentary on the New Testament
AGJU	Arbeiten zur Geschichte des antiken Judentums und des Urchristentums
AnBib	Analecta biblica
ANTC	Abingdon New Testament Commentaries
AOTC	Apollos Old Testament Commentary
ArBib	The Aramaic Bible
AusBR	*Australian Biblical Review*
BBB	Bonner biblische Beiträge
BBR	*Bulletin for Biblical Research*
BCOTWP	Baker Commentary on the Old Testament Wisdom and Psalms
BDAG	W. Arndt, F. W. Danker, W. Bauer and F. W. Gringrich, *A Greek–English Lexicon of the New Testament and Other Early Christian Literature*, 3rd ed, Chicago, 2000
BDF	F. Blass, A. Debrunner and R. W. Funk, *A Greek Grammar of the New Testament and Other Early Christian Literature*, Chicago: University of Chicago Press, 1961
BDS	BIBAL Dissertation Series
BECNT	Baker Exegetical Commentary on the New Testament
BETL	Bibliotheca ephemeridum theologicarum lovaniensium
Bib	*Biblica*
BibInt	*Biblical Interpretation*
BIS	Biblical Interpretation Series
BJRL	*Bulletin of the John Rylands University Library of Manchester*
BTB	*Biblical Theology Bulletin*
BZ	*Biblische Zeitschrift*
BZAW	Beihefte zur Zeitschrift für die alttestamentliche Wissenschaft
BZNW	Beihefte zur Zeitschrift für die neutestamentliche Wissenschaft
CahRB	Cahiers de la Revue biblique
CBET	Contributions to Biblical Exegesis and Theology
CBQ	*Catholic Biblical Quarterly*
CBR	*Currents in Biblical Research*
CNT	Commentaire du Nouveau Testament
ConBNT	Coniectanea neotestamentica or Coniectanea biblica: New Testament Series

DJG	*Dictionary of Jesus and the Gospels*
DNTB	*Dictionary of New Testament Background*
DOTP	*Dictionary of the Old Testament: Pentateuch*
DOTWPW	*Dictionary of the Old Testament: Wisdom, Poetry and Writings*
ELL	*Encyclopedia of Language and Linguistics*
ETL	*Ephemerides theologicae lovanienses*
ExpTim	*Expository Times*
FRLANT	Forschungen zur Religion und Literatur des Alten und Neuen Testaments
FTS	Frankfurter Theologische Studien
GSC	Geneva Series Commentary
HTKNT	Herders Theologischer Kommentar zum Neuen Testament
HTR	*Harvard Theological Review*
HvTSt	*Hervormde teologiese studies*
IBS	*Irish Biblical Studies*
ICC	International Critical Commentary
ISBL	Indiana Studies in Biblical Literature
ITS	International Theological Studies
IVPNTC	IVP New Testament Commentary
JATS	*Journal of the Adventist Theological Society*
JBL	*Journal of Biblical Literature*
JETS	*Journal of the Evangelical Theological Society*
JJS	*Journal of Jewish Studies*
JLS	*Journal of Literary Semantics*
JOTT	*Journal of Translation and Textlinguistics*
Jprag	*Journal of Pragmatics*
JPTSS	Journal of Pentecostal Theology Supplement Series
JQR	*Jewish Quarterly Review*
JRadRef	*Journal from the Radical Reformation*
JSNT	*Journal for the Study of the New Testament*
JSNTSup	Journal for the Study of the New Testament: Supplement Series
JSPSup	Journal for the Study of the Pseudepigrapha: Supplement Series
JTI	*Journal of Theological Interpretation*
JTISupp	Journal of Theological Interpretation Supplements
Jud	*Judaica*
LD	Lectio divina
LL	*Language and Literature*
LNTS	Library of New Testament Studies
LSTS	Library of Second Temple Studies
MNTS	McMaster New Testament Studies
NA²⁷	Nestle and Aland, *Novum Testamentum Graece*, 27th edition, Stuttgart, 1996
NA²⁸	Nestle and Aland, *Novum Testamentum Graece*, 28th edition, Stuttgart, 2012
NAC	New American Commentary
NCB	New Century Bible
Neot	*Neotestamentica*

NETS	New English Translation of the Septuagint
NGS	New Gospel Studies
NIBCNT	New International Biblical Commentary on the New Testament
NICNT	New International Commentary on the New Testament
NICOT	New International Commentary on the Old Testament
NIDOTTE	*New International Dictionary of Old Testament Theology and Exegesis*
NIGTC	New International Greek Testament Commentary
NLC	New London Commentary
Notes	*Notes on Translation*
NovT	*Novum Testamentum*
NovTSup	Supplements to Novum Testamentum
NRSV	New Revised Standard Version
NSBT	New Studies in Biblical Theology
NTL	New Testament Library
NTS	*New Testament Studies*
NTT	New Testament Theology
ÖTK	Ökumenischer Taschenbuch-Kommentar
OTL	Old Testament Library
PBM	Paternoster Biblical Monographs
PBNS	Pragmatics & Beyond New Series
PCNT	Paideia Commentaries on the New Testament
Penguin	Penguin New Testament Commentaries
PNTC	Pillar New Testament Commentary
RAEI	*Revista Alicantina de Estudios Ingleses*
RB	*Revue biblique*
RfR	*Review for Religious*
RNT	Regensburger Neues Testament
RPh	*Revue de philologie, de litterature et d'histoire anciennes*
RSR	*Recherches de science religieuse*
SAC	Studies in Antiquity and Christianity
SBLDS	Society of Biblical Literature Dissertation Series
SBLMS	Society of Biblical Literature Monograph Series
SBLSP	*Society of Biblical Literature Seminar Papers*
SBLStBL	Society of Biblical Literature Studies in Biblical Literature
SBS	Stuttgarter Bibelstudien
SBT	Studies in Biblical Theology
SHS	Scripture and Hermeneutics Series
SNT	Studien zum Neuen Testament
SNTA	Studiorum Novi Testamenti Auxilia
SNTSMS	Society for New Testament Studies Monograph Series
SNTSU	*Studien zum Neuen Testament und seiner Umwelt*
SOTBT	Studies in Old Testament Biblical Theology
SP	Sacra pagina
Str-B	Strack, H. L., and P. Billerbeck, *Kommentar zum Neuen Testament aus Talmud und Midrasch*, 6 vols., Munich, 1922–61
StudBT	*Studia Biblica et Theologica*

SVTQ	*St. Vladimir's Theological Quarterly*
TDNT	*Theological Dictionary of the New Testament*
Them	*Themelios*
THKNT	Theologischer Handkommentar zum Neuen Testament
THOTC	Two Horizons Old Testament Commentary
TJ	*Trinity Journal*
TNTC	Tyndale New Testament Commentaries
TPINTC	TPI New Testament Commentaries
TynBul	*Tyndale Bulletin*
TZ	*Theologische Zeitschrift*
UCLWPL	*UCL Working Papers in Linguistics*
WBC	Word Biblical Commentary
WMANT	Wissenschaftliche Monographien zum Alten und Neuen Testament
WTJ	*Westminster Theological Journal*
WUNT	Wissenschaftliche Untersuchungen zum Neuen Testament
ZAW	*Zeitschrift für die alttestamentliche Wissenschaft*
ZNW	Zeitschrift für die neutestamentliche Wissenschaft und die Kunde der älteren Kirche

Chapter 1

INTRODUCTION

Jerusalem and its temple are important to Luke–Acts. Luke's Gospel has more references to the city than the other Gospels,[1] and both locations play an important role in the narrative, with many references to the city and temple unique to Luke.[2] It begins with several episodes set in the temple (1.8-22; 2.22-38, 46-49), and the climactic final temptation of Jesus is also located there (4.9-12); the middle of the Gospel is dominated by a journey to Jerusalem (9.51–19.27), and when Jesus arrives he teaches in the temple daily (19.47); the Gospel closes with the apostles gathered in the temple (24.53). In addition, Luke relocates some events into the temple that Mark and Matthew record as occurring elsewhere.[3] The concern with the temple continues in the beginning of Acts. Chapters 1–7 are located in Jerusalem with the disciples regularly teaching in the temple (3.11–4.2; 5.20-26, 42). It is only after the death of Stephen (who is accused of speaking against the temple, 6.13-14) that the narrative moves beyond the city, but even then it occasionally returns to Jerusalem or the temple (Acts 15; 17.24; 21.15–23.22).

Luke–Acts contains both positive and negative statements about the temple. It is affirmed as the place of revelation, prayer, watchful expectancy for Messianic salvation, and teaching (Lk. 1.8-22; 2.22-38, 46-49);

---

1. Ἱεροσόλυμα or Ἱερουσαλήμ occur 13 times in Matthew, 10 in Mark, 12 in John and 31 in Luke, with a further 59 occurrences in Acts. Luke refers to the temple about the same number of times as Matthew and slightly more than Mark. For details see Peter Head, 'The Temple in Luke's Gospel', in *Heaven on Earth*, ed. T. Desmond Alexander and Simon J. Gathercole (Carlisle: Paternoster, 2004), 106–109.

2. See the list of references to Jerusalem in Bruce N. Fisk, 'See My Tears: A Lament for Jerusalem (Luke 13:31–35; 19:41–44)', in *The Word Leaps the Gap: Essays on Scripture and Theology in Honor of Richard B. Hays*, ed. J. Ross Wagner, Christopher Kavin Rowe, and A. Katherine Grieb (Grand Rapids: Eerdmans, 2008), 150–52.

3. E.g. the discourse of Lk. 21; N. H. Taylor, 'The Jerusalem Temple in Luke–Acts', *HvTSt* 60, no. 1/2 (2004): 475.

what is more, Jesus and the disciples habitually meet or teach there (Lk. 19.47; Acts 3.11-26; 5.12, 20-21).[4] Yet, as Luke's narrative progresses it becomes a place where the teaching of Jesus and the Apostles was opposed (Lk. 19.47; 20.1-47; Acts 4.1-22; 5.17-42),[5] eventually serving as the location of Paul's final arrest (Acts 21.30).[6] Most importantly, Luke also records apparently critical statements about the temple in the so-called laments over Jerusalem (Lk. 13.34-35; 19.41-44; 21.20-24; 23.28-31) and the speech of Stephen (Acts 7).[7]

Stephen's speech is a significant turning point in Luke's narrative, and it focuses on the temple and the early Christian attitudes to it.[8] Effectively, it is Luke's final word on the matter because the references to pagan temples in Acts 17 and Paul's arrest in Acts 21 do not add anything significant to Stephen's argument. In explaining how the early Christian movement and the temple parted company, Acts 7 draws together several narrative and theological threads from Luke's Gospel and expands upon them; any engagement with Luke's theology of the temple needs to pay significant attention to it.

The Focus of the Study

It is the proposal of this study that Luke's temple theology in Acts 7 can only be properly understood *intratextually* and *intertextually*. The reading needs to be *intratextual* because, while it needs to be understood in relation to the entire narrative of Luke–Acts, it especially needs to be read with the sayings of Jesus about Jerusalem and the temple, principally Lk. 13.34-35; 19.41-44; 21.20-24; 23.28-31.[9] All of these have a Lukan

---

4. Head, 'Temple', 109–11; J. Bradley Chance, *Jerusalem, the Temple, and the New Age in Luke–Acts* (Macon: Mercer University Press, 1988), 82–85.

5. Geir Otto Holmås, '"My House Shall Be a House of Prayer": Regarding the Temple as a Place of Prayer in Acts within the Context of Luke's Apologetical Objective', *JSNT* 27, no. 4 (2005): 402.

6. F. F. Bruce, *The Acts of the Apostles: The Greek Text and Introduction with Commentary*, 3rd ed. (Leicester: Apollos, 1990), 16, 450, regards the slamming of the temple gates on that occasion as highly symbolic.

7. Paul also criticises pagan temples in Acts 17.24 by repeating some words of Stephen; see Steve Walton, 'A Tale of Two Perspectives? The Place of the Temple in Acts', in Alexander and Gathercole, eds., *Heaven on Earth*, 143.

8. It also discusses the law, but the prime focus is on the temple (see Chapter 7).

9. Some scholars regard Lk. 17.37 as a reference to the Roman army (Frederick W. Danker, *Jesus and the New Age: A Commentary on St. Luke's Gospel* [Philadelphia: Fortress, 1972], 183; Lloyd Gaston, *No Stone on Another: Studies in the*

emphasis: three of them are unique to Luke, and the fourth (13.34-35) has been moved to a new setting. Luke paves the way for reading these texts with Acts 7 by associating Jesus' death with his apparently anti-temple prophetic speech in Lk. 13.31-35, and then delaying the accusation of Jesus speaking against the temple until the charge against Stephen in Acts 6.14; unlike Matthew and Mark, Luke does not mention it during Jesus' trials.[10] This requires a two-way intratextual reading: Acts 7 is understood in the light of the Gospel, but the Gospel's message is completed by Acts 7. Such a reading is not without precedent, and the unity of Luke–Acts has been a scholarly consensus for some time.[11] In addition to other literary

Significance of the Fall of Jerusalem in the Synoptic Gospels, NovTSup 23 [Leiden: Brill, 1970], 353), but Lk. 17.20-37 is not primarily about the fall of Jerusalem. Like Lk. 21, it is a parallel to Mk 13 and Mt. 24, but it has been separated from the material about Jerusalem in Lk. 21; see Steven L. Bridge, *'Where the Eagles Are Gathered': The Deliverance of the Elect in Lukan Eschatology*, JSNTSup 240 (London: Sheffield Academic, 2003), 13–15.

10. Robert C. Tannehill, *The Narrative Unity of Luke–Acts*, 2 vols. (Minneapolis: Fortress, 1986–90), 2:94. Its absence from the trials is more than Luke wanting Lk. 22.66-71 to focus on christological issues, as suggested by Taylor, 'Temple', 476–77.

11. Since Henry J. Cadbury, *The Making of Luke–Acts* (London: SPCK, 1961; orig. pub., 1927), and defended in the collections of essays in Joseph Verheyden, ed. *The Unity of Luke–Acts*, BETL 142 (Leuven: Leuven University Press, 1999); and David P. Moessner, ed. *Jesus and the Heritage of Israel* (Harrisburg, PA: Trinity Press International, 1999). This consensus is seen in the vast number of monographs and articles addressing the books as a narrative and theological unit, and is assumed in many commentaries, especially Luke Timothy Johnson, *The Acts of the Apostles*, SP 5 (Collegeville, MD: Liturgical Press, 1992); idem, *The Gospel of Luke*, SP 3 (Collegeville, MD: Liturgical Press, 1991); and Tannehill, *Narrative Unity*. For a helpful review of scholarship on unity, see Michael F. Bird, 'The Unity of Luke–Acts in Recent Discussion', *JSNT* 29, no. 4 (2007); Patrick E. Spencer, 'The Unity of Luke–Acts: A Four-Bolted Hermeneutical Hinge', *CBR* 5, no. 3 (2007), and the summary of the issues in Joseph Verheyden, 'The Unity of Luke–Acts: What Are We Up To?', in Verheyden, ed., *The Unity of Luke–Acts*. The consensus is not without opposition; see Mikeal C. Parsons and Richard I. Pervo, *Rethinking the Unity of Luke and Acts* (Minneapolis: Fortress, 1993); C. Kavin Rowe, 'History, Hermeneutics and the Unity of Luke–Acts', *JSNT* 28, no. 2 (2005); Andrew F. Gregory and C. Kavin Rowe, *Rethinking the Unity and Reception of Luke and Acts* (Columbia: University of South Carolina Press, 2010). The main case against unity is made along two lines. First, it questions that there is a unified genre across both books; see the overview in Thomas E. Phillips, 'The Genre of Acts: Moving Toward a Consensus?', *CBR* 4, no. 3 (2006). Second, there is little evidence for Luke and Acts being read together in antiquity; see Andrew F. Gregory, *The Reception of Luke and Acts in the Period Before Irenaeus: Looking for Luke in the Second Century*, WUNT 2/169 (Tübingen: Mohr Siebeck,

parallels between the books,[12] Luke and Acts have a unified narrative aim through the two volumes, with narrative trajectories spanning the two books.[13] More significantly, Luke's Gospel omits some of Mark's material, but includes it in the narrative of Acts where it has more space for development, for instance, the purity law of Mk 7.1-23 in Acts 10, and the abbreviated citation of Isa. 6.9-10 in Lk. 8.10b is expanded in Acts 28.23-28.[14] All of this suggests that the two books were written to be read together.[15]

The reading also needs to be *intertextual* because of the role that the Old Testament (OT) plays in all of these texts. Far from having predominantly Gentile concerns, Luke's familiarity with and frequent use of the

2003), and the discussion in Rowe, 'History'. In response, Acts does not seem typical of any genre; instead, it is a novel genre because there is little precedent for Luke's kind of succession narrative across two volumes involving ascension and heavenly enthronement (see Charles H. Talbert and P. Stepp, 'Succession in Mediterranean Antiquity: The Lukan Milieu', *SBLSP* 37 [1998]; Charles H. Talbert and P. Stepp, 'Succession in Mediterranean Antiquity: Luke–Acts', *SBLSP* 37 [1998]; Vernon K. Robbins, 'The Claims of the Prologues and Graeco-Roman Rhetoric: The Prefaces to Luke and Acts in Light of Graeco-Roman Rhetorical Strategies', in Moessner, ed., *Jesus and the Heritage of Israel*, 65; Phillips, 'Genre'), so Luke probably deviates from typical genre conventions. Concerning the second point, reception history cannot decide the issue; see the arguments of Luke T. Johnson, 'Literary Criticism of Luke–Acts: Is Reception-History Pertinent', *JSNT* 28, no. 2 (2005).

12. Including parallel lives of Jesus, Peter and Paul, see Richard B. Rackham, *Acts of the Apostles*, 9th ed. (London: Methuen, 1922), xlvii–xlix, and the further detail in Steve Walton, *Leadership and Lifestyle: The Portrait of Paul in the Miletus Speech and 1 Thessalonians*, SNTSMS 108 (Cambridge: Cambridge University Press, 2000), 35–40.

13. For instance, the Gentile mission is introduced in the infancy narrative but only fulfilled in Acts; see Gregory E. Sterling, '"Opening the Scriptures": The Legitimation of the Jewish Diaspora and the Early Christian Mission', in Moessner, ed., *Jesus and the Heritage of Israel*, 214–15. See also Tannehill, *Narrative Unity*.

14. Daniel Marguerat, 'Luc-Actes: une unité à construire', in Verheyden, ed., *The Unity of Luke–Acts*, 62–63. This also happens with OT quotations: Koet lists Isa. 49.6 in Lk. 2.28-32 and Acts 13.47; Isa. 53.12 in Lk. 22.37 and Acts 8.32-33. Bart J. Koet, 'Isaiah in Luke–Acts', in *Isaiah in the New Testament*, ed. Steve Moyise and Maarten J. J. Menken (London: T&T Clark, 2005), 80. See also Spencer, 'Unity', 357–58.

15. Acts' preface refers back to the Gospel (see Loveday C. A. Alexander, 'The Preface to Acts and the Historians', in *History, Literature and Society in the Book of Acts*, ed. Ben Witherington [Cambridge: Cambridge University Press, 1996], 79–82, 89–92), something common in Graeco-Roman works of more than one volume; and Acts 28 functions as the conclusion to both volumes (see Loveday C. A. Alexander, 'Reading Luke–Acts from Back to Front', in Verheyden, ed., *The Unity of Luke–Acts*).

Septuagint (LXX) stems from his understanding of Jewish perspectives,[16] and it is critical that he is interpreted with this in mind, especially when dealing with something as important to Judaism as the Jerusalem temple. Throughout his writings Luke uses scripture to demonstrate how the story of Jesus fits into the larger story of Israel,[17] and the great density of quotations and allusions to the LXX in the laments and Acts 7 shows that the OT plays a central role in his argument about the fate of the city. Prior studies of the temple in Luke–Acts have not made enough of these intratextual and intertextual associations.

Of course, such a reading of the Jerusalem temple in Luke–Acts is a selective reading, but with the large number of references to the city and temple in Luke–Acts such choices have to be made. The selection of texts here is a deliberate attempt to focus on the apparently *temple-critical* material because these texts are the subject of the greatest scholarly debate when attempting to reconstruct a Lukan view of the temple. The aim is not to reconstruct Luke's temple theology, it is more limited and solely directed at identifying the focus and extent of Luke's apparent temple-criticism; this information will then be helpful in defining Luke's overall theology more accurately. Of course, many scholars have attempted to describe Luke's overall temple theology, and it is important to review their views, paying particular attention to the apparently *temple-critical* texts.

---

16. Luke is often assumed to have a Gentile focus (e.g., Hans Conzelmann, *The Theology of St. Luke*, trans. Geoffrey Buswell [London: Faber, 1960]; Ernst Haenchen, *The Acts of the Apostles: A Commentary*, trans. R. M. Wilson [Oxford: Blackwell, 1971]), though this assumption has been challenged by many, including Robert L. Brawley, *Luke–Acts and the Jews: Conflict, Apology, and Conciliation* (Atlanta: Scholars Press, 1987), and Bart J. Koet, *Five Studies on Interpretation of Scripture in Luke–Acts*, SNTA (Leuven: Leuven University Press, 1989), 156–60. Joseph A. Fitzmyer, *Gospel According to Luke: A New Translation with Introduction and Commentary*, AB 28–28A, 2 vols., (New York: Doubleday, 1981–85), 1:42 thinks Luke was a non-Jewish Semite; E. Earle Ellis, *The Gospel of Luke*, NCB (London: Oliphants, 1966), 52–53, regards him as a Hellenistic Jew. It is also possible that he was a Gentile god-fearer. Whatever his origins, it is likely that he had a diaspora synagogue background because of his familiarity with the LXX; see Ben Witherington, *The Acts of the Apostles: A Socio-Rhetorical Commentary* (Grand Rapids: Eerdmans; Carlisle: Paternoster, 1998), 54.

17. Joel B. Green, *The Theology of the Gospel of Luke*, NTT 3 (Cambridge: Cambridge University Press, 1995), 24–28.

Luke's View of Jerusalem and the Temple

There are places where Luke discusses Jerusalem, not the temple (e.g., Lk. 19.41-44; 21.20-24); although some scholars argue that discussion of the temple needs to be dissociated from discussion of the city, this is not necessary.[18] References to the destruction of the temple and the city are mutually interpretive, with references to Jerusalem often occurring together with specific material about the temple. The references to the city in Lk. 21.20-24 occur in the context of predictions of the destruction of the temple (21.5-7); and Luke 19.41-44 needs to be interpreted in the light of the temple action (19.45-46). In any case, it is difficult to differentiate the temple and Jerusalem theologically: the city is special because the temple is its social/cultural/religious organising focus. One cannot conceive of a destroyed city without God's abandonment of the temple, and one cannot consider a desecrated temple having no effect on Jerusalem.[19] The discussion of the temple therefore needs to be taken together with the discussion of the city.

For some scholars, Luke is uniformly positive about the temple. For example, Francis Weinert regards it as a place of communication and communion,[20] and Bradley Chance describes the temple achieving its eschatological fulfilment (without being replaced) as Jesus enters the temple in Luke 19 and makes it his own.[21] But their engagement with the more critical material is limited: Chance does not examine Acts 7 and all of the laments, and although Weinert examines them, he does so through his positive interpretive grid.[22]

A longer list of scholars regards Luke as more negative about the temple. According to Klaus Baltzer, the temple was replaced by Jesus; he argues that as Jesus was present in the temple so the glory was present

---

18. Notably Conzelmann, *Theology*, 74–79; Peter W. L. Walker, *Jesus and the Holy City: New Testament Perspectives on Jerusalem* (Grand Rapids: Eerdmans, 1996), 57–112 (who separates the temple and city in the laments but reviews the data together); Head, 'Temple', 106–109.

19. Chance, *Jerusalem*, 2.

20. Francis. D. Weinert, 'The Meaning of the Temple in Luke–Acts', *BTB* 11 (1981); 'Luke, the Temple, and Jesus' Saying About Jerusalem's Abandoned House', *CBQ* 44 (1982); 'Luke, Stephen, and the Temple in Luke–Acts', *BTB* 17, no. 3 (1987).

21. Chance (*Jerusalem*) maintains that Jerusalem is the hub of the church's mission. Chance is followed by Ron C. Fay, 'The Narrative Function of the Temple in Luke–Acts', *TJ* 27, no. 2 (2006).

22. As does Cyprian Robert Hutcheon, '"God Is with Us": The Temple in Luke–Acts', *SVTQ* 44, no. 1 (2000).

(arguing his case by reading Luke in the light of Ezekiel); but he does not focus on the laments and Stephen's speech.[23] Most others emphasise that Jesus was rejected: Hans Conzelmann argues that the temple became a profane building, destined for destruction after the rejection of Jesus (who occupied the temple as its rightful owner after cleansing it).[24] Cornelius van de Waal also emphasises rejection, but although his account observes patterns between the Gospel and Acts, he does not explore the laments and Acts 7.[25] Charles Giblin does examine the laments and is sensitive to the development of the narrative,[26] but his study does not give enough emphasis to Acts 7. He does not think it expands on the Gospel judgements because it has no prediction of destruction of the temple; therefore, he only gives it five pages in an appendix without sufficient attention to the OT background.[27] Nicholas Taylor does review the laments and Acts 7 as part of a wider review of the temple in Luke–Acts, and notes that Acts 6–7 establishes the link between the absence of the divine in the temple and the rejection of Jesus, but Acts 7 is not interpreted in the light of the Gospel.[28] Peter Walker examines the whole of the narrative of Luke–Acts and argues that Luke's original positive description of the temple at the beginning of the Gospel is reversed as he shows how it has failed (beginning with Lk. 13.35); similarly, Acts 7 is not opposed to what the temple was, but to what it has become. This work is significant because of the emphasis that he gives to the four laments and Acts 7; nevertheless, he does not clearly refer back to the laments in order to interpret the content of Acts 7, and he does not give adequate focus to the use of the OT.[29] More

---

23. He notes that Acts 7 is important but has no space to explore it; see Klaus Baltzer, 'The Meaning of the Temple in the Lukan Writings', *HTR* 58, no. 3 (1965).

24. Conzelmann, *Theology*, 75–78.

25. C. Van der Waal, 'The Temple in the Gospel According to Luke', *Neot* 7 (1973).

26. Luke 13.34-35 is mainly discussed as part of the narrative background to the other texts; see Charles H. Giblin, *The Destruction of Jerusalem According to Luke's Gospel: A Historical-Typological Moral* (Rome: Biblical Institute Press, 1985), esp. 4–5.

27. Ibid., 108–12.

28. N. H. Taylor, 'Stephen, the Temple, and Early Christian Eschatology', *RB* 110, no. 1 (2003); 'Luke–Acts and the Temple', in Verheyden, ed., *The Unity of Luke–Acts*; and 'Temple'.

29. He notes the use of Isaiah and 1 Kgs 8 in Acts 7, and notes Dodd's view of the use of prophetic texts in the laments; see C. H. Dodd, 'The Fall of Jerusalem and the "Abomination of Desolation"', in *More New Testament Studies*, ed. C. H. Dodd (Manchester: Manchester University Press, 1968). But the intertextual relationships to these texts is not really explored; see Walker, *Jesus*, 57–112.

recently, Peter Head (on Luke) and Steve Walton (on Acts) contribute chapters to a volume on the temple in biblical theology. In Luke, the temple is seen as the place for prayer and revelation especially in the light of the eschatological events of Jesus life, but it is under judgement because of the rejection of Jesus.[30] Walton evaluates how Stephen's speech offers a critique of the Jerusalem temple before demonstrating how the function of the temple is taken over by Jesus.[31] While both recognise the importance of the Acts narrative in understanding the Gospel, no link is made between Acts 7 and the laments because of the format of the separate essays.

Plan for This Study

There is a need to detail Luke's apparently temple-critical material by investigating Jesus' sayings together with their expansion in Acts 7, and to do this in relation to the use of the OT in these texts. By examining the overall message of Luke's critical material over the temple it is possible to give more precise definition to what is being criticised, and this is important information for the debate over Luke's overall view of the temple.

This study will pursue this objective in the following way. Chapter 2 will engage with the scholarship on Luke's use of the OT in order to define how to examine the Lukan material against its OT allusions. Chapters 3–6 will engage sequentially with Jesus' sayings about the fate of Jerusalem and its temple (Lk. 13.34-35; 19.41-44; 21.20-24; 23.28-31). Chapter 7 examines Acts 7, with a particular focus on how it interacts with the texts in Luke's Gospel.

---

30. Head, 'Temple', 109–19.
31. Walton, 'Tale'. Reitzel also emphasises that Jesus replaces the temple in Luke–Acts, demonstrating this with a fanciful sevenfold division of the narrative; see Frank X. Reitzel, 'St. Luke's Use of the Temple Image', *RfR* 38, no. 4 (1979). Also note Barrett who argues that Luke is inconsistent in Acts with regard to the temple. C. K. Barrett, 'Attitudes to the Temple in the Acts of the Apostles', in *Templum Amicitiae: Essays on the Second Temple Presented to Ernst Bammel*, ed. William Horbury, JSNTSup 48 (Sheffield: JSOT, 1991).

Chapter 2

THE OLD TESTAMENT IN LUKE–ACTS

Luke's use of the OT has been the subject of much scholarly discussion.[1] Attention has focused on different aspects, broadly following a shift in methodological interests from textual and historical-critical to literary approaches,[2] with attention moving from the Lukan *Vorlage*, to quotation, allusion and literary patterns. Many of these approaches have made significant contributions to our understanding of Lukan use of the OT, but no single one is capable of providing a comprehensive description of Lukan hermeneutics. This is usually because they examine an aspect of Luke's textual re-use to the exclusion of others. It is helpful to review the most significant contributions before detailing the approach taken in this study.

Luke–Acts and the Septuagint

It is generally accepted that Luke used a Greek OT related to what is today identified as the LXX in the Alexandrian form.[3] His citations are typically

---

1. No title for the text which Luke quoted is without difficulty. Nevertheless despite its anachronistic nature, 'Old Testament' is perhaps the simplest term to use; see the discussion in Dennis L. Stamps, 'The Use of the Old Testament in the New Testament as a Rhetorical Device: A Methodological Proposal', in *Hearing the Old Testament in the New Testament*, ed. Stanley E. Porter, MNTS (Grand Rapids: Eerdmans, 2006), 10–11. For a helpful review older scholarship of Luke's use of the OT, see Darrell L. Bock, *Proclamation from Prophecy and Pattern: Lucan Old Testament Christology*, JSNTSup 12 (Sheffield: JSOT, 1987), 13–46; for recent summaries see David W. Pao and Eckhard J. Schnabel, 'Luke', in *Commentary on the New Testament Use of the Old Testament*, ed. G. K. Beale and D. A. Carson (Grand Rapids: Baker Academic, 2007), 251–53, and, in the same volume, I. Howard Marshall, 'Acts', 513–27.

2. An observation made by Peter Mallen, *The Reading and Transformation of Isaiah in Luke–Acts*, LNTS 367 (London: T&T Clark, 2008), 4.

3. William K. L. Clarke, 'The Use of the Septuagint in Acts', in *The Beginnings of Christianity*, ed. F. J. Foakes Jackson and Kirsopp Lake, 5 vols. (London: Macmillan,

close to the LXX, and where the LXX and the Hebrew Masoretic text (MT) differ he follows the LXX (e.g., the citation of Amos 9.11-12 in Acts 15.16-18).[4] The occasions where the quotations differ from known Greek MSS (notably Lk. 2.23; 7.27; 8.10; 20.38; Acts 4.11; 7.7b) are either explained by lapses in memory, Lukan theological necessity, or use of an alternative text; it is difficult to decide between these options.[5] Although it is possible that Luke was making use of early Christian collections of texts,[6] there is no clear evidence of testimonia use in the texts under consideration in this study.[7] For this reason, this study engages with

---

1920–33). See also the discussion in Bock, *Proclamation*, 13–16; Joseph A. Fitzmyer, 'The Use of the Old Testament in Luke–Acts', *SBLSP* 31 (1992): 533–34; Luke Timothy Johnson, *Septuagintal Midrash in the Speeches of Acts (the Pere Marquette Lecture in Theology 2002)* (Milwaukee: Marquette University Press, 2002), 13–18, 47–51.

4. Tim McLay, *The Use of the Septuagint in New Testament Research* (Grand Rapids: Eerdmans, 2003), 17–23.

5. Helmer Ringgren, 'Luke's Use of the Old Testament', *HTR* 79 (1986): 229, suggests faulty memory; McLay, *Use*, 27–28, discusses alternative MSS. See Fitzmyer, 'Use', 534, for the list of texts; others are added by Max Wilcox, 'The Old Testament in Acts 1–15', *AusBR* 4 (1956).

6. I.e., testimonia; see J. Rendel Harris, *Testimonies*, 2 vols. (Cambridge: Cambridge University Press, 1916); Martin C. Albl, *And Scripture Cannot Be Broken: The Form and Function of the Early Christian Testimonia Collections*, NovTSup 96 (Leiden: Brill, 1999). For oral testimonia the classic description is C. H. Dodd, *According to the Scriptures: The Sub-Structure of New Testament Theology* (London: Fontana, 1952).

7. It is possible that a tradition of texts could lie behind the eschatological discourse in Lk. 21, Lars Hartman, *Prophecy Interpreted: The Formation of Some Jewish Apocalyptic Texts and of the Eschatological Discourse Mark 13*, ConBNT 1 (Lund: Gleerup, 1966); David Wenham, *The Rediscovery of Jesus Eschatological Discourse*, Gospel Perspectives 4 (Sheffield: JSOT, 1984), 51–134, 75–218; Allan J. McNicol, *Jesus' Directions for the Future: A Source and Redaction-History Study of the Use of the Eschatological Traditions in Paul and in the Synoptic Accounts of Jesus' Last Eschatological Discourse*, NGS 9 (Macon: Mercer, 1996), 67–192. E.g., the use of the OT in Revelation and the eschatological discourse might be based on some common tradition, with Zech. 12.3 LXX and Dan. 8.13 used by both Lk. 21.24b and Rev. 11.2b; see Paul T. Penley, *The Common Tradition Behind Synoptic Sayings of Judgment and John's Apocalypse: An Oral Interpretive Tradition of OT Prophetic Material*, LNTS 424 (London: T&T Clark, 2010), 90–99. However, is difficult to disentangle any such textual tradition behind Lk. 21 from dependence on the Jesus tradition, and there is no clear evidence of a testimonia behind Lk. 21.20-28. The most helpful criteria for identifying that a quotation comes from a *collection* are described in Albl, *Scripture*, 66–67.

Luke's use of the LXX, not the MT.⁸ Rahlfs LXX is used throughout, and the New English Translation of the Septuagint is used for all translations of the OT.

Jewish Exegesis

Part of the discussion of the place of Jewish forms of exegesis in Luke's use of the OT has centred on the role of *midrash*.⁹ Although this debate has been complicated by different definitions of midrash,¹⁰ the conclusions are relatively clear: Luke's Gospel might use some midrashic elements in order to interpret the life of Jesus through OT texts, but it is not a midrash itself because the Gospel is not primarily an interpretation of the OT – it is an account of Jesus' life.¹¹ In addition to midrash, Charles Kimball notes that the Lukan Jesus uses many of the exegetical techniques common to the Judaism of his time, using introductory formulae, *pesher*-like formulae, and two of Hillel's exegetical rules (*gezerah shawah*, and *bin 'ab mikatub 'ehad*).¹² But the Lukan Jesus differs from contemporary

---

8. A similar approach is taken by others, e.g., Kenneth D. Litwak, *Echoes of Scripture in Luke–Acts: Telling the History of God's People Intertextually*, JSNTSup 282 (London: T&T Clark, 2005), 6–7; James A. Meek, *The Gentile Mission in Old Testament Citations in Acts: Text, Hermeneutic, and Purpose*, LNTS 385 (London: T&T Clark, 2008), 4–5; Mallen, *Transformation*, 4–5.

9. For detail on Jewish exegesis see Craig A. Evans, 'Midrash', in *DJG*, 544–48; David Instone Brewer, *Techniques and Assumptions in Jewish Exegesis before 70 CE* (Tübingen: Mohr, 1992).

10. For *Midrash* see Instone Brewer, *Techniques*, 3.

11. Craig A. Evans and James A. Sanders, 'Gospels and Midrash: An Introduction to Luke and Scripture', in *Luke and Scripture: The Function of Sacred Tradition in Luke–Acts*, ed. Craig A. Evans and James A. Sanders (Minneapolis: Fortress, 1993), 1–4; Craig A. Evans, 'Luke and the Rewritten Bible: Aspects of Lukan Hagiography', in *The Pseudepigrapha and Early Biblical Interpretation*, ed. James H. Charlesworth and Craig A. Evans, JSPSup 14 (Sheffield: JSOT, 1993); Bock, *Proclamation*, 18–19; E. Earle Ellis, *The Old Testament in Early Christianity: Canon and Interpretation in the Light of Modern Research* (Tübingen: J. C. B. Mohr [Paul Siebeck], 1991), 91–101. It was argued by John Drury, *Tradition and Design in Luke's Gospel: A Study in Early Christian Historiography* (Atlanta: John Knox, 1976), esp. 48, that Luke uses midrashic creation from the OT to fill in gaps in Mark and Matthew, but this is widely criticised; see Charles A. Kimball, *Jesus' Exposition of the Old Testament in Luke's Gospel*, JSNTSup 94 (Sheffield: JSOT, 1994), 19–21 esp. n. 24.

12. Kimball, *Exposition*, 197–99.

Judaism by producing radically different interpretations, with abbreviated and less stylised application.[13] It is, perhaps, no surprise that these techniques are present if Luke is reproducing the Jesus tradition, and Luke was also familiar with such techniques from the synagogue.[14] However, such techniques do not give a complete account of Luke's use of scripture; Kimball's specific focus highlights the Jewish exegetical approaches to the OT in particular texts, but there are other approaches to the OT elsewhere in Luke–Acts.

The Fulfilment of Prophecy in Quotation and Typology

For many scholars the main Lukan use of the OT is in the fulfilment of prophecy. Their attention has usually been fixed on quotations and texts which demonstrate that Jesus is the promised Messiah, and Luke was thought to be using the OT with a christocentric and apologetic *proof-from-prophecy* or *promise–fulfilment* hermeneutic.[15] While different scholars use different terminology to refer to the process, they fundamentally agree that Luke uses the OT to show how it is fulfilled in the events (or people) of Luke–Acts.[16] They are right that fulfilment is present in

---

13. Ibid., 200.
14. C. K. Barrett, 'Luke/Acts', in *It Is Written: Scripture Citing Scripture: Essays in Honour of Barnabas Lindars*, ed. D. A. Carson and H. G. M. Williamson (Cambridge: Cambridge University Press, 1988), 241–42.
15. Conzelmann, *Theology*, 157–62; Cadbury, *Making*, 303–305, and its classic presentation in Paul Schubert, 'The Structure and Significance of Luke 24', in *Neutestamentliche Studien Für Rudolf Bultmann*, ed. Walther Eltester, BZNW 21 (Berlin: Töpelmann, 1957), 173–86.
16. While some have distinguished between scripture's apologetic function and proof from prophecy function, Barrett is surely right that they amount to the same thing: Barrett, 'Luke/Acts'. For older studies, see Nils A. Dahl, 'The Story of Abraham in Luke–Acts', in *Studies in Luke–Acts: Essays Presented in Honor of Paul Schubert*, ed. Leander E. Keck and J. Louis Martyn (Nashville: Abingdon, 1966); Jacques Dupont, *Études sur Les Actes des Apôtres*, LD (Paris: Éditions du Cerf, 1967); and the discussion and bibliography in Bock, *Proclamation*, 27–37. More recent contributions include Fitzmyer, 'Use', 537; Brigid C. Frein, 'Narrative Predictions, Old Testament Prophecies and Luke's Sense of Fulfilment', *NTS* 40, no. 1 (1994); Kimball, *Exposition*; Gert J. Steyn, *Septuagint Quotations in the Context of the Petrine and Pauline Speeches of the Acta Apostolorum*, CBET (Kampen: Kok Pharos, 1995); William Kurz, 'Promise and Fulfilment in Hellenistic Jewish Narratives and in Luke and Acts', in Moessner, ed., *Jesus and the Heritage of Israel*; Stanley E. Porter, 'Scripture Justifies Mission: The Use of the Old Testament in Luke–Acts', in Porter, ed., *Hearing the Old Testament in the New Testament*; Meek, *Mission*.

many texts (e.g., Isa. 61.1-2 is fulfilled in Lk. 4.18-21, and Isa. 53.12 in Lk. 22.37),[17] and right that Luke is interested in fulfilled prophecy (he reports prophecies which are fulfilled later in his narrative),[18] but this does not make prophecy fulfilment the *only* theme of Lukan hermeneutics or even the *major* theme.[19] Quotations are used for other purposes too.[20] Those scholars who argue that fulfilment is universally present have generally concentrated on certain types of text. For example, Darrell Bock examines christological texts in Luke–Acts because he regards this as the most important Lukan OT usage,[21] but such selectivity limits the usefulness of his study in describing Luke's overall hermeneutical approach.

Where fulfilment is present there are three aspects of Luke's approach to note. First, the OT texts which Luke seems to regard as predictive were not universally accepted in the same way by his contemporaries. As Kenneth Litwak points out, in Luke 24 it is notable that Jesus explained the scriptures to the disciples, he did *not* explain the events and how they fitted with any prior understanding of scripture; he offered a new hermeneutical lens (his death and resurrection) with which to interpret texts not understood in this way before.[22] Second, some OT texts are not used to show fulfilment in Luke's narrative; instead, they achieve a fulfilment beyond Luke's time; in such cases the people of the narrative still have

---

17. Robert L. Brawley, *Text to Text Pours Forth Speech: Voices of Scripture in Luke–Acts*, ISBL (Bloomington: Indiana University Press, 1995), 58.

18. Luke 1.13-17, 67-79, 26-37; 9.22, 44; 24.48-49; Acts 11.27-28a: Charles H. Talbert, 'Promise and Fulfilment in Lucan Theology', in *Luke–Acts: New Perspectives from the Society of Biblical Literature Seminar*, ed. Charles H. Talbert (New York: Crossroad, 1984), 94–95.

19. Ibid.

20. In categorising quotations, James Meek identified 44 of 78 texts as prophetic, see Meek, *Mission*, 14–20. Despite his focus on fulfilment, Martin Rese noted that the OT can be used to offer an explanation of an NT event (his *hermeneutical* category, discussing Joel in Acts 2.17-21); see Martin Rese, *Alttestamentliche Motive in der Christologie des Lukas*, SNT 1 (Gütersloh: G. Mohn, 1969), 36–38.

21. Bock, *Proclamation*.

22. Litwak, *Echoes*, 118–19. This argument is part of Litwak's attempt to prove that there is no promise–fulfilment in Luke–Acts, something he achieves, in part, by devising a restrictive definition of promise-fulfilment and then undermining it (15–17). Others make similar points. Donald H. Juel, *Messianic Exegesis: Christological Interpretation of the Old Testament in Early Christianity* (Philadelphia: Fortress, 1988), 173; Richard B. Hays, *Reading Backwards: Figural Christology and the Fourfold Gospel Witness* (Waco: Baylor University Press, 2014), 55–57; and, especially in texts about messianic suffering, Mallen, *Transformation*, 177.

a response to make to the words of the prophecy.²³ Third, although it is possible to show where a text seems to function as showing fulfilment of prophecy, it does not follow that this is what Luke *meant* by using that prophecy (i.e. that he meant to use the prophecy as a proof).²⁴ To assume this, as Charles Talbert observes, is to see prophecy abstracted from its first-century audience who could regard prophecy as having a role in requiring ethical behaviour as well as in simply proving something.²⁵

Typology can also emphasise the role of scripture fulfilment, and Rebecca Denova places it as part of the eschatological fulfilment of the promises made to Israel within Luke–Acts.²⁶ For her, certain traits present in OT characters or events are typologically fulfilled in the Lukan narrative (e.g., Lk. 4.16-30 begins a development of a theme of rejection with Jesus as a type of the Elijah figure, and the apostles successors like Elisha). Luke's scripture citations play a crucial role in emphasising the precedent for such typological fulfilment.²⁷ Like Darrell Bock, she has shown that typology is present in places in Luke–Acts,²⁸ yet her study contains some unconvincing typological links,²⁹ and her emphasis on it fails to persuade, in part, because of textual selectivity.

Allusion and Intertextuality

Others take a more literary approach and emphasise the complex networks of allusions to the OT, from explicit quotation through to subtle allusion. While the term *intertextuality* is often used to describe such relationships, in NT studies this term has moved some way from the original description

---

23. Steyn, *Quotations*, 232; Craig A. Evans, 'Old Testament in the Gospels', in *DJG*, 586–87.

24. That would be a confusion of emic and etic approaches, for which see Steve Moyise, *Evoking Scripture: Seeing the Old Testament in the New* (London: T&T Clark, 2008), 126 n. 1.

25. Talbert, 'Prophecy', 95–99.

26. Rebecca I. Denova, *The Things Accomplished Among Us: Prophetic Tradition in the Structural Pattern of Luke–Acts*, JSNTSup 141 (Sheffield: Sheffield Academic, 1997).

27. Ibid., 92–93, 112–24. For citation as precedent, see 112; for the example, see 126–41. For a discussion on whether the historical Jesus presented himself as an Elijah-like prophet with regard to the law see John P. Meier, *A Marginal Jew*, ABRL, 5 vols. (New York: Doubleday, 1991–2015), 4:565–67.

28. Bock, *Proclamation*, 49, 109–10, and examples throughout Chapter 3 of Bock's study.

29. E.g., Peter as leader of the twelve, developing Elisha ploughing with twelve oxen (1 Kgs 17.19). See Denova, *Things*, 141.

of Julia Kristeva and the semiotic relationship between two texts that she describes (where every text is a rewriting of prior texts).[30] The interest in biblical intertextuality was stimulated by the ground-breaking work of Richard Hays, and intertextuality is frequently anchored to the subtle but evocative relationships between texts which he describes – the entering of an echo-chamber where the voice of the prior text is heard echoing.[31]

Inevitably, these intertextual relationships must involve some *continuity* between the NT and the prior text. For example, Joel Green notes that Luke's birth narratives use similar stories to those in the Abraham cycle,[32] where the echoes of the prior account ring in the Lukan one and spell out its significance: this is the continuation of the OT story, and the present acts of God are in line with his previous acts of redemption.[33] But intertextual theory is not just about textual continuity, something which Robert Brawley explores in Luke–Acts by combining aspects of the intertextual approaches of Harold Bloom and John Hollander.[34] Bloom described a discontinuous relationship between two texts with every text correcting a previous text.[35] For Bloom, a strong text would so overcome

---

30. Julia Kristeva, *Desire in Language: A Semiotic Approach to Literature and Art*, trans. Leon S. Roudiez (Oxford: Blackwell, 1980), 36–37, 66. The limitations with Kristeva's approach are discussed in Litwak, *Echoes*, 48–51.

31. Richard B. Hays, *Echoes of Scripture in the Letters of Paul* (New Haven: Yale University Press, 1989). His analysis builds on John Hollander, *Figure of Echo: A Mode of Allusion in Milton and After* (Berkeley: University of California Press, 1981). For helpful reviews of biblical intertextuality, see Steve Moyise, 'Intertextuality and the Study of the Old Testament in the New', in *The Old Testament in the New: Essays in Honour of J. L. North* (Sheffield: Sheffield Academic, 2000); Patricia Tull Willey, *Remember the Former Things: The Recollection of Previous Texts in Second Isaiah*, SBLDS 161 (Atlanta: Scholars Press, 1997), 57–84.

32. Joel B. Green, 'The Problem of a Beginning: Israel's Scriptures in Luke 1–2', *BBR* 4 (1994).

33. Ibid., 75–77. This is not typology because there is no one to one relationship between any OT and NT character (pp. 66, 76–77).

34. Brawley, *Text*, 5–14; Hollander, *Figure*; Harold Bloom, *The Anxiety of Influence: A Theory of Poetry*, 2nd ed. (New York; Oxford: Oxford University Press, 1997).

35. He described six revisionary categories: *clinamen*, the redirection of the meaning of the precursor in a twist (Bloom, *Anxiety*, 19–45); *tessera*, the completion of the meaning of the precursor as if it were incomplete (48–73); *Kenosis*, an emptying-out of the precursor's meaning (77–93); *daemonization*, a revision which raises the prior text meaning to a higher level (99–112); *askesis*, where the text pulls away from the prior text, allowing the prior text to fade and die (115–36); and *apophrades*, the return of the prior text after its demise (139–55).

and revise its precursor that continuity is lost and it denies that it was built on a previous text; such strong texts revise the prior text but *never* fulfil it. Brawley demonstrates that the NT takes a revisionary stance towards *some* OT texts throughout his work; for example, in Isa. 5.1-7 the Lord offers the vineyard to destruction, but in Lk. 20.9-19 the owner preserves this vineyard and destroys the tenants.[36] But the NT is not a strong text in Bloom's terms for it does not seek to overcome the OT but rather expresses fulfilment of it, and in order to incorporate this continuity, Brawley turns to Hollander.[37] Hollander's work was the basis for Hays' approach, and describes the interaction between a text and a prior text as echoes bouncing back and forth between the texts synchronically, resulting in a 'new figuration'.[38] The meaning of the prior text is altered by this figuration, but so is the meaning of the evoking text: each text influences the other. So, for a reader, the meaning does not lie in either text in isolation but it is discovered by noting 'how the two texts reverberate with each other'.[39] For Brawley, Luke–Acts revises the use of the OT (in a manner described by Bloom) but the OT is not thereby denied; the OT text seemingly replies with a revision of its own, adapting the interpretation of the prior text in the Lukan passage.[40] In these ways the intertextual allusions lead the reader to a richer understanding of the text.[41]

Brawley notes that the reverberative connections between texts open up a rich world of interpretive possibility by connecting the current text to not only the prior text, but also to that text's context, thereby producing more connections than are immediately obvious from the words in the citing text. For example, the evocation of the parable of the vineyard in Lk. 20.9-19 is able to lead the reader beyond Isa. 5.1-7 to the world of Israelite history because it refers to the story of Israel.[42] Extrapolating from this, an

---

36. Brawley, *Text*, 40–41. For other examples see pp. 99–100, 113, 116, 119.
37. Ibid., 12–13.
38. Hollander, *Figure*, 31, 43, 111, quotation ix; and Hays, *Echoes*, 16–19.
39. Brawley, *Text*, 8.
40. Ibid., 12–13.
41. Within biblical studies, intertextuality is not always used in this way. Steve Moyise describes three applications of intertextuality: *Intertextual Echo*, the influence of even subtle allusions on a biblical text; *Dialogical Intertextuality*, where the relationship between the quoting and prior text occurs in both directions; and *Postmodern Intertextuality*, which does not attempt to define how the texts interact – it simply emphasises that all readers bring their own prior texts with them. The second category is consistent with the approach described above and leads to the most stimulating readings. See Moyise, 'Intertextuality', 17–18, 25–32.
42. Brawley, *Text*, 32–39.

allusion to the life of Abraham could connect with a specific part of the Abraham cycle, and then proceed to the context of the whole of his life, or to a theme associated with Abraham (e.g., faithfulness or circumcision). Connections produced by intertextual echoes may also evoke for the reader non-rational things like emotion, a sense of belonging, or a sense of identity. In the latter case this is because intertextual allusions require readers to be aware of the prior text in order to detect them, meaning that a reader's recognition of the link connotes that they share a textual history with the writer, and this builds a sense of shared community.[43]

While such intertextual relationships are undoubtedly present in Luke–Acts,[44] two observations need to be made. First, as has been noted before, the texts that are selected for analysis by a scholar direct the results that are achieved; subtle or complex intertextual uses of scripture are more likely to be seen in certain evocative textual environments. They are an important part of Luke's approach, but they do not describe all of it. Second, such approaches raise questions about how the reader should interpret these intertexts. When is a textual link too subtle for a reader to be reasonably expected to notice it? How much of the prior text's context is required for an adequate interpretation of the textual link? Are there any principles that can guide an interpreter to hearing appropriate echoes?

The Interaction of Scripture and the Narrative

Luke is a skilled storyteller who uses narrative as a vehicle to communicate his theology.[45] Because such a narrative requires a careful structure, and because the OT is important to Luke, it should be no surprise that scholars have argued that the OT provides structure to Luke's narrative. There are three ways that this is said to happen.

Structural Frameworks

Thomas Brodie has written extensively on the concept of *mimesis*, a technique where a writer consciously imitates the narrative content or style of a prior author (something supposedly used frequently in Graeco-Roman literature where imitation was a virtue).[46] For Brodie, such imitation is

---

43. An example in ibid., 95.
44. See also Hays, *Reading Backwards*, 55–74.
45. Joel B. Green, 'Learning Theological Interpretation from Luke', in *Reading Luke: Interpretation, Reflection, Formation*, ed. Craig G. Bartholomew, Joel B. Green, and Anthony C. Thiselton, SHS 6 (Grand Rapids: Zondervan, 2005), 56–61.
46. Thomas Brodie has written on this extensively; see, e.g., Thomas L. Brodie, 'Luke 7, 36–50 as an Internalization of 2 Kings 4, 1–37: A Study in Luke's Use of

the essential aspect of the use of the OT in Luke–Acts; quotations are 'cherries on top'.[47] His clearest example is the use of stories from the Elijah and Elisha cycle to form a narrative backbone to Luke–Acts (where Jesus is like Elijah),[48] but he describes others. David Moessner describes similar narrative patterns in the journey narrative of Lk. 9.51–19.44, arguing that there is a thematic coherence with the narrative of the Exodus in Deuteronomy which reveals Jesus as a prophet like Moses.[49] Gregory Bloomquist has also proposed that Luke is using mimesis in Lk. 21.5-36, where Jesus becomes one of the prophets in his denunciation of the city.[50]

What makes this approach distinct from typology is the effect that the OT has on the structure of Luke–Acts, where imitation of the OT goes beyond speech and quotation and affects entire narratives.[51] But while *some* of the Lukan stories do have *some* structural parallels with the OT narrative *at certain points*, the evidence does not suggest that Luke–Acts is arranged in this fashion. Brodie's argument relies on the establishment of multiple parallels between the accounts in the OT and Luke–Acts, and many are unconvincing.[52]

Rhetorical Imitation', *Bib* 64, no. 4 (1983); 'Towards Unraveling the Rhetorical Imitation of Sources in Acts: 2 Kings 5 as One Component of Acts 8, 9–40', *Bib* 67, no. 1 (1986); 'Luke's Use of the Elijah–Elisha Narrative', in *The Elijah–Elisha Narrative in the Composition of Luke*, ed. John S. Kloppenborg and Jozef Verheyden, LNTS 493 (London: Bloomsbury T&T Clark, 2014); and especially, *The Birthing of the New Testament. The Intertextual Development of the New Testament Writings* (Sheffield: Sheffield Phoenix, 2004).

47. Thomas L. Brodie, 'Intertextuality and Its Use in Tracing Q and Proto-Luke', in *The Scriptures in the Gospels*, ed. C. M. Tuckett (Leuven: Leuven University Press/Uitgeverij Peeters, 1997), 469.

48. Well summarised in Brodie, 'Elijah–Elisha'.

49. David P. Moessner, *Lord of the Banquet: The Literary and Theological Significance of the Lukan Travel Narrative* (Minneapolis: Fortress, 1989). A similar conclusion is reached in Christopher F. Evans, 'The Central Section of Luke's Gospel', in *Studies in the Gospels: Essays in Memory of R. H. Lightfoot*, ed. Dennis Eric Nineham (Oxford: Blackwell, 1955).

50. L. Gregory Bloomquist, 'Rhetorical Argumentation and the Culture of Apocalyptic: A Socio-Rhetorical Analysis of Luke 21', in *The Rhetorical Interpretation of Scripture: Essays from the 1996 Malibu Conference*, ed. Stanley E. Porter and Dennis L. Stamps, JSNTSup 180 (Sheffield: Sheffield Academic, 1999), 187–88.

51. See the helpful discussion in Gert J. Steyn, 'Luke's Use of ΜΙΜΗΣΙΣ', in Tuckett, ed., *The Scriptures in the Gospels*, 553.

52. He even suggests that differences are signs of a parallel in places; see Brodie, 'Internalization', 470–72, and *Birthing*, 307.

A Theological Framework
David Pao argues that the OT is used in Acts for the establishment of a theological framework for interpretation drawn from the Isaianic New Exodus cluster of hopes.[53] These hopes provide 'controlling motifs' for the Lukan narrative and serve as a hermeneutical lens for its interpretation.[54] The framework is formed in three ways: first, the citation of Isa. 40.3-5 at the beginning of the narrative (Lk. 3.4-6) serves to evoke all of Isaiah 40–55 and the Isaianic New Exodus themes (because it does so in Jewish writing)[55] and therefore acts as a hermeneutical lens showing the importance of these themes to Luke.[56] The ὁδός of God's salvific activity in Isaiah is then further employed to refer to the Christian community (e.g. Acts 9.2; 19.9, 23; 22.4; 24.14, 22).[57] Second, Isaiah is quoted at key moments in the narrative where it serves to explain the identity of the Christian community.[58] Third, four themes of the Isaianic New Exodus from Isaiah 40 are developed in Acts;[59] of these, Luke emphasises the mission to the gentiles, making it the goal of the New Exodus (Lk. 3.4-6; 24.47; Acts 1.6-8) with the message going *to* the nations rather than the nations coming to Jerusalem.

For Pao's proposal to work there needs to be some Lukan adaptation of Isaianic hopes, a theme which Peter Mallen explores by demonstrating transformation of two significant Isaianic themes. First, Luke–Acts emphasises the minor Isaianic theme of active mission into Gentile territories while ignoring both the dominant Isaianic model of Gentile pilgrimage to Jerusalem and the references to the judgement of the nations.[60] Secondly,

---

53. David W. Pao, *Acts and the Isaianic New Exodus* (Grand Rapids: Baker Academic, 2000), 10. For these hopes see also Max Turner, *Power from on High: The Spirit in Israel's Restoration and Witness in Luke–Acts*, JPTSup 9 (Sheffield: Sheffield Academic, 1996), 247; N. T. Wright, *The New Testament and the People of God*, Christian Origins and the Question of God 1 (London: SPCK, 1992), 268-79.

54. Pao, *Acts*, 249–50, quotation 49.

55. Ibid., 37, 41–44.

56. Ibid., 37, 41–59.

57. Ibid., 59–68.

58. E.g., Lk. 4.16-30; 24.44-49; Acts 1.8; 13.46-47; 28.25-28. See ibid., 70–110.

59. (a) The true people of God are defined and Israel is restored; (b) the word of God functions as the agent of the New Exodus; (c) the anti-idol polemic of Isaiah is developed showing that Jesus is Lord over all nations and gods; (d) the transformation of the Isaianic vision with respect to the mission to the Gentiles. Ibid., 122–42, 147–73, 182–89, 199–202, 218–22, 227–29.

60. Mallen, *Transformation*, 103–14. In Luke–Acts, Jerusalem is judged (Lk. 21.20-24).

it is Israel, not the nations, which undergoes a prophetic critique because of its rejection of salvation (e.g., Isa. 66.1-2a is quoted in Acts 7.49-50 to critique the temple, and Isa. 49.6 is used in Acts 13.47 to comment on Israel rejecting Jesus).[61] In this way, there are occasions where the Lukan narrative – rather than the Isaianic context – provides the correct interpretation for a citation (e.g., the reapplication of the mission of Isaiah 61 to both outsiders and Gentiles at the close of Jesus' speech in Lk. 4.25-27), but even here an awareness of the Isaianic context is still important in order to see what has been transformed. Mallen may place more emphasis on the Lukan narrative and Pao more emphasis on the Isaianic context, but essentially they agree that the context of the hopes and expectations of Isaiah are essential to the force of Luke's narrative (even if Luke transforms them).[62] This effectively provides an Isaianic framework for Luke.[63]

Peter Doble argues for a framework from Psalms.[64] They are frequently cited,[65] explicitly referred to as being important for understanding Jesus (Lk. 24.44), and they are particularly concentrated in the passion narrative and the speeches of Peter (Acts 2.14-36; 4.1-31) and Paul (Acts 13.16-31).[66] Their structural and hermeneutical role is demonstrated in the two psalms which link Luke and Acts: Psalm 118 is used by Jesus to frame a question in Lk. 20.17, and Peter gives an answer in Acts 4.11; Jesus' question from Psalm 110 (in Lk. 20.41-44) is answered by Peter in Acts 2.32-36.[67] In addition, the Psalms are strongly linked to Luke's Davidic theme (a trajectory beginning in Lk. 1.27; 2.11 and continuing until Acts 15.13-18), and this forms a lens through which Luke–Acts is to be read.[68] This linkage creates a rich repository of theology about a suffering and rejected one, which Luke mines in the parallelism between the lives of

---

61. Ibid., 114–18.

62. Methodologically Mallen begins with key Lukan themes and sees how they relate to Isaiah; Pao does the reverse.

63. The framework is clearer with Pao, but still present in Mallen; see Mallen, *Transformation*, Chapter 3.

64. Peter Doble, 'Luke 24.26, 44 – Songs of God's Servant: David and His Psalms in Luke–Acts', *JSNT* 28, no. 3 (2006), and 'The Psalms in Luke–Acts', in *The Psalms in the New Testament*, ed. Steve Moyise and Maarten J. J. Menken (London: T&T Clark, 2004).

65. There are fourteen quotations and many allusions.

66. Doble, 'Songs', 271–73.

67. Ibid., 271; Doble, 'Psalms', 88.

68. Doble, 'Songs', 273–74.

David and Jesus in the early Acts speeches.[69] These speeches use the psalms in a rich intertextual sense, their multiple allusions and quotations form the 'warp' and 'weft' of Luke's argument',[70] and they are 'signals of his narrative's theological *substructure*, the essential body of scripture revealing God's plan now fulfilled in Jesus'.[71]

Doble is surely correct about the importance of the Psalms to Luke's passion narrative and the speeches in chs. 2, 4, and 13 of Acts; he is also correct about their important role in structuring the discussion of Jesus' passion and messianic claims. But this does not require them to be the overall narrative structure. The case for Isaianic New Exodus hopes is also persuasive, especially with Mallen's adaptation, even if they are not all controlling.[72] The Psalms are commonly found in the speeches of Acts to give the early church kerygma of the suffering Messiah, but not in the Acts narrative where the Isaianic case is stronger.[73] The Davidic Messiah is perhaps the central christological concern of Luke–Acts,[74] but his christology concerns more than Jesus as Davidic Messiah,[75] and Luke–Acts is about more than christology.[76] Neither Isaiah nor the Psalms control the whole of Luke's narrative, they both exert influence over the narrative structure in different parts: deciding between them is a matter of choosing

---

69. Ibid., 275. The theology of a suffering Messiah is therefore from psalms and not Isaiah.

70. Doble, 'Psalms', 90. For the details of the speeches, see 90–112.

71. Ibid., 90, italics original.

72. Pao discusses mainly Acts, but his themes originate in the Gospel, where Mark L. Strauss, *The Davidic Messiah in Luke–Acts: The Promise and Its Fulfillment in Lukan Christology*, JSNTSup 110 (Sheffield: Sheffield Academic, 1995), and Turner, *Power*, make a good case for its presence.

73. Interestingly, away from a speech, Isaiah plays an important role in describing Christ's suffering (Acts 8.32-33).

74. See also Strauss, *Messiah*.

75. It also involves Lordship; see Douglas Buckwalter, *The Character and Purpose of Luke's Christology*, SNTSMS 89 (Cambridge: Cambridge University Press, 1996); Darrell L. Bock, *A Theology of Luke and Acts: Biblical Theology of the New Testament* (Grand Rapids: Zondervan, 2012), 169–76. Bock argues that the focus moves from Messiah to Lord during Acts, a position that is problematic; see Christopher M. Tuckett, 'The Christology of Luke–Acts', in Verheyden, ed., *The Unity of Luke–Acts*, 150. Jesus is also a Prophet; see Luke Timothy Johnson, *Prophetic Jesus, Prophetic Church: The Challenge of Luke–Acts to Contemporary Christians* (Grand Rapids: Eerdmans, 2011). In addition, Jesus' Spirit anointing is for New Exodus as well as Messianic empowering; see Turner, *Power*, 188–266.

76. Among other things, the Gentile mission is also a crucial theme of Acts.

between christology and the mission of the church as a dominant theme of Luke–Acts, but this is not necessary. Their narrative structures interweave with each other, possibly with additional Deuteronomic emphases,[77] to produce the whole narrative. This is means that, at times, Isaiah might be a dominant hermeneutical force in an argument, and at other times Psalms will take this role.

A Reading Framework
Kenneth Litwak uses intertextuality to propose a form of narrative framework which guides the context for the interpretation of the text.[78] He adapts Deborah Tannen's concept of *reading frames*;[79] such frames describe how readers typically make sense of a narrative through their previous experiences of reading, and how certain parts of a text form a frame which enables readers to know what to expect in the current text by indicating which prior reading experiences are most relevant.[80] The frames performing this function are often at the beginning of a text, but other types of text can also do it (e.g., repetition of things which a narrator says or fails to say).[81] For Litwak, intertextual relationships play this role, providing hermeneutical keys to unlock the text, both for the narrative as a whole (in the opening and closing chapters of Luke–Acts) or for individual pericopae.[82] For example, a reading frame is established by the intertextual relationships between the annunciation stories in Lk. 1.5-38 and the accounts of children promised to barren couples in the OT; this leads the reader to expect the children in Luke's account to be significant for God, just like those in the OT.[83]

In some respects, Litwak is utilising an alternative vocabulary to describe a recognised process (that the evocation of a prior context is important for interpreting a text), but his contribution shows how the OT can influence reader expectations of a whole narrative. Such contextual signals (or reading frames) are important, and Litwak's work indicates

---

77. Moessner, *Lord*.
78. Litwak, *Echoes*, 2.
79. Deborah Tannen, 'What Is a Frame? Surface Evidence for Underlying Expectations', in *Framing in Discourse*, ed. Deborah Tannen (Oxford: Oxford University Press, 1993); adapted in Litwak, *Echoes*, 55–61.
80. Tannen, 'Frame', 16.
81. Ibid., 41–51, who refers to viewers of a film but the principles apply to written texts too.
82. Litwak, *Echoes*, 56, 205.
83. E.g., Gen. 11.30; 18.11a; Judg. 13.2; 1 Kgs 1.3-12. See ibid., 70–81.

which allusions might have a framing role. First, they occur in strategic places in the text, like the beginning of a story or in repeated phrases.[84] Second, many of the texts Litwak uses are treated as 'type-scenes', where strong stories or motifs are evoked (this is the effective end result of his recording a string of allusions and reducing their significance to their common elements).[85] This suggests that general allusions to stories or concepts may have the greatest framing power.[86]

Despite the usefulness of reading frames, Litwak overemphasises their importance by claiming that it can account for all the use of allusion and quotation in Luke–Acts, a contention which partly results from his concentration on key framing chapters in Luke–Acts where one would expect such scriptural use. Allusions do more than create reading frames – their content typically contributes to the meaning of the quoting text too.

Rhetoric

It is likely that Luke employed contemporary Graeco-Roman rhetorical techniques because such ideas had permeated as far as Palestine when he wrote.[87] An examination of Luke's use of rhetoric offers the possibility of showing what the author is attempting to draw the attention of the reader to. Yet, despite this, rhetorical techniques have only been applied to the use of the OT by the NT relatively recently.[88] Part of the problem with the

---

84. As suggested by Tannen, 'Frame', 41–42.
85. Litwak, *Echoes*, 70–81.
86. It is possible, therefore, that the Septuagintalisms in Luke–Acts may act primarily as a reading frame to draw the reader's attention to the OT world as a suitable context for understanding events in the narrative. For Septuagintalisms, see Fitzmyer, *Luke*, 1:114–16; Brian S. Rosner, 'Acts and Biblical History', in *The Book of Acts in Its First Century Setting. Vol. 1, The Book of Acts in Its Ancient Literary Setting*, ed. Bruce W. Winter and Andrew D. Clark (Grand Rapids: Eerdmans, 1993), 68–70; Kimball, *Exposition*, 17.
87. Martin Hengel, *Judaism and Hellenism: Studies in Their Encounter in Palestine During the Early Hellenistic Period*, trans. John Bowden, 2 vols. (London: SCM, 1974), 1:65–78.
88. For rhetorical approaches, see Dennis L. Stamps, 'Rhetoric', in *Dictionary of New Testament Background*, ed. Craig A. Evans and Stanley E. Porter (Leicester: InterVarsity Press, 2000), 953–56. For application to Luke–Acts, see Todd C. Penner, 'Narrative as Persuasion: Epideictic Rhetoric and Scribal Amplification in the Stephen Episode in Acts', in *SBLSP* 35 (1996); David P. Moessner and David L. Tiede, 'Conclusion: "And Some Were Persuaded..."', in Moessner, ed., *Jesus and*

application of rhetorical theory to the quotation of scripture is the paucity of discussion on quotation within Greek theoretical literature on rhetoric.[89] As a result, any approach taken relies on the insight of modern theorists whose discussions emphasise its role in increasing vividness in writing, on creating distance between the writer and a quoted opinion, and in creating solidarity with the readership.[90]

There are two scholars whose work is interesting in this regard. John Paul Heil draws a distinction between citations in 1 Corinthians where Paul seemingly expects his readers to be aware of the OT and others where he does not.[91] In the more general citations it is not possible to determine *exactly* where the quotation comes from (because similar terms or themes come from more than one place) and the rhetorical force of such quotations is simply that it comes from scripture, without requiring recognition of the precise text.[92] This may still require some contextual knowledge, perhaps of a biblical theme or cluster of motifs, but not of a particular text.

For Christopher Stanley, quotations in the letters of Paul only function at this rhetorical level. He argues that Paul's readers were too unfamiliar with the LXX, mainly through illiteracy and the scarcity of biblical texts;[93] as such, they would not understand the content of the OT text, and even

---

the Heritage of Israel, 368; Bloomquist, 'Culture of Apocalyptic', and the awareness of rhetoric within Witherington, *Acts*. For notable applications to the OT elsewhere in the NT, see Christopher D. Stanley, 'The Rhetoric of Quotations: An Essay on Method', in *Early Christian Interpretation*, ed. Craig A. Evans and James A. Sanders, JSNTSup 148 (Sheffield: Sheffield Academic, 1997); idem, *Arguing with Scripture: The Rhetoric of Quotations in the Letters of Paul* (New York/London: T&T Clark, 2004); and the different outcome in Stamps, 'Use'.

89. Only present in Aristotle, *Rhet.* 1.15.3, 13-17; Quintilian, *Inst.* 2.7.4; and the quotation of Homer by ancient writers. See Christopher D. Stanley, 'Paul and Homer: Greco-Roman Citation Practice in the First Century CE', *NovT* 32, no. 1 (1990); idem, 'Rhetoric', 45 n. 1; idem, 'Use', 27–30.

90. Herbert H. Clark and Richard J. Gerrig, 'Quotations as Demonstrations', *Language* 66, no. 4 (1990), which was appropriated for biblical studies by Stanley, 'Rhetoric'.

91. John Paul Heil, *The Rhetorical Role of Scripture in 1 Corinthians*, SBLStBL 15 (Atlanta: Society of Biblical Literature, 2005), 9–10.

92. For examples, see ibid., 66, 70.

93. Stanley, *Scripture*, 38–61. His argument proceeds against what he sees as ten assumptions common in Pauline scholarship, but these are the two critical reasons for the purposes here.

less appreciate its context. The power of a quotation, therefore, depends upon its rhetorical force in the setting in which Paul used it; the OT context is not critical for interpretation.[94] But Stanley's approach over-estimates the problem of illiteracy, and under-estimates the knowledge of the LXX in the churches.[95] As far as Luke is concerned, he seems to expect that converts become versed in scripture as part of catechesis,[96] and teachers in the churches are likely to have explained the significance of allusions to all. In addition to this, the paucity of ancient discussion about quotations as rhetoric suggests that quotations were not used for purely rhetorical purposes; this is supported by the importance of the content (and, to some extent, the context) of many OT allusions to the argument of NT texts. Despite this, Stanley makes an important contribution by emphasising how quotations contribute to the rhetorical force of a NT text. He is also correct in emphasising that different readers approach texts on different levels,[97] and that overly complex textual interactions would have been beyond many readers.

Summary

The use of scripture in Luke–Acts is therefore complex: it includes formal quotation, subtle intertextual relationships, and theological and narrative uses. The clear lines of definition favoured by some scholars are the result of their focus on certain types of text and the application of particular methods; an examination of christological texts is likely to unearth a fulfilment theme, and complex literary approaches to literary allusions draw attention to complex textual interactions. There is much to affirm in these various approaches, but none of them describe all allusions, and their downplaying of alternatives seems short-sighted. Luke is too diverse

---

94. Ibid.
95. See the detailed arguments in Brian J. Abasciano, 'Diamonds in the Rough: A Reply to Christopher Stanley Concerning the Reader Competency of Paul's Original Audiences', *NovT* 49 (2007).
96. Christoph W. Stenschke, *Luke's Portrait of Gentiles Prior to Their Coming to Faith*, WUNT 2/108 (Tübingen: Mohr Siebeck, 1999), 339. The reading and teaching of scripture was probably a central part of synagogue worship; see Stephen K. Catto, *Reconstructing the First-Century Synagogue: A Critical Analysis of Current Research*, LNTS 363 (London: T&T Clark, 2007), 116–25.
97. Something he demonstrates by evaluating Paul's quotations of the OT from the perspective of three different hypothetical audiences with different knowledge of scripture (see the rationale in Stanley, *Scripture*, 65–71).

in his use of scripture for one approach to describe it all. While it is clear that the content and context of OT texts can play a critical role in the interpretation of a NT text, it is also clear that the function they play will differ from text to text (demonstrating fulfilment, creating literary echoes, or providing a hermeneutical grid). At times, much of the OT context is required for interpretation, at others little.

Old Testament Allusions in This Study

Some scholars seem to analyse every intertext as far as possible, searching its context for further layers of meaning;[98] others, like Stanley,[99] deny that the readers have competence to notice intertexts or notice subtlety of argument drawn from the OT context. The best approach is to steer a path between these two extremes, and a way can be found to do that by considering how Luke's readers analyse texts. This can give a helpful basis for making an interpretive decision in difficult texts.

The Audience and Reading the Old Testament

This study examines Luke–Acts from the perspective of the reader. Of course, the only access available to this audience is through the text, by inferring the readership that Luke was writing for; however, despite being a reconstructed audience, it is likely that such inferred readers have considerable overlap with the real audience.[100] Luke–Acts was written for a wide readership,[101] and Luke's real readers were a heterogenous group with different abilities and experiences.[102] These real readers were not the

---

98. An example is the explicit reading of all of the OT context of the evoked psalms in the Markan passion narrative because there is no reason *not* to. See Stephen P. Ahearne-Kroll, *The Psalms of Lament in Mark's Passion: Jesus' Davidic Suffering*, SNTSMS 142 (Cambridge: Cambridge University Press, 2007), 27.

99. Stanley, *Scripture*.

100. For a helpful discussion of Luke's probable readership, see Craig S. Keener, *Acts: An Exegetical Commentary*, 4 vols. (Grand Rapids: Baker Academic, 2012–2015), 1:423–34. It is likely that they had a synagogue background, and knew the LXX. See ibid., 1:428; Mikeal C. Parsons, *Acts*, PCNT (Grand Rapids: Baker, 2008), 20, and the discussion in Joseph B. Tyson, *Images of Judaism in Luke–Acts* (Columbia: University of South Carolina Press, 1992), 35–36.

101. See the essays in Richard Bauckham, ed. *The Gospels for All Christians: Rethinking the Gospel Audiences* (Grand Rapids: Eerdmans, 1998).

102. Kathy R. Maxwell, *Hearing Between the Lines: The Audience as Fellow-Worker in Luke–Acts and Its Literary Milieu*, LNTS 425 (London: T&T Clark, 2010), 14.

idealized readers that literary theory typically recreates, and not many of them would follow the intricacies of Luke's argument as idealized readers would.[103] The approach in this study therefore needs to account for this heterogeneity. It also needs to address a couple of important issues concerning how readers approach allusions. First, which texts would a reader notice? This is especially important when a Lukan phrase has similarity to several OT texts: Would the reader notice all of them,[104] some of them, or make links to biblical stories or motifs (e.g., the Isaianic New Exodus) instead of texts? Second, how much of the OT context would a reader explore for meaning?

In order to give a theoretical basis for a discussion of how a reader would proceed to interpret texts (and to facilitate an interpretation that avoids the extremes above) it is helpful to consider how a reader's mind processes information, and *relevance theory* offers a useful theoretical basis for doing this.

Relevance Theory
Relevance theory is a linguistic or communicative theory that offers a helpful account of human communication, detailing how the mind processes utterances;[105] as such, it can give a useful framework to understand how a reader of Luke–Acts would view Luke's use of the OT. Relevance theory's focus has been primarily on spoken communication,

---

103. See the discussion in Benjamin J. Lappenga, *Paul's Language of Ζῆλος: Monosemy and the Rhetoric of Identity and Practice*, BIS 137 (Leiden: Brill, 2015), 50–51.

104. Many commentaries list all of the potential texts but do not indicate whether they are all similarly important for interpretation.

105. The most important presentation of the theory is to be found in Dan Sperber and Deirdre Wilson, *Relevance: Communication and Cognition*, 2nd ed. (Oxford: Blackwell, 1995), which has some refinements from the 1986 first edition. Several important essays are gathered in Deirdre Wilson and Dan Sperber, ed., *Meaning and Relevance* (Cambridge: Cambridge University Press, 2012), including details of experimental testing of the theory; see, in the same volume, Jean-Baptiste Van der Henst and Dan Sperber, 'Testing the Cognitive and Communicative Principles of Relevance', in *Meaning and Relevance*. Among many summaries, the following are helpful: Neil Smith and Deirdre Wilson, 'Introduction', *Lingua* 87, no. 1 (1992); Deirdre Wilson and Dan Sperber, 'Relevance Theory', in *Handbook of Pragmatics*, ed. Laurence Horn and Gregory Ward (Oxford: Blackwell, 2003). There is a regularly updated bibliography at http://www.ua.es/personal/francisco.yus/rt.html.

but it has been applied with considerable benefit to texts,[106] and it is increasingly used in biblical studies.[107]

Relevance theory describes communication as happening through inference,[108] in a process directed by *relevance*. A communication is

---

106. Christine Richards, 'Inferential Pragmatics and the Literary Text', *JPrag* 9, no. 2–3 (1985). For the benefit of relevance theory in literary texts, see Anne Furlong, 'Relevance Theory and Literary Interpretation' (Ph.D. diss., University College London, 1996), and also David Trotter, 'Analysing Literary Prose: The Relevance of Relevance Theory', *Lingua* 87, no. 1–2 (1992); Nam Sun Song, 'Metaphor and Metonymy', in *Relevance Theory: Applications and Implications*, ed. Robyn Carston and Seiji Uchida, PBNS 37 (Amsterdam: Benjamins, 1998); Seiji Uchida, 'Text and Relevance', in *Relevance Theory: Applications and Implications*, ed. Robyn Carston and Seiji Uchida, PBNS 37 (Amsterdam: Benjamins, 1998); Adrian Pilkington, *Poetic Effects: A Relevance Theory Perspective*, PBNS 75 (Amsterdam: Benjamins, 2000). Keith Green argues that relevance theory cannot explain the more stylistic and less dialogical communication of texts; see Keith Green, 'Relevance Theory and the Literary Text: Some Problems and Perspectives', *JLS* 22, no. 3 (1993): 210. Yet texts do not signal that they require different communicative rules so there should be no reason to treat them differently; see Tzvetan Todorov, *Genres in Discourse*, trans. Catherine Porter (Cambridge: Cambridge University Press, 1990), 1–12; Stephen W. Pattemore, *The People of God in the Apocalypse: Discourse, Structure and Exegesis*, SNTSMS 128 (Cambridge: Cambridge University Press, 2004), 23.

107. See, e.g., Tim Meadowcroft, 'Relevance as a Mediating Category in the Reading of Biblical Texts: Venturing Beyond the Hermeneutical Circle', *JETS* 45, no. 4 (2002); Pattemore, *People*; Gene L. Green, 'Relevance Theory and Biblical Interpretation', in *The Linguist as Pedagogue: Trends in the Teaching and Linguistic Analysis of the Greek New Testament*, ed. Stanley E. Porter and Matthew Brook O'Donnell (Sheffield: Sheffield Phoenix, 2009); Gene L. Green, 'Relevance Theory and Theological Interpretation: Thoughts on Metarepresentation', *JTI* 4, no. 1 (2010); Joseph D. Fantin, *The Lord of the Entire World: Lord Jesus, a Challenge to Lord Caesar?* (Sheffield: Sheffield Phoenix, 2011); Yael Klangwisan, *Earthing the Cosmic Queen: Relevance Theory and the Song of Songs* (Eugene: Pickwick, 2014); Lappenga, *Language*. It is also significant in translation; see Ernst-August Gutt, 'Unraveling Meaning: An Introduction to Relevance Theory', *Notes* 112 (1986); idem, "Approaches to Translation: Relevance Theory," in *Encyclopedia of Language and Linguistics*, ed. Keith Brown (Oxford: Elsevier, 2006); Karen H. Jobes, 'Relevance Theory and the Translation of Scripture', *JETS* 50, no. 4 (2007).

108. Communication is not simply a matter of encoding into words the speaker's thoughts, then decoding them so that they are reproduced in the hearer's mind; see Sperber and Wilson, *Relevance*, 3–5. While relevance theory's concern for inference is shared with pragmatic theories (especially those of Paul Grice), it is not simply a development of them; see Dan Sperber and Deirdre Wilson, 'Introduction: Pragmatics', in Wilson and Sperber, eds., *Meaning and Relevance*.

relevant if the explicit content of the communication together with what it implies modifies the context or *cognitive environment* of the hearer to produce new *contextual effects*; in other words, it is relevant if it adds new information to what the hearer already knows.[109] Utterances are made with the presumption that they are relevant to the hearer, and human cognitive processes proceed by searching for this relevance.[110] The degree of relevance is defined in terms of a balance between maximising the contextual effects achieved, and minimising the mental effort required to process them.[111] So, on hearing new information, the hearer presumes the utterance to be relevant and searches through their cognitive environment, their network of contexts, to see where the utterance is relevant;[112] these contexts will include both the wider context of the utterance, and so-called encyclopaedic information (chunks of data associated with a concept which are accessed *en-masse*, including cultural beliefs, personal opinion, and experiences).[113] Some of these contexts will require less effort to process than others because they are more immediately accessible;[114] in order to minimise effort, a person will begin the search for cognitive effects with the most available context and proceed from there. Because the interpretive goal is *optimal relevance*, a hearer will stop searching once relevance has been achieved; in other words, they will not examine

109. Sperber and Wilson, *Relevance*, 48, 58, 108–109.
110. Ibid., 260–79.
111. 'Extent condition 1: An assumption is relevant to an individual to the extent that the positive cognitive effects achieved when it is optimally processed are large. Extent condition 2: An assumption is relevant to an individual to the extent that the effort required to achieve these positive cognitive effects is small.' Ibid., 265–66. For a fuller discussion see also pp. 118–71.
112. These do not have to be things that the person is thinking about at the time of an utterance, only things that the person is capable of accessing (referred to as facts or assumptions that are *manifest* to the interpreter). For successful communication, the speaker and hearer need to have the same facts or assumptions manifest to them, and the speaker needs to be aware that the hearer has these things manifest to them. For spoken utterances it can also include the physical environment. Ibid., 38–46, 138.
113. Adrian Pilkington has suggested that if mental images could be included in these encyclopaedic entries, then other data could also be included such as affective states and emotions; see Adrian Pilkington, 'Metaphor Comprehension: Some Questions for Current Account in Relevance Theory', in *Explicit Communication: Robyn Carston's Pragmatics*, ed. Belén Soria and Esther Romero (Basingstoke: Palgrave Macmillan, 2010), 164–65.
114. Some information is only attainable through an indirect route involving the activation of other encyclopaedic information first; see Sperber and Wilson, *Relevance*, 137.

further contexts for greater or additional relevance because this would require further processing effort.[115] This is a critical observation for the current study.

From a relevance perspective, when an utterance alludes to another utterance, it does so through linguistic similarity or shared content; such common content is effectively the sharing of implications between the two texts, and the more implications the texts have in common, the closer their resemblance.[116] A hearer noting such utterances does not need to assume they are identical; instead, 'following the relevance-theoretic comprehension procedure, he should start deriving implications that might plausibly be shared with the original, and stop when he has enough to satisfy his expectation of relevance'.[117] A reader will stop searching for possible interpretations when one which fulfils expectations of relevance is found. For this reason, a reader would stop at the most accessible context when reading an allusion in Luke. So, if relevance can be attained in the most available text, then a reader will not proceed to process other possible allusions no matter how many there are; if relevance is attained with less effort through a motif, story or theme, then a reader will not proceed to process the verse itself. For this reason, it is critical to evaluate which contexts would have been the most accessible to the first-century reader.

But there is more to interpreting OT allusions than this; in order to describe how a reader would handle the more allusive intertextual allusions it is helpful to draw on relevance theory's discussion of metaphors.[118] The interpretation of metaphors, just like all utterances, relies on *explicature* and *implicature*. Explicatures are assumptions that arise as a development

---

115. Deirdre Wilson, 'Relevance and Understanding', in *Language and Understanding*, ed. Gillian Brown (Oxford: Oxford University Press, 1994), 44–50.

116. Deirdre Wilson, 'Metarepresentation in Linguistic Communication', in Wilson and Sperber, eds., *Meaning and Relevance*, 244. Human communication has the ability to form mental *representations* about a state of affairs or a concept. Quotations are a form of *metarepresentation*, 'a representation of a representation: a higher-order representation with a lower-order representation embedded within it'. They concern the 'ability to form *thoughts* about *attributed* thoughts'. See ibid., 230, for both quotations; see also the summary in Green, 'Relevance Theory', 82–84.

117. Wilson, 'Metarepresentation', 244.

118. There is some similarity in how allusions and metaphor are processed; see Pattemore, *People*, 37–38. See also Eva María Almazán García, 'Dwelling in Marble Halls: A Relevance-Theoretic Approach to Intertextuality in Translation', *RAEI* 14 (2001): 10–13.

of the logical form of the utterance;[119] implicatures are everything except the explicatures.[120] Implicatures can add greatly to the cognitive effects produced certain types of utterances, such as indirect answers to questions. For example, when asked if they would drive a Mercedes, if a person responds, 'I wouldn't drive ANY expensive car', the answer 'no' is not explicit, it depends on the implicature, something which follows from the explicature of the utterance and contextual information (Mercedes are expensive).[121] The speaker intends the hearer to reach this implicature in order for the question to be answered, but it requires more processing effort than the answer 'no'. In return, it offers an increase in contextual effects through further implicatures, varying in strength from stronger ones that a speaker clearly intended (e.g. she would not drive a Bentley), to weaker ones (e.g. she is unlikely to go on an expensive cruise).[122] There is no clear distinction between stronger and weaker implicatures, they fall on a spectrum, but the weaker the implicature the more responsibility a hearer must take for forming it.[123]

Metaphors encourage the reader to explore the context further than a literal statement: their presence signals that optimal relevance is not achieved without expending increased processing effort, and in return they yield increased cognitive effects through implicature.[124] Some will be at the strong end of the spectrum, where the reader is almost 'forced to supply them';[125] others will be weaker (with the weakest arising from contexts apparent to the reader alone).[126] A writer may not have in mind all of the implicatures that a reader arrives at, but the communication should

---

119. 'An assumption communicated by an utterance *U* is *explicit* if and only if it is a development of a logical form encoded by *U*' (Sperber and Wilson, *Relevance*, 182, italics original).

120. Ibid., 182, 93–202.

121. For the example quoted here, see ibid., 194–95.

122. Ibid., 196–99.

123. Ibid., 199–200.

124. Ibid., 230–43; Adrian Pilkington, 'Introduction: Relevance Theory and Literary Style', *LL* 5, no. 3 (1996): 158–59; idem, *Effects*, 85–90; Song, 'Metaphor', 87–95; Markus Tendahl and Raymond W. Gibbs Jr., 'Complementary Perspectives on Metaphor: Cognitive Linguistics and Relevance Theory', *JPrag* 40, no. 11 (2008); Sperber and Wilson, 'Meaning'.

125. Adrian Pilkington, 'Poetic Effects', *Lingua* 87, no. 1–2 (1992): 36.

126. Some metaphors rely on the experience that a reader has of certain things, or an emotion which the reader recalls; see Pilkington, *Effects*, 36–38, 183–84; Furlong, 'Relevance', 94–97.

direct the reader to the kind of implicatures the writer intends – but the interpretive decision rests with the reader. It is only by noting the important implicatures that optimal relevance is achieved; however, if a reader goes beyond this and looks for further relevance in other implicatures, then this goes beyond the manifest communication of the author (something more typical of interested-party interpretations).[127]

In this way, allusions to the OT can evoke a series of implicatures of different strengths. There are three additional points that need to be made about metaphors which all apply to allusion.

First, although all metaphors rely on implicature, some have a more expansive range than others. *Poetic metaphors* are characterised by a wide range of weaker implicatures that are essential to optimal relevance.[128] The precise weak implicatures that readers attain may differ from reading to reading but the range of these weak implicatures is part of the intended communication of the metaphor.[129] The writer often enlarges the encyclopaedic information that goes with such metaphors in the text in order to guide the reader's interpretation;[130] they can be the subject of several lines and can be examined repeatedly (sometimes requiring more than one reading to appreciate their richness).[131] Other metaphors have a relatively fixed meaning: 'he is a gorilla' is a metaphor typically associated with aggression, and even a zoologist would hear it in this way, despite having encyclopaedic information about gorillas that contradicts it. The zoologist would access its fixed meaning and stop the search for relevance there because this is the route of least processing effort.[132] Such contexts are *metarepresented* as a belief by a particular group, and are readily available to people who are a part of that group; metaphors will often be interpreted this way if they have a lot of sentimentality attached to them, their concept is vague,[133] or they are associated with strongly held beliefs.[134]

Second, metaphor interpretation can be modified as a text progresses. Theorists describe *ad hoc* concepts, which are temporary clusters of thoughts arranged around a key concept such as the collection of

127. The best discussion of this is Furlong, 'Relevance', 189–204.
128. Pilkington, 'Introduction', 159.
129. Sperber and Wilson, 'Meaning', 121–22.
130. Pilkington, *Effects*, 42–43, 102–103; Song, 'Metaphor', 94–95.
131. Repeated exposure enlarges the web of implicatures by adding to the encyclopaedic entries associated with the metaphor, Pilkington, *Effects*, 105.
132. See ibid., 112–18; the example is his.
133. Pilkington, 'Effects', 44.
134. Ibid., 40.

implicatures which gather around a metaphor.[135] Once formed, these *ad hoc* concepts are capable of modification as new information becomes apparent, meaning that the reference of the metaphor can be made either broader or narrower.[136] In this way, complex metaphors can be re-evaluated as the reader continues in the text.

Third, metaphors can also raise other kinds of weak implicatures, including emotional responses, or the evocation of a mood or atmosphere.[137] In addition, quotations can also signal the attitude of the speaker toward the attributed thought or utterance (e.g., approval, criticism or ridicule).[138]

Proposing a Method for Interpreting Intertextuality
With this description of how a reader's mind processes information, it is possible to address the interpretation of the OT allusions in this study. While they are not followed sequentially in the chapters that follow, there are three aspects to the interpretive task.

(i) Identification of possible interpretive contexts.
An allusion to the OT can be signalled in several ways: verbal repetition and distinctive phrases are the most common, but motifs and ideas can also signal OT texts, and 'setting, plot, form and genre' can contribute.[139] Once these are noted, the potential OT intertexts can be identified, and NA[28] and the commentaries form a useful starting point for this.

(ii) Identification of the most available context.
Because readers evaluate the most accessible contexts first, it is important to identify which contexts would have involved the least processing effort. Richard Hays' criteria are useful in this, especially the *availability* of the text to the writer and reader, and the *volume* of the allusion (the

---

135. For further explanation, see Tendahl and Gibbs, 'Perspectives', 1832–39; Pilkington, *Effects*, 96–108; Sperber and Wilson, 'Meaning', 120–22.
136. Tendahl and Gibbs, 'Perspectives', 1832–33.
137. Pilkington, 'Introduction', 159.
138. Wilson, 'Metarepresentation', 249–53; Eun-Ju Noh, *Metarepresentation: A Relevance-Theory Approach* (Amsterdam: Benjamins, 2000), 91–98; Sperber and Wilson, *Relevance*, 237–43.
139. Benjamin D. Sommer, *A Prophet Reads Scripture: Allusion in Isaiah 40–66* (Stanford: Stanford University Press, 1998), 11; genre is also noted in Tull Willey, *Things*, 63. The quotation is from Brawley, *Text*, 125, who also notes that certain textual formulations suggest that a literal reading is insufficient, encouraging the reader to explore intertextual relationships. Ibid., 65–66.

distinctiveness or length of the phrase that echoes an OT text).[140] However, it is possible that other contexts are more accessible; for instance, the frequent liturgical use of a text may make it come to a reader's mind more quickly. On occasions where more than one text is alluded to by the same phrase, then it is possible that the reader would find relevance in a biblical theme common to these two texts rather than in the texts themselves. But if a reader does not find enough cognitive effects in the most immediate intertext, then the reader will move on, perhaps to other texts.

(iii) Interpreting the intertext.
The selected text can now be evaluated. However, in doing this it is important to note whether the intertext would have a relatively fixed meaning for the audience, or whether it functions like a poetic metaphor. Attention needs to be paid to signals in the text that suggest how it is to be interpreted, and to further information in the developing narrative text that modifies the *ad hoc* concepts that have arisen in interpreting the intertext.

Having said all this, relevance theory will not be required for every text. Although its principles govern all interpretive actions, it does not need to be applied to many of the intertexts in this study. However, where there is debate about the likely intertext, or where there is debate about how much of the OT context to take notice of, relevance theory will provide a helpful basis for making a decision.

---

140. Hays, *Echoes*, 29–32. Recurrence is also helpful in making a text more noticeable to the reader.

Chapter 3

LUKE 13.31-35:
THE REJECTED PROPHET AND SAVIOUR

The first apparently temple-critical material appears in the speech of Lk. 13.34-35. It is the only lament shared with Matthew's Gospel (Mt. 23.37-39);[1] Luke's version has some differences in wording, but the changed location of the saying is more notable.[2] Matthew combines it with the wisdom saying of Mt. 23.34-36 (paralleled in Lk. 11.49-51) and has it in Jerusalem, not the journey narrative where Luke locates it. Although it is unlikely it was originally related to the wisdom saying, because Luke does not tend to split Q sayings,[3] its position in Luke's journey narrative looks like a Lukan relocation.[4] Its placement has two important effects upon interpretation. First, it is attached to 13.31-33 through the catchword 'Jerusalem', meaning that the two sayings relate together as a close unit, and need to be interpreted together. Second, the placement of 13.31-35 in the journey to Jerusalem locates the saying long before other sayings about the temple. It is used both to create a sense of expectancy over what will happen in Jerusalem, and to introduce themes which are picked up later in the narrative. Its principal themes are addressed in turn.

1. For a reconstruction of the Q text, see Kim Huat Tan, *The Zion Traditions and the Aims of Jesus*, SNTSMS 91 (New York: Cambridge University Press, 1997), 102–104.

2. Luke's brood is feminine singular, he omits ἔρημος and the modifier ἀπ' ἄρτι, he uses the infinitive ἐπισυνάξαι (not ἐπισυναγαγεῖν with an indicative), and includes ἥξει ὅτε. The textual evidence for this is uncertain, but its inclusion is the more difficult reading; see Bruce M. Metzger, *A Textual Commentary on the Greek New Testament*, 2nd ed. (Stuttgart: United Bible Societies, 1994), 138.

3. George R. Beasley-Murray, *Jesus and the Kingdom of God* (Grand Rapids: Eerdmans; Exeter: Paternoster, 1986), 304; in addition, Mt. 23.34-36 is a prose passage and Mt. 23.37-39 is more typical of a prophetic-poetic style. See also Penley, *Tradition*, 137–39.

4. Fitzmyer, *Luke*, 2:1034; Darrell L. Bock, *Luke*, BECNT, 2 vols. (Grand Rapids: Baker Academic, 1994–96), 2:1243–45.

Jesus a Rejected Prophet

It has been clear since Lk. 9.22 that Jesus expected to die, but the conversation between Jesus and the Pharisees in 13.31-33 adds that his death would be that of a rejected prophet. Jesus' phrase, οὐκ ἐνδέχεται προφήτην ἀπολέσθαι ἔξω Ἰερουσαλήμ (13.33), sounds as much like a proverb as it does hyperbole; similarly, Ἰερουσαλὴμ Ἰερουσαλήμ, ἡ ἀποκτείνουσα τοὺς προφήτας καὶ λιθοβολοῦσα τοὺς ἀπεσταλμένους πρὸς αὐτήν sounds like a reference to tradition. Both are likely to signal to a reader that OT tradition is important for interpretation, but no OT verse has significantly similar language. However, several OT verses do refer to the murder of people in Jerusalem.[5]

Three verses describe specific events: Jer. 33.20-23 (26.20-23 ET)[6] has some conceptual parallels, describing the killing of the prophet Uriah in Jerusalem;[7] Jer. 45.4-6 (38.4-6 ET) refers to an attempt on Jeremiah's life in Jerusalem, but he is not killed; and 2 Chron. 24.20-21 describes the death of Zechariah the priest by stoning in the court of the Jerusalem temple.[8]

Other verses are more general: 4 Kgdms 21.16 refers to King Manasseh filling Jerusalem with innocent blood,[9] something which Josephus (*Ant.* 10.38) understood to include prophets. But even if Josephus reflects popular interpretation, this verse says more about Manasseh than it does about the danger of being a prophet. Other verses (3 Kgdms 18.4, 13; 19.10, 14; Jer. 2.30; Neh. 9.26) acknowledge the general killing of the prophets, and there are references in the later tradition (e.g., *Jub.* 1.12), but apart from the reference to the death of Isaiah by a wood-saw (*Mart. Isa.* 5.1-14) these texts do not state that the deaths are in Jerusalem – they simply confirm that prophets suffer a violent death. However, Jerusalem is centrally important to Luke's saying, and no reader would find relevance in an intertext without Jerusalem after the threefold repetition in 13.33-34.

Although none of these texts have enough similarity to Lk. 13.34 to make them a context for finding relevance, Lk. 11.49-51 has a similar generalisation about the death of the prophets, and occurs very close in the Lukan narrative. It is likely that the search for relevance would begin here.

---

5. Tan, *Zion*, 75–76; Pao and Schnabel, 'Luke', 336; Fisk, 'Tears', 154–55.
6. All OT verse references use the LXX.
7. Tan, *Zion*, 75–76, favours this as the chief parallel.
8. Noted by Pao and Schnabel, 'Luke', 336.
9. Following the LXX, 1–4 Kingdoms will be used instead of 1–2 Samuel and 1–2 Kings.

Lk. 11.49-51:

⁴⁹διὰ τοῦτο καὶ ἡ σοφία τοῦ θεοῦ εἶπεν· ἀποστελῶ εἰς αὐτοὺς προφήτας καὶ ἀποστόλους, καὶ ἐξ αὐτῶν ἀποκτενοῦσιν καὶ διώξουσιν, ⁵⁰ἵνα ἐκζητηθῇ τὸ αἷμα πάντων τῶν προφητῶν τὸ ἐκκεχυμένον ἀπὸ καταβολῆς κόσμου ἀπὸ τῆς γενεᾶς ταύτης, ⁵¹ἀπὸ αἵματος Ἄβελ ἕως αἵματος Ζαχαρίου τοῦ ἀπολομένου μεταξὺ τοῦ θυσιαστηρίου καὶ τοῦ οἴκου· ...

⁴⁹Therefore also the Wisdom of God said, 'I will send them prophets and apostles, some of whom they will kill and persecute', ⁵⁰so that this generation may be charged with the blood of all the prophets shed since the foundation of the world, ⁵¹from the blood of Abel to the blood of Zechariah, who perished between the altar and the sanctuary. ...[10]

Luke 11.49-51 is closer than any of the OT texts, but it is likely that a reader would not stop here because there is a need to interpret the significance of the stoning in Lk. 13.34. This form of execution is not mentioned in Lk. 11.51, but with the information associated with Lk. 11.51 activated it is highly likely that a reader would begin to access the contextual information associated with the death of Zechariah in 2 Chron. 24.20-21 (as above), where the stoning reference can be understood.[11] It is likely that this is the Zechariah referred to in 11.49 because he was the last martyr of the Hebrew canon, here paired with the first (Abel in Gen. 4.1-12), and because both their deaths call for vengeance (2 Chron. 24.22; Gen. 4.10).[12] Zechariah son of Jehoiada is also likely to come to mind

10. Unless otherwise stated, all quotations from the NT are from NRSV.

11. Zechariah is a priest, not a prophet, but that should not discourage seeing the allusion: he utters a prophet-like warning under the influence of the spirit (and, for Luke, the Spirit is the 'Spirit of Prophecy'; see Turner, *Power*). Luke 11.51 also calls him a prophet, although this is in a broad sense; see I. Howard Marshall, *The Gospel of Luke: A Commentary on the Greek Text*, NIGTC (Exeter: Paternoster, 1978), 506.

12. The doubt around the identity of this figure usually arises because of Matthew's account where he is called Zechariah son of Barachiah (Mt. 23.35). This figure has been identified with several people but the best option is a conflation of the individual of Zech. 1.1 with Zechariah son of Jehoiada (2 Chron. 24.20-22). See the discussion in, W. D. Davies and Dale C. Allison, *A Critical and Exegetical Commentary on the Gospel According to Saint Matthew*, ICC, 3 vols. (Edinburgh: T&T Clark, 1988–97), 3:318–19; but also J. M. Ross, 'Which Zechariah?', *IBS* 9, no. 2 (1987); Bock, *Luke*, 2:1123–24. This is likely to be Matthew's alteration of Q because of the amount of Matthew's redaction in this section; see Marshall, *Gospel*, 506; Siegfried Schulz, *Q: Die Spruchquelle der Evangelisten* (Zurich: Theologischer Verlag, 1972), 338 n. 120.

because his murder was well-known,[13] and his tomb probably stood in the Kidron valley, reminding people of the event.[14]

Interpreted against this background, it is likely that the reader would understand the saying as building on Lk. 13.33 and its expectation that Jesus would die as a rejected prophet in Jerusalem; Lk. 13.34 repeats that the prophets die in Jerusalem with the strong implicature that this is a deplorable act. Yet, because the reader is encouraged to explore further contexts in the search for relevance, there will be other implicatures; these will arise especially through the shared contextual implications of Lk. 13.34 and its intertexts.[15] First, Zechariah was killed for his message that God would abandon the people (resonating with the temple abandonment in Lk. 13.35) because the people had abandoned God. Their abandonment was a reference to their idolatry, and it is therefore likely to be a strong implicature that Jesus is a prophet like Zechariah who will be killed for his criticism of idolatry. Second, Zechariah was killed in the temple courts, and this associates the death of Jesus with the temple, albeit as a weaker implicature.[16]

The idea of Jesus as a prophet continues throughout Luke–Acts (Lk. 4.24; 7.16, 39; 24.19; Acts 3.22-23; 7.37),[17] and Jesus also acts as a prophet in many of the texts in the present study, but the theme of Jesus' death as a rejected temple-prophet is more fully dealt with in Stephen's speech, where it will be discussed further.

A Prophetic Evocation of Restoration or Exile

Having aligned himself with the rejected prophets, Jesus prophesies about the future of Jerusalem in Lk. 13.34-35. There are similarities between the form of Lk. 13.34 and typical OT prophetic reproaches,[18] and

---

13. There is memory of the event in *Liv. Proph.* 23.1; *b. Giṭ.* 57b; *b. Sanh.* 96b; *Eccl. Rab.* on 3.16; on 10.4. See Davies and Allison, *Matthew*, 3:319 n. 51.

14. Luke 11.47-48 may refer to this tomb; see Fisk, 'Tears', 154.

15. Commentators such as Pao and Schnabel ('Luke', 336) and Marshall (*Gospel*, 573) limit the thrust of Jesus' words here to stating that Jesus, as a prophet, should die in Jerusalem. But this does not go far enough.

16. Fisk, 'Tears', 158, notes some of these links, but mainly notes that both preached judgement without observing the similarities in message.

17. J. Severino Croatto, 'Jesus, Prophet Like Elijah, and Prophet-Teacher Like Moses in Luke–Acts', *JBL* 124, no. 3 (2005); Johnson, *Prophetic Jesus*.

18. The audience is repeatedly named; the crime is announced using participles; and a simile is used to show God's actions. See Schulz, *Q*, 352 n. 210.

Lk. 13.35a represents the subsequent threat.[19] Such similarities caused Robert Miller to comment that, 'Were it not for the actual accusation hurled at Jerusalem, the saying could pass for an OT citation'.[20] Such a genre evocation reinforces the prophetic context of the sayings as drawn from the OT.

The Rejection of Gathering

Lk. 13.34:

...ποσάκις ἠθέλησα ἐπισυνάξαι τὰ τέκνα σου ὃν τρόπον ὄρνις τὴν ἑαυτῆς νοσσιὰν ὑπὸ τὰς πτέρυγας, καὶ οὐκ ἠθελήσατε

...How often have I desired to gather your children together as a hen gathers her brood under her wings, and you were not willing!

The image of a bird sheltering its young under her wings in Lk. 13.34 is a common image of divine protection in the OT.[21] Several psalms utilise it:[22]

---

19. Introduced by ἰδού, a term used in LXX (1 Kgdms 2.31; 2 Kgdms 12.11; 3 Kgdms 11.31; Ezek. 5.8): Robert J. Miller, 'The Rejection of the Prophets in Q', *JBL* 107, no. 2 (1988): 234.
20. Ibid., although he also notes evidence of Christian additions in λέγω ὑμῖν. See also Giblin, *Jerusalem*, 37–40.
21. Several scholars have found a reference to wisdom in Lk. 13.34. See, e.g., Odil Hannes Steck, *Israel und das gewaltsame Geschick der Propheten: Untersuchungen zur Überlieferung des deuteronomistischen Geschichtsbildes im Alten Testament, Spätjudentum und Urchristentum*, WMANT 23 (Neukirchen-Vluyn: Neukirchener Verlag, 1967), 230–31; Rudolf Bultmann, *The History of the Synoptic Tradition*, trans. John Marsh, rev ed. (Oxford: Blackwell, 1968), 114–15; John S. Kloppenborg, *The Formation of Q: Trajectories in Ancient Wisdom Collections*, SAC (Philadelphia: Fortress, 1987), 228; Ronald A. Piper, *Wisdom in the Q-Tradition: The Aphoristic Teaching of Jesus*, SNTSMS 61 (Cambridge: Cambridge University Press, 1989), 164–56). This, however, seems to be unlikely; see Marshall, *Gospel*, 573–74; Miller, 'Prophets', 325–27; Tan, *Zion*, 110–12.
22. These allusions are noted by many commentaries; those noting them all include Marshall (*Gospel*, 575) and Bock (*Luke*, 2:1249). Other commentaries noting some of the allusions include Alfred Plummer, *A Critical and Exegetical Commentary on the Gospel According to S. Luke*, ICC, 5th ed. (Edinburgh: T&T Clark, 1922), 352; Pao and Schnabel, 'Luke', 336; John Nolland, *Luke*, WBC 35A–C, 3 vols. (Dallas: Word, 1989–93), 2:742. Notably, NA[28] only notes Ps. 35.8 of these psalms; NA[27] notes none.

Ps. 16.8 (17.8 ET):[23]

φύλαξόν με ὡς κόραν ὀφθαλμοῦ· ἐν σκέπῃ τῶν <u>πτερύγων</u> σου σκεπάσεις με.

Guard me as the eye's pupil; with your wings' shelter you will shelter me.[24]

Ps. 35.8:

ὡς ἐπλήθυνας τὸ ἔλεός σου, ὁ θεός· οἱ δὲ υἱοὶ τῶν ἀνθρώπων ἐν σκέπῃ τῶν <u>πτερύγων</u> σου ἐλπιοῦσιν.

How you increased your mercy, O God! But the sons of men will hope in the shelter of your wings.

Ps. 56.2:

Ἐλέησόν με, ὁ θεός, ἐλέησόν με, ὅτι ἐπὶ σοὶ πέποιθεν ἡ ψυχή μου καὶ ἐν τῇ σκιᾷ τῶν <u>πτερύγων</u> σου ἐλπιῶ, ἕως οὗ παρέλθῃ ἡ ἀνομία.

Have mercy on me, O God; have mercy on me, because in you my soul trusts and in the shadow of your wings I will hope until lawlessness passes by.

Ps. 60.5:

παροικήσω ἐν τῷ σκηνώματί σου εἰς τοὺς αἰῶνας, σκεπασθήσομαι ἐν σκέπῃ τῶν <u>πτερύγων</u> σου...

I will sojourn in your covert forever, find shelter in the shelter of your wings.

Ps. 62.8:

ὅτι ἐγενήθης βοηθός μου, καὶ ἐν τῇ σκέπῃ τῶν <u>πτερύγων</u> σου ἀγαλλιάσομαι.

because you became my helper, and in the shelter of your wings I will rejoice.

But these clearly differ to Luke: they refer to the shadow (σκέπη, σκιά) of YHWH's wings rather than ὑπὸ τὰς πτέρυγας; they are human observations or requests for shelter or protection, not a divine declaration of desire to shelter (as Luke); they do not use the verb ἐπισυνάγω; and

---

23. Unless otherwise indicated, psalm references are to the LXX; references to the ET or MT in the secondary literature will be adapted to LXX verse references. References in the later Jewish literature which specifically refer to the MT will be given as MT.

24. All English quotations of the LXX are from NETS.

all except Ps. 35.8 refer to a single person sheltering. The language of Ps. 90.4 is a little closer:[25]

> ἐν τοῖς μεταφρένοις αὐτοῦ ἐπισκιάσει σοι, καὶ <u>ὑπὸ τὰς πτέρυγας</u> αὐτοῦ ἐλπιεῖς· ὅπλῳ κυκλώσει σε ἡ ἀλήθεια αὐτοῦ.
>
> with the broad of his back he will shade you, and under his wings you will find hope; with a shield his truth will surround you.

Yet despite Luke's frequent allusion to these psalms there is not enough similarity for any of them to be the first textual link where a reader would find relevance. Ruth 2.12 has similar language and is similarly excluded:[26]

> ἀποτείσαι κύριος τὴν ἐργασίαν σου, καὶ γένοιτο ὁ μισθός σου πλήρης παρὰ κυρίου θεοῦ Ισραηλ, πρὸς ὃν ἦλθες πεποιθέναι <u>ὑπὸ τὰς πτέρυγας</u> αὐτοῦ.
>
> May the Lord repay you for your work, and may your recompense be full from the Lord, God of Israel, to whom you came, to put your trust under his wings!

Deuteronomy 32.11 has two key parallel lexical terms (νοσσιά and πτέρυξ):[27]

> ὡς ἀετὸς σκεπάσαι <u>νοσσιὰν</u> αὐτοῦ καὶ ἐπὶ τοῖς νεοσσοῖς αὐτοῦ ἐπεπόθησεν, διεὶς τὰς <u>πτέρυγας</u> αὐτοῦ ἐδέξατο αὐτοὺς καὶ ἀνέλαβεν αὐτοὺς ἐπὶ τῶν μεταφρένων αὐτοῦ.
>
> Like an eagle to protect his brood, he too yearned for his young; spreading his wings, he received them and bore them aloft on his back;

Notably, the bird in Deut 32.11 is ἀετός, not Luke's ὄρνις; it has masculine pronouns for the brood, not feminine; and the eagle is training its young in flight, which is different to the language of protection in Luke.[28]

---

25. NA[28], and several commentaries, including Marshall, *Gospel*, 575; Bock, *Luke*, 2:1249; Pao and Schnabel, 'Luke', 336; Johnson, *Luke*, 219; James R. Edwards, *The Gospel According to Luke*, PNTC (Nottingham: Apollos, 2015), 407.

26. Noted by Marshall, *Gospel*, 575; Pao and Schnabel, 'Luke', 336; Bock, *Luke*, 2:1249; Nolland, *Luke*, 2:742; Edwards, *Luke*.

27. The intertext favoured by Jerome, as noted in Plummer, *Luke*, 352; NA[28]; and several commentaries, including Marshall, *Gospel*, 575; Johnson, *Luke*, 219; Pao and Schnabel, 'Luke', 336.

28. For the activity of the eagle, see Richard D. Nelson, *Deuteronomy: A Commentary*, OTL (Louisville: Westminster John Knox, 2002), 372.

Isaiah 31.5 is closer still:²⁹

ὡς ὄρνεα πετόμενα, οὕτως ὑπερασπιεῖ κύριος ὑπὲρ Ιερουσαλημ καὶ ἐξελεῖται καὶ περιποιήσεται καὶ σώσει

Like birds flying, so the Lord will shield Ierousalem; he will deliver and preserve and save it.

The two words in common with Luke are significant ones (ὄρνις and Ἰερουσαλήμ), and there is some conceptual similarity in the imagery that stresses protection (a mother bird at her nest when a predator is near).³⁰ The contextual similarity is especially pronounced in Isaiah's expansion of the divine protective activity: where Luke has one verb (ἐπισυνάγω), Isaiah has four (ὑπερασπίζω, ἐξαιρέω, περιποιέω and σῴζω) in his call for Israel to repent, to abandon her alliance with Egypt, and to trust in YHWH. But a reader is unlikely to locate relevance here alone because there is not the immediate link with the images of wings in Lk. 13.34, imagery which is fundamental and found in other texts.

So, none of these texts are distinctive enough to be the sole intertext.³¹ It is more likely that the interpretive context for these words in Luke would be in the motif of YHWH's care of his people; this idea was common enough in the OT and is present in several later Jewish texts,³² and as such was commonly available to the group of people that the readers of the Gospel belonged to.³³ This is the context where the intertext would find relevance.³⁴

Having made this link, there are four aspects which would contribute to the understanding. The first two relate to similarities between the

---

29. NA²⁸, and commentaries, including Bock, *Luke*, 2:1249; Plummer, *Luke*, 352; Marshall, *Gospel*, 575.

30. John N. Oswalt, *The Book of Isaiah Chapters 1–39*, NICOT (Grand Rapids: Eerdmans, 1986), 570–73.

31. 2 Esdras 1.30 also uses the image of a hen but this is clearly a Christianised later text; Jacob M. Myers, *I and II Esdras: Introduction, Translation and Commentary*, AB 42 (New York: Doubleday, 1974), 155.

32. Pao and Schnabel, 'Luke', 336, lists *1 En.* 39.7; *Sipre Deut.* 296.3; 306.4; 314.1; *b. Soṭah* 13b; *Pesiq. Rab Kah.* 16.1; *Pesiq. Rab.* 14.2. Pao and Schnabel also note that it was sometimes used to describe proselytes coming for shelter under the wing of the Shekinah, listing: *'Abot R. Nat.* 12a; *Sipra Qed.* Pq. 8.205; *Sipre Num.* 80.1; *Sipre Deut.* 32.2; *b. 'Abod. Zar.* 13b; *b. Šabb.* 31a; *Gen. Rab.* 47.10; *Pesiq. Rab.* 14.2, but these ideas are too late to be considered here.

33. Metarepresented, in relevance theory terms.

34. This is the effective conclusion of most commentaries when they list several of the texts above.

contexts of Lk. 13.34 and the OT. First, the imagery is typically used for protection from a real threat – whether personal attacks in the psalms or national threat of judgement – and Jesus would therefore be understood as speaking about his ability to defend from real threat, not offer spiritualised protection. Second, while YHWH may provide the shelter, there is a human responsibility for receiving it. This is made especially clear through the parallel uses of θέλω to describe Jesus' desire, and the desire of the Jerusalemites.

The other two arise where Jesus' saying departs from OT imagery. Third, Jesus' image of a hen is unique in the Jewish literature,[35] and this maternal adaptation is likely to find relevance through an implicature which emphasises the love which Jesus has for the city and his desire to protect them. This passion is also emphasised by the use of the double vocative Ἰερουσαλήμ Ἰερουσαλήμ (a construction used in 2 Kgdms 18.33; Jer 22.29).[36] Fourth, Luke uses the verb ἐπισυνάγω, which is not present in the OT sheltering intertexts. As Christopher Evans points out, ἐπισυνάγω is normally associated with restoration hopes describing the gathering of Israel in the LXX (in Pss 105.47; 146.2; 2 Macc. 1.27; 2.18; Isa. 52.12; its related term συνάγω is used in Isa. 27.12; Zech. 2.10); in addition, ἐπισυνάγω is used in an eschatological sense in the NT in Mt. 24.31 (and the parallel Mk 13.27), and its cognate, ἐπισυναγωγή, is used eschatologically in 2 Thess. 2.1.[37] While the idea of protection and salvation is clearly present in the metaphor, the deliberate use of ἐπισυνάγω raises implications of the restoration hopes of the eschatological ingathering of the people: this raises eschatological expectancy over Jesus' actions in Jerusalem,[38] and makes it clear that this is the salvation that the people of the city reject.[39]

---

35. Tan, *Zion*, 111, it is found in Christianised later texts; see, e.g., 2 Esd. 1.30.
36. Bock, *Luke*, 2:1248-49.
37. Both terms are used with a more mundane meaning elsewhere: ἐπισυνάγω in Mk 1.33; Lk. 12.1; and ἐπισυναγωγή in Heb. 10.25. See Christopher F. Evans, *Saint Luke*, TPINTC (London: SCM, 1990), 564, and also Werner Foerster, 'Ἐπισυναγωγή', *TDNT* 7:842; Bridge, *Eagles*, 54.
38. Richard Bauckham, 'The Restoration of Israel in Luke–Acts', in *Restoration: Old Testament, Jewish, and Christian Perspectives*, ed. M. Scott, JSJSup 7 (Leiden: Brill, 2001), 457-58.
39. The conclusions of N. T. Wright that the saying refers to Jesus offering to save Jerusalem are fundamentally correct, but there is no clear evidence in the OT contexts for the imagery of a farmyard fire which he uses to show this salvation comes at the expense of Jesus' life, N. T. Wright, *Jesus and the Victory of God*, Christian Origins and the Question of God 2 (London: SPCK, 1996), 570-51.

The Abandonment of the House to Exile
The consequence of this rejection immediately follows: ἰδοὺ ἀφίεται ὑμῖν ὁ οἶκος ὑμῶν (Lk. 13.35). In order to understand this text it is important to identify the meaning of ὁ οἶκος, and to determine what intertexts underlie it. There are four possibilities for the meaning of ὁ οἶκος:

(i) The temple: while the lament is addressed to Jerusalem, the temple is the centre of the city and οἶκος is commonly used for the temple in the OT (e.g., 3 Kgdms 9.1-9; 2 Chron. 7.19-22; Jer. 7.10-14; 33.4-6 [26.4-6 ET]; Ezek. 10.18),[40] and in Luke (6.4; 11.51; 19.46).[41] This is, perhaps, the most obvious referent and it remains the favoured interpretation of several scholars.[42]

(ii) The city: John Nolland argues that οἶκος has a general reference to the whole city because it is taken that way in Jer. 22.1-8, which he regards as an important intertext.[43] Similarly, David Moessner argues that abandonment in Lk. 13.35 is the typical Deuteronomistic term for the destruction of the city because God has abandoned it to its enemies.[44]

(iii) The nation of Israel: where it refers to the '"household" of Jerusalem', the centre of the whole nation of people who are opposing God.[45]

(iv) The Judean leadership: Francis Weinert regards Jer. 22.5 as the intertext to Lk. 13.35a, and because the house in Jer. 22.1-2 referred to the royal household, then the equivalent in Luke must be the leaders of the people in Jerusalem.[46]

---

40. For references (except Ezek. 10.18), see Tan, *Zion*, 114.

41. Though Luke uses other terms too. See Head, 'Temple', 108.

42. Thomas W. Manson, *The Sayings of Jesus as Recorded in the Gospels According to St. Matthew and St. Luke, Arranged with Introduction and Commentary* (London: SCM, 1949), 127 (as both the temple and the Jewish commonwealth); Norval Geldenhuys, *Commentary on the Gospel of Luke*, NLC (London: Marshall, Morgan & Scott, 1950), 384; C. H. Dodd, *The Parables of the Kingdom*, rev. ed. (London: Nisbet, 1935), 44–45; Werner Georg Kümmel, *Promise and Fulfilment: The Eschatological Message of Jesus*, trans. Dorothea M. Barton, 2nd ed. (London: SCM, 1961), 80–81; Joachim Jeremias, *The Parables of Jesus. Revised Edition*, trans. S. H. Hooke, 3rd ed. (London: SCM, 1963), 167–68; Ellis, *Luke*, 191; Wright, *Victory*, 571; Head, 'Temple', 113–14; Fisk, 'Tears', 162–64; Marcus J. Borg, *Conflict, Holiness, and Politics in the Teachings of Jesus* (Harrisburg, PA: Trinity Press International, 1998), 194.

43. Nolland, *Luke*, 2:742.

44. Moessner, *Lord*, 23 n. 133. See also the discussion in Steck, *Israel*, 228; Marshall, *Gospel*, 576.

45. Joel B. Green, *The Gospel of Luke*, NICNT (Grand Rapids: Eerdmans, 1997), 539, including the quotation. See also, Pao and Schnabel, 'Luke', 336.

46. Weinert, 'Luke', 74–76. See also Fitzmyer, *Luke*, 2:1037; Giblin, *Jerusalem*, 42; Bock, *Proclamation*, 326 n. 115.

There are good reasons for thinking that the temple is in view.[47] First, Jesus addresses Jerusalem in the second person in 13.34 (σου ... ἠθελήσατε) meaning that in 13.35 ὑμῶν refers to Jerusalem;[48] in that case ὁ οἶκος is *Jerusalem's* house, and therefore cannot be the city or the nation, it is most likely the temple.[49] Second, Ps. 117.26 (which is cited in Lk. 13.35) concludes by referring to the temple using οἶκος,[50] as does 2 Chron. 24.21; the term is therefore an important link between these intertexts.[51] Third, if Jer. 22.5 is not the major intertext behind Lk. 13.35 (as argued below) then it cannot control the meaning of ὁ οἶκος (against the city and Judean leadership hypothesis).[52] While ὁ οἶκος referring to the temple does not affect the explicit meaning of the saying (because if the city is abandoned so is the temple, and vice versa), it does influence the implicatures gained in reading the text.

Turning to the possible intertexts, the most commonly noted intertexts are from Jeremiah.[53]

Jer. 12.7:

Ἐγκαταλέλοιπα τὸν οἶκόν μου, ἀφῆκα τὴν κληρονομίαν μου, ἔδωκα τὴν ἠγαπημένην ψυχήν μου εἰς χεῖρας ἐχθρῶν αὐτῆς.

I have forsaken my house; I have let go of my heritage; I have given my beloved soul into the hands of her enemies.

While this has οἶκος and ἀφίημι in common with Luke, these terms are not in the same clause, and Jeremiah's verb for abandonment (ἐγκαταλείπω) is a little stronger than Luke's ἀφίημι.[54] An alternative is Jer. 22.5:

---

47. Marshall objected that ὁ οἶκος ὑμῶν cannot refer to *your* temple because the only pronominal suffix that 'house' ever takes when referring to the temple in the OT is one referring to God. See Marshall, *Gospel*, 576. However, this is not true in the case of ὁ οἶκος, τό ἅγιον ἡμῶν in Isa. 64.10-11; see Tan, *Zion*, 114–15.

48. Fisk, 'Tears', 163. The change from singular σου to plural ἠθελήσατε is because of the collective noun Ἰερουσαλήμ.

49. While it *could* be the leadership, this is excluded by the other points here.

50. Fisk, 'Tears', 163–64.

51. Dale C. Allison, *The Intertextual Jesus: Scripture in Q* (Harrisburg, PA: Trinity Press International, 2000), 128.

52. And even if it was the intertext, it is debatable whether Jeremiah's meaning trumps contextual meaning in Luke; see Head, 'Temple', 113; Fisk, 'Tears', 163.

53. While NA[27] has both Jer. 12.7 and 22.5, NA[28] only has Jer. 12.7. Both texts are noted by Pao and Schnabel, 'Luke', 336–37; Fisk, 'Tears', 160–66; Bock, *Luke*, 2:1250. Jeremiah 22.5 is also noted by Fitzmyer, *Luke*, 2:1036; Nolland, *Luke*, 2:742.

54. Fisk, 'Tears', 160.

ἐὰν δὲ μὴ ποιήσητε τοὺς λόγους τούτους, κατ' ἐμαυτοῦ ὤμοσα, λέγει κύριος, ὅτι εἰς ἐρήμωσιν ἔσται ὁ <u>οἶκος</u> οὗτος.

But if you will not do these words, by myself I have sworn, says the Lord, that this house shall become a desolation –

The only lexical similarity with Lk. 13.35 is οἶκος; unlike Mt. 23.38, Luke has no ἔρημος to parallel Jeremiah's ἐρήμωσιν, and because of that there is no clear textual link here.[55] Bruce Fisk thinks that other parallels between Luke and Jeremiah make the case stronger, but the examples he notes are not clear at this stage of the Lukan narrative – they only become noticeable when Jesus weeps in 19.41.[56]

An alternative depiction of the departure of YHWH from the temple is in Ezekiel.[57] Some specific verses have been proposed as likely candidates.[58]

Ezek. 10.18-19:

[18]καὶ ἐξῆλθεν δόξα κυρίου ἀπὸ τοῦ οἴκου καὶ ἐπέβη ἐπὶ τὰ χερουβιν, [19]καὶ ἀνέλαβον τὰ χερουβιν τὰς πτέρυγας αὐτῶν καὶ ἐμετεωρίσθησαν ἀπὸ τῆς γῆς ἐνώπιον ἐμοῦ ἐν τῷ ἐξελθεῖν αὐτὰ καὶ οἱ τροχοὶ ἐχόμενοι αὐτῶν καὶ ἔστησαν ἐπὶ τὰ πρόθυρα τῆς πύλης οἴκου κυρίου τῆς ἀπέναντι, καὶ δόξα θεοῦ Ισραηλ ἦν ἐπ' αὐτῶν ὑπεράνω.

[18]And the glory of the Lord went out from the house and mounted upon the cheroubin, [19]and the cheroubin lifted up their wings, and they were borne aloft from the earth before me when they went out together with the wheels beside them, and they stood at the entry of the opposite gate of the house of the Lord, and the glory of God of Israel was upon them from above.

---

55. See Head, 'Temple', 113. Several Lukan manuscripts contain ἔρημος (e.g., D N Δ Θ Ψ f^{13}); however, its omission is more likely to be original because it is more difficult reading, and it is not present in several significant witnesses ($\mathfrak{P}^{45vid, 75}$ ℵ A B L W f^1). See Fitzmyer, *Luke*, 2:1036; Metzger, *Commentary*, 138.

56. E.g., Jer. 22.10 and Lk. 23.28-29. Fisk also notes that Jeremiah, Lamentations and Baruch were influential on other contemporary Jewish writing; see Fisk, 'Tears', 160–66.

57. Psalm 68.26 has also been suggested, e.g., by NA[28]; Bock, *Luke*, 2:1250, but it relies on ἐρημόω and refers to an abandoned camp. It is best discounted.

58. Josef Ernst, *Das Evangelium nach Lukas*, RNT (Regensburg: Friedrich Pustet, 1977), 434, notes Ezek. 8.6 (though this is not close in LXX); 11.23. Fisk, 'Tears', 160 n. 45, notes Ezek. 10.18-19, but he prefers Jeremiah. More general are Beasley-Murray, *Kingdom*, 305 (Ezek. 10.1-22, 22-25); Wright, *Victory*, 331 (Ezek. 10); and Borg, *Conflict*, 194 (similar to events in Ezekiel and Jeremiah).

Ezek. 11.23:

καὶ ἀνέβη ἡ δόξα κυρίου ἐκ μέσης τῆς πόλεως καὶ ἔστη ἐπὶ τοῦ ὄρους, ὃ ἦν ἀπέναντι τῆς πόλεως.

and the glory of the Lord ascended from the midst of the city and stopped on the mountain that was opposite the city.

The lexical links to these verses are limited to οἶκος in Ezek. 10.18-19. This should make it no more obvious to the reader than Jeremiah, but there are a couple of reasons why it might be closer. The force of οἶκος becomes magnified when the whole of ch. 10 of Ezekiel is regarded as the intertext: not only is οἶκος relatively common in the chapter (five occurrences), but the chapter also describes the departure of the Lord from the temple in powerful and highly visual terms. This actual departure (rather than Jeremiah's warnings) is closer to the imminent sense of Jesus' saying conveyed by Luke's use of the present tense. In addition, if Luke had wanted the reader to think of Jer. 22.5, then he would surely have included ἐρημός. As it stands, Ezekiel 10 is at least as likely as Jeremiah as a context, probably more likely.

It may not matter whether the reader turns to Jeremiah, Ezekiel or a generalised recall of prophetic sayings about divine abandonment of the temple: they all have in common the abandonment by YHWH at the time of the exile, and it is likely that this is where the relevance of the phrase would be found. In each case, the accompanying contextual information associates the abandonment with the destruction of the city, and with the sin of the people: Ezekiel addressed idolatry,[59] and Jeremiah injustice and idolatry.[60] Such concepts would enrich the interpretation obtained by the reader, and this is probably where the search for relevance would stop because it is likely to fulfil expectations of optimal relevance for the phrase – there are no clear signals in the Lukan text that further relevance can be achieved by expending further processing effort in accessing a particular OT context.

---

59. Stephen L. Cook, 'Cosmos, *Kabod*, and Cherub: Ontological and Epistemological Hierarchy in Ezekiel', in *Ezekiel's Hierarchical World: Wrestling with a Tiered Reality*, ed. Stephen L. Cook and Corrine L. Patton (Atlanta: Society of Biblical Literature, 2004), 188–89.

60. Jeremiah 5.26-29; 6.13; 7.5-6; 22.17 and idolatry in Jer. 22.9. See Fisk, 'Tears', 161–62. Jeremiah is critical of the priests for their failure in showing the people their sin, Lena-Sofia Tiemeyer, 'The Priests and the Temple Cult in the Book of Jeremiah', in *Prophecy in the Book of Jeremiah*, ed. Hans M. Barstad and Reinhard Gregor Kratz, BZAW 388 (Berlin: de Gruyter, 2009).

Jesus is therefore referring to the abandonment of the temple, the departure of the glory, with the associated concepts that it is an event like the exile, happening because of the sin of the people. What makes this statement particularly marked is its association with the rejection of Jesus and his offer of protection.[61] The rejection of Jesus is then further emphasised in the following words.

The Identification of Jesus as Saviour

The end of the oracle has a verbatim quotation of six words from Ps. 117.26: εὐλογημένος ὁ ἐρχόμενος ἐν ὀνόματι κυρίου. Its only introduction in the Lukan text is εἴπητε, which marks it out as a representation of the thoughts of the Jerusalemites, not as a quotation; however, its highly distinctive language is sufficient to identify this well-known OT text. There are two issues that require discussion. First, how will the reader understand the psalm quotation? Second, Lk. 13.35 identifies these words as spoken by the people of Jerusalem at some point in the future – when will this be?

The Psalm Quotation

Among the implicatures which would contribute to the relevance of this quotation for the reader, four stand out.

---

61. 1 Thessalonians 2.14-16 also refers to the Jewish leaders killing Jesus and the prophets, and it associates this with ἔφθασεν δὲ ἐπ' αὐτοὺς ἡ ὀργὴ εἰς τέλος. Some regard this as a prophetic reference to the destruction of the Jerusalem temple, but the most natural way to take ἔφθασεν is with a past reference. Pearson argues that these verses are a later interpolation referring to the historical destruction of the temple. Birger A. Pearson, '1 Thessalonians 2:13–16: A Deutero-Pauline Interpolation', *HTR* 64, no. 1 (1971). This, however, is unconvincing, and it is more likely to be a reference to a recent event that Paul's readers would be aware of. For exegetical argument to support this, see Gene L. Green, *The Letters to the Thessalonians*, PNTC (Leicester: Apollos, 2002), 141–50; and Charles A. Wanamaker, *The Epistles to the Thessalonians: A Commentary on the Greek Text*, NIGTC (Grand Rapids: Eerdmans, 1990), 112–19; Abraham J. Malherbe, *The Letters to the Thessalonians: A New Translation with Introduction and Commentary*, AB 32B (New York: Doubleday, 2000), 172–79, and the bibliography there. For a detailed case for an eschatological perspective, and an evaluation of interpolation, see David Luckensmeyer, *The Eschatology of First Thessalonians* (Göttingen: Vandenhoeck & Ruprecht, 2009), 152–67. Without a clear reference to the temple, this text does not contribute anything substantial to the argument in Luke–Acts.

(i) Jesus as the Messiah
Although the term ὁ ἐρχόμενος is variously understood as the eschatological prophet, an Elijah figure, the Son of Man, or the Messiah, this does not require that it simply expresses 'the essence of all Jewish eschatological hope' in Lk. 13.35, as John Nolland concludes.[62] The reader would interpret this potentially polyvalent term in the context which is most manifest, the context of Psalm 117.

A good case can be made for this psalm (and other Hallel psalms) being understood with a messianic and eschatological reference later in the Second Temple period because several texts demonstrate this: *b. Pesaḥ.* 118b (Ps. 118.1 MT); *b. Pesaḥ.* 118a (Ps. 115.1 MT); *Midr. Ps.* 36 §6 (Ps. 118.27 MT); *Pesiq. Rab Kah.* 17.7 (Ps. 118.15 MT); and *y. Ber.* 4d (2.4) (Ps. 118.27-28 MT).[63] These are late texts (no earlier than the late second century), and there are no quotations of Psalm 118 (MT) in earlier literature that prove the same application in Jesus' time.[64] However, this does not exclude its messianic use in the first century because the interpretation in these later texts developed from a growing messianic use of these psalms.[65] The original setting of the psalm was quite possibly an annual enthronement ritual involving the king,[66] and because of this it is commonly classified as a royal psalm. If this is the case, then it is likely that by Jesus' day this psalm would have been understood as referring

---

62. Nolland, *Luke*, 1:328–29, quotation 329.
63. J. Ross Wagner, 'Psalm 118 in Luke–Acts: Tracing a Narrative Thread', in *Early Christian Interpretation of the Scriptures of Israel: Investigations and Proposals*, ed. Craig A. Evans and James A. Sanders, JSNTSup 148 (Sheffield: Sheffield Academic, 1997), 158, and the discussion on 157–61. Other scholars agree; see Joachim Jeremias, *The Eucharistic Words of Jesus*, trans. Norman Perrin (London: SCM, 1966), 255–61; Barnabas F. C. Lindars, *New Testament Apologetic: The Doctrinal Significance of the Old Testament Quotations* (London: SCM, 1961), 169–85; Brent Kinman, *Jesus' Entry into Jerusalem: In the Context of Lukan Theology and the Politics of His Day* (Leiden: Brill, 1995), 57–58; Allison, *Jesus*, 163; Andrew Brunson, *Psalm 118 in the Gospel of John: An Intertextual Study on the New Exodus Pattern in the Theology of John*, WUNT 2/158 (Tübingen: Mohr Siebeck, 2003), 22–101.
64. Wagner, 'Psalm', 159.
65. For details on the Jewish use of the psalm, see Brunson, *Psalm 118*, 22–101. He cautiously accepts these later texts as contributory evidence for a first-century messianic use, as does Wagner, 'Psalm', 157–61.
66. E.g., the autumn festival; see Sigmund Mowinckel, *The Psalms in Israel's Worship*, trans. D. R. Ap-Thomas, 2 vols. (Oxford: Blackwell, 1962), 2:118–21, 70, 80–81, 245; Mitchell J. Dahood, *Psalms*, 3 vols., AB 16–17A (Garden City: Doubleday, 1965–70), 3:155; Leslie C. Allen, *Psalms 101–150*, WBC 21 (Waco: Word, 1983), 163–65. A liturgy for this is proposed by James A. Sanders, 'A Hermeneutic

to the Messiah because the arrangement of the psalms by the post-exilic editor is 'highly eschatological in nature',[67] with the royal psalms pointing to the messianic hope (because the Messiah is the obvious reference when there has been no king in Jerusalem for a long time).[68] In addition to this, the frequent use of the psalm in the NT with a messianic reference means that a Christian reader of the citation in Lk. 13.35 is likely to interpret it in a messianic way: however readers from other Jewish backgrounds might interpret it, in the Christian community it was messianic.[69]

So the psalm quotation would be understood as a reference to people recognising Jesus as Messiah, and praising God. But this cannot be all that the reader would understand: optimal relevance demands more, because such a meaning could be conveyed without a quotation. The extra processing effort that the quotation requires will be matched with more implicatures which will include the following, from strongest to weakest.

(ii) Association with Eschatological Hopes of Liberation
It is quite likely this psalm had a place in Jewish liturgy as part of the Egyptian Hallel, and would have been sung at the feasts of Tabernacles and Passover.[70] Although the evidence for this is in the Mishnah,[71] liturgical practice is typically fairly constant, and it is likely that the psalm also had this role in Jesus' day (see the hint of it in Mk 14.26).[72] These very familiar contexts would be accessed in the search for the meaning of the quotation in Lk. 13.35. Both of these feasts concern God's acts of deliverance for his people,[73] and it is notable that the New Exodus cluster

---

Fabric: Psalm 118 in Luke's Entrance Narrative', in Evans and Sanders, eds., *Luke and Scripture*, 146–47. For a description of the festival and the role of the psalm, see Brunson, *Psalm 118*, 26–34.

67. Brevard S. Childs, *Introduction to the Old Testament as Scripture* (Philadelphia: Fortress, 1979), 518.

68. Ibid., 516; Wagner, 'Psalm', 159.

69. Wagner, 'Psalm', 161.

70. Allen, *Psalms 101–150*, 134; for details see Solomon Zeitlin, 'The Hallel: A Historical Study of the Canonization of the Hebrew Liturgy', *JQR* 53, no. 1 (1962).

71. For Tabernacles see *m. Sukkah* 3.9; 4.1, 5, 8; for Passover and its meal, *m. Pesaḥ.* 5.7; 10.5-7. See Wagner, 'Psalm', 160. For a comprehensive overview of Ps 117 in these contexts, see Brunson, *Psalm 118*, 45–101.

72. As argued in Wagner, 'Psalm', 160 n. 22, citing Craig A. Evans ('Early Rabbinic Sources and Jesus Research', *SBLSP* 34 [1995]: 56) in support.

73. For evidence for the eschatological significance of Tabernacles, see Brunson, *Psalm 118*, 45–58, including Zech. 14 describing the celebration of Tabernacles in the renewed temple; there are also eschatological developments of Tabernacles themes in *1 En.* 60 and *Jub.* 16.

of hopes for return from Exile made an association between Passover and the first exodus.[74] Such liturgical settings for the psalm would encourage it to be read with a focus on God's eschatological deliverance,[75] with a return from exile theme close at hand for the reader because of the use of ἐπισυνάγω in Lk. 13.34.

(iii) Association with the Temple
Psalm 117 is processional, and the participants in the psalm enter the temple and proceed to the altar (117.19-27);[76] more notably, the verse quoted continues with a welcome from the temple (εὐλογήκαμεν ὑμᾶς ἐξ οἴκου κυρίου, 117.26). It is highly likely that this temple association would form part of the psalm's weaker implicatures because of the context of its discussion in Luke 13, and its use in temple processionals at the feast of Tabernacles.

(iv) Liturgical Setting
Finally, the use of a psalm for the words spoken by the people in Lk. 13.35 encourages the reader to develop implicatures that these words would be spoken in a formalised setting, because of the liturgical associations of these words. These implicatures would be weaker, but their role in the narrative is an important one because they create audience expectation about what might happen, and encourage the exploration of ideas that the later narrative might develop.

Other weaker implicatures might gather around these, but the principal expectation generated by this psalm quotation is of a recognition of Jesus as Messiah, God's eschatological agent of deliverance (perhaps incorporating New Exodus hopes).[77] The question arises: When is this likely to happen?

---

74. Ibid., 63–82, taking ideas expressed by Wright, *New Testament*, 269–72, although Wright's whole return from exile thesis is not necessary for the point to stand. Ezekiel the Tragedian, *Exagoge* 188–92, associated the feast with hopes for deliverance, and later rabbinic writing referred to Passover as the time when God acted on behalf of Israel, expecting messianic deliverance to happen at the time of the feast. See Brunson, *Psalm 118*, 57–58.

75. Wagner, 'Psalm', 160.

76. Brunson, *Psalm 118*, 36.

77. Le Donne notes a rejection motif in the NT use of the psalm, with the psalm used to indict the Jerusalem leadership in Lk. 13.35. Anthony Le Donne, 'The Improper Temple Offering of Ananias and Sapphira', *NTS* 59, no. 3 (2013): 351. He is correct that the psalm is used for these reasons, but the main function of the psalm here is to show the future greeting of the Messiah in Jerusalem; it is the later uses that develop the rejection theme.

The Timing of the Utterance

Jerusalem is informed that it will not see Jesus again until it utters the psalm quotation. Because the abandonment of the house in Lk. 13.34 seems to occur while the coming one is absent from Jerusalem, most commentators understand the timing of this utterance to be at the parousia.[78] For some, these are words of judgement on Jerusalem: the opportunity for repentance is past and the people will not see Jesus again until they speak the psalm's words, presumably from fear, at the parousia.[79] But this interpretation requires that the joyful εὐλογημένος of the psalm becomes a word of fear uttered by those under judgement, and there is no precedent for a wicked person uttering a blessing when the Messiah comes.[80] Others suggest that the words are uttered joyfully because Jerusalem will then know salvation and accept her Messiah.[81] But such certainty of future hope would take the sting right out of the oracle of judgement.[82]

Dale Allison's alternative proposal is that the oracle is seen as a conditional prophecy detailing certain conditions which Jerusalem is required to meet.[83] Grammatically it is possible for οὐ μὴ ἴδητέ με ἕως [ἥξει ὅτε] εἴπητε to be understood in this way: ἕως is not only temporal but conditional, with the phrase functioning in a similar manner to a negative condition. It could be translated as 'you will not see me *unless* you say', effectively meaning that when his people bless the Messiah, he will come.[84] Allison surveys an impressive range of rabbinic texts which show a similar contingency in the time of the eschaton, and argues that the structure of Lk. 13.35 can be understood in this manner.[85] Allison's interpretation makes good sense of the oracle: there is hope in the possibility of repentance, but without repentance the judgement remains.[86] However, the timing of this event at the eschaton is questionable.

---

78. E.g., Marshall, *Gospel*, 577; Bock, *Proclamation*, 117–21; Strauss, *Messiah*, 315–17.

79. Manson, *Sayings*, 128; Gaston, *Stone*, 455.

80. Dale C. Allison, 'Matt. 23:39 = Luke 13:35b as Conditional Prophecy', *JSNT* 18 (1983): 75–76; Tan, *Zion*, 116.

81. Geldenhuys, *Luke*, 383; Ernst, *Lukas*, 434; Marshall, *Gospel*, 577. Plummer sees it as the salvation of Jews throughout time, not at the parousia. See Plummer, *Luke*, 353.

82. See Allison, 'Prophecy', 76–77; Tan, *Zion*, 116–18; Fisk, 'Tears', 167.

83. Allison, 'Prophecy', 76–77.

84. For the translation, see Fisk, 'Tears', 169.

85. Allison, 'Prophecy', 77–80. Bruce Fisk has demonstrated that in Luke–Acts clauses containing a negative condition and a subordinate clause introduced by ἕως can be either conditional or unconditional. See Fisk, 'Tears', 168–69.

86. He is followed by Tan, *Zion*, 115–18; Green, *Gospel*, 538; Fisk, 'Tears', 166–70.

The same words from Ps. 117.26 are also spoken at the arrival of Jesus in Jerusalem in Lk. 19.38, meaning that the referent of Lk. 13.35 could be Jesus' entry into Jerusalem.[87] Those favouring the parousia argue against this on several fronts: it denies the temporal sequence of 13.35 (Jerusalem sees Jesus *after* the house is abandoned); the people do not utter the words in Lk. 19.38, only the disciples do; and it would make the whole oracle anticlimactic, with Jesus effectively saying the obvious, 'you will not see me until I arrive in Jerusalem'.[88] But at least on a literary level there is a good case. This solution does not deny the temporal sequence of 13.35, because while ἀφίεται is a present tense it can convey a futuristic sense.[89] It is a *threat* of judgement which hangs over Jerusalem in the time of Jesus' absence before Luke 19, not the actual abandonment of the house before the parousia. If they welcome Jesus and accept the shelter under his wings, then disaster can still be averted; if not, their fate is sealed. The sense then becomes: 'You were not willing to gather under my wings. See, your house will become desolate. And I tell you, you will not see me unless you say, "blessed is he who comes in the name of the Lord"'. If they welcome him, then they will truly perceive Jesus as Messiah who will save the people, and the judgement of abandonment will not happen; if they do not utter the words, then the temple's fate is certain.[90]

This approach takes seriously the position of Lk. 13.34-35 in the journey narrative before the entry to the city,[91] and gives sufficient weight to the narrative force of the psalm quotation – its reuse in Luke 19 forms an interpretive bridge between the chapters. A reference to seeing him at the time of the entry is neither obvious nor anticlimactic – quite the reverse. It is the proper climax of the journey narrative and the preparation for the events leading to the cross.

Conclusion

The lament of Lk. 13.34-35 introduces some important themes, especially those of Jesus' rejection as a prophet and a saviour. The context of the

---

87. Lindars, *Apologetic*, 172; Eduard Schweizer, *The Good News According to Luke* (London: SPCK, 1984), 230–31; Green, *Gospel*, 538–39; Wagner, 'Psalm', 163; Dietrich Rusam, *Das Alte Testament bei Lukas*, ZNW 112 (Berlin: de Gruyter, 2003), 224; John T. Carroll, *Luke: A Commentary*, NTL (Louisville: Westminster John Knox, 2012).
88. Fisk, 'Tears', 167; see also the discussion in Marshall, *Gospel*, 577.
89. BDF, §323; Marshall, *Gospel*, 576.
90. This does not exclude a further chance at the parousia. See Fisk, 'Tears', 168.
91. Brunson, *Psalm 118*, 114–15.

oracle makes it clear that Jesus expected to be rejected in Jerusalem as a prophet, and the reference to the persecution of past prophets in 13.34 draws the reader's attention to Lk. 11.49-51, and through this verse to the story of Zechariah in 2 Chron. 24.20-21. The association with this prophet raises the suggestion that Jesus' prophetic message might contain criticisms of worship practices associated with the temple (including idolatry) and that this will be a contributing factor in his death. Although the detail of his prophetic message is not given in this chapter, Jesus does predict the abandonment of the temple.

Jesus will also be rejected as a saviour. The saying ποσάκις ἠθέλησα ἐπισυνάξαι τὰ τέκνα σου ὃν τρόπον ὄρνις τὴν ἑαυτῆς νοσσιὰν ὑπὸ τὰς πτέρυγας echoes a motif common in the OT – of protection from real threat – but Jesus' offer requires a response from the people. The language used evokes restoration hopes of the ingathering of Israel from exile, but the saying evokes other exilic language too. In referring to the abandonment of ὁ οἶκος ὑμῶν, Jesus refers to the temple in language echoing the exilic prophets, bringing to mind implicatures of the past disaster and the sin which led to it. The final part of the oracle uses a quotation of Ps. 117.26 which plays a crucial role in the narrative. It raises reader expectancy over the significance of the arrival of Jesus in Jerusalem, and whether the people would welcome him as the Messiah and agent of God's eschatological salvation, or whether they would reject him, as Jesus predicted. This quotation also forms a literary link with Lk. 19.38. Luke 13.34-35 therefore provides an introduction to the relationship of Jesus and the fall of Jerusalem: this chapter's themes are developed in the subsequent sayings of Jesus over Jerusalem and Acts 7, where implicit material becomes more apparent.

Chapter 4

LUKE 19.29-46:
THE REJECTED MESSIAH AND THE TEMPLE

The second saying (Lk. 19.41-44) is spoken as Jesus enters the city, before going to the temple and casting out the sellers. This narrative context is crucial for its interpretation, for as with the cursing of the fig tree in Mk 11.12-14, 20-24, the temple action and its preceding event (the lament) are mutually interpretive.[1] In addition, both the lament and the temple action look back to the entry to the city, so this must be examined first.

The Non-Triumphal Entry (Luke 19.29-40)

The entry of Jesus into Jerusalem is the climax of the journey narrative in Luke's Gospel; for the people who welcome Jesus it is a joyous occasion where they cry out the words of Ps. 117.26.[2] While this psalm quotation is the crucial moment in the entry narrative, it is prepared for by an allusion to another text as Luke describes the arrival of Jesus at the city.

The Arrival of the King
Luke's account of Jesus' arrival in Jerusalem does not quote Zech. 9.9 (unlike Mt. 21.5; Jn 12.15), but it does allude to it.

> <u>Χαῖρε</u> σφόδρα, θύγατερ Σιων· κήρυσσε, θύγατερ Ιερουσαλημ· ἰδοὺ ὁ βασιλεὺς σου ἔρχεταί σοι, δίκαιος καὶ σῴζων αὐτός, πραΰς καὶ ἐπιβεβηκὼς ἐπὶ ὑποζύγιον καὶ <u>πῶλον</u> νέον.
>
> Rejoice greatly, O daughter Sion! Proclaim, O daughter Ierousalem! Behold, your king comes to you, just and salvific is he, meek and riding on a beast of burden and a young foal.

---

1. Brent Kinman, 'Lukan Eschatology and the Missing Fig Tree', *JBL* 113, no. 4 (1994), argues that Luke omitted the cursing of the fig tree because it is too negative about the temple, but Luke criticises aspects of temple practice elsewhere so it is more likely that it is omitted because the lament serves his purposes better.
2. For a defence of authenticity of the account, see Tan, *Zion*, 138–43.

Like Zechariah, Luke uses πῶλος (in 19.30, 33, 35), and χαίρω (Lk. 19.37);[3] Luke's animal is unridden (Lk. 19.30), a periphrasis of the new colt of Zech. 9.9;[4] and crucially, Jesus uses the colt for only the last mile or so of the journey, demonstrating that this is a symbolic ride, where 'scripture was not cited but enacted'.[5] It is highly likely that a reader will regard this text as an intertext.[6] It is certainly closer than the two commonly noted alternatives. Genesis 49.11 is not likely because the disciples untie the colt, not tie it;[7] and 3 Kgdms 1.28-53 is unlikely because it concerns a journey away from (not towards) Jerusalem, and it has a different word for the beast, with no entry motif.[8]

Zechariah 9.9 is therefore the clearest intertext, in part alluded to through Jesus' actions. Brent Kinman is right that its 'coming king' ideas 'did not come out of thin air' but were a development of traditions in 3 Kingdoms 1 and Gen. 49.11.[9] However, this does not mean that the other texts pop into view (as Kinman suggests); instead, the search for relevance will proceed from the conceptual information associated with Zech. 9.9 to information associated with the tradition. In this way, an OT type scene is evoked, a familiar narrative complete with expectations for what should happen – a reading frame, to use Kenneth Litwak's term.[10] This makes manifest the idea of enthronement from the texts discussed above, and from other historical events (such as Judas

---

3. Luke 19.35 has ἐπιβιβάζω not the ἐπιβαίνω of Zech. 9.9; while they share a semantic domain, it cannot be given as evidence of deliberate allusion.

4. Green, *Gospel*, 684–85.

5. Tan, *Zion*, 151.

6. As NA[28]; Sanders, 'Fabric', 141–42; Green, *Gospel*, 685; R. T. France, *Jesus and the Old Testament: His Application of Old Testament Passages to Himself and His Mission* (Vancouver: Regent College Publishing, 1998), 105; Wagner, 'Psalm', 165; Pao and Schnabel, 'Luke', 354; but not NA[27].

7. A text proposed by Joseph Blenkinsopp, 'The Oracle of Judah and the Messianic Entry', *JBL* 80 (1961). It creates messianic expectations for Marshall, *Gospel*, 712; Green argues that Luke parodies it Green, *Gospel*, 684. For reasons to reject it, see Fitzmyer, *Luke*, 2:1248–49.

8. Noted in Schweizer, *Luke*, 298; Bock, *Luke*, 2:1556; Kinman, *Entry*, 49–54, 91–94, 109–13. For reasons to dismiss it, see Pao and Schnabel, 'Luke', 354–55. Luke also omits a specific reference to David in the greeting given to Jesus (compare to Mt. 21.9; Mk 11.10). For other possible allusions, see Kinman, *Entry*, 58–64; Pao and Schnabel, 'Luke', 355, but there are not sufficient links for any of them to be evoked.

9. Kinman, *Entry*, 93, 108–109, the quotation is from 108.

10. Litwak, *Echoes*, 56, 205.

Maccabaeus).[11] This type scene creates expectations for the welcome that Jesus will receive as king, and within this type scene Zech. 9.9 has the loudest voice.[12] The implicatures that will arise through Zech. 9.9 concern the arrival in Zion of the Lord's agent, the king, who ushers in peace (because the king approaching Zion in Zechariah fulfils the book's expectation that God will act).[13] This emphasises the rightful expectation of the city, a delight as God sends his royal saviour. This reinforces the wider narrative at the end of the journey where Jesus is called the Davidic heir (Lk. 18.38-39), and brings salvation (19.9), but is also the rejected king of the parable of the pounds (19.11-27).[14]

Echo of Luke 13.35
It is in this framework of expectation that Luke introduces the quotation from Ps. 117.26, quoting the same words as Lk. 13.35 with an insertion of ὁ βασιλεύς (Lk. 19.38). As a well-known text, this quotation would be readily recognised, and the reader's search for relevance would begin with the prior use of these words in Lk. 13.35 because this is the most immediately available context.[15] This is a greeting of the psalm's messianic king (the insertion of ὁ βασιλεύς makes this clear to the reader); but the reader will also find implicatures, including the thought that this is the occasion that Jesus was talking about in Lk. 13.35, the crucial time when Jerusalem would either accept or reject him. This is just the sort of semi-liturgical setting imagined in Lk. 13.35. Jesus is entering the city, re-enacting Zech. 9.9; it is, therefore, an appropriate context for the city

---

11. David R. Catchpole, 'The "Triumphal" Entry', in *Jesus and the Politics of His Day*, ed. Ernst Bammel and C. F. D. Moule (Cambridge: Cambridge University Press, 1984), 319–22.

12. Such riding a colt is typically a royal right, though there are traditions of rabbis doing it; see J. Duncan M. Derrett, 'Law in the New Testament: The Palm Sunday Colt', *NovT* 13, no. 4 (1971); Kinman, *Entry*, 51.

13. Kinman, *Entry*, 54.

14. David L. Tiede, *Prophecy and History in Luke–Acts* (Philadelphia: Fortress, 1980), 78; John T. Carroll, *Response to the End of History: Eschatology and Situation in Luke–Acts*, SBLDS 92 (Atlanta: Scholars Press, 1988), 97–99; Brent Kinman, 'Parousia, Jesus' "A-Triumphal" Entry, and the Fate of Jerusalem (Luke 19:28–44)', *JBL* 118, no. 2 (1999): 284–89.

15. See the previous chapter. An alternative context is its use in liturgy at Pentecost and Tabernacles; see Brunson, *Psalm 118*, 45–101. Although Passover was approaching, its use there was mainly at the meal, and Luke omits references to branches that could evoke thoughts of Tabernacles, so neither is as obvious as Lk. 13:35. Note that not all the psalm is evoked, against Sanders, 'Fabric', 141.

to welcome him. In addition, it would raise implicatures that this is the time for the greeting to come from the temple (as implied by the psalm in Lk. 13.35).

But there is a twist to the narrative. Although the words from Lk. 13.35 are uttered, they are not uttered by the whole city even though the allusions of the entry narrative create the expectation that they would be. Luke's welcome is restricted to the disciples (τό πλῆθος τῶν μαθητῶν, Lk. 19.37) and not the larger indeterminate crowds of Mt. 21.8-9 and Mk 11.8-9.[16] The significance of this becomes apparent with the quotation of Ps. 117.26, and the subsequent attempt of the Pharisees to silence the disciples: it is *only* the followers of Jesus who welcome him, not the city.[17]

Just as the crowds do not welcome Jesus, the expected cry does not come from the temple and its leadership (εὐλογήκαμεν ὑμᾶς ἐξ οἴκου κυρίου, Ps. 117.26).[18] This absence of temple greeting is emphasised in Jesus' statement in Lk. 19.40: if the disciples were silent, then the stones would cry out, a reference to calling out in praise and welcome.[19] These are most likely to be the stones of the temple itself, crying out in celebration;[20] after all, the words which the stones would utter are the words which should come from the temple.[21]

Summary

Far from being a triumphal entry, as the event is commonly understood, it is a non-triumphal entry, as Brent Kinman identified, though one with a

---

16. Despite the translation of the NRSV, 'people kept spreading their cloaks on the road' (Lk. 19.36), there is no reference to *people* doing this: the only antecedent for ὑπεστρώννυον is the disciples.

17. Wagner, 'Psalm', 167. Matthew and Mark omit the pharisaic rebuke of Lk. 19.39.

18. See Kinman, *Entry*, 97–98; and 'Parousia', 290–93.

19. Bock, *Luke*, 2:1559–60; Green, *Gospel*, 688. Cicero's report of his welcome in Rome had walls showing their joy, see Kinman, *Entry*, 100–101.

20. Sanders, 'Fabric', 150. This is a better reading than the principal alternatives: seeing it as an intertextual link to Hab. 2.11 (so Plummer, *Luke*, 449; Gerhard Schneider, *Das Evangelium nach Lukas*, ÖTK 3 [Gütersloh: Mohn; Würzburg: Echter-Verlag, 1977], 387; Fitzmyer, *Luke*, 2:1252; Pao and Schnabel, 'Luke', 356) or seeing it as the future stones of the Jerusalem temple crying out in judgement against the city who sinned (so Gaston, *Stone*, 359; Danker, *Luke*, 198; Ernst, *Lukas*, 528; Wagner, 'Psalm', 168). For arguments against, see Green, *Gospel*, 688 n. 27; Kinman, *Entry*, 99. The words of 19.40 are celebratory in tone, not judgemental.

21. Sanders, 'Fabric', 150.

background in Jewish messianic expectancy, not Graeco-Roman parousia (as Kinman thought).[22] The narrative now proceeds to explain the significance of this event and its consequences for Jerusalem.

The Lament (Luke 19.41-44)

The Jerusalem saying of Lk. 19.41-44 is an oracle with similarity to the OT, evoking the form of two genres of OT text. First, it is a 'threat oracle' like that of the pre-exilic prophets.[23] There are three elements: (1) an 'address' or 'summons' detailing who is being accused (Jerusalem); (2) an 'indictment' which describes the crimes for which they are found guilty (Lk. 19.42a, 44b); and (3) the 'threat', 'warning' or 'sentence' (Lk. 19.43-44a). Second, the tears which Jesus shed draw to mind Jeremiah the weeping prophet (Jer. 8.23 [9.1 ET]; 13.17; 14.17), and several other OT texts (e.g., 4 Kgdms 8.11; Neh. 1.4; Ps 136.1 [137.1 ET]).[24] None of these are likely to be seen as an intertext on their own, but Lk. 19.41-44 shares enough with these sorts of texts for it to be interpreted with them as a lament.[25] Bridging these two forms, it is best thought of as a threat-lament. Following the format of the threat oracle, there are two parts that need consideration: the indictment, and the threat.

---

22. There is no distinctive Graeco-Roman vocabulary or background for Kinman's thesis to stand. For Graeco-Roman background, see Kinman, *Entry*, Chapter 3; and, 'Parousia', 279–80.

23. Marcus J. Borg, 'Luke 19:42–44 and Jesus as Prophet', *Forum* 8, no. 1–2 (1992): 104–105.

24. Johnson, *Luke*, 298; Pao and Schnabel, 'Luke', 356; Bock, *Luke*, 2:1560. For Jeremiah, see also Fisk, 'Tears', 165.

25. A link noted by many, e.g., Manson, *Sayings*, 319–22; Gaston, *Stone*, 359; Bock, *Luke*, 2:1561. Some note the closeness of the oracle to Jeremiah (Gaston, *Stone*, 359–60; Tiede, *Prophecy*, 83), and Fisk ('Tears', 164–65) links the laments to Jeremiah more generally. But although there are similarities, there are not sufficient links to show that Jesus is paralleled with Jeremiah. The links are clearer in Matthew's Gospel, see Michael Knowles, *Jeremiah in Matthew's Gospel: The Rejected Prophet Motif in Matthaean Redaction*, JSNTSup 68 (Sheffield: JSOT, 1993); David M. Moffitt, 'Righteous Bloodshed, Matthew's Passion Narrative, and the Temple's Destruction: Lamentations as a Matthean Intertext', *JBL* 125, no. 2 (2006). Luke has fewer quotations from Jeremiah to sustain the link, and links with other prophets like Zechariah (13.33-34). So, while Jeremiah is an important context, it is not the dominant one.

The Indictment Against Jerusalem
The indictment contains two phrases:

Lk. 19.42:

...εἰ ἔγνως ἐν τῇ ἡμέρᾳ ταύτῃ καὶ σὺ τὰ πρὸς εἰρήνην· νῦν δὲ ἐκρύβη ἀπὸ ὀφθαλμῶν σου

Lk. 19.44:

...ἀνθ' ὧν οὐκ ἔγνως τὸν καιρὸν τῆς ἐπισκοπῆς σου

Both criticise the people for not recognising something, and both contain a temporal marker suggesting that they should be treated as two aspects of one charge. This charge is wrapped around the threat, serving to maintain focus on the indictment through repetition and expansion in what is, perhaps, the clearest statement of the charge in the Gospel.[26]

The form of this oracle might lead a reader to expect that τὰ πρὸς εἰρήνην (19.42) should be interpreted against a more specific context than the general Lukan soteriological concept,[27] but the phrase does not occur in the LXX. It does occur in *T. Jud.* 9.7, and once elsewhere in the NT (Lk. 14.32), referring to terms of peace in a military situation,[28] but it is unlikely that this is enough to satisfy expectations of relevance – it simply repeats the words. The reader of Lk. 19.42 needs to understand the specific reference to peace used here, and it is likely to be found through an immediately available textual context, ἐν οὐρανῷ εἰρήνη in Lk. 19.38.[29] This saying was spoken on the same day, as ἐν τῇ ἡμέρᾳ ταύτῃ implies. Although the Lukan use of ἡμέρα is broad, that does not exclude it referring to the day of the entry;[30] its reference might extend beyond the day of the non-triumphal entry to include the on-going rejection of Jesus to his death that it marks, but it is still important to note the decisiveness of this particular day as a point of no return (marked by 'now' in 19.42).[31]

Having made the connection to Lk. 19.38, relevance would be found in the contextual information associated with this verse. The disciples' words (ἐν οὐρανῷ εἰρήνη καὶ δόξα ἐν ὑψίστοις) are a celebration about what is to

---

26. Tiede regards it as the 'most explicit "explanation"' in the NT, but from a *post eventum* perspective; see Tiede, *Prophecy*, 81.
27. For the concept, see Green, *Gospel*, 690.
28. Evans, *Luke*, 579.
29. Kinman, 'Parousia', 290.
30. Fisk, 'Tears', 172, argues that it does exclude it.
31. Green, *Gospel*, 690.

be achieved in heaven by Jesus' death,³² which brings peace between God and humanity;³³ but there is more to it than this. The optimal relevance of these words includes implicatures found in their relation to Lk. 2.14, which shares εἰρήνη and δόξα ἐν ὑψίστοις. The different location of the peace in these texts is noteworthy: in 2.14 the angels promise that Jesus' birth will bring peace on earth, but 19.38 has peace in heaven. When 19.38 is viewed in this context, it leads to implicatures that Jerusalem would have received peace if it had recognised Jesus as the figure of Zech. 9.9 – but they did not, and the expected 'peace on earth' is absent from Jerusalem.³⁴ With this contextual context activated, failing to know 'the things which make for peace' (19.42) is equated with failing to embrace the agent of God who brings peace and salvation to Jerusalem. But this context is also expanded, because 19.42 adds that peace is now 'hidden from their eyes', in heaven and not in their experience.

Turning to 19.44, the days or times of visitation in the LXX either refer to times of judgement (e.g., Isa. 10.3, Jer. 6.15; 10.15)³⁵ or blessing (e.g., Gen. 50.24-25; Exod. 3.16; Wis. 3.13).³⁶ The statement in Lk. 19.44 (ἀνθ' ὧν οὐκ ἔγνως τὸν καιρὸν τῆς ἐπισκοπῆς σου) is not about a time of judgement, so relevance will not be found in any of the judgement texts,³⁷ even if Jeremiah 6 lies in the background for the rest of the oracle.³⁸

---

32. Nolland, *Luke*, 3:927.
33. Marshall, *Gospel*, 715–16.
34. Johnson, *Luke*, 298. This makes better sense of the phrase than Jesus bringing with him the peace stored in heaven (John M. Creed, *The Gospel According to St. Luke: The Greek Text with Introduction, Notes, and Indices* [London: Macmillan, 1930], 240); or that it is a temporary withdrawal of peace in order to make Jesus vulnerable (Dhyanchand Carr, 'Jesus, the King of Zion: A Traditio-Historical Enquiry into the So-Called "Triumphal" Entry of Jesus' [Ph.D. diss., Kings College, London, 1980], 271–75).
35. Fitzmyer, *Luke*, 2:1259 (Jer. 6.15; 10.15); and NA²⁸ (Jer. 6.15; Wis. 3.7, but the latter probably reuses Isaiah and Jeremiah traditions).
36. Job 10.12 in NA²⁸. For lists of OT texts, see Johnson, *Luke*, 299; Pao and Schnabel, 'Luke', 357; Marshall, *Gospel*, 719.
37. Bock, *Luke*, 2:1563–64.
38. Adrian Hastings, *Prophet and Witness in Jerusalem: A Study of the Teaching of St. Luke* (London: Longmans, 1958), 116–20 finds 19.41-46 indebted to Jer. 6–7. There are other parallels between Jer. 6 and Jesus' threat-lament: discipline coming upon Jerusalem in Jer. 6.6, 8; anger poured out on infants in 6.11; and the absence of peace in 6.14. It is notable that the language in Jer. 6.15 (ἐν καιρῷ ἐπισκοπῆς αὐτῶν) is similar, but the visitation is different. See Bock, *Luke*, 2:1563; Pao and Schnabel, 'Luke', 356–57.

The relationship of the indictment in 19.44 to that in 19.42 is too strong for this saying to be anything other than a missed visitation of blessing. Although none of the texts listed are close enough to be a specific intertext, their concept of a time of divine visitation will enrich the encyclopaedic information attached to the phrase in Lk. 19.44, meaning that it will find relevance in the peace and eschatological redemption which comes when the Lord visits his people.[39]

The Textual Background of the Threat

This prophetic threat oracle is carefully structured into five separate threats separated by καί,[40] each has a violent verb at the beginning for emphasis, followed by a personal pronoun.[41]

Clause 1: ἥξουσιν ἡμέραι ἐπὶ σὲ καὶ παρεμβαλοῦσιν οἱ ἐχθροί σου χάρακά σοι
Clause 2: καὶ περικυκλώσουσίν σε
Clause 3: καὶ συνέξουσίν σε πάντοθεν,
Clause 4: καὶ ἐδαφιοῦσίν σε καὶ τὰ τέκνα σου ἐν σοί,
Clause 5: καὶ οὐκ ἀφήσουσιν λίθον ἐπὶ λίθον ἐν σοί, ...

As Jaques Dupont points out, this fivefold use of καί with nine possessives follows a common Aramaic pattern.[42] This, together with the observation that its language (except for συνέχω) is atypical for Luke,[43] suggests that Luke is using traditional material with little redaction,[44] quite possibly going back to a spoken original of Jesus. It also suggests that this is not *ex eventu* material based on reports of the fall of the city;[45] the similarities between Luke and the historical account in Josephus (the barricade against the city and the destruction of the city walls) are general descriptions of a siege.[46] It is significant that Luke does not have much of the information that Josephus includes, such as, the preservation of some of the wall, the earthworks (τὰ χώματα), the burning temple gates, and the battering of the

39. Steven M. Bryan, *Jesus and Israel's Traditions of Judgement and Restoration*, SNTSMS 117 (Cambridge: Cambridge University Press, 2002), 22. See also Pao and Schnabel, 'Luke', 357, who note the importance of the texts of visitation for blessing.
40. Jacques Dupont, 'Il n'en sera pas laissé pierre sur pierre (Marc 13,2; Luc 19,44)', *Bib* 52 (1971): 312.
41. Green, *Gospel*, 689.
42. Dupont, 'Pierre', 312.
43. Nolland, *Luke*, 3:931–32.
44. Dupont, 'Pierre'; Fitzmyer, *Luke*, 2:1253.
45. As Bultmann, *History*, 123, thought.
46. Bock, *Luke*, 2:1562. See Josephus, *War* 5.466; 5.502-11; 7.1-4, 375-77.

Antonia Fort;⁴⁷ therefore, the military language is more likely from OT descriptions of the destruction of Jerusalem, as C. H. Dodd proposed, not from reports of the historical event.⁴⁸

The description in Lk. 19.43-44 contains several technical terms for military siege which are NT *hapax legomena*: παρεμβάλλω is used in military contexts for enclosing an area and, when associated with χάραξ (the second *hapax legomenon*), it refers to erecting a palisade or siege-works.⁴⁹ Περικυκλόω refers to surrounding a besieged city,⁵⁰ and ἐδαφίζω, denotes the destruction of something by tearing it to the ground.⁵¹ While these terms are all used in the LXX in military contexts, there are no texts that combine all of these terms together;⁵² in addition, while several LXX texts detail sieges using a series of clauses, none use the combination of imagery that Luke does. While this means that no single text stands behind all the imagery, there are, however, several texts which could be intertexts for part of the imagery.

(i) Parallels to Luke 19.43
There are three frequently suggested texts.⁵³ Ezekiel 4.2 has five clauses describing different aspects of the siege process:

καὶ δώσεις ἐπ' αὐτὴν περιοχὴν καὶ οἰκοδομήσεις ἐπ' αὐτὴν προμαχῶνας καὶ περιβαλεῖς ἐπ' αὐτὴν χάρακα καὶ δώσεις ἐπ' αὐτὴν παρεμβολὰς καὶ τάξεις τὰς βελοστάσεις κύκλῳ.

And you shall give an enclosure against it and build siege walls against it and cast a palisade against it and give camps against it and line up the batteries of war engines all around.

---

47. Josephus, *War* 5.466; 6.24-28, 93, 228; 7.1-4, 375-77. See Fitzmyer, *Luke*, 2:1255; and the omissions of other things one may expect (cannibalism, pestilence and fire) noted by Wright, *Victory*, 349.
48. Dodd, 'Studies'; and supported by Dupont, 'Pierre', 312; Borg, 'Luke 19:42-44', 102–103; Bock, *Luke*, 2:1562-63.
49. BDAG, 775, 1078.
50. Ibid., 802.
51. Ibid., 275.
52. The same is true of the Greek Pseudepigrapha and Josephus. For a list of where these NT *hapax legomena* appear in the OT, see Bock, *Luke*, 2:1562 n. 18.
53. All three are noted in Green, *Gospel*, 691; Pao and Schnabel, 'Luke', 356. Ezekiel 4.2 in NA²⁸ (but not NA²⁷); F. Flückiger, 'Luk 21.20-24 und die Zerstörung Jerusalems', *TZ* 28 (1972); Fitzmyer, *Luke*, 2:1258; Giblin, *Jerusalem*, 56. Isaiah 29.3 in NA²⁸; Marshall, *Gospel*, 718; Bock, *Luke*, 2:1562; François Bovon, *L'Évangile Selon Saint Luc 19,28–24,53*, CNT, 2nd Series, 3D (Geneva: Labor et Fides, 2009), 42. Isaiah 37.33 by Fitzmyer, *Luke*, 2:1258.

The concepts in this text show similarities with Luke's first three clauses, and it has lexical links with Luke's first two clauses: in the first, χάραξ and παρεμβολή (a cognate of Luke's Παρεμβάλλω); and in the second, κύκλος has some relation to περικυκλόω; but the other vocabulary is not particularly close. It is the closest intertext.

Isaiah 29.3 and 37.33 are similar:

Isa. 29.3:

καὶ <u>κυκλώσω</u> ὡς Δαυιδ ἐπὶ σὲ καὶ βαλῶ περὶ σὲ <u>χάρακα</u> καὶ θήσω περὶ σὲ πύργους

And like Dauid I will surround you; I will lay ramparts around you and set up towers around you.

Isa. 37.33:

διὰ τοῦτο οὕτως λέγει κύριος ἐπὶ βασιλέα Ἀσσυρίων Οὐ μὴ εἰσέλθῃ εἰς τὴν πόλιν ταύτην οὐδὲ μὴ βάλῃ ἐπ' αὐτὴν βέλος οὐδὲ μὴ ἐπιβάλῃ ἐπ' αὐτὴν θυρεὸν οὐδὲ μὴ <u>κυκλώσῃ</u> ἐπ' αὐτὴν <u>χάρακα</u>.

Therefore thus says the Lord concerning the king of the Assyrians: He shall not come into this city nor cast a missile against it nor bring a shield against it nor set up a rampart around it.

Both contain χάραξ and κυκλόω, but the relationship that this offers to Luke's clauses 1–2 is undermined because Isa. 29.3 is not about Jerusalem, and Isa. 37.33 concerns what YHWH says the king of Assyria will *not* do.

There are two other LXX verses which use παρεμβάλλω (like Luke's first clause), and a word related to περικυκλόω (from the second), but neither are about Jerusalem being sacked:[54] Jer. 27.29 refers to a besieged Babylon (using the adverb κυκλόθεν);[55] 1 Macc. 15.13-14 refers to Antiochus surrounding Dora (using κυκλόω). Still others are more distant: Ezek. 21.27 (21.22 ET) has a series of statements about putting up siegeworks (using χάραξ twice) but only parallels the first Lukan clause.[56] 4 Kingdoms 6.14 describes the king of Syria surrounding (περικυκλόω) the city of Elisha, but this linguistic link with clause 2 is its only parallel; and Jer. 52.5 has only a general concept of a city under siege with no lexical links.[57]

54. Both noted by Dodd, 'Studies', 77.
55. Κυκλόθεν is used three times in the NT (Rev. 4.3, 4, 8).
56. Green, *Gospel*, 691.
57. Four Kingdoms 6.14 in Nolland, *Luke*, 3:931; Pao and Schnabel, 'Luke', 356. Jeremiah 52.5 in Green, *Gospel*, 691; Pao and Schnabel, 'Luke', 356; Bovon,

(ii) Parallels to Luke 19.44

The violent language of Luke's fourth and fifth clauses is typical of descriptions of siege settings within the OT, but not evocative of a single text. Among the several OT texts which have similarity, the most significant are Hos 10.14; 14.1 (10.14; 13.16 ET) because of their reference to two generations of people.[58] Although Luke's σε καὶ τὰ τέκνα σου could refer the city and her inhabitants (Jerusalem has daughters in Lk. 23.38), it is more likely that the phrase refers to two generations of city inhabitants. There are two reasons for this: first, the oracle's 'you' is best understood as the people who have not recognised the 'things that make for peace' in 19.42, implying people and not the city; and second, this reading does not require two different meanings of the verb ἐδαφίζω, as city and inhabitants would.[59]

> Hos. 10.14:
>
> ...ὡς ἄρχων Σαλαμαν ... ἐν ἡμέραις πολέμου μητέρα ἐπὶ τέκνοις ἠδάφισαν.
>
> ...as the ruler Salaman ... in the days of battle, dashed a mother to the ground with her children.
>
> Hos. 14.1:
>
> ...καὶ τὰ ὑποτίτθια αὐτῶν ἐδαφισθήσονται, καὶ αἱ ἐν γαστρὶ ἔχουσαι αὐτῶν διαρραγήσονται.
>
> ...and their nurslings shall be dashed to the ground, and their pregnant ones ripped open.

Although these verses refer to Israel and Samaria respectively, they both use ἐδαφίζω. Hosea 10.14 is closer because it refers to a mother and child (τέκνον, like Luke), and Luke does not refer to the gashing open of pregnant women from Hos. 14.1 (this is graphic imagery which Luke

---

Luc, 39 n. 12. Dodd adds Josh. 7.9 (using περικυκλόω), and 1 Kgdms 23.8; 2 Macc. 9.2 (with συνέχω in a military context, but this is a fairly common Lukan word), but these do not have any other reason to be favoured. See Dodd, 'Studies', 77.

58. NA[28]; Fitzmyer, *Luke*, 2:1258 (not Hos 14.1); Bock, *Luke*, 2:1563; Pao and Schnabel, 'Luke', 356.

59. Ἐδαφίζω means either destroying something by dashing it to the ground, or razing a city to total destruction (BDAG, 275). If σε refers to the city then these meanings have to be combined and such a conflation seems awkward. Alternatively καὶ τὰ τέκνα σου could be circumstantial, 'while your children are in you', but this is unlikely in the parallelism and structure of the saying. See the discussion in Marshall, *Gospel*, 718–19; Bock, *Luke*, 2:1563.

would have been well-served to include if he wanted to evoke the text, despite this being not uncommon practice in ancient warfare).⁶⁰ Other verses have been suggested, but although both the oracle against Babylon in Ps. 136.9, and that against Thebes and Nineveh in Nah. 3.10 use ἐδαφίζω, they employ νήπιος for the children.⁶¹

Clause 5 has only 2 Kgdms 17.13 as a possible intertext: this shares λίθος and the concept of city destruction, but it does not have Luke's distinctive λίθον ἐπὶ λίθον.⁶² In the absence of other texts it might be an interpretive context for a reader, but it is not strongly evoked and this limits its role.

Finding the Interpretive Context
The language of Lk. 19.43-44 suggests that OT contexts are important for interpretation, but no single text echoes all of its imagery. Certain texts are closer than others: Ezek. 4.2 is closer than the alternatives for the first three clauses, and Hos 10.14 is closer than others in the fourth clause. But while they are closer, there are not enough textual signals to make them exclusive contexts for interpretation. Some readers might single them out and add extra implicatures, but it is more likely that relevance would be found in the general context of OT prophetic texts of city destruction, typified by those discussed above. This is reinforced by the oracle's evocation of the genre of a threat oracle. This does not mean that implicatures are restricted: the repeated echoing of different aspects of city destruction functions like a poetic metaphor, encouraging the exploration of the motifs which OT texts of city destruction have in common. This results in a range of weaker implicatures. The only exception to this is the last clause, where 2 Kgdms 17.13 is the only possible text, but it has no specific correlation to Luke's phrasing, and its place in the final clause about destruction is likely to mean that the reader achieves relevance without examining it in too much detail.

The text will therefore be interpreted as a warning of city destruction, but several implicatures will be added to this. First, an evocation of the prior destruction of Jerusalem activates the disaster of the exile as an

---

60. See 4 Kgdms 15.16; Amos 1.13.
61. Both noted by NA²⁸; Fitzmyer, *Luke*, 2:1258; Bock, *Luke*, 2:1563; Pao and Schnabel, 'Luke', 356–57. Psalm 136.9 by Giblin, *Jerusalem*, 56. Nahum 3.10 by Marshall, *Gospel*, 718. 4 Kgdms 8.12 is more distant, with a different verb and noun, and a reference to pregnant women.
62. Noted in NA²⁸. Nolland, *Luke*, 3:932, rejects it. The reference to Jerusalem as a heap of ruins in the MT of Mic. 3.12, noted by Pao and Schnabel, 'Luke', 357, is not present in the LXX so must be discounted.

interpretive context,[63] not only for this immediate text, but also when future verses in Luke–Acts echo back to this text. With this exilic context activated, information related to it is readily accessible for the reader. Second, just as the previous destruction of the city occurred because of the sin of the people, so does the event Jesus refers to. The sin is not detailed in the threat oracle, but the indictment of 19.42, 44 indicates what it is, as do references later in the narrative. Further processing in specific contexts (especially Hos. 10.14) might add an implicature that the Jerusalemites are in denial about this state of affairs, just as the people of Hosea's day.[64] Third, the military action against the city is the result of divine judgement on Israel, just like the action against cities in the OT. Fourth, the evocation of these past events connotes an element of the totality of the destruction that goes beyond the words. Fifth, it reinforces the picture of Jesus as a prophet, reminding the reader of the sayings of Lk. 13.31-35 and all that they imply. Sixth, because the temple was the dwelling place of God,[65] the total destruction of the city is only possible if God has already abandoned his temple, as stated in Lk. 13.35.

Summary

The unifying thread running through these two pericopae is the failure of Jerusalem to receive Jesus (a theme also present in the parables of Lk. 19.11-27 and 20.9-18). The entry narrative used Ps. 117.26 to show that it was the climactic, eschatological moment referred to by Jesus in Lk. 13.35 – but the leadership in Jerusalem missed it. The subsequent threat-lament explains that the city ignored the offer of peace that came with Jesus and faces military calamity instead (19.42); this rejection of Jesus is a rejection of God's salvation. Luke 13.35 spoke of the abandonment of the temple and in doing so evoked exilic themes; Lk. 19.41-44 expands on those themes and shows that the abandoned temple will lead to the desolation of the city. But this is not an indictment of all of Jerusalem, Luke–Acts is not so sweeping in judgement;[66] it is focused on the temple system and its leadership, and the temple action expands on this by describing the specific sins associated with the temple.

---

63. The historical event behind Jesus' oracle is the fall of Jerusalem in 586 BCE; see Dodd, 'Studies', 79.
64. Douglas Stuart, *Hosea–Jonah*, WBC 31 (Waco: Word, 1987), 172.
65. Or the dwelling of his glory: Pss. 19.3; 25.8; 77.68-69; 127.5; 131.13-14; 133.3; 134.21; Isa. 6.1; Jer. 38.6; Amos 1.2; Tob. 1.4; *Jub.* 1.28. This list of texts comes from Borg, *Conflict*, 175 n. 4.
66. Green, *Gospel*, 689.

The Action in the Temple (Luke 19.45-46)

The meaning of Jesus' actions in the temple remains an area of considerable debate.[67] There is a broad consensus that it was a symbolic action, a small-scale action carrying great significance;[68] but debate surrounds three aspects. First, discussion focuses on whether it was an act of cleansing, which either objected to the commercial trade impinging on the purity of worship and sacrifice,[69] or which rejected the corrupt business practices and profiteering of the temple authorities.[70] Second, debate questions how it functioned as an eschatological event. For some, Jesus was not criticising the temple at all but enacting its destruction because for the new temple to be built, the old must go;[71] others recognise a critique mixed with symbolic destruction based on the cessation of sacrifice.[72] Alternatively,

---

67. Helpful reviews include Tan, *Zion*, 164–96; Bryan, *Jesus*, 206–25; James D. G. Dunn, *Jesus Remembered*, Christianity in the Making 1 (Grand Rapids: Eerdmans, 2003), 636–40; Nicholas Perrin, *Jesus the Temple* (London: SPCK; Grand Rapids: Baker, 2010), 80–99; Jostein Ådna, 'Jesus and the Temple', in *Handbook for the Study of the Historical Jesus*, ed. Tom Holmén and Stanley E. Porter, 4 vols. (Leiden: Brill, 2011), 3:2654–72. 'Temple action' is a more neutral term than 'cleansing of the temple'.

68. E. P. Sanders, *Jesus and Judaism* (London: SCM, 1985), 70; Borg, *Conflict*, 182; Green, *Gospel*, 692–93. Against S. G. F. Brandon, *Jesus and the Zealots: A Study of the Political Factor in Primitive Christianity* (Manchester: Manchester University Press, 1967), 333–34. If it was more than a small-scale event then it would have met with swift Roman reprisals. See Tan, *Zion*, 164–65.

69. Hans Dieter Betz, 'Jesus and the Purity of the Temple (Mark 11:15-18): A Comparative Religion Approach', *JBL* 116, no. 3 (1997); Maurice Casey, 'Culture and Historicity: The Cleansing of the Temple', *CBQ* 59, no. 2 (1997).

70. Morna Hooker, 'Traditions About the Temple in the Sayings of Jesus', *BJRL* 70 (1988); Richard Bauckham, 'Jesus' Demonstration in the Temple', in *Law and Religion: Essays on the Place of the Law in Israel and Early Christianity*, ed. Barnabas Lindars (Cambridge: James Clarke, 1988); Craig A. Evans, 'Jesus' Action in the Temple: Cleansing or Portent of Destruction?', *CBQ* 51, no. 2 (1989); Bock, *Luke*, 2:1572–73; Tan, *Zion*, 174–87.

71. Sanders, *Jesus*, 61–71; followed by Paula Fredriksen, *Jesus of Nazareth, King of the Jews: A Jewish Life and the Emergence of Christianity* (London: Macmillan, 1999), 207–12.

72. Especially John Dominic Crossan, *The Historical Jesus: The Life of a Mediterranean Jewish Peasant* (Edinburgh: T&T Clark, 1991), 357–58, where Jesus enacts a temporary cessation of the cult. For Jostein Ådna, the cult was disrupted because Jesus was ultimately the new sin offering; the refusal of the leaders to repent meant the temple was heading for destruction (Jostein Ådna, 'Jesus' Symbolic Act in the Temple [Mark 11:15–17]: The Replacement of the Sacrificial Cult by His Atoning

the temple was not in a state to function as the eschatological temple and required cleansing (it was not an enacted destruction).[73] Third, there is discussion about the emphasis it places on Jesus' messianic identity. For example, N. T. Wright argues that Jesus prophetically enacted a temporary cessation of sacrifice in a 'royal' action where he is the king who had 'ultimate authority over the temple', including authority to rebuild it.[74] Others focus on Jesus without the eschatological stress, regarding it as preparatory for Jesus' teaching ministry.[75]

The above approaches have typically been concerned with the historical Jesus and have focused on the fuller account in Mk 11.15-17. While Luke is dependent on Mark, he has a substantially truncated version of events, only retaining one of the four Markan actions of Jesus (driving out the sellers).[76] This means that the double quotations of Isa. 56.7 and Jer. 7.11 are more prominent in Luke's account, and so interpretation of the quotations is of primary importance.[77] In addition, the words of the threat-lament over Jerusalem also have a significant role in understanding

---

Death', in *Gemeinde ohne Tempel / Community without temple: zur Substituierung und Transformation des Jerusalemer Tempels und seines Kults im Alten Testament, antiken Judentum und frühen Christentum*, ed. Beate Ego, Armin Lange, and Peter Pilhofer, WUNT 118 [Tübingen: Mohr Siebeck, 1999]; idem, *Jesu Stellung zum Tempel*, WUNT 2/119 [Tübingen: Mohr Siebeck, 2000], 381–86; idem, 'Jesus', 3:2670). For the action as disruption of sacrifice, see also Jacob Neusner, 'Money-Changers in the Temple: The Mishnah's Explanation', *NTS* 35, no. 2 (1989); Kurt Paesler, *Das Tempelwort Jesu: die Traditionen von Tempelzerstörung und Tempelerneuerung im Neuen Testament*, FRLANT 184 (Göttingen: Vandenhoeck & Ruprecht, 1999), 244–45.

73. Bauckham, 'Demonstration'; Tan, *Zion*, 174–86. For others it is purification for its role in welcoming the Gentiles, see Joachim Jeremias, *Jesus' Promise to the Nations: The Franz Delitzsch Lectures for 1953*, SBT (London: SCM, 1958), 65–66; James D. G. Dunn, *The Partings of the Ways: Between Christianity and Judaism and Their Significance for the Character of Christianity* (London: SCM, 1991), 47–49. Perrin blends eschatological and cleansing approaches; see Perrin, *Jesus*, 89–113.

74. Wright, *Victory*, 422–24, 490–93, the quotation is from 492. For Ben Witherington, *The Christology of Jesus* (Minneapolis: Fortress, 1990), 113–15, it reveals Jesus' self-identity as Messiah.

75. So he could take up residence there, Conzelmann, *Theology*, 77–78. Similarly, Schweizer, *Luke*, 302; Johnson, *Luke*, 301–302.

76. For Mark's account, see the discussion and bibliography in Timothy C. Gray, *The Temple in the Gospel of Mark: A Study of Its Narrative Role* (Grand Rapids: Baker Academic, 2008), 25–30.

77. See Borg, *Conflict*, 184–85, who regards the words as of primary importance in all Synoptic Gospel accounts.

the temple action because of Luke's placement of it immediately prior to the temple action. This significance of Jesus' words is underlined by the attempted arrest of Jesus over his words in 19.47. In this way, Jesus continues to act as the rejected prophet of Lk. 13.31-35.

The Old Testament Quotations

The words of Jesus in Lk. 19.46 are a composite quotation of Isa. 56.7 and Jer. 7.11 linked through a common phrase ὁ οἶκός μου,[78] and marked by a clear introductory formula.

Isa. 56.7	Lk. 19.46
... ὁ γὰρ <u>οἶκός μου οἶκος προσευχῆς</u> κληθήσεται πᾶσιν τοῖς ἔθνεσιν,	λέγων αὐτοῖς· γέγραπται· καὶ ἔσται <u>ὁ οἶκός μου οἶκος προσευχῆς</u>, ...
Jer. 7.11	Lk. 19.46
μὴ <u>σπήλαιον λῃστῶν</u> <u>ὁ οἶκός μου</u>, οὗ ἐπικέκληται τὸ ὄνομά μου ἐπ' αὐτῷ ἐκεῖ, ἐνώπιον ὑμῶν ...	... <u>ὁ οἶκός μου</u> οἶκος προσευχῆς, ὑμεῖς δὲ αὐτὸν ἐποιήσατε <u>σπήλαιον λῃστῶν</u>.

There are two adaptations of the Isaiah quotation: the reference to all the nations is omitted,[79] and the verb is changed from κληθήσεται to ἔσται.[80] Although the Jeremiah quotation is truncated, its identification is assured because σπήλαιον λῃστῶν is a distinctive phrase found nowhere else in the LXX or Pseudepigrapha, and it has ὁ οἶκός μου.

The combination of these two quotations contrasts the idealised vision of the temple as a house of prayer with its reality as a robbers' den. There are three signals in the text that indicate that optimal relevance goes beyond its explicit statement; rather, the reader is required to expend extra processing effort in exploring the quotations in return for a series

---

78. Koet, 'Isaiah', 86 n. 27. There are good arguments that these words have their origin in Jesus tradition; see Hooker, 'Traditions'; Tan, *Zion*, 181–85.

79. Like Mt. 21.13; but Mk 11.17 retains them.

80. Retained by Matthew and Mark. A few manuscripts (C² 1241 1424) read κληθήσεται, but this is most likely conforming to other texts.

of implicatures. First, the introductory formula, γέγραπται, is more than a signal that the quotations lend scriptural authority to Jesus' argument because there is no argument apart from the quotations; it therefore draws attention to the importance of the OT context of the quotations. Second, the quotations are an explanation of a significant event, but their language does not offer a direct explanation; this signals that they require analysis against the OT context to give further detail. Third, it is a composite quotation, and optimal relevance requires proper evaluation of the contribution of their juxtaposition. The implicatures that arise will be in three principal areas.

The Temple as the Centre of Resistance to the Eschatological Event
The quotation of Isa. 56.7 would be understood primarily in an eschatological sense because it is a thorough-going eschatological text.[81] In its original context, Isa. 56.7 is part of an announcement of salvation, an expectation of coming deliverance (56.1) when those currently excluded from worship – including eunuchs (56.4-5) and foreigners (56.6-7) – would be gathered to worship in the eschatological temple, the 'house of prayer' (56.7). As such, it is part of the expression of hope for the ending of the exile (56.8), a central part of Jewish restoration theology and something important to Jesus' message.[82] This eschatological emphasis is likely to be close at hand for the reader to explore because of the eschatological focus of Jesus' entry to Jerusalem in Lk. 19.29-44. It is seen in three main places: (1) the reference to peace in 19.42, which evoked the eschatological hopes of Luke 1–2; (2) Ps. 117.26 (quoted in Lk. 19.38) expresses eschatological hopes of the messianic deliverer; and (3) Lk. 19.44 referred to the day of visitation, a term with eschatological connotations.[83] In this way, the quotation of Isa. 56.7 would be understood to refer to Jesus's expectations of the eschatological function of the temple (οἶκος) compared to what he finds in the temple.

However, this comparison alone does not satisfy expectations of relevance; that requires more clarity to the point Jesus is making. But what is that point? Richard Bauckham argues that Jesus can hardly be criticising the leaders of the contemporary Jerusalem temple for it not *being* the eschatological temple: he thinks that while Isa. 56.7 does refer

---

81. Bryan, *Jesus*, 222; Perrin, *Jesus*, 85. It was typically thought to refer to the eschatological temple; see Ådna, *Jesu*, 276–87.

82. For this aspect of Jesus' message, see Wright, *Victory*, especially 418; Dale C. Allison, *Jesus of Nazareth: Millenarian Prophet* (Minneapolis: Fortress, 1998); Bryan, *Jesus*, 221–25.

83. Bock, *Luke*, 2:1563.

to the eschatological temple, Jesus quotes it to suggest that the eschatological fulfilment was also God's purpose for the Jerusalem temple all the time. In other words, any Gentiles coming to the temple should have been permitted in anticipation of the future welcome they would receive in the eschaton.[84] Kim Tan disagrees; he thinks that an application to the contemporary temple cannot be supported because the pilgrimage of Gentiles to the eschatological temple is the main force of Isa. 56.7[85] – Jesus' use of Isaiah is therefore to show that the temple is too corrupt to become the eschatological temple (even though the time has come). Instead of being renewed, it is set for destruction.[86] This does not go far enough for Steven Bryan, who challenges Bauckham's assumption that Jesus could not be criticising the authorities of the historical temple for it not being the eschatological temple. Bryan argues that this 'was precisely Jesus' point: he indicts the Temple because, though the time of fulfilment had come, the Temple was clearly not the eschatological Temple'.[87] In other words, it is not just that 'the Temple was disqualified from *becoming* the eschatological Temple', but that 'Jesus employs Israel's restoration traditions *to indict the Temple for failing already to be* the eschatological Temple'.[88] But Bryan's analysis needs to be modified slightly. In Lk. 13.34, Jesus' statement about his desire to gather Jerusalem under his wings evoked end-of-exile imagery of eschatological gathering, and Lk. 19.28-44 showed that Jerusalem refused to welcome Jesus as the agent of this gathering. In doing this they have refused to be part of the eschatological age which Jesus inaugurates. The quotation of Isa. 56.7 should be viewed against this context: it is not so much criticising the temple for failing to be the eschatological temple, it is criticising the leaders for *refusing to allow* the temple to become the eschatological temple, by refusing to welcome the eschatological age which Jesus brought.[89]

But there is more to it than this. If Luke had included πᾶσιν τοῖς ἔθνεσιν (as Mk 11.17) then Isaiah's discussion of the temple and Gentiles would

---

84. Bauckham, 'Demonstration', 85.
85. Tan, *Zion*, 189–90.
86. Ibid.
87. Bryan, *Jesus*, 222–23, the quotation is from 222. For Bryan, this was clear because the nations were not coming to the temple. Like most scholars, he focuses more on the Markan account and therefore includes the reference to 'all nations' that Luke omits.
88. Ibid., 222–23.
89. Ådna notes that there is a refusal to respond to Jesus' eschatological call, but maintains that this is because of clinging to old worship patterns; see Ådna, 'Jesus', 3:2669.

be a dominant context for the reader; without it the reader's attention falls on the house of prayer first.[90] This is significant and foregrounds the importance of right worship in the eschatological temple, a contextual link strengthened by Luke's change of Isaiah's 'will be called' to 'will *be* a house of prayer'. It is notable that the Jerusalem temple was a place for the prayer of the righteous in Lk. 1.10, 13; 2.28-32, 37;[91] in addition, Simeon and Anna lived in a prayerful, watchful expectancy for the revelation of salvation (Lk. 2.25-38). All this stands in stark contrast with both the rejection of salvation in Lk. 19.38-47, and the accusation of prayerlessness in 19.46. The temple is also the place where they rejected revelation about salvation: Luke's Gospel shows the temple as a place for divine revelation, where Jesus taught and the teachers were amazed (e.g., Lk. 2.41-49). This teaching context is brought to mind when Jesus resumed teaching in the temple in Lk. 19.47, but the leaders then planned his death.[92] This contrast continues when the disciples later pray and teach in the temple; however, at this point it is enough to note that prayer and revelatory teaching are rejected in the temple, something Jesus criticises.[93]

The Temple as a 'Den of Thieves'
The quotation of Jer. 7.11 is also important.[94] The force of σπήλαιον λῃστῶν in the Lukan context is a comparison of the temple as a house (of prayer) or a den (of thieves); it is not primarily a characterisation of the

---

90. It is unlikely that this phrase is omitted because Luke wrote after 70 CE (against C. K. Barrett, 'The House of Prayer and the Den of Thieves', in *Jesus und Paulus: Festschrift Für Werner Georg Kümmel*, ed. E. Earle Ellis and Erich Gräßer [Göttingen: Vandenhoeck & Ruprecht, 1975], 15; Étienne Trocmé, 'L'expulsion des marchands du Temple', *NTS* 15, no. 1 [1968]: 6; Bovon, *Luc*, 4:44–45) because he does not omit 'House of prayer' either. If it cannot be for the Gentiles, then it cannot be for prayer. See Wright, *Victory*, 418 n. 185. For alternative reasons for omission, see Tan, *Zion*, 191; Bock, *Luke*, 2:1579.

91. It is also a place for piety (Lk. 1.5-6; 2.22-24, 39, 41-42) and sacrifice (Lk. 1.11; 2.24). Holmås, 'House', 406, 408–409.

92. Green, *Gospel*, 694. There is a constant period of teaching in the temple beginning in Lk. 19.45 (Chance, *Jerusalem*, 60–62), but it is going beyond the textual evidence to say that the temple action prepares for this teaching (as Conzelmann, *Theology*, 75–76), or to say that Jesus restores it for its eschatological role (Chance, *Jerusalem*, 58).

93. Such rejection is consistent with their rejection of Jesus' message throughout Luke's Gospel (e.g., 4.16-30; 14.1-24). For Jesus' teaching as revelatory, see Lk. 10.21-24. See Green, *Gospel*, 694. For prayer in Acts, see Holmås, 'House'.

94. Steven Bryan regards the two texts as summing up two strands of scripture tradition: a restoration strand and a judgement strand. See Bryan, *Jesus*, 217.

activity of the people as praying or thieving.⁹⁵ That being said, λῃστής plays an important role in characterising the problem with the temple through implicature: it might be assumed that 'den of robbers' points to financial wrongdoing or corruption of some kind, and although there are three arguments for this, they are not persuasive.

First, if there was a commonly held view that the temple authorities were corrupt, then the relevance of Jesus' saying would immediately be found in this metarepresented idea. Craig Evans argues that such a view was commonly held and represented in a series of texts which are spread over many years.⁹⁶ Before the time of Jesus, the high priest was said to rob the poor (1QpHab 8.12; 9.5; 10.1; 12.10), to have gained great wealth (1QpHab 8.8-12; 9.4-5), and to have defiled the sanctuary (1QpHab 12.8-9).⁹⁷ Roughly contemporary with Jesus, *As. Mos.* 7.6-10 refers to priestly corruption,⁹⁸ and Josephus noted both priestly extortion (*Ant.* 20.180-81) and the great wealth of the temple (*Ant.* 14.105, 110).⁹⁹ Later rabbinic writings contain similar criticism (even citing it as the reason for the demise of the Second Temple).¹⁰⁰ But while ideas of corruption were undoubtedly present in the Christian community, the evidence presented does not mean that corruption was the *dominant* idea. The early Christian community did not explain the demise of the temple in the same terms as Jewish texts; and although the Lukan Jesus refers to corruption in his critique of the Jewish leaders,¹⁰¹ they are not his only criticism, and they

---

95. Tom Holmén, *Jesus and Jewish Covenant Thinking*, BIS 55 (Leiden: Brill, 2001), 325, notes: 'It is not a "den robber" that is at issue here but a "robber den". The Markan text does not identify the people with "robbers" but the Temple with the "den".' The same is true of Luke.

96. Craig A. Evans, 'Jesus' Action in the Temple and Evidence of Corruption in the First-Century Temple', in *Jesus and His Contemporaries: Comparative Studies*, ed. Craig A. Evans, AGJU 25 (Leiden: Brill, 1995); idem, 'Cleansing'; idem, 'Cave', from which the data below is taken.

97. Evans, 'Evidence', 337–38.

98. Ibid., 340–41, Evans dates this to the early first century.

99. For further references see ibid., 338–40.

100. 'As to Jerusalem's first building, on what account was it destroyed? Because of idolatry and licentiousness and bloodshed which was in it. But as to the latter building we know that they devoted themselves to Torah and were meticulous about tithes. On what account did they go into exile? *Because they loved money* and hated one another' (*t. Menaḥ.* 13.22B–D, cited in Perrin, *Jesus*, 96 n. 50, italics are Perrin's). Other texts include *b. Pesaḥ.* 57; *t. Zebaḥ.* 11.16-17; *b. Yebam.* 86a-b; *b. Ketub.* 26a; *y. Ma'as. Š.* 5.15. See Evans, 'Cleansing', 258–59, and, 'Evidence', 327–37.

101. Specifically, the wealth of the temple (21.5), and the wrongful financial actions of those in power (20.47–21.2).

are not his greatest criticism. The rejection and murder of the Messiah, and the false leadership of the people are far more significant (19.14, 27; 20.9-19, 46-47). So, even if such a metarepresentation did exist for some groups, it is not a metarepresented idea in the Christian community, and it would not govern interpretation of Jer. 7.11.

Second, Nicholas Perrin argues that Jeremiah 7 was understood as referring to stealing. *Targum Jeremiah* 7.9 reads, '*thieves (gānōbîm), killers of persons, adulterers, men who* swear falsely […]'; the verb to steal (גְּנֹב) in the Hebrew text of Jer. 7.9 has been interpreted in the Aramaic version so that 'the addressees are specifically defined by their sin of thievery'.[102] But adulterers and swearers are similarly defined in that text, meaning that the sin of the people in Jeremiah was not understood to be exclusively financial. Perrin notes other adaptations of the Hebrew to refer to financial wrongdoing in the Targum. For example, *T. Jer.* 23.11 refers to 'both *scribe* and priest have *stolen their ways*…',[103] adapting references to prophet (scribe) and ungodliness (stolen their ways), and he presumes this refers to bribery.[104] But none of this requires a financial understanding of Jeremiah 7 because other sins are mentioned in the targum; especially notable is the continuation of *T. Jer.* 7.11 (omitted by Perrin), which has a focus on idolatry: '…and offer up incense to Ba'al, and to follow *the idols of the nations* which you have not known…'[105] Most significantly, the targum does not interpret Jer. 7.11 with an emphasis on financial wrongdoing, as Robert Hayward observes in the notes to his translation: 'Hebrew has: "a den of robbers." *Tg.* has, literally, "a synagogue of the wicked".'[106] Perrin also notes that the actions of Jesus (in Mark) are focused on the financial aspects of the temple,[107] but such observations do not help in Luke's Gospel.[108] Neither the context of Jeremiah, nor the

---

102. Perrin, *Jesus*, 93. This is his citation of Robert Hayward's translation of the Targum in Robert Hayward, *The Targum of Jeremiah: Translated, with a Critical Introduction, Apparatus, and Notes*, ArBib 12 (Edinburgh: T&T Clark, 1987), 70, adding '(*gānōbîm*)'; italics are original and indicate deviation of Aramaic from Hebrew.

103. Hayward, *Targum of Jeremiah*, 112, italics original.

104. Perrin, *Jesus*, 93. See also Evans, 'Cleansing', 268–69, who cites *T. Jer.* 8.10 as evidence that thieving was the usual understanding of Jer. 7 before 70 CE. None of these demonstrate that theft overshadows other crimes in the interpretation of Jeremiah before 70 CE.

105. Hayward, *Targum of Jeremiah*, 70, italics original.

106. Ibid., 71.

107. Perrin, *Jesus*, 92.

108. Other readings of Mark's criticism are also possible; see Sanders, *Jesus*, 61–65; Green, *Gospel*, 693.

context of Luke, demands that financial wrongdoing is the most manifest context for the reader to find implicatures.

Third, it could be argued that ληστής implies theft and dishonesty.[109] But such an interpretation robs ληστής of much of its first-century linguistic emphasis where it usually had the meaning of brigand, bandit or even insurrectionist; its connotations included violence, and it was not the usual word for corrupt practice.[110] This does not require that Luke used it to refer to insurrectionists, but it does suggest some violence.[111]

Instead, the reader is likely to find implicatures through an engagement with the context of Jeremiah 7. This chapter is the well-known temple sermon of the prophet, and it contains a biting attack on idolatry and murder as well as stealing and oppression (Jer. 7.6, 9).[112] As such, its focus is not against the temple itself, nor against the cult; it is the worshippers who are the problem, and its leaders who promote the behaviour.[113] They thought that the temple secured them protection (despite their wrongdoing) because the presence of YHWH was there, a theology based on promises of YHWH in texts like Isa. 37.33-35 and Ps 131.6-10. Jeremiah attacked the assumption that such promises restricted the judgement of God against them, saying, 'Do not trust in yourselves with deceptive words, because they will not benefit you at all, when you say: "A shrine of the Lord, a shrine of the Lord it is"' (Jer. 7.4).[114] The temple had become a σπήλαιον ληστῶν, a hideaway for the guilty where they sheltered between wrongful acts.[115] Because this is the phrase that Luke repeats, this is where the search for relevance would begin in Jeremiah 7, and it would continue in related contexts. This leads to two significant implicatures. First, the rejection and murder of Jesus: Lk. 19.41-44 emphasised the significance of the rejection of Jesus, and 19.47 explicitly states that the chief priests, scribes, and leaders desire to kill Jesus. This implicature resonates with

---

109. As Evans, 'Cleansing', 267–68.

110. BDAG, 594. See the discussion in Barrett, 'House', 15–16; Wright, *Victory*, 420; and the use in Josephus, *Ant.* 14.415; 15.345-48.

111. Barrett, 'House', 16. Some argue that the temple is associated with anti-Roman resistance (Borg, *Conflict*, 186 n. 59; Wright, *Victory*, 420) but the case for this cannot be made on the use of ληστής alone.

112. Ådna, 'Jesus', 3:2669, notes that Jer. 7.11 is about idolatry.

113. Peter C. Craigie, Page H. Kelley, and Joel F. Drinkard, *Jeremiah 1–25*, WBC 26 (Dallas: Word, 1991), 121; Tiemeyer, 'Priests', 257–58.

114. See William McKane, *A Critical and Exegetical Commentary on Jeremiah*, ICC, 2 vols. (Edinburgh: T&T Clark, 1986–96), 1:162–63; Walter Brueggemann, *A Commentary on Jeremiah: Exile and Homecoming* (Grand Rapids: Eerdmans, 1998), 77–78.

115. John Bright, *Jeremiah*, AB 21 (New York: Doubleday, 1965), 56.

the violent connotations of λῃστής, and picks up on Jeremiah's murder charge.[116] Second, idolatry: this is because of the implicature about wrongful worship in Isa. 56.7, and its presence in Jeremiah.[117] The idea of corruption will probably be added to these, but as a weaker implicature. The subsequent sayings of Jesus, and Stephen's speech, will develop these themes, but in Luke 19 they form the implicatures of the charge.

So, rather than focusing on the corruption of the Jerusalem leadership (with the corollary that the temple needs to be cleansed), the strongest implicatures of the phrase are found in the violent rejection of Jesus and the idolatry of the leaders of the temple, together with the temple being the centre of such activity, while the leaders thought its divine protection covered them. Some of their trust may have been in the sacrificial cult, as Jostein Ådna suggests, but the cult itself does not seem to be Jesus' target:[118] his actions did not attack it, nor did he speak against it. In casting out the sellers, he performed a symbolic cessation of the daily business of the temple, but in a way which did not profane the cult.[119] The relationship between Jesus' death and the cult is not resolved at this point, and interpretive decisions about this must await the input of Acts 7. However, it is possible to be confident that Jesus did not cleanse the temple from corruption – his actions were more consistent with an enacted prophecy of destruction, especially because 19.46 quotes Jeremiah 7, a text predicting destruction.

The Relationship of the Eschatological Temple and Jesus
Finally, it remains to discuss the relationship between Jesus and the temple, specifically whether there are also implicatures of Jesus as a temple-builder.[120] While it is logical to assume that any rebuilding of

---

116. Gray, *Temple*, 37–38.

117. Some might argue that the issue with idolatry could be linked to imagery on coins within the temple, whether this is the imperial image (Lk. 20.21-25) or that on Tyrian shekels; see Peter Richardson, 'Why Turn the Tables? Jesus' Protest in the Temple Precincts', *SBLSP* 31 (1992). However, this is unlikely. The focus here is not on the coins: Luke does not record activities of Jesus that direct attention to the coins in the temple action, nor does Jesus' language point in that direction. Rather, attention is on other aspects of temple worship, as discussed above.

118. Ådna, 'Act', 470; idem, *Jesu*, 381–86. For Paesler, *Tempelwort*, 260–61, the cult is implicitly perverted to idolatry by the people rejecting Jesus.

119. Animal trade was an essential part of temple business (Sanders, *Jesus*, 61–65) and stopping it would symbolise the end of sacrifice and temple activity. See Neusner, 'Money-Changers', 289–90; Wright, *Victory*, 423–24.

120. As Wright, *Victory*, 422–24, 90–93.

the temple would first require the old one to be destroyed, no texts actually predict a figure who will either destroy the temple or predict its destruction before rebuilding.[121] Instead, the destruction of the old temple happens through an act of divine judgement (Mic. 3.12; Jer. 7.26; *Sib. Or.* 3.265-81; 4.115-18; *Apoc. Abr.* 27; *2 Bar.* 1–8; *4 Bar.* 1–4),[122] and this is exactly what Luke recorded: the predictions of the Lukan Jesus about the fall of the temple are those of a prophet, not what Jesus would perform himself.

In terms of rebuilding, there is a long line of Jewish tradition about a new temple being constructed in the eschaton (e.g. Tob. 14.5; 2 Macc. 2.7; *1 En.* 24–25; 89–90; *Jub.* 1.15-17; 1QM 2.5-6; 7.10; 4QpPs 37 3.11; 11QTemple 29.8-10);[123] and other non-biblical texts expected a redeeming figure associated with the temple (Josephus, *Ant.* 18.4.1; *War* 6.5.2).[124] In addition, both Zechariah 6 and *Psalms of Solomon* 17 associate the renewal of the temple with the messianic king,[125] and James Dunn has noted that there was an expectation that the Messiah would cleanse the temple (basing this upon Mal. 3.1-4; *Jub.* 4.26; *Pss. Sol.* 17.30).[126] But while such texts have an important place within Jewish expectation, they are remarkably silent within Luke 19, despite the royal imagery of Zech. 9.9 in the entry narrative. This means that Jesus is not portrayed as a royal figure who rebuilds the temple even though Luke recounts a royal entry into the city.[127] It is quite possible that these texts have been deliberately silenced to give focus to other things. Significantly, Luke–Acts does not have false witnesses claiming that Jesus said he would rebuild the temple (as Mt. 26.61; Mk 14.58); nor does Luke have such a strong association of Jesus with David in the entry narrative (Jesus is not greeted with 'Blessed is the coming kingdom *of our father David*' as Mk 11.10, or 'Hosanna to the *Son of David!*' as Mt. 21.9). All this means that Jesus is not clearly associated with Solomon the temple-builder in Luke's account.[128]

121. Evans, 'Cleansing', 249–50.
122. Bauckham, 'Demonstration', 87.
123. Sanders, *Jesus*, 77–90.
124. Bock, *Luke*, 1573 n. 3, who also cites the list from Sanders.
125. Wright, *Victory*, 427–28.
126. Dunn, *Parting*, 48, also including 11QT 29.8-10.
127. The psalm quotation of Lk. 20.17 is not about Jesus as the chief stone of a renewed temple, it is a reference to vindication through the resurrection. See Nolland, *Luke*, 3:953.
128. Anthony Le Donne, 'Diarchic Symbolism in Matthew's Procession Narrative: A Dead Sea Scrolls Perspective', in *Early Christian Literature and Intertextuality*, ed. Craig A. Evans and H. Daniel Zacharias, LNTS 391 (London: T&T Clark, 2009), makes this association in Matthew by reading Zech. 9.9 together with 3 Kgdms 1.

Conclusion

In the second lament over Jerusalem (19.41-44) Jesus is again a prophet, speaking about the fate of Jerusalem and its temple, and doing so in words which are typical of an OT threat or lament; in 19.45-46 he then enacts the prophetic destruction of the temple. Yet despite the prophetic message, Jesus is not rejected as a prophet in this chapter – he is rejected as Messiah and saviour.

The words of the threat-lament in 19.41-44 are of critical importance, and echo the OT. Despite the large number of possible intertexts, it is likely that the reader would pay particular attention to a couple of texts (especially Ezek. 4.2 and Hos. 10.14), and interpret the words in the context of the prophets discussing the exile. This leads to a whole range of implicatures about the coming disaster, principal among which are that Jerusalem's destruction will be total, a result of divine judgement for the sin of the people, and preceded by the divine abandonment of the temple. His lament also indicts his hearers for their sin, principally their refusal to accept Jesus as the saviour: they failed to recognise the time of visitation (19.44), and because they did not recognise the coming peace they will inevitably face military catastrophe.

The words of this threat-lament are only fully appreciated when seen in their narrative context against the entry narrative (19.28-39) and the temple action (19.45-46). The entry narrative begins with Jesus' symbolic ride into the city; this is an evocation of Zech. 9.9, expecting that Jesus would be welcomed as king, as God's saviour, just as the figure who brings peace in Zechariah. With the quotation of Ps. 117.26, Luke indicates that this is the time spoken about in Lk. 13.35; the welcome Jesus receives is from his followers alone, not the city, and the welcome from the temple in Ps. 117.26 does not happen. The temple action gives more detail about the criticism of temple practice, and Luke's truncated report of this event emphasises the combined quotation of Isa. 56.7 and Jer. 7.11. These point to several strong implicatures: the eschatological age brought by Jesus is rejected, and the leaders of the temple are criticised for failing to allow the temple to become the eschatological temple. What is more, it is a den for those who assume that divine protection covers them, and Jesus' enacted destruction of the temple shows that it does not. There are also implicatures of idolatry associated with the temple, just as there were in Lk. 13.33-35, and accusations that true worship is neglected (with a focus on prayer and revelatory teaching), but these are not developed further at this point.

While Luke 19 demonstrates the significance of Jesus' rejection, and begins to show the relationship of the temple authorities to this, the relationship of the death of Jesus, the temple and the sin of the leadership must await further definition in Acts 7.

Chapter 5

LUKE 21.20-28:
THE SON OF MAN AND JERUSALEM

The eschatological discourse of Luke 21 focuses on Jerusalem and its temple;[1] its opening discussion and the disciples' question are both focused solely on the temple without a further eschatological horizon (Lk. 21.5-7).[2] The discourse is also set in the temple,[3] making it part of Jesus' temple teaching that began in 19.46; much of this teaching criticised the Jerusalem

---

1. For significant engagements with Lk. 21, see Bridge, *Eagles*, 115–40; Andrew R. Angel, *Chaos and the Son of Man: The Hebrew Chaoskampf Tradition in the Period 515 BCE to 200 CE*, LSTS 60 (London: T&T Clark, 2006), 135–39; Edward Adams, *The Stars Will Fall from Heaven: Cosmic Catastrophe in the New Testament and Its World*, LNTS 347 (London: T&T Clark, 2007), 172–80; Giblin, *Jerusalem*, 87–92; John Nolland, '"The Times of the Nations" and a Prophetic Pattern in Luke 21', in *Biblical Interpretation in Early Christian Gospels. Vol. 3, The Gospel of Luke*, ed. Thomas R Hatina, LNTS 376 (London: T&T Clark, 2010); Bloomquist, 'Culture of Apocalyptic'; John T. Baldwin, 'Reimarus and the Return of Christ Revisited: Reflections on Luke 21:24b and Its Phrase "Times of the Gentiles" in Historicist Perspective', *JATS* 11, no. 1–2 (2000); Anthony F. Buzzard, 'Luke's Prelude to the Kingdom of God: The Fall of Jerusalem and the End of the Age – Luke 21:20-33', *JRadRef* 4, no. 4 (1995); M. Morgen, 'Lc 17.20-37 et Lc 21,8-11.20-24: "Arrière-Fond Scripturaire"', in *The Scriptures in the Gospels*, ed. C. M. Tuckett (Leuven: Leuven University Press/Uitgeverij Peeters, 1997); Vittorio Fusco, 'Problems of Structure in Luke's Eschatological Discourse (Luke 21:7–36)', in *Luke and Acts*, ed. Gerald O'Collins and Gilberto Marconi (New York: Paulist Press, 1993); Kimball, *Exposition*, 187–96.

2. Ellis, *Luke*, 243; Schweizer, *Luke*, 314; Nolland, *Luke*, 3:990; Fitzmyer, *Luke*, 2:1331. Some challenge this and see a wider reference, e.g., Marshall, *Gospel*, 762; Bock, *Luke*, 2:1663; and Fusco argues the temple is the focus of the question, but this does not exclude the parousia as part of the answer. Fusco, 'Problems', 73–74. This is a specific reference to the temple, not the more general reference to buildings of Mk 13.1-2; see Chance, *Jerusalem*, 116.

3. Not the Mount of Olives, as Mk 13.3; Mt. 24.3. See Fitzmyer, *Luke*, 2:1330.

leadership (e.g., the parable of the tenants, 20.9-18;[4] and scribal behaviour, 20.46–21.4),[5] and the abrupt transition in 21.5 suggests that Luke 21 develops similar themes.[6]

The oracle reaches its climax in 21.20, where the questions of the introduction find their answer: πότε οὖν ταῦτα ἔσται is answered by ὅταν in 21.20, and τί τὸ σημεῖον ὅταν μέλλῃ ταῦτα γίνεσθαι is addressed in the events of 21.20.[7] This unique Lukan material in Lk. 21.20-24, addressing the fate of the city, forms the main area of interest for this chapter.[8] Many of the scholarly debates concerning the eschatological discourse cannot be discussed here,[9] but the use of cosmic disaster language requires attention because 21.25-28 is of crucial importance. It is the conclusion here that these verses refer to the fall of Jerusalem, rather than the parousia, and they are taken as part of the narrative unit. With that in mind, the chapter proceeds by examining Lk. 20.20-24 and 25-28 in turn.

The Fate of the City: Luke 21.20-24

The description of the fall of the city in 21.20-24 is detailed but not so specific that it must have been composed after the event; it is more likely that Luke based his account on an alternative source.[10] Whatever that

---

4. See Evans, 'Vineyard'. There is some temple-critical content to this parable, but it does not add to the overall discussion in these chapters.

5. Green, *Gospel*, 731.

6. Ibid., 733. It is likely to be addressed to the same group as Lk. 20.45 because Luke does not indicate a change in audience (which is his usual practice); see Giblin, *Jerusalem*, 75.

7. Luke 21.20 is when Jerusalem's desolation has come near (ἤγγικεν), a time for fleeing (21.21); the first answer is not given by ὅταν in 21.9 because they are told not to be afraid, and the time is not near (ἤγγικεν, 21.8). The events of 21.20 are also the signs enquired about; this question is not answered in 21.8-9 and 21.12-19.

8. The material is structurally independent of Mark; see Ellis, *Luke*, 244. It has some phrases in common with Mk 13.14-19: Ὅταν δὲ ἴδητε (Lk. 21.20 / Mk 13.14); τότε οἱ ἐν τῇ Ἰουδαίᾳ φευγέτωσαν εἰς τὰ ὄρη (Lk. 21.21 / Mk 13.14); ταῖς ἐν γαστρὶ ἐχούσαις καὶ ταῖς θηλαζούσαις ἐν ἐκείναις ταῖς ἡμέραις (Lk. 21.23 / Mk 13.17); and οἱ ἐν ταῖς χώραις μὴ εἰσερχέσθωσαν (Lk. 21.21) is similar to ὁ εἰς τὸν ἀγρὸν μὴ ἐπιστρεψάτω (Mk 13.16). The other material is uniquely Lukan with a focus on the city under siege.

9. See the summary of scholarly views in George R. Beasley-Murray, *Jesus and the Last Days: The Interpretation of the Olivet Discourse* (Peabody, MA: Hendrickson, 1993). On pp. 298–303 Beasley-Murray discusses the sources behind the discourse. See also the comments in Nolland, *Luke*, 3:984.

10. In Luke using historical sources after the event, see Josef Zmijewski, *Die Eschatologiereden des Lukas-Evangeliums. Eine traditions- und redaktionsgeschichtliche Untersuchung zu Lk 21, 5-36 und Lk 17, 20-37*, BBB 40 (Bonn: Hanstein,

source may be, his account is strongly evocative of the OT prophetic tradition,[11] and it is vital to identify the specific OT contexts that are echoed.

The Old Testament Background
(i) Luke 21.20

Ὅταν δὲ ἴδητε κυκλουμένην ὑπὸ στρατοπέδων Ἰερουσαλήμ, τότε γνῶτε ὅτι ἤγγικεν ἡ ἐρήμωσις αὐτῆς

When you see Jerusalem surrounded by armies, then know that its desolation has come near.

The first clause contains a phrase unique to the NT (κυκλουμένην ὑπὸ στρατοπέδων),[12] but κυκλόω and στρατόπεδον do not occur together in the LXX. Similarly, while the words κυκλόω and Ἰερουσαλήμ occur together three times in the LXX, these are not in a military context;[13] and of the seven uses of στρατόπεδον in the LXX, only Jer. 41.1 [ET 34.1] has any similarity with Lk. 21.20. Nevertheless, it has insufficient linguistic or contextual resemblance to be a clear intertext.[14] Isaiah 29.3 is closer:[15]

καὶ κυκλώσω ὡς Δαυιδ ἐπὶ σὲ καὶ βαλῶ περὶ σὲ χάρακα καὶ θήσω περὶ σὲ πύργους

And like Dauid I will surround you; I will lay ramparts around you and set up towers around you.

1972), 190–92; Fitzmyer, *Luke*, 2:1343; Danker, *Luke*, 212–13. For alternative sources see Geldenhuys, *Luke*, 533; Bock, *Luke*, 2:1675; Marshall, *Gospel*, 770–71; this source could go back to the historical Jesus. See also the discussion in N. H. Taylor, 'The Destruction of Jerusalem and the Transmission of the Synoptic Eschatological Discourse', *HvTSt* 59, no. 2 (2003): 303–305.

11. Dodd, 'Studies', who argued the LXX was Luke's source, not Mark or the historical events.

12. Κυκλόω also occurs in Jn 10.24; Acts 14.20; Heb. 11.30; στρατόπεδον is a NT *hapax legomenon*.

13. 2 Chronicles 23.2; 1 Macc. 6.7; Zech. 14.10.

14. Nolland, *Luke*, 3:1000, notes the possibility of this verse. Other verses with στρατόπεδον are: 2 Macc. 8.12; 9.9; *3 Macc.* 6.17; *4 Macc.* 3.13; Wis. 12.8; 48.12 (41.12 ET). Hartman, *Prophecy*, 230 n. 29 examines Hebrew texts whose words can be translated στρατόπεδον, but this goes beyond Luke's use of the LXX.

15. Nolland, *Luke*, 3:1000; Pao and Schnabel, 'Luke', 376.

It might have some conceptual similarity but there is insufficient similarity with Luke's distinctive phrasing for it to be readily accessible as an intertext above the general concept Luke echoes.

Daniel 12.11 (containing βδέλυγμα τῆς ἐρημώσεως) has been proposed as an intertext for the second phrase,[16] but while clearly related to Mk 13.14,[17] Luke's omission of βδέλυγμα makes a relationship unlikely.[18] The same is true of 1 Macc. 1.54 (with βδέλυγμα ἐρημώσεως).[19] Other options include Jer. 51.22 (44.22 ET), which contains reference to desolation of the land (ἡ γῆ ὑμῶν εἰς ἐρήμωσιν);[20] and Jer. 51.6 (44.6 ET),[21] which associates Jerusalem and other Judean cities with desolation (ἐρήμωσις). All this makes it conceptually closer, but it does not mention it drawing near, and that is vital imagery in Luke. There are other verses with ἐρήμωσις (Ps. 72.19; 2 Chron. 36.21; Jer. 4.7),[22] but none mention drawing near, and none are close enough lexically. It is therefore unlikely that a reader would explore any of these individual texts, instead relevance would be found in the generalised context of city desolation described by these verses. It is important to note that the language and concepts of Lk. 21.20 are similar enough to Lk. 19.40-44 to bring that threat-lament to mind; although it does not use κυκλόω, 19.43 has περικυκλόω, and it refers to the same event. The significance of this will be discussed below.

(ii) Luke 21.21

> τότε οἱ ἐν τῇ Ἰουδαίᾳ φευγέτωσαν εἰς τὰ ὄρη
> καὶ οἱ ἐν μέσῳ αὐτῆς ἐκχωρείτωσαν
> καὶ οἱ ἐν ταῖς χώραις μὴ εἰσερχέσθωσαν εἰς αὐτήν
>
> Then those in Judea must flee to the mountains,
> and those inside the city must leave it,
> and those out in the country must not enter it;

The three imperative phrases in Lk. 21.21 also echo familiar prophetic language of city capture without referring to a specific text. The first

---

16. Pao and Schnabel, 'Luke', 376.
17. R. T. France, *The Gospel of Mark: A Commentary on the Greek Text*, NIGTC (Carlisle: Paternoster, 2002), 522. Daniel 12.11 LXX has τὸ βδέλυγμα τῆς ἐρημώσεως, and Dan. 11.31 LXX (and Theodotian Dan. 12.11) have βδέλυγμα ἐρημώσεως.
18. In addition, Daniel's focus is more on the temple than the city.
19. Noted in Pao and Schnabel, 'Luke', 376.
20. Nolland, *Luke*, 3:1000.
21. Ibid.
22. Bock, *Luke*, 2:1676.

phrase's fleeing to the mountains evokes an image in Gen. 19.17, 19; Judg. 1.34; 6.2; 1 Kgdms 23.19; 26.1; 3 Kgdms 22.17; Isa. 15.5; Jer. 16.16; 27.6; 30.2 (50.6; 49.8 ET); Lam. 4.19; Ezek. 7.16; Amos 5.19-20; Nah. 3.18; Zech. 14.5; 1 Macc. 2.28; 2 Macc. 5.27;[23] but none of these texts is striking on its own.[24] The other two phrases are also common in warfare (e.g., Jer. 21.8-10; 41.21 [34.21 ET]; 52.7),[25] but none are close enough to be an exclusive intertext.

(iii) Luke 21.22

> ὅτι ἡμέραι ἐκδικήσεως αὗταί εἰσιν τοῦ πλησθῆναι πάντα τὰ γεγραμμένα
>
> 'for these are days of vengeance, as a fulfilment of all that is written.'

The phrase ἡμέραι ἐκδικήσεως could echo a couple of OT verses. Hosea 9.7 accuses Israel of forsaking YHWH and his prophet leading to judgement:

> ἥκασιν αἱ ἡμέραι τῆς ἐκδικήσεως, ἥκασιν αἱ ἡμέραι τῆς ἀνταποδόσεώς σου...
>
> the days of punishment have come; the days of your recompense have come...

This text has the closest LXX parallel to the phrase in Lk. 21.22, leading several commentators to identify this verse as an intertext.[26] Another possibility is Jer. 28.6 (51.6 ET), which uses the similar καιρὸς ἐκδικήσεως to describe a call for flight from a doomed city,[27] but it is not as close as Hos. 9.7 lexically, and its city is Babylon. Other texts noted in NA[28] have the singular 'day of vengeance' or a more general reference to the judgement of YHWH, including Deut. 32.35 (ἐν ἡμέρᾳ ἐκδικήσεως) and Jer. 26.10 (46.10 ET, ἡμέρα ἐκδικήσεως). Of all of these texts, Hos. 9.7 is the closest intertext and it is likely that a reader would identify it.

---

23. Marshall, *Gospel*, 772; Nolland, *Luke*, 3:1001; Bock, *Luke*, 2:1677; Pao and Schnabel, 'Luke', 376.

24. 1 Maccabees 2.28 is the closest with a reference to an abandoned city.

25. Nolland, *Luke*, 3:1001; Pao and Schnabel, 'Luke', 376.

26. Including Nolland, *Luke*, 3:1001; Fitzmyer, *Luke*, 2:1342; Green, *Gospel*, 739; Morgen, 'Lc 17.20-37', 319; Pao and Schnabel, 'Luke', 376.

27. Nolland, *Luke*, 3:1001; Pao and Schnabel, 'Luke', 376, who both note that the Hebrew term translated as ἐκδικήσεως in Jer. 51.6 (נְקָמָה) is closer to the meaning of the phrase in Lk. 21 than the term translated with the same word in Hos. 9.7 (פְּקֻדָּה). But this argument is questionable as Luke uses the LXX.

However, the subsequent reference to the scriptures in the plural (τοῦ πλησθῆναι πάντα τὰ γεγραμμένα) will affect how readers interpret the oracle. First, it encourages the interpretation of ἡμέραι ἐκδικήσεως against a general scriptural background rather than a single verse; so ἡμέραι ἐκδικήσεως is likely to evoke the general concept of the time of the Lord's vengeance whether against Israel or her enemies,[28] with the specific contribution of Hosea limited to the covenant-disobedience of Israel that exists in its setting. Second, the reference to the scriptures encourages the reader to expend more processing effort to explore the OT context of the rest of the oracle because these verses expand the theme of 'days of vengeance'. As readers explore these biblical themes they will add various weak implicatures.

(iv) Luke 21.23

οὐαὶ ταῖς ἐν γαστρὶ ἐχούσαις καὶ ταῖς θηλαζούσαις ἐν ἐκείναις ταῖς ἡμέραις· ἔσται γὰρ ἀνάγκη μεγάλη ἐπὶ τῆς γῆς καὶ ὀργὴ τῷ λαῷ τούτῳ

Woe to those who are pregnant and to those who are nursing infants in those days! For there will be great distress on the earth and wrath against this people;

The two participle phrases in Lk. 21.23 have no clear linguistic OT parallel, despite the distinctive phrases ἀνάγκη μεγάλη and ὀργὴ τῷ λαῷ τούτῳ; however, two texts do have conceptual parallels. First, the nature of the destruction suggests the terrible plagues, disasters and exile spoken of in Deut. 28.58-68 in its discussion of the consequences of covenant disobedience;[29] the relationship with the covenant is made stronger by the reference to the land in Lk. 21.23, and ὀργή is frequently used in the context of covenant curses in the OT.[30] Second, the reference to nursing infants and pregnant women brings to mind the similar imagery in Lk. 19.44.

---

28. Giblin, *Jerusalem*, 87, adds the following texts: Ezek. 9.1; Sir. 5.7; Jer. 27.21; 28.6 (50.31; 51.6 ET); Exod. 7.4; 12.12; Num. 33.4, in addition to the above. NA[28] (not NA[27]) adds 3 Kgdms 9.6-9; Mic. 3.12; Dan. 9.26, which also describe general judgement.

29. Bock, *Luke*, 2:1679 n. 31; Pao and Schnabel, 'Luke', 376–77. For Deut. 28 and covenant, see J. Gordon McConville, *Deuteronomy*, AOTC 5 (Leicester: Apollos; Downers Grove: InterVarsity, 2002), 409–10.

30. It conceptually recalls Deut. 28.64. See Bock, *Luke*, 2:1679 n. 31.

(v) Luke 21.24

καὶ πεσοῦνται στόματι μαχαίρης
καὶ αἰχμαλωτισθήσονται εἰς τὰ ἔθνη πάντα,
καὶ Ἰερουσαλὴμ ἔσται πατουμένη ὑπὸ ἐθνῶν,
ἄχρι οὗ πληρωθῶσιν καιροὶ ἐθνῶν.

they will fall by the edge of the sword
and be taken away as captives among all nations;
and Jerusalem will be trampled on by the Gentiles,
until the times of the Gentiles are fulfilled.

The final verse contains four phrases which strongly evoke exilic themes; no OT text clearly matches all of them but two verses parallel more than one clause of the verse each:[31]

Jer. 20.4-6:

⁴διότι τάδε λέγει κύριος Ἰδοὺ ἐγὼ δίδωμί σε εἰς μετοικίαν σὺν πᾶσι τοῖς φίλοις σου, καὶ <u>πεσοῦνται</u> ἐν <u>μαχαίρᾳ</u> ἐχθρῶν αὐτῶν, καὶ οἱ ὀφθαλμοί σου ὄψονται, καὶ σὲ καὶ πάντα Ιουδαν δώσω εἰς χεῖρας βασιλέως Βαβυλῶνος, καὶ μετοικιοῦσιν αὐτοὺς καὶ κατακόψουσιν αὐτοὺς ἐν <u>μαχαίραις</u>· ⁵καὶ δώσω τὴν πᾶσαν ἰσχὺν τῆς πόλεως ταύτης καὶ πάντας τοὺς πόνους αὐτῆς καὶ πάντας τοὺς θησαυροὺς τοῦ βασιλέως Ιουδα εἰς χεῖρας ἐχθρῶν αὐτοῦ, καὶ ἄξουσιν αὐτοὺς εἰς Βαβυλῶνα. ⁶καὶ σὺ καὶ πάντες οἱ κατοικοῦντες ἐν τῷ οἴκῳ σου πορεύσεσθε ἐν <u>αἰχμαλωσίᾳ</u>, καὶ ἐν Βαβυλῶνι ἀποθανῇ καὶ ἐκεῖ ταφήσῃ, σὺ καὶ πάντες οἱ φίλοι σου, οἷς ἐπροφήτευσας αὐτοῖς ψευδῆ.

⁴for this is what the Lord says: Behold, I am assigning you to deportation with all your friends, and they shall fall by their enemies' dagger, and your eyes shall see it. And I will give you and all Iouda into the hands of the king of Babylon, and they shall deport them and shall cut them down with daggers. ⁵And I will give all the strength of this city and all its toils and all the treasures of the king of Iouda into the hands of his enemies, and they shall bring them into Babylon. ⁶And as for you and all who live in your house – you shall go in captivity, and in Babylon you shall die, and there you shall be buried, you and all your friends, to them to whom you have prophesied lies.

---

31. Other possibilities include Ezra 9.7 (see NA[28]), which contains dying with the sword (ῥομφαίᾳ) and captivity (αἰχμαλωσίᾳ), but the cognate αἰχμαλωσίᾳ is the only close link to Lk. 21.24. Jeremiah 39.1-10 (MT) has some similarity (noted by Pao and Schnabel, 'Luke', 377), but the significant material is omitted in the LXX translation (Jer. 46.1-3). Isaiah 10 and Jer. 50–52 contain other judgements against Jerusalem. See Nolland, *Luke*, 3:1004.

It has two references to being cut down by a sword (one using πίπτω, like Luke, but none with the distinctive στόματι μαχαίρης); and it has three references to deportation, two use μετοικίζω (20.4) and the other the cognate noun of the Lukan αἰχμαλωτίζω (20.6).[32]

Ezekiel 39.23 also parallels to the first two clauses of Lk. 21.24:[33]

καὶ γνώσονται πάντα τὰ ἔθνη ὅτι διὰ τὰς ἁμαρτίας αὐτῶν ἠχμαλωτεύθησαν οἶκος Ισραηλ, ἀνθ' ὧν ἠθέτησαν εἰς ἐμέ, καὶ ἀπέστρεψα τὸ πρόσωπόν μου ἀπ' αὐτῶν καὶ παρέδωκα αὐτοὺς εἰς χεῖρας τῶν ἐχθρῶν αὐτῶν, καὶ ἔπεσαν πάντες μαχαίρᾳ.

And all the nations shall know that, because of their sins, the house of Israel was taken captive, because they dealt treacherously with me, and I averted my face from them and gave them over into the hands of their adversaries, and they all fell by dagger.

Its αἰχμαλωτεύω is similar to αἰχμαλωτίζω, and it refers to all the nations in a separate clause; while it has πίπτω and μάχαιρα it does not contain the distinctive στόματι μαχαίρης. Joel Green argues that this verse is about judgement through the enemies of Israel and therefore similar in concept to Luke's trampling by nations;[34] though not explicitly stated in the text, this might be enough to favour it as a prime intertext. However, Luke's distinctive descriptive language does not point clearly to either of these verses,[35] it points to a range of additional texts and motifs.

Πεσοῦνται στόματι μαχαίρης. Many texts in the LXX refer to death by the sword: some do not use the characteristic στόματι μαχαίρης (e.g., Isa. 3.25; 13.15; 65.12; Jer. 14.12-18; 16.4);[36] others do (e.g., Gen. 34.26; Josh. 19.48; 2 Kgdms 15.14; Sir. 28.18; Jer. 21.7).[37] Sirach 28.18 might be the closest lexically (it has ἔπεσαν ἐν στόματι μαχαίρας)',[38] but the phrase is not the same as Lk. 21.24, and it is unlikely that it is significantly close enough to make this wisdom text more obvious than the general motif (especially when the motif appears in OT prophetic texts). It is more likely that a general motif is echoed.

---

32. Nolland, *Luke*, 3:1002; Pao and Schnabel, 'Luke', 377.
33. Bock, *Luke*, 2:1680; Green, *Gospel*, 739.
34. Green, *Gospel*, 739.
35. Morgen, 'Lc 17.20-37', 320, notes that there is not one clear intertext here, but many.
36. As suggested by Johnson, *Luke*, 324.
37. NA[28] has Gen. 34.26; Sir. 28.18; Jer. 21.7.
38. Fitzmyer, *Luke*, 2:1346; Nolland, *Luke*, 3:1002; Bock, *Luke*, 2:1680.

Αἰχμαλωτισθήσονται εἰς τὰ ἔθνη πάντα has many possible parallels in the OT as a general concept. Deuteronomy 28.41; 4 Kgdms 24.14; Isa. 5.13; 46.2; Jer. 15.2; 22.22; Ezek. 12.3; Mic 1.16; Amos 9.4; Zech. 14.2 all use either the cognate noun αἰχμαλωσία or the adjective αἰχμάλωτος to refer to exile, but none of them stands out from among the others.[39] Ezekiel 32.9 is closer lexically:[40]

καὶ παροργιῶ καρδίαν λαῶν πολλῶν, ἡνίκα ἂν ἄγω αἰχμαλωσίαν σου εἰς τὰ ἔθνη εἰς γῆν, ἣν οὐκ ἔγνως.

And I will provoke the heart of many peoples, when I take your captivity into the nations, into a land that you did not know.

It has a cognate noun of αἰχμαλωτίζω and a reference to the nations, but it is not as close as Deut. 28.64:[41]

καὶ διασπερεῖ σε κύριος ὁ θεός σου εἰς πάντα τὰ ἔθνη ἀπ' ἄκρου τῆς γῆς ἕως ἄκρου τῆς γῆς, καὶ δουλεύσεις ἐκεῖ θεοῖς ἑτέροις, ξύλοις καὶ λίθοις, οὓς οὐκ ἠπίστω σὺ καὶ οἱ πατέρες σου.

And the Lord your God will disperse you to all nations, from an end of the earth to an end of the earth, and there you shall be subject to other gods, of wood and stone, which you and your fathers did not know.

It does not use αἰχμαλωτίζω, and its exile is about dispersal, not captivity; nonetheless, it refers to a form of exile with εἰς πάντα τὰ ἔθνη, and it is a verse close at hand for the reader because of the reference to Deut. 28.58-68 in Lk. 21.23. But even if the reader notices this verse, it is likely that its interpretation will be limited to the familiar metarepresentation of the idea of exile as a result of covenant unfaithfulness. This general interpretation is encouraged by Luke's interpretive comment that these things are fulfilment of πάντα τὰ γεγραμμένα.

Ἰερουσαλὴμ ἔσται πατουμένη ὑπὸ ἐθνῶν. Despite Luke's distinctive language (πατέω occurs five times in the NT) there are no verses with πατουμένη ὑπὸ ἐθνῶν in the LXX, and no likely parallels using πατέω;[42]

---

39. Hartman, *Prophecy*, 231 n. 29; Johnson, *Luke*, 324, have this list. Bock, *Luke*, 2:1680, adds 1 Macc. 10.33 and Tob. 1.10, which both use αἰχμαλωτίζω, but do not have sufficient contextual association. The reference to nations in a separate clause is not enough to distinguish Zech. 14.2.

40. NA[28].

41. Favoured by Gaston, *Stone*, 361; Fitzmyer, *Luke*, 2:1346; Nolland, *Luke*, 3:1002.

42. Isaiah 25.10; 26.6; Zech. 10.5 use πατέω in a military sense but are not conceptually close.

all possible intertexts use καταπατέω. Isaiah 63.18; 1 Macc. 3.45, 51; 4.60; 2 Macc. 8.2 use the verb in the context of trampling Jerusalem or the temple; Zech. 12.3; *Pss. Sol.* 17.22 (17.25) add a reference to the nations.[43]

> Zech. 12.3:
>
> καὶ ἔσται ἐν τῇ ἡμέρᾳ ἐκείνῃ θήσομαι τὴν Ιερουσαλημ λίθον καταπατούμενον πᾶσιν τοῖς ἔθνεσιν· πᾶς ὁ καταπατῶν αὐτὴν ἐμπαίζων ἐμπαίξεται, καὶ ἐπισυναχθήσονται ἐπ' αὐτὴν πάντα τὰ ἔθνη τῆς γῆς.
>
> And it shall be on that day, I will make Ierousalem a trampled stone for all the nations; everyone who tramples it when mocking shall mock. And all the nations of the earth shall be gathered against it.
>
> *Pss. Sol.* 17.22:
>
> ...καθαρίσαι Ιερουσαλημ ἀπὸ ἐθνῶν καταπατούντων ἐν ἀπωλείᾳ,
>
> ...to purify Ierousalem from nations that trample her down in destruction,

The closest is Zech. 12.3,[44] because it refers to the threat of trampling, not its resolution. However, it is unlikely that Zech. 12.3 is an exclusive intertext because the reader is not directed toward it specifically: Luke's language does not pick up on key phrases from Zechariah (e.g., λίθον καταπατούμενον or ἐπισυναχθήσονται ἐπ' αὐτὴν πάντα τὰ ἔθνη τῆς γῆς).[45]

So, while it is possible that a reader would search for relevance in this text, it is more likely that relevance would be found quickly in the concept of Gentile defilement of the city, something which is common in OT prophetic texts.[46]

Ἄχρι οὗ πληρωθῶσιν καιροί ἐθνῶν. There are several texts in the LXX referring to a divine limit to judgement, including Dan. 8.13-14; 12.7; Tob. 14.5.[47] The closest lexically is Tob. 14.5 ('until the time when the time of the appointed times will be completed', ἕως πληρωθῶσιν καιροὶ

---

43. For lists of potential intertexts, see NA[28] (except Maccabees); see also the discussions in Fitzmyer, *Luke*, 2:1346–47; Bock, *Luke*, 2:1680; Nolland, *Luke*, 3:1002; Green, *Gospel*, 739; Chance, *Jerusalem*, 134. Nolland and Green do not include the *Psalms of Solomon*.

44. The main intertext in Fitzmyer, *Luke*, 2:1344; Nolland, *Luke*, 3:1002; Pao and Schnabel, 'Luke', 377; Morgen, 'Lc 17.20-37', 321. Present in NA[28].

45. In the MT, Jerusalem is made a 'heavy rock' not a 'trampled stone'.

46. A concept present in texts which do not refer to trampling, e.g., Ps. 78.1. See NA[28]; Chance, *Jerusalem*, 134.

47. NA[28] adds Jer. 25.29 (32.15 LXX) to this list and omits Dan. 8.13-14. See also Pao and Schnabel, 'Luke', 377.

τοῦ αἰῶνος), but it is not close enough. It is likely that a reader would find relevance in the main emphasis of any of these parallels, the establishment of divine limits.

Interpretation

Luke 21.20-24 clearly reflects the OT, with every phrase repeating themes from scripture, but this does not require that it is interpreted in the light of specific verses. If Luke wanted to draw a specific verse to the attention of his readers, then he would have reproduced more of its distinctive elements, but instead he uses distinctive phrases that do not echo particular texts. Of course, arguments can be made that particular OT verses are closer to a NT phrase than any other, but this is not the point. The issue is whether a reader would move beyond the most accessible context (the OT motif) to search for relevance in specific verses; it is likely that a reader would not, because sufficient cognitive effects can be found in the general motif to satisfy expectations of relevance (especially because of the general appeal to the scriptures in 21.22).

Having said that, some verses are clearly identified, especially Deut. 28.58-68 and Hos. 9.7, and these will be explored by the reader. In addition, three specific links are made back to Lk. 19.41-44 and its description of the same event: Lk. 21.6 (οὐκ ἀφεθήσεται λίθος ἐπὶ λίθῳ), which echoes 19.44 (οὐκ ἀφήσουσιν λίθον ἐπὶ λίθον), and the two links discussed above (in 21.20 and 21.23).[48] This connection to Luke 19 means that the contextual information associated with Luke 19 will be activated when interpreting the message of Luke 21, and Luke 21 will either expand or constrain the implicatures from Luke 19. Although Lk. 21.20-24 clearly foretells the destruction of Jerusalem, its use of OT motifs adds four main implicatures.

First, it evokes themes of exile. Its language is similar to Lk. 19.42-44 in describing catastrophic military action, and its OT motifs draw parallels back to the exile and the previous destruction of Jerusalem. The piling of image upon image, and motif upon motif has the effect of evoking a whole series of implicatures, many of them weak. These implicatures do not require expansion here because they are similar to those discussed in the last two chapters (including ideas of judgement, totality of destruction, divine abandonment and Gentile military action),[49] and there will also be a host of associated weak implicatures about personal danger, threats

---

48. There is also a possible connection back from ἡμέραι ἐκδικήσεως αὗταί εἰσιν (21.22).

49. Such ideas are foregrounded by the rare use of ὀργή by Jesus in 21.23. For divine judgement, see Hartman, *Prophecy*, 231.

of displacement from the city, and desire to avoid the event. To such imagery, this chapter adds the need of the inhabitants to escape the city, their removal to captivity, and Gentile defilement of the city (albeit limited temporally). This is highly evocative of the past exile,[50] and it drives home the completeness of the destruction, the human consequences, and the inevitable abandonment of the city by God. Whether or not the first-century Jews believed themselves to have returned from exile, such words uttered within the temple must have had a significant effect;[51] Jerusalem was no longer a safe place from judgement.

Second, it evokes covenant unfaithfulness. The evocation of Deut. 28.58-68 raises disobedience to the covenant as the cause for the distress because this OT text has a focus on covenant; Hos. 9.7 makes a similar association. Such unfaithfulness is likely to be the emphasis of τοῦ πλησθῆναι πάντα τὰ γεγραμμένα in 21.22, the statement sandwiched between the evocation of Hosea and Deuteronomy. The oracle is not specific about what this disobedience is, and it is left for the reader to enlarge upon the idea through the creation of weak implicatures (with the hope that the later narrative gives some clarity), but ideas of covenant breaking will enrich the accusations in Luke 19 (especially the rejection of Jesus) because of the link between the texts. There may be more to it than this, and a reader is invited to think of how the scriptures refer to vengeance on unfaithfulness: it is not that any specific text is evoked, but this theme is rich in a host of OT texts (e.g., Lev. 26.31-33; Deut. 28.49-57; 32.35; 3 Kgdms 9.6-9; Isa. 10.3; 34.8; 61.2; 63.4; Jer. 5.29; 6.1-8; 7.8-15; 26.10 [46.10 ET]; 27.27 [50.27 ET]; 33.19 [26.19]; 28.6 [51.6 ET]; Ezek. 9.1; Dan. 9.26; Hos. 9.7; Mic 3.12; Zech. 8.1-8; 11.6; Sir. 5.7).[52]

Third, it adds the on-going rejection of Jesus, through the rejection of the disciples.[53] Asked about the destruction of the temple, Jesus does not answer the disciples until Lk. 21.20; in the interim he speaks about persecution (Lk. 21.12-19). The persecutors are not identified in 21.12 (third person plural verbs are used without a subject), and this invites the reader to form a range of implicatures about their identity as the narrative progresses: these will include associations derived from the rejection of Jesus (through links back to Lk. 19), but they will await further definition in Acts where the persecution is detailed.

50. Johnson, *Luke*, 324.
51. Pao and Schnabel, 'Luke', 374, referencing the ideas expressed in Wright, *New Testament*, 268–71, 299–301.
52. For these texts see Hartman, *Prophecy*, 231 n. 29; Bock, *Luke*, 2:1678; Green, *Gospel*, 739; Pao and Schnabel, 'Luke', 376.
53. A point well made by Walker, *Jesus*, 75–76; see also Green, *Gospel*, 738.

Fourth, the repetition of prophetic language reemphasises the place of Jesus as a prophet who speaks about the fate of Jerusalem and its temple.[54] This is set up by an introduction to the chapter in the prophetic style (21.6),[55] and continued through the content of the material.

Cosmic Disturbances: Luke 21.25-28

The majority of scholars think Lk. 21.25-28 refers to the parousia at the end of the age;[56] for some this event is separated from the destruction of the city by a significant amount of time,[57] though others think the two events are more closely related,[58] and others steer a middle course.[59] However, this view is not a consensus.

---

54. Bock, *Luke*, 2:1680; Thomas R. Hatina, 'The Focus of Mark 13:24-27 – The Parousia, or the Destruction of the Temple?', *BBR* 6 (1996): 50, speaking about Mk 13, but the same applies here.

55. For the prophetic style, see Fusco, 'Problems', 85.

56. The discussion is usually about Mark 13. For an overview, see Beasley-Murray, *Days*, 1–349. For a recent discussion and further bibliography, see Adams, *Stars*, 137–39; Hatina, 'Focus', 43 n. 1. Those interpreting Lk. 21.25–28 as parousia include: Walter Grundmann, *Das Evangelium nach Lukas*, THKNT 3, 2nd ed. (Berlin: Evangelische Verlagsanstalt, 1961), 384–85; Plummer, *Luke*, 483–85; Schweizer, *Luke*, 320–29; Geldenhuys, *Luke*, 337–38; Ellis, *Luke*, 245; Johnson, *Luke*, 327–31; Bovon, *Luc*, 152–56; Marshall, *Gospel*, 774–75; Fitzmyer, *Luke*, 2:1349; Bock, *Luke*, 2:1682–86; Nolland, *Luke*, 3:1005–1007; Danker, *Luke*, 212–14; Evans, *Luke*, 752–56; Michael D. Goulder, *Luke: A New Paradigm*, JSNTSup 20 (Sheffield: Sheffield Academic, 1994), 713–14; Judith Lieu, *The Gospel of Luke*, Epworth Commentaries (Peterborough: Epworth, 1997), 170–71; A. R. C. Leaney, *A Commentary on the Gospel According to St Luke* (London: A. & C. Black, 1958), 262.

57. Classically the delay of the parousia, as discussed in Conzelmann, *Theology*, 74; also described in Georg Braumann, 'Die lukanische Interpretation der Zerstörung Jerusalems', *NovT* 6, no. 2 (1963). John Carroll argues Luke is correcting a mistaken understanding that the fall of the city was an end-time event, and that Luke therefore separated the parousia and the fall of the city; see Carroll, *History*, 107–17. See also Ruthild Geiger, *Die Lukanischen Endzeitreden: Studien zur Eschatologie des Lukas-Evangeliums* (Bern: Herbert Lang; Frankfurt: Peter Lang, 1973), 249.

58. Robert Maddox, *The Purpose of Luke–Acts* (Göttingen: Vandenhoeck & Ruprecht, 1982), 120–21. Buzzard, 'Prelude', thinks the fall of the city refers to a future event (not 70 CE). Still others think the fall of the city was an eschatological event, but not part of the consummation of history

59. For Green, *Gospel*, 731, the destruction of the city is an eschatological event, separate to the consummation of history, but that end is described in imminent terms.

Scholars such as N. T. Wright and R. T. France, regard the language of cosmic disturbance as a metaphor for political upheaval on the stage of world history, so Mk 13.26 and parallels refer to the fall of Jerusalem, not the parousia.[60] This is not a recent development; indeed, it is consistently present in the literature since the nineteenth century.[61] Significantly, while supporters of this view all agree that the verses refer to a political event (not the parousia), they disagree about the specific event. For example, among recent contributors, Bas Van Iersel argues Mk 13.24-25 refers to the fall of pagan idols;[62] C. S. Mann and Peter Bolt argue that it refers to cosmic signs at Jesus' crucifixion;[63] and for Keith Dyer it is about political changes in the east after the fall of Jerusalem.[64] The argument over whether Lk. 21.25-27 refers to a historical or eschatological event hinges on how the language would have been understood, and this needs to be reviewed before examining the contribution that the structure of Luke 21 makes to the debate.

Cosmic Disaster Language

Wright argues that the kind of language in Lk. 21.25-27 has its origins in the OT prophets, in passages such as Isaiah 13, whose 'language about

60. France, *Jesus*, 227–39; idem, *Mark*, 530–37; Wright, *New Testament*, 280–338. They are joined by Hatina, 'Focus', on Mark; Jeffrey A. Gibbs, *Jerusalem and Parousia: Jesus' Eschatological Discourse in Matthew's Gospel* (Saint Louis: Concordia Academic Press, 2000), 167–204; Alistair I. Wilson, *When Will These Things Happen? A Study of Jesus as Judge in Matthew 21–25*, PBM (Carlisle: Paternoster, 2004), 109–58, on Matthew; and in Luke's Gospel, Angel, *Chaos*, 125–39.

61. Joseph A. Alexander, *The Gospel According to Mark*, GSC (Edinburgh: Banner of Truth Trust, 1960 [orig. 1858]); James S. Russell, *The Parousia, a Critical Inquiry into the New Testament Doctrine of Our Lord's Second Coming* (Bradford: Kingdom Publications, 1996 [orig. 1877]), 80–82; Ezra P. Gould, *A Critical and Exegetical Commentary on the Gospel According to St. Mark*, ICC (Edinburgh: T&T Clark, 1896), 250–51; Philip Carrington, *According to Mark: A Running Commentary on the Oldest Gospel* (Cambridge: University Press, 1960), 280–83; R. V. G. Tasker, *The Gospel According to St. Matthew: An Introduction and Commentary*, TNTC (Leicester: Inter-Varsity Press, 1961), 225–27. See also the others mentioned in France, *Jesus*, 234 n. 26.

62. Bas Van Iersel, 'The Sun, Moon and Stars of Mark 13, 24–25 in a Greco-Roman Reading', *Bib* 77 (1996): 89–90.

63. C. S. Mann, *Mark: A New Translation with Introduction and Commentary*, AB 27 (Garden City: Doubleday, 1986), 530–32; Peter G. Bolt, *The Cross from a Distance: Atonement in Mark's Gospel*, NSBT 18 (Leicester: Apollos, 2004), 125–26.

64. Keith D. Dyer, *The Prophecy on the Mount: Mark 13 and the Gathering of the New Community*, ITS 2 (Bern: Peter Lang, 1998), 230.

sun, moon and stars being darkened or shaken has as its primary referent a set of cataclysmic events *within* the space-time universe, and not an event which will bring that universe to its utter end'.[65] Later Jewish apocalyptic writers also used similar imagery to describe calamitous events within history (e.g., *Apoc. Abr.* 12.3-10; *2 Bar.* 36.1–37.1).[66] Wright argues such writers had an interpretive framework where the restoration of Israel was an event within history, not at the end of history,[67] and while they looked to the end of the present world order where the pagans held power – and used cosmological language to refer to that – they did not look for the end of the 'space-time world'.[68] So Wright does not think that the prophets had one eye on the future 'day of the Lord' (unlike George Caird), their metaphors had no basis in future expectation.[69] All this means that 'such language cannot be read in a crassly literalistic way without doing it great violence'.[70] France argues similarly: 'The phrases which make up these verses are part of a stock-in-trade of Old Testament prophecy, and they are used to describe especially political disasters, and the destruction of cities and nations, particularly those which played a leading role'.[71]

Wright and France are correct that there are many places in the OT where cosmic signs are used to refer to an event of judgement within history:[72] Isa. 13.10 uses cosmological language to describe the coming day of the Lord in Babylon;[73] Isa. 34.4 uses similar portents for judgement on Edom;[74] Ezek. 32.7 refers to Egypt; Amos 8.9 to Israel; and Joel 3–4 to Judah and other nations. Similar language is used to describe the defeat of political and religious entities in later Jewish writings (e.g., *1 En.* 1.5; 6.2-8; 12.3-6; 14.3-6; 15.4-16; 80.4-7; *2 En.* 7.18; *Jub.* 4.15; 5.1; *T. Levi* 4.1-5; *T. Reub.* 5.6-7; *T. Naph.* 3.5; *Sib. Or.* 3.796).[75]

---

65. Wright, *Victory*, 209, italics original.
66. Wright, *New Testament*, 281.
67. Ibid., 285.
68. Ibid., 297–99, 333, the quotation is a phrase used on pp. 299, 300.
69. George Caird argues that biblical writers believed in a literal end of the world, though end-of-the-world language was metaphor for historical events; see George B. Caird, *The Language and Imagery of the Bible* (London: Duckworth, 1980), 256-58. See the discussion in Adams, *Stars*, 9.
70. Wright, *New Testament*, 284.
71. France, *Jesus*, 233.
72. For more detail, see Wilson, *Things*, 124–27; Hatina, 'Focus', 53–59.
73. Heavenly bodies are either the pagan deities of Babylon (Oswalt, *Isaiah 1–39*, 1:609), or a metaphor for judgement (Wilson, *Things*, 124; Hatina, 'Focus', 55).
74. A literal reading demands that thorns can overrun a stronghold (34.13) after celestial bodies are destroyed (34.4)! See Wilson, *Things*, 125.
75. The list is from Hatina, 'Focus', 57 n. 61.

However, this interpretation of the imagery has been questioned by Edward Adams.[76] Against Wright, he argues that a Jewish mind would entertain the ideas of the end of the world, and disputes that there was a 'linguistic convention' of the use of language of cosmic disaster for political events;[77] he also maintains that if Wright had looked closer at later Jewish disaster texts then this would have been clear. He states: 'It is a common view that later apocalyptic writers who took over the cosmic disaster imagery of the biblical prophets used it in a more clear-cut final sense than perhaps their biblical forerunners had done'.[78] Adams makes some helpful observations, but his case is overstated in three significant parts of his argument: in the use of metaphor; the presence of eschatological interpretation in the texts; and the hermeneutical significance of later Jewish texts in interpreting the language in the NT.

(i) The Role of Metaphor
Adams interprets cosmic destruction language metaphorically; it involves re-use of flood imagery, or language of cosmic disturbance associated with the 'day of the Lord',[79] and it is possible because the Jews had a conception of the destruction of the world.[80] But, for Adams, the language of destruction still refers to general destruction, not a historical event: so in texts with an apparent eschatological reference, the metaphors refer to cosmic or global catastrophe. Even where texts refer to localised judgement (e.g., Isa. 13.9-13; 34.4; Jer. 4.23-28; Joel 1.1–2.27; Mic 1.3-4; Nah. 1.2-8; Zeph. 1.2-3), Adams does not think the language has an exclusively local focus:[81] he interprets the language as a particularisation of generalised eschatological destruction. In other words, the language encourages the reader first to imagine the coming generalised disaster (typically on a global or cosmic level), and through this to interpret the historical event as a particular example.[82] But even if a case was made for

---

76. Adams, *Stars*, especially 10–16. See also the earlier arguments of Dale C. Allison, 'Jesus and the Victory of Apocalyptic', in *Jesus and the Restoration of Israel: A Critical Assessment of N. T. Wright's Jesus and the Victory of God*, ed. C. C. Newman (Carlisle: Paternoster, 1999), and the counter-arguments of Wilson, *Things*, 122–23.

77. Adams, *Stars*, 10.

78. Ibid., 11.

79. E.g., ibid., 17, see also the examples of flood imagery on p. 57 and day of the Lord on p. 36.

80. Ibid., 12–14.

81. Ibid., 25–51.

82. Ibid., 36–44, 156, using the approach of Paul R. Raabe, 'The Particularizing of Universal Judgment in Prophetic Discourse', *CBQ* 64, no. 4 (2002).

the Jews having such a conception of destruction, this does not require that language of celestial disturbance or flood was usually used to refer to such future global or universal destruction.[83] The language can function as a metaphor for historical events without requiring the reader to envisage a particularisation of eschatological judgement; it can also compare the event in calamity with cosmic events without implying that those events were going to happen.[84] It all depends on how the metaphor was commonly used, and heavenly bodies were rich metaphors whose encyclopaedic information incorporated other deities. It is therefore significant to note that Adams pays little attention to *Chaoskampf* language.

Andrew Angel's examination of Jewish and Christian texts in the period 515 BCE to 200 CE concludes that there is a continuing use of the Hebrew *Chaoskampf* tradition (HCT) during this time, something that Adams almost entirely misses. Angel defines *Chaoskampf* as 'the battle of the warrior god with the monstrous forces of chaos';[85] he notes its origins in ancient Near-Eastern mythology and observes the role of the chaos waters, chaos monsters and the divine warrior in the OT, where he thinks it describes God's action *within* history.[86] Celestial signs, therefore,

---

83. Jews had some conception of destruction (e.g., the flood story) but it was typically accompanied by expectations of the remaking of creation (as Adams, *Stars*, 12–14 with notes). While this means that a Jewish expectation of a this-worldly future must incorporate *some* understanding of destruction, it does not require that destruction has a dominant place. There is typically continuity (the flood story involves continuity through the inhabitants of the ark and the re-making of the *same* creation), and there is not an end of the space-time world (agreeing with Wright) because of Jewish this-worldly eschatology. Whatever global or cosmic destruction might mean to an ancient Jewish mind, it has to be defined within these limits.

84. Caird, *Language*, 256–57.

85. Angel, *Chaos*, 1. The theory goes back to Gunkel, see the summary in H. Gunkel, 'The Influence of Babylonian Mythology Upon the Biblical Creation Story', in *Creation in the Old Testament*, ed. Bernhard W. Anderson (Philadelphia: Fortress, 1984). See the discussion in Frederick J. Mabie, 'Chaos and Death', in *Dictionary of the Old Testament Wisdom, Poetry, and Writings*, ed. Tremper Longman and Peter Enns (Nottingham: IVP, 2008), 41–54; David Tsumura, *Creation and Destruction: A Reappraisal of the Chaoskampf Theory of the Old Testament* (Winona Lake: Eisenbrauns, 2005); Rebecca S. Watson, *Chaos Uncreated: A Reassessment of the Theme of "Chaos" in the Hebrew Bible*, BZAW 341 (Berlin: de Gruyter, 2005).

86. Angel, *Chaos*, 1–19. The texts are many, including divine warrior imagery in Deut. 33.26; Pss 17.12; 67.35; 103.3 (18.11; 68.34; 104.3 ET); Isa. 19.1; 66.15; and his defeat of the chaos water or monsters in Pss 17.6-19; 73.12-17; 76.18-21 (18.5-18; 74.12-17; 77.17-21 ET). He finds divine warrior imagery in Isa. 8.5-8; 17.12-14; 30.7; Jer. 5.22b; 38.36 (31.35 ET); Amos 9.3; Nah. 1.3-5 and Hab. 3.1-15. This means

often accompany the movement of the divine warrior (e.g., Isa. 13.10; Joel 4.15; Ezek. 32.7; Hab 3.10-11).[87] He goes on to amass a catalogue of texts using HCT imagery in the Dead Sea Scrolls, and in later wisdom and apocalyptic writings;[88] he also argues that such imagery is present in the NT, including Mark 13 and Luke 21.[89] Angel's thesis might be built on an overly broad definition of HCT (where a reference to sea *or* the divine is enough without a requirement for battle imagery),[90] but there is quite a variation in the use of chaos language across Jewish literature,[91] and Angel's cases are well argued. This means that the imagery often present in 'day of the Lord' or flood imagery would be interpreted against the HCT tradition, and it is this very imagery that is present in Lk. 21.25-27.

(ii) Eschatological Interpretation in Texts
Adams exaggerates the frequency of reference to cosmic destruction, especially in later Jewish texts. In part this is because his study is focused on texts that use language of disaster in apparently eschatological contexts,[92] and this makes them appear more prevalent than they are. This means that he misses texts that use this language for clearly historical events (e.g., Josephus, *Ant.* 5.60, 205; 6.27),[93] and those using it for the giving of Torah (Josephus, *Ant.* 3.80; Pseudo-Philo, *L.A.B.* 11.5; 23.10; 32.7-8).[94]

Even in texts that Adams thinks refer to the eschaton or cosmic catastrophe, the reference is frequently historical. Because he misses HCT imagery in the prophetic literature, he misses its use to describe victories

that it is present in the psalms of the royal cult and the pre-exilic prophets. See also the discussion in Walter Brueggemann, *Theology of the Old Testament: Testimony, Dispute, Advocacy* (Minneapolis: Fortress, 1997), 657.

87. Angel, *Chaos*, 121.
88. Ibid., 37–161.
89. Also in Mt. 8.23-27; 14.22-23; Mk 4.35-41; 6.45-52; Lk. 8.22-25; Jn 6.16-21 (ibid., 21, 160).
90. As noted by John J. Collins, review of *Chaos and the Son of Man: The Hebrew Chaoskampf Tradition in the Period 515 BCE to 200 CE*, *JJS* 58 (2007): 338; Angel does not stick to the stricter ideas of Gunkel.
91. Watson, *Chaos*; and demonstrated by several of the essays in Norman C. Habel, ed. *The Earth Story in the Psalms and the Prophets*, vol. 4 (Sheffield: T&T Clark; Cleveland: Pilgrim Press, 2001).
92. Andrew R. Angel, 'The Son of Man: Jesus, Eschatology and Mission', *Anvil* 26, no. 3–4 (2009): 225–28.
93. Exegesis detailed in Angel, *Chaos*, 184–88; see also the list of texts in Hatina, 'Focus', 57 n. 61.
94. Angel, *Chaos*, 166–79, 181–82.

of YHWH within history – for instance, Isaiah 24–27,[95] and the divine warrior imagery in Micah 1 and Joel 4.15 (3.15 ET).[96] He also argues for an eschatological interpretation in later texts; for example, 1QH 11.19-36 and *T. Mos.* 10.4-6. In the former, Adams notes the praise of the psalmist that God rescued him and brought him into the community (11.19-28), and then argues that the focus becomes the final eschatological battle, with a destroying flood of fire, and a theophany described by shaking (11.29-36).[97] But it is more likely that it all refers to the fate of the psalmist or his community with these two sections of the psalm balancing each other. 11.19-28 describes the restoration of the psalmist despite facing death and evil; 11.29-36 uses language of the victory of the divine warrior over chaos to express the same thing.[98] Similarly, Adams argues that *T. Mos.* 10.4-6 describes a theophany using OT language of cosmic catastrophe (10.4-6), and the exaltation of Israel among the stars (10.9-10). Although both descriptions are metaphors, he argues that stars mean stars (10.9), and therefore other elements of the universe are meant in 10.4-6; as such, it refers to 'final eschatological events'.[99] But this is imagery of the chaos waters fleeing from the divine warrior who comes with signs of heavenly disruption, and it describes a historical event: the defeat of a Gentile nation (10.7). The exaltation of Israel to the heavens is a metaphor for them receiving victory from God, and gazing down on the slain in battle.[100]

Taking HCT imagery into account, Angel excludes an eschatological focus throughout his analysis, concluding that: 'The imagery generally refers to God's intervention in history to establish his covenant and to God's creation of the world, …there is little to no warrant for thinking that the imagery has been eschatologized in this period'.[101] John Collins argues that Angel's definition of eschatology is perhaps too strict, leading him to exclude eschatology too often;[102] others (like Frederick Mabie) are more open to the possibility of eschatological interpretations, and think that while HCT imagery is typically historicised in the historical books,

---

95. Ibid., 5, 13–15. It is notable that Adams thinks Isa. 24 is an example of a more developed eschatological outlook; see Adams, *Stars*, 44–50.

96. Angel, *Chaos*, 121, 51, 53.

97. Adams, *Stars*, 69–71.

98. See the more detailed argument in Angel, *Chaos*, 50–54.

99. Adams, *Stars*, 71–74, the quotation is from 74.

100. Angel, *Chaos*, 119–25. A historical event is also favoured by Wright, *New Testament*, 304–306; Hatina, 'Focus', 57. This is a notable text because of similar language to Lk. 21.25-27.

101. Angel, *Chaos*, 200 and the summary on 191–200.

102. Collins, 'Chaos', 339.

it can have an eschatological feel in certain apocalyptic contexts.[103] But even if there is some eschatological reference, this is not the same as exclusive eschatological reference;[104] for the purposes here it is enough to note that there are sufficient persuasive cases where HCT imagery is used for historical events (e.g., 1QH 11.19-36; *T. Mos.* 10.4-6) to mean that Adams overstates the frequency of eschatological use.

(iii) The Significance of Later Texts
For Adams, the use of the language of disaster by later Jewish writers plays a vital role in understanding contemporary Jewish usage at the time of the NT:[105]

> Even if the originally intended meaning of the catastrophe language in Isaiah 13; 34, etc., could be established with absolute certainty, subsequent post-biblical Jewish usage of this kind of language (from the third century BCE to the end of the first century CE) has to be regarded as more important for interpreting Mk 13.24-25, and the fact remains that this evidence does not support a narrow socio-political reading of these verses.[106]

He regards this later use as eschatological, and concludes that is how texts like Lk. 21.25-27 would be understood. But it is unlikely that NT readers would turn to the later Jewish writings to interpret the imagery they are presented with, partly because the OT writings would have been more available (e.g., through use in liturgical settings), but mainly because the NT texts echo OT texts. A reader will interpret the NT language in the context which is most manifest: if a NT text alludes to a later Jewish apocalypse, then relevance will be found in that context; if it alludes to the OT prophets (or uses their motifs) then the reader will search there. Jesus' eschatological discourse's allusions are clearly to the OT prophets (see below), so that is where its interpretation will be, not in later writings.[107]

Of course, Adams prioritises the later writings because their interpretations are supposedly more representative of contemporary Jewish thought in the NT period, but the evidence does not suggest that they express a

---

103. It can have an occasional mythopoeic use; see Mabie, 'Chaos', 50–52; R. T. France sees some eschatological reference in some later texts; see France, *Mark*, 533 n. 8.

104. The texts are not exclusively eschatological, as noted by Collins, 'Chaos', 339.

105. Adams, *Stars*, 18–19, 156. This distinction is also noted as a crucial hermeneutical difference in Wilson, *Things*, 109–31.

106. Presumably also for Lk. 21; see Adams, *Stars*, 156.

107. Wilson, *Things*, 155.

significantly different approach to the imagery. There are two aspects to this. First, there is no unambiguous evidence that later writings reused OT texts with a historical referent and made them refer to eschatological events (as Adams suggests), because in some cases an echo of specific verses refers to a local event, not an eschatological one (e.g., *T. Mos.* 10.4-6 echoing Isa. 13.10 and Joel 2.10, 31 [LXX]).[108] Second, the evidence does not suggest that the later writers universally use the language eschatologically (as above); if anything, the majority of texts with HCT imagery apply it in a local or historical setting. This means that contemporary Jews did not have a default interpretation of such texts as eschatological. More importantly, early Christian communities interpreted such language in a historical manner. There is little doubt that they also had future eschatological concerns, as texts like 1 Corinthians 15 and 1 Thess. 4.13-18 demonstrate, but this does not mean that they used cosmic destruction or HCT language exclusively to describe eschatological events. HCT language could be used for future events (e.g., Acts 1.9-11 and 1 Thess. 4.13-18 refer to cloud transportation),[109] but it appears frequently with a local reference (e.g., Rev 12.1-17; 13.1-18; Mt. 8.23-27; Mk 4.35-41; 6.47-52; Lk. 8.22-25; Jn 6.16-21; Eph 6.11-17; 1 Thess. 5.8).[110]

So, interpretation is not as clear-cut as Adams argues: although there may be some eschatological uses, historical readings persist, and they are preferred for HCT language. This means that NT texts need to be interpreted on a case-by-case basis.

Cosmic Language in Luke 21.25-27
The language of Lk. 21.25-27 is best read as referring to a historical context, and there are four reasons for this. First, genre signals are important in creating reader expectation about how to read a text, and although some modern readers think Luke 21 is an apocalypse, its distinctive prophetic

---

108. Adams, *Stars*, 73, regards this as an example of an echo for eschatological purposes. Also note that *1 En.* 1.3b-9 has similarities with Mic. 3.1 (because of the repetition of τακήσονται ὡς κηρὸς ἀπὸ προσώπου πυρὸς ἐν φλογί) (see ibid., 55–58), and it uses motifs of theophany from the OT. It is commonly seen eschatologically, though Hatina, 'Focus', 57 n. 61 includes *1 En.* 1.5 among texts with a local reference.

109. 2 Peter 3.5-13 also has a future reference (Richard Bauckham, *Jude, 2 Peter*, WBC 50 [Waco: Word, 1983], 314–22). Hebrews 12.25-29 uses cosmic shaking from the Sinai theophany in what is typically seen as an eschatological reference, though ultimately with a contemporary exhortatory purpose. See Harold W. Attridge, *The Epistle to the Hebrews: A Commentary on the Epistle to the Hebrews*, Hermeneia (Philadelphia: Fortress, 1989), 378–83.

110. List from Angel, *Chaos*, 197–98. For Revelation, see ibid., 139–48.

language about Jerusalem defines its overall genre. There are no signals that 21.25-27 departs from this prophetic genre because its language is consistent with prophecy. It might have some similarities with apocalyptic, but the differences are greater: it does not include crucial elements like a revelation from a heavenly being, and it does not have the typical mention of a supernatural world.[111] What is more, the introduction in Lk. 21.5-7 creates a this-worldly expectation for the entire discourse, and apocalyptic elements would be out of place. This encourages a historical application of the imagery. Second, Lk. 21.25-27 specifically allude to texts from the OT prophets (see below), and because this language has a historical reference in these prophets, it would be understood in the same way in Luke 21. Third, cosmic destruction language can be used for eschatological events in the NT, but this is usually clearly signalled in the text. The setting of Luke 21 is a discussion about the fate of the city and its temple with no signal that the referent has changed in Lk. 21.25. Fourth, Luke–Acts does not have a strong emphasis on the eschatological future: that is not to say that it is absent, but it does not develop eschatological themes greatly. It is especially significant that Acts 2.17-21 uses the cosmic language of Joel 3.1-5 (2.28-32 ET) to refer to an event of eschatological significance, but occurring within history.

Structure
The structure of the oracle provides further evidence for Lk. 21.25-27 referring to a historical event that is not separated in time from the events of Lk. 21.20-24. The discourse is an answer to a question about time, and temporal markers are used to separate sections within it.[112] There are clear temporal markers at Lk. 21.20 (ὅταν δὲ ἴδητε) and 21.27 (καὶ τότε ὄψονται) – both involving verbs of perception, and both referring to fresh

---

111. According to the definition of the SBL genre project; see John J. Collins, 'Introduction: Towards the Morphology of a Genre', *Semeia* 14 (1979): 9; adapted in Adela Yarbro Collins, 'Introduction: Early Christian Apocalypticism', *Semeia* 36 (1986): 7). For further differences between the eschatological discourse and apocalyptic, see Hatina, 'Focus', 46–47; his discussion centres on Mark which he regards as paranesis (pp. 47–53). Luke 21 has some paraenetic features (warnings in 21.8, 9, 12-19, advice in 21.21, and exhortation in 21.28), but it is more clearly prophecy, especially in the light of 21.20-24. For a helpful recent discussion of the issues (in Matthew), see Wilson, *Things*, 109–32.

112. The best discussion about structure remains Fusco, 'Problems'. The discussion in Nolland, 'Nations', 143–44, is helpful, even if the conclusions are debatable. Giblin, *Jerusalem*, 79, offers an alternative structure divided through 'he said', but this is limited value; see Fusco, 'Problems', 74–77.

events. If Lk. 21.24 and 21.25 refer to different events, then there should be a similar temporal marker between them, but there is not, unless ἄχρι οὗ πληρωθῶσιν καιροί ἐθνῶν (21.24) is understood as one.[113]

The temporal function of this phrase would be easier to determine if it was clearer what it pointed to. Scholars variously identify the καιροί ἐθνῶν as a period of Gentile dominance when they will occupy the city of Jerusalem,[114] whose end brings reversal of fortune for Jerusalem;[115] the time of Gentile mission;[116] a time when the Gentiles are at the fore of the God's world plans;[117] and a time of judgement of the Gentiles.[118] John Nolland makes his case for the judgement of the Gentiles by reviewing its syntax, and concludes that the phrase refers to 'the *arrival* of what are called καιροί ἐθνῶν (lit. "times of nations")'.[119] In other words, although the phrase has a focus on fulfilment, it is when the time is fulfilled that the καιροί ἐθνῶν begins; for Nolland, this is a time of judgement for the nations. His interpretation of the syntax is convincing, and it makes Gentile dominance an unlikely reading; the Gentile mission is also unlikely because Luke 21 is otherwise negative about the Gentiles, and the mission would require ἔθνος to have a second meaning in 21.24.[120]

So does this make the phrase a temporal separator at 21.24? For Nolland it does not mark a transition as such, it is an elaboration dealing with the Gentile equivalent of the events of Lk. 21.20-24. While this is not a temporal marker (like 21.27), it creates a movement to events subsequent to the fall of the city in 21.20-24;[121] but this is not a necessary

---

113. Nolland, 'Nations', 144–45; Fusco, 'Problems', 86–87. Both note that there is not a strong break here but both argue that the 'times of the Gentiles' introduces some form of separation.

114. Marshall, *Gospel*, 773–74; Fitzmyer, *Luke*, 2:1347; Evans, *Luke*, 751–52; Walker, *Jesus*, 100–101.

115. For Ellis, *Luke*, 245, this extends to the parousia.

116. Zmijewski, *Eschatologiereden*, 217–18, an interpretation possibly driven by Mk 13.10.

117. Bock, *Luke*, 2:1680–82; Green, *Gospel*, 739 (incorporating elements of dominance in the city and the Gentile mission).

118. Nolland, 'Nations'. There are other approaches. For instance, Plummer, *Luke*, 483, lists six. Baldwin, 'Reimarus', has an unlikely reconstruction explained through parallels to Daniel and Rev. 11.2. See the reviews of scholarly opinions and bibliography in Giblin, *Jerusalem*, 89; Nolland, 'Nations', 141–46.

119. Nolland, 'Nations', 137, italics original. He reviews the similar language in Mk 1.15, and time phrases with passive verbs of fulfilment.

120. Ibid., 141–45. He also argues against it on the basis of temporal separators in the text.

121. Ibid., 144–46.

conclusion. Typically ἄχρι οὗ and a subjunctive is used for the cessation of an event, as well as to prepare for the next event:[122] while it marks the beginning of the times of the Gentiles, that does not require that its narrative function is to drive the narrative forward to that event. Its function is to provide a temporal limit to the events of 21.20-24, showing that it is not an indefinite state of affairs:[123] its end will come, simultaneously bringing a fulfilment of Jesus' prophetic words (πληρωθῶσιν), and judgement on the nations who are used in judgement of Jerusalem. As such, this phrase is almost a parenthesis to the main message, before cosmic language is used to describe the fall of the city. The important issue in 21.24 is what happens *before* the καιροί ἐθνῶν because the focus is on Israel, not on the nations; the same is true in 21.25. This means that the future verb (ἔσονται) in 21.25 does not require a future reference beyond 21.24, because 21.24 has three future indicatives and 21.23 one, all describing concurrent events; 21.25 is better read as a description of events concurrent with 21.23-24. In addition, there is no necessity for the portents of Lk. 21.25 to be a future escalation of the cosmic crisis over Jerusalem that 21.9-11 represents – it is more likely that they refer to the same event, expanding its description.[124]

This way of reading the text makes more sense of the repeated use of 'these things' throughout the oracle (21.7, 12, 28, 31, 32), a phrase which also has structural significance. It echoes back to the opening question in 21.7, a question exclusively about the temple; this suggests that the event of 21.28 is some part of its fulfilment, and that everything between 21.20 (the beginning of the reply about the temple's fate) and 21.28 are about the same thing. The phrase is also used in 21.31, 32, and taking it as a reference to the city provides a better explanation of how it happens within a generation than if it included eschatological events.

The Intertexts
(i) Luke 21.25-26

> [25]Καὶ ἔσονται σημεῖα ἐν ἡλίῳ καὶ σελήνῃ καὶ ἄστροις, καὶ ἐπὶ τῆς γῆς συνοχὴ ἐθνῶν ἐν ἀπορίᾳ ἤχους θαλάσσης καὶ σάλου, [26]ἀποψυχόντων ἀνθρώπων ἀπὸ φόβου καὶ προσδοκίας τῶν ἐπερχομένων τῇ οἰκουμένῃ, αἱ γὰρ δυνάμεις τῶν οὐρανῶν σαλευθήσονται.

---

122. Giblin, *Jerusalem*, 90; BDF, §383 (2).
123. Fitzmyer, *Luke*, 2:1347; Walker, *Jesus*, 100–101.
124. Both points against Nolland, 'Nations', 144.

²⁵There will be signs in the sun, the moon, and the stars, and on the earth distress among nations confused by the roaring of the sea and the waves. ²⁶People will faint from fear and foreboding of what is coming upon the world, for the powers of the heavens will be shaken.

The imagery of Lk. 21.25-26 is vivid and strongly reminiscent of OT prophetic language – this is enough to create an expectation that optimal relevance will only be found through exploration against an OT context. But, just like Lk. 21.20-24 and 19.41-44, there is no single verse which parallels all of the material in these verses, though Joel 3.3-4 (2.30-31 ET) comes closest.[125]

καὶ δώσω τέρατα ἐν τῷ οὐρανῷ καὶ ἐπὶ τῆς γῆς, αἷμα καὶ πῦρ καὶ ἀτμίδα καπνοῦ· ὁ ἥλιος μεταστραφήσεται εἰς σκότος καὶ ἡ σελήνη εἰς αἷμα πρὶν ἐλθεῖν ἡμέραν κυρίου τὴν μεγάλην καί ἐπιφανῆ.

I will give portents in the sky and on earth: blood and fire and the vapor of smoke. The sun shall be turned to darkness, and the moon to blood, before the great and notable day of the Lord comes.

These verses follow a similar order to Lk. 21.25-26: celestial signs, earthly events, a further reference to heavenly events, then a reference to salvation which parallels 21.28 (ὃς ἂν ἐπικαλέσηται τὸ ὄνομα κυρίου, σωθήσεται, Joel 3.5). Although Luke uses σημεῖα for the heavenly signs, not the τέρας in modern versions of Joel, Luke probably had a version of Joel which contained σημεῖα in relation to the earth (see Acts 2.19).[126] Luke also repeats καὶ ἐπί τῆς γῆς. However, the metaphors about events on earth are different, and Joel does not mention the sea; although both have heavenly signs, Joel does not have shaking, and has more detail on other heavenly signs. Despite this, it is likely that these verses are part of the interpretive context, with other verses alluded to through specific Lukan phrases.

Σημεῖα ἐν ἡλίῳ καὶ σελήνῃ καὶ ἄστροις. The description of celestial signs in Lk. 21.25 is general and four texts are possible intertexts in addition to Joel 3.3-4. While both Isa. 13.10 and Ezek. 32.7 refer to heavenly bodies darkening, the heavenly bodies are the only lexical link and they are in a different order to Luke (ἄστρον, ἥλιος, and σελήνη) with intervening

---

125. NA²⁸; Pao and Schnabel, 'Luke', 378; Bock, *Luke*, 2:1682; Fitzmyer, *Luke*, 2:1349; Nolland, *Luke*, 3:1005.

126. Stuart, *Hosea*, 257.

text between them; it is unlikely Luke is specifically directing attention to them.[127] Isaiah 34.4 refers to falling stars without reference to sun or moon; it is very close to Mt. 24.29 and Mk 13.25 but not Lk. 21.25. Joel 4.15 (3.15 ET) is closer:[128]

ὁ ἥλιος καὶ ἡ σελήνη συσκοτάσουσιν, καὶ οἱ ἀστέρες δύσουσιν φέγγος αὐτῶν

The sun and the moon shall grow dark, and the stars shall shed their brightness.

It presents the bodies in the same order as Luke and simply refers to them being darkened – this makes it closer than any other text. Additionally, the reference to the Lord calling from Jerusalem and the shaking of the heavens and earth (albeit using σείω) in Joel 4.16 serve to increase the volume of this verse. If any single verse functions as an intertext, then this is the likely candidate (along with Joel 2.10 which has almost identical language), otherwise it is only the concept of celestial signs (especially in OT HCT texts) that is evoked.

Language of Distress and Fear. The dual descriptions about distress and confusion over the sea (21.25), and fear over what is happening (21.26), contain distinctive language. Ἀπορία (21.25) and ἀποψύχω (21.26) are NT *hapax legomena*, and συνοχή (21.25) only occurs elsewhere in 2 Cor. 2.4, but these words do not appear together in any OT text to suggest it is an intertext. The closest are Isa. 24.19 and 8.22.[129]

Isa. 24.19:

ταραχῇ ταραχθήσεται ἡ γῆ, καὶ ἀπορίᾳ ἀπορηθήσεται ἡ γῆ

The earth will be troubled with trouble, and the earth will be perplexed with perplexity.

---

127. Texts noted by Bock, *Luke*, 2:1682; Fitzmyer, *Luke*, 2:1349; Nolland, *Luke*, 3:1005; Green, *Gospel*, 740; Samuel Tobias Lachs, *A Rabbinic Commentary on the New Testament: The Gospels of Matthew, Mark, and Luke* (Hoboken: KTAV, 1987), 385–86; Pao and Schnabel, 'Luke', 378. The distress of Isa. 13.7-8 is not close enough to Lk. 21.26 to increase the volume of the intertext, nor is the reference to captivity among the nations in Ezek. 32.

128. Bock, *Luke*, 2:1682.

129. Isaiah 24.19 in NA[28]; Fitzmyer, *Luke*, 2:1349; Pao and Schnabel, 'Luke', 378; Nolland, *Luke*, 3:1005. Isaiah 8.22 in Green, *Gospel*, 740.

Isa. 8.22:

...καὶ ἰδοὺ θλῖψις καὶ στενοχωρία καὶ σκότος, <u>ἀπορία</u> στενὴ καὶ σκότος ὥστε μὴ βλέπειν...

...but look: affliction and distress and darkness – dire straits and darkness so that they cannot see...

Both contain ἀπορίᾳ, but otherwise use different language to Luke to describe distress. Isaiah 24.19 is closer than Isa. 8.22 because it refers to the earth (without ἐπί), and Isa. 24.18 has shaking (σείω and earth, not σαλεύω and heavens), but there are not enough signals in Lk. 21.25 for this to be the main intertext. This is principally because the distress in Lk. 21.25 is associated with nations, peoples or distress over the sea, and Isa. 24.19 does not refer to them.

Ἤχους θαλάσσης καὶ σάλου. There are several LXX texts which refer to the sea and the waves in what is typically an image of chaos,[130] but none match the words or phrase used in 21.25. Some have two words in common, but include κῦμα, which Luke omits: Ps. 64.8 has ὁ συνταράσσων τὸ κύτος τῆς <u>θαλάσσης</u>, <u>ἤχους</u> κυμάτων αὐτῆς;[131] Ps. 88.10 has τοῦ κράτους τῆς <u>θαλάσσης</u>, τὸν δὲ <u>σάλον</u> τῶν κυμάτων;[132] and Isa. 51.15 has τὴν <u>θάλασσαν</u> καὶ <u>ἠχῶν</u> τὰ κύματα αὐτῆς.[133] There is little to choose between them lexically, although the reference to ταραχθήσονται τὰ ἔθνη in Ps. 64.8 does increase the volume a little. What goes against any of them being found as an intertext is their reference to YHWH as the one who creates the waves, which is different to Lk. 21.25 where the seas are a destructive force. Jeremiah 28.42 is closer (ἀνέβη ἐπὶ Βαβυλῶνα ἡ <u>θάλασσα</u> ἐν <u>ἤχῳ</u> κυμάτων αὐτῆς, καὶ κατεκαλύφθη); it has the same words as the other texts but refers to destruction of a city.[134] Psalm 45.4 is a far more significant verse:[135]

---

130. Angel, *Chaos*, 41, 69.
131. NA[28]; Bock, *Luke*, 2:1682.
132. Pao and Schnabel, 'Luke', 378; Bock, *Luke*, 2:1682.
133. This verse is as close as those commonly noted in the literature. Other options are more remote: Isa. 5.30 has some words in common (ὡς φωνὴ θαλάσσης κυμαινούσης with <u>ἀπορία</u> in a subsequent clause) but describes a voice in sea-like terms, not the sea's destructive power; Isa. 17.12 is no closer. Isaiah 5.30 and 17.12 noted in Green, *Gospel*, 740; Pao and Schnabel, 'Luke', 378; Isa. 5.30 in Bock, *Luke*, 2:1682.
134. See also Ps. 106.23-32; Jer. 5.22; 31.35; 38.36, which use similar terms.
135. NA[28]; Pao and Schnabel, 'Luke', 378; Bock, *Luke*, 2:1682; Fitzmyer, *Luke*, 2:1349; Nolland, *Luke*, 3:1005.

<u>ἤχησαν</u> καὶ ἐταράχθησαν τὰ ὕδατα αὐτῶν, ἐταράχθησαν τὰ ὄρη ἐν τῇ κραταιότητι αὐτοῦ...

Their waters roared and were troubled; the mountains were troubled by his force

It refers to chaos waters (τὰ ὕδατα), but this parallels θάλασσα in the previous verse, meaning that it has similar imagery to Lk. 21.25 with a roaring and troubled sea (ἠχέω is a cognate of the Lukan ἦχος). Although it does not have the parallelism of sea and waves of other texts, it does have two things that distinguish it. First, its sea is a powerful destructive force, like Lk. 21.25; Luke has nations distressed over the sea (21.25) and afraid of coming events (21.26), the psalm has distressed mountains (with Israel unafraid, Ps. 45.3). Second, Ps. 45.7 goes on to state ἐταράχθησαν <u>ἔθνη</u>, ἔκλιναν βασιλεῖαι· ἔδωκεν φωνὴν αὐτοῦ, <u>ἐσαλεύθη</u> ἡ γῆ. The nations are troubled, and there is shaking (using the same term as Lk. 21.26, but about the earth, not heaven). With these links, Psalm 45 is the closest intertext for the sea imagery and the associated fear of Lk. 21.24-25.

Αἱ γὰρ δυνάμεις τῶν οὐρανῶν σαλευθήσονται. Despite the distinctive imagery, this phrase does not repeat any LXX text, although Codex B and Lucian have Isa. 34.4 in the form τακήσονται πᾶσαι <u>αἱ δυνάμεις τῶν οὐρανῶν</u>, which is very close to Luke.[136] If this text is a preservation of a Greek text that Luke knew then it is very likely to be an intertext, but that is uncertain; in the LXX form (ἑλιγήσεται ὁ <u>οὐρανὸς</u> ὡς βιβλίον, καὶ πάντα τὰ ἄστρα πεσεῖται) it is not close enough.[137] There are two other possibilities. First, Hag. 2.6-7:[138]

> ⁶διότι τάδε λέγει κύριος παντοκράτωρ Ἔτι ἅπαξ ἐγὼ σείσω <u>τὸν οὐρανὸν</u> καὶ <u>τὴν γῆν</u> καὶ τὴν <u>θάλασσαν</u> καὶ τὴν ξηράν· ⁷καὶ συσσείσω πάντα τὰ <u>ἔθνη</u>, καὶ ἥξει τὰ ἐκλεκτὰ πάντων τῶν ἐθνῶν, καὶ πλήσω τὸν οἶκον τοῦτον δόξης, λέγει κύριος παντοκράτωρ.

> ⁶For this is what the Lord Almighty says, Once again I will shake the sky and the earth and the sea and the dry land, ⁷and I will shake all the nations, and the choice things of all the nations shall come, and I will fill this house with splendor, says the Lord Almighty.

---

136. See the discussion in Fitzmyer, *Luke*, 2:1350; Pao and Schnabel, 'Luke', 378.
137. It is noted in Nolland, *Luke*, 3:1006; Bock, *Luke*, 2:1683–84 (neither discuss textual forms), and in Fitzmyer, *Luke*, 2:1350; Pao and Schnabel, 'Luke', 378.
138. NA²⁸.

It refers to the heavens, the earth and the sea, but the shaking happens in all three, and uses σείω not σαλεύω. It refers to τὰ ἔθνη with a similar meaning to Luke, despite them being shaken, not fearful. But it is not likely to be a primary intertext, especially because of the order of material in Luke. The distinctive aspect of Haggai 2 is the shaking, but this is the last thing mentioned in Lk. 21.25-26. If Luke mentioned shaking before the other phrases, then the other similarities might support the tentative evocation of Haggai through the shaking heavens, but Luke's order does not encourage spotting a Haggai allusion, especially because Haggai does not mention δυνάμεις τῶν οὐρανῶν.

Second, Joel 2.10, which in addition to being similar to the reference to sun, moon and stars in Lk. 21.25, has a reference to shaking heavens:[139]

...καὶ σεισθήσεται ὁ οὐρανός, ὁ ἥλιος καὶ ἡ σελήνη συσκοτάσουσιν, καὶ τὰ ἄστρα δύσουσιν τὸ φέγγος αὐτῶν.

...and the sky shall be shaken. The sun and the moon shall grow dark, and the stars shall shed their brightness.

However, it uses σείω not σαλεύω, and does not refer to δυνάμεις τῶν οὐρανῶν; it is no closer than the other options, and it similar to Joel 4.16 (3.16 ET). It is likely to have been accessed as part of the general concept of cosmic events in OT prophetic texts, which is where the search for relevance is most likely to be undertaken, but is unlikely to be selected as the only text.

There is one other text which must be considered as a potential parallel. Andrew Angel argues that Jer. 38.35-37 (31.35-37 ET) is important because it is the only LXX text which refers to sun, moon and stars together with a reference to the sea and waves (κῦμα).[140] He notes that there is little lexical similarity between Lk. 21.25 and Jer. 38.36 LXX, such that one cannot call it a quotation. Nevertheless, he argues that the similar imagery is 'so close that it is reasonable to conclude that Luke shapes his picture of the *Chaoskampf* in such a way as to recall Jer. 31.35-37'.[141] It does contain a link between the fate of Israel and cosmic signs, but there is no reference to the fear of the peoples, no reference to shaking, and Luke's distinctive phrasing does not encourage its exploration in place of the other contexts mentioned above. However, this text (and the

---

139. Ibid.
140. Angel, *Chaos*, 136–37.
141. Ibid., 137.

ideas behind it) would form part of the contextual information accessed by a reader once the context of OT cosmic destruction is explored. It is this OT concept that is the most accessible interpretive context for the reader, with the addition of the specific verses noted above.

(ii) Luke 21.27

καὶ τότε ὄψονται τὸν υἱὸν τοῦ ἀνθρώπου ἐρχόμενον ἐν νεφέλῃ μετὰ δυνάμεως καὶ δόξης πολλῆς.

Then they will see 'the Son of Man coming in a cloud' with power and great glory.

It is well accepted that there is a literary relationship between τὸν υἱὸν τοῦ ἀνθρώπου ἐρχόμενον ἐν νεφέλῃ in Lk. 21.27 and Dan. 7.13:

ἐθεώρουν ἐν ὁράματι τῆς νυκτὸς καὶ ἰδοὺ ἐπὶ τῶν <u>νεφελῶν</u> τοῦ οὐρανοῦ ὡς <u>υἱὸς ἀνθρώπου</u> ἤρχετο, καὶ ὡς παλαιὸς ἡμερῶν παρῆν, καὶ οἱ παρεστηκότες παρῆσαν αὐτῷ.

I was watching in the night visions, and lo, as it were a son of man was coming upon the clouds of heaven. And he came as far as the ancient of days, and the attendants were present with him.

There are differences: Luke refers to the Son of Man (SM), to coming ἐν νεφέλῃ, and adds an interpretive μετὰ δυνάμεως καὶ δόξης πολλῆς without reference to the throne scene. In addition the order of the SM and the clouds is inverted, but the distinctive imagery of SM and clouds makes a connection sure.[142]

The Interpretation

The language of Lk. 21.25-27 is evocative of the OT, especially prophetic texts of cosmic disturbance referring to events within history. In Luke's context, these verses continue to describe the fall of Jerusalem but use a different set of metaphors building upon 21.20-24. The rich biblical

---

142. There is no space to discuss the Son of Man problem here. Several scholars have challenged that when Jesus used the Aramaic *bar (e)nash(a)* he would have been understood as using a circumlocution for himself and not pointing to Dan. 7. The definite noun in the NT was a decision made by the first Christians. See Maurice Casey, *The Solution to the "Son of Man" Problem*, LNTS 343 (London: T&T Clark, 2007), especially 67–81, 261–62. For the NT use see the reply of Angel, 'Jesus', 227. However, Lk. 21.27 refers to Dan. 7.13, whatever the historical Jesus may have meant, Casey, *Solution*, 54.

language means that optimal relevance will only be achieved through engagement with the OT context, and there are three ways that this will happen.

(1) Most of the imagery in Lk. 21.25-26 (especially that of heavenly disturbance) does not unambiguously point to a particular OT text. With the exception of the verses discussed in points 2 and 3 below, optimal relevance does not require engagement with specific texts because relevance is likely to be achieved in the common ideas associated with this metaphorical language. Whether the reader searches first in any of the texts (e.g., Joel 2.10; 4.15; Isa. 13.10), or simply in their common biblical language, the reader is likely to find relevance in this language as typical HCT imagery, and not explore further.[143] In the OT, the use of σαλεύω for shaking and the plural form of οὐρανός typically refer to theophany rather than the 'day of the Lord',[144] but they do not occur together in a single phrase in the LXX, and there is some fluidity in how the terminology is used.[145] Because Lk. 21.25-26 is set in a context of strongly judgemental language (21.20-24) and refers to the fall of the city, the motifs in 21.25-26 most likely refer to YHWH bringing judgement.[146] Three sets of implicatures arise from this use of language for judgement: first, it is a deliberate action of God who will come, bearing judgement. Second, it is a catastrophic event of great significance, just like the events in the prophets. Third, it places Jesus among the prophets. In each case a reader will also develop some associated weaker implicatures.

(2) Other imagery points more directly to specific texts. The maritime imagery of Lk. 21.25 is typical of OT chaos imagery;[147] this imagery was normally historicised with the chaos seas referring to the enemies of Israel, and YHWH as the divine warrior who overcomes these

---

143. For the language as typical of HCT, see Angel, *Chaos*, 135–36.

144. Joseph Verheyden, 'Describing the Parousia: The Cosmic Phenomena in Mk 13,24–25', in *The Scriptures in the Gospels*, ed. C. M. Tuckett (Leuven: Leuven University Press/Uitgeverij Peeters, 1997), 543–44.

145. Ibid. For YHWH coming as a warrior god on the Day of the Lord, see Gerhard von Rad, *Old Testament Theology*, trans. D. M. G. Stalker, 2 vols. (New York: Harper & Row, 1962–65), 2:119–25; for theophany see the discussion in Beasley-Murray, *Kingdom*, 3–16; Hartman, *Prophecy*, 71–74.

146. When such language is used for judgement in the OT, it is clearly stated; Verheyden, 'Parousia', 531.

147. Adams, *Stars*, 176, though he does not pursue it. See also Angel, *Chaos*, 136; Nolland, *Luke*, 3:1005.

enemies.[148] Psalm 45 is a good example: this liturgical hymn describes cosmic disaster with mounting threat from the chaos seas (45.1-4),[149] followed by a more local threat to Zion (45.5-8),[150] and it looks to the divine warrior to overcome them.[151] This trust in YHWH forms the central message of the psalm;[152] YHWH resides in the city (Ps. 45.6), where his presence stills the storms which rage against it.[153] Zion is therefore inviolable.[154] This encyclopaedic information was well-enough known for it to have been immediately available for the Lukan reader on thinking about the psalm after its citation in Lk. 21.25-26, especially

148. E.g., 1QH 10.12-16; 11.6-18; possibly in Wis. 5.17-23. Angel, *Chaos*, 40–42, 44–50, 89–92. At Qumran it referred to the Jerusalem establishment as enemies of the community. For HCT as historicized, see the discussion above, and also Caird, *Language*, 229–31; Leslie J. Hoppe, *The Holy City: Jerusalem in the Theology of the Old Testament* (Collegeville, MD: Liturgical Press, 2000), 29–31; Mabie, 'Chaos', 50.

149. Peter C. Craigie, *Psalms 1–50*, WBC 19 (Waco: Word Books, 1983), 344.

150. Geoffrey Grogan, *Psalms*, THOTC (Grand Rapids: Eerdmans, 2008), 100–101. The original reference might not have been to Zion, but the psalm quickly took Jerusalem as referent; see John Goldingay, *Psalms*, 3 vols., BCOTWP (Grand Rapids: Baker Academic, 2006–2008), 2:65–66.

151. J. J. M. Roberts, 'Zion in the Theology of the Davidic–Solomonic Empire', in *Studies in the Period of David and Solomon and Other Essays*, ed. T Ishida (Tokyo: Yamakawa-Shuppausha, 1982), 102. For the chaos waters, see Brueggemann, *Theology*, 656–57. Both Tsumura (*Creation*, 156–63) and Watson (*Chaos*, 115–17) challenge usual ideas of a battle between YHWH and chaos in this psalm, but YHWH is clearly shown as victorious over the sea and the nations; see the fuller discussion in H. Wayne Jr. Ballard, *The Divine Warrior Motif in the Psalms*, BDS 6 (North Richland Hills: Bibal, 1999); John Day, *Yahweh and the Gods and Goddesses of Canaan* (Sheffield: Sheffield Academic, 2002).

152. Goldingay, *Psalms*, 2:67–68.

153. For YHWH as victorious in Zion in Ps. 45, see John H. Hayes, 'The Tradition of Zion's Inviolability', *JBL* 82, no. 4 (1963); Ben C. Ollenburger, *Zion, the City of the Great King: A Theological Symbol of the Jerusalem Cult* (Sheffield: JSOT, 1987), 15–22, 64; Brueggemann, *Theology*, 656–57; Goldingay, *Psalms*, 2:67–69; Craigie, *Psalms 1–50*, 344; Adams, *Stars*, 29–30; Watson, *Chaos*, 135.

154. Richard J. Clifford, *The Cosmic Mountain in Canaan and the Old Testament* (Cambridge: Harvard University Press, 1972), 142–57; Hayes, 'Tradition'; Ollenburger, *Zion*, 64–80; Hoppe, *City*, 37–38; Moshe Weinfeld, 'Zion and Jerusalem as Religious and Political Capital: Ideology and Utopia', in *The Poet and the Historian: Essays in Literary and Historical Biblical Criticism*, ed. Richard E. Friedman (Chico: Scholars Press, 1983), 103. These are similar hopes to those described in Jer. 31 and referred to by Angel, *Chaos*, 136–37.

because of the liturgical use of the psalm in a temple setting, where it reminded the worshipper about the salvation brought by YHWH, who dwells in Zion as king.[155] In Lk. 21.25-26, the allusion to the psalm through its maritime imagery (and in the context of describing the fall of Jerusalem) will encourage the reader to explore the psalm's context and create implicatures of Zion's importance, its inviolability, and of YHWH's role in defending it because of his residence there.

The chaos theme is also alluded to in Lk. 21.26, where the powers of the heavens are shaken. The meaning of this term is a little uncertain: if δυνάμεις τῶν οὐρανῶν refer to the armies of God, then they are suffering a set-back (just as Jerusalem, which is assailed by the chaos sea).[156] But this does not seem likely: the language is not taken from Psalm 45 such that it necessarily develops its maritime imagery on a cosmic scale, nor is it likely to be a Lukan invention in the middle of such rich OT imagery. Most probably it is alluding to the OT concept of the heavens shaking (or possibly to Isa. 34.4, in the variant noted above), in which case it refers to what those texts refer to: the heavenly bodies (and the powers behind them) shaking in the presence of YHWH as he comes.[157] As such, this phrase adds to the general picture of cosmic disturbance; it is also reversal of the created order and a return to chaos.[158] However, the repeated reference to heavenly signs in 21.25-26 suggests that optimal relevance requires exploration against more specific interpretive contexts. The recent reference to Zion (through the allusion to Ps. 45) draws attention to two texts in Joel which juxtapose heavenly signs and Zion: first, Joel 3.5 (2.32 ET) describes Zion as a place of security and seeming inviolability;[159] second, Joel 4.16 (3.16 ET) has the Lord crying out from Zion with the heavens trembling in response. This reinforces the implicatures that Zion is supposedly inviolable and that God's salvation for his people should arise from the city. Both of these implicatures are subsequently challenged.

---

155. Brueggemann, *Theology*, 656–57; for HCT and the establishment of the Jerusalem temple, see Angel, *Chaos*, 35.

156. Angel, *Chaos*, 136.

157. This is the interpretation when 21.25-27 is understood as referring to the Parousia; see Bovon, *Luc*, 153–54; Fitzmyer, *Luke*, 2:1350; Marshall, *Gospel*, 775. See also the discussion of the use of shaking and heavens in theophany and judgement in Verheyden, 'Parousia', 543–44.

158. Fitzmyer, *Luke*, 2:1350.

159. Leslie C. Allen, *The Books of Joel, Obadiah, Jonah and Micah*, NICOT (London: Hodder & Stoughton, 1976), 102.

It is clear from this oracle that Zion is no longer inviolable, it will be laid bare.[160] In addition, several other implicatures are formed. First, not only is Zion about to be destroyed, but the divine warrior is not going to arise from it. Second, if chaos is winning over Israel, then it is doing so because God is permitting it.[161] This is truly an act of divine judgement,[162] and the divine warrior, rather than coming to the aid of Zion, is judging it.[163] Third, this resurgence of chaos is easily equated with a return to exile because the exile was understood as a time when chaos reigned.[164] Fourth, this is an event of great significance, as indicated by the global destruction language.[165] Jerusalem, and especially its temple, were understood as the centre of the earth, the place where heaven and earth met;[166] its destruction was truly of global significance (affecting all nations, 21.25). This destruction signals an end to this role, and as the Lukan narrative progresses he demonstrates how Christian theology redefines the *axis mundi*.

(3) The coming SM in Lk. 21.27 is separated from the description of the fall of Jerusalem in 21.20-26 by the temporal marker τότε ὄψονται. This describes a short timeframe because the subjects of ὄψονται are present during the fall of the city, and the subjects of 21.28 are, most naturally, Jesus' hearers.[167] Luke 21.27 does not refer to the parousia because its

---

160. Walker, *Jesus*, 72–73, stresses that Jerusalem is no longer a safe place, but he does not share the exegesis above.

161. Because he is the one who holds the sea in place; see Marshall, *Gospel*, 775. There was an ambiguity in the HCT with the chaos sea understood as opposed to God but also under his control; see Angel, *Chaos*, 17–19.

162. Green, *Gospel*, 738–39; Fitzmyer, *Luke*, 2:1342–44. For the divine warrior fighting against Israel, see Brad E. Kelle, 'Warfare Imagery', in Longman and Enns, eds., *Dictionary of the Old Testament Wisdom, Poetry, and Writings*, 830.

163. For the divine warrior, including as judge of Israel, see Ballard, *Divine Warrior*, especially 84–85.

164. Walter Brueggemann, 'Weariness, Exile and Chaos: A Motif in Royal Theology', *CBQ* 34, no. 1 (1972); idem, 'Kingship and Chaos: A Study in Tenth Century Theology', *CBQ* 33, no. 3 (1971).

165. Crispin Fletcher-Louis argues that cosmic language is used here because the temple is a micro-cosmos and the destruction of the temple requires language of cosmic destruction. Crispin H. T. Fletcher-Louis, 'The Destruction of the Temple and the Relativization of the Old Covenant: Mark 13:31 and Matthew 5:18', in *The Reader Must Understand: Eschatology in Bible and Theology*, ed. Mark Elliott and Kent Brower (Nottingham: Apollos, 1998), 156–62. But this does not follow as HCT language is commonly used for historical events of great significance.

166. Hoppe, *City*.

167. Against Fusco, 'Problems', 89, who thinks it is Luke's readers.

language is most naturally interpreted like 21.25-26 as referring to a historical event at the time of the fall of Jerusalem. When seen this way, the SM reference is often taken to refer to the vindication of Jesus which comes about at the fall of the temple in 70 CE, because Daniel 7 is about the vindication of the people of God through a SM figure.[168] But this is not the best way to interpret it. The observation that Daniel 7 concerns vindication is true: it is a dream-vision,[169] its four beasts from the sea are literary representations of oppressing kings, and the SM is a representation of the people of Israel. The SM travels to heaven (not earth), and is presented before the Ancient of Days,[170] where he is vindicated.[171] While this is true of Daniel 7, in later Jewish interpretations ideas of vindication were joined by the concept of judging Israel's enemies,[172] and the SM became a figure who defeated those opposing the righteous of God, thereby bringing peace and vindication to the righteous.[173] Such later conceptions do not automatically take priority in the interpretation of the SM in Lk. 21.27, especially as Dan. 7.13 is alluded to: both the original context of Daniel and the later conceptions form part of the contextual information associated with the SM reference, and the particular elements within the Lukan setting are important in directing the reader to the correct interpretive context.

Bearing this in mind, there are several things that that can be deduced from the imagery in Lk. 21.27. First, the coming of the SM is towards earth because it makes more sense that the subjects of ὄψονται (21.27) are the people on earth who have suffered the disasters (they are the subjects of two indicatives in 21.24) than the δυνάμεις τῶν οὐρανῶν (21.26) witnessing an

---

168. Wright, *Victory*, 360–68, 510–19; France, *Jesus*, 169–71, 235–36; idem, *Mark*, 530–37 (though not writing specifically about Lk. 21).

169. John Goldingay, *Daniel*, WBC 30 (Dallas: Word Books, 1989), 146.

170. Hatina, 'Focus', 60–61; Wright, *Victory*, 361; but this cannot be to pressed this too far because the language is highly symbolic; see George B. Caird and Lincoln D. Hurst, *New Testament Theology* (Oxford: Clarendon Press, 1994), 377. See also Dunn, *Remembered*, 748, who thinks the Daniel scene is in heaven, but notes the debate around the locations in the Synoptic re-use of the text.

171. Wright, *New Testament*, 291–97; see also Hatina, 'Focus', 60–61, and the discussion in Wilson, *Things*, 127–30.

172. Hatina, 'Focus', 61; noting John J. Collins, *Daniel: A Commentary on the Book of Daniel*, Hermeneia (Minneapolis: Fortress, 1993), 79–89.

173. John J. Collins, *The Scepter and the Star: The Messiahs of the Dead Sea Scrolls and Other Ancient Literature* (New York: Doubleday, 1995), 68. See the discussion in Hatina, 'Focus', 61–62, for whom he is God's son (*4 Ezra* 13) and the anointed one (*1 En.* 48.10; 52.4). See also Thomas B. Slater, 'One Like a Son of Man in First-Century Judaism', *NTS* 41, no. 2 (1995).

arrival in heaven (the subjects of an indicative in 21.26).[174] This is because τότε ὄψονται forms a parallel with 21.28 where the people are invited to look heavenward, and because the structural marker καὶ τότε ὄψονται (21.27) moves the focus back to the events on earth (because these phrases answer the question of 21.7). Second, the coming of the SM emphasises his role in bringing salvation, as 21.28 makes clear. His coming is separated from the events of 21.26 by τότε ὄψονται, therefore he cannot be regarded as bringing judgement on the temple or the city. Although salvation of the righteous and judgement on their oppressors inevitably go together, the emphasis in Lk. 21.27-28 is on salvation. Third, Lk. 21.27 refers to the SM ἐρχόμενον...μετὰ δυνάμεως καὶ δόξης πολλῆς. These terms are not in Dan. 7.13 to describe the coming, and Dan. 7.14 has ἐξουσία (a term related to δύναμις) and δόξα as descriptions of what the enthroned SM receives; for the SM to come with power and great glory suggests that he has already been enthroned. The SM in Lk. 21.27 is therefore not approaching the Ancient of Days for vindication, but is coming subsequent to that event. Fourth, it is possible that the reader would form the implicature that the SM is coming as the divine warrior because 21.25-27 contain two motifs commonly associated with the divine warrior: chaos imagery and cloud transport.[175] The likelihood of the reader forming this implicature increases if there is a use of divine warrior imagery to describe Jesus within the early Christian community (as some scholars argue),[176] and if the SM is seen as a divine warrior figure (whether in Daniel 7,[177] or more tentatively, Mk 13).[178]

174. Marshall, *Gospel*, 775–76.

175. For this imagery, and YHWH as divine warrior, see Tremper Longman, 'The Divine Warrior: The New Testament Use of an Old Testament Motif', *WTJ* 44, no. 2 (1982); Ballard, *Divine Warrior*; Thomas R. Yoder Neufeld, *Put on the Armour of God: The Divine Warrior from Isaiah to Ephesians*, JSNTSup 140 (Sheffield: Sheffield Academic, 1997).

176. As argued by Longman, 'Warrior', 91–192; Timothy G. Gombis, 'Ephesians 2 as a Narrative of Divine Warfare', *JSNT* 26, no. 4 (2004); Bruce A. Stevens, 'Divine Warrior in the Gospel of Mark', *BZ* 31 (1987); Paul B. Duff, 'The March of the Divine Warrior and the Advent of the Greco-Roman King: Mark's Account of Jesus' Entry into Jerusalem', *JBL* 111, no. 1 (1992).

177. Where he conquers over chaos, like in ancient Near Eastern parallels, see Collins, *Daniel*, 286–91.

178. Andrew Angel argues that μετὰ δυνάμεως πολλῆς (Mk 13.26) could suggest an approach with a great army (the phrase means this in Isa. 36.2; 1 Macc. 7.10-11; 9.60; 11.63; 12.24, 42; 13.12). If so, then this suggests the SM is the divine warrior at its head; see Angel, *Chaos*, 127–28. The SM also sends out angels in Mk 13.27, and this is a divine function; see Craig A. Evans, *Mark 8:27–16:20*, WBC 34B (Nashville: Thomas Nelson, 2001), 329.

These factors may well be enough for readers to form the implicature and thereby enrich their understanding of the events of Lk. 21.27, but it is not an association given explicitly in the text. If a reader did not make this association, the other points remain: the SM is coming to earth, post-enthronement, and is bringing God's salvation in the face of rising chaos.

As such, the imagery is not consistent with the vindication of the SM in the fall of the city.[179] Instead, Lk. 21.27 describes the coming of the SM to earth (for salvation of his people) after his enthronement.[180] This is a salvation for the followers of Christ as the temple is destroyed, and therefore it brings their vindication; as such, it has parallels with the setting of Dan. 7.13 in the time of temple desolation at the time of Antiochus.[181] Beyond this, it is important to note a further strong implicature of the imagery in Lk. 21.27-28. The response to the rising chaos manifested against Jerusalem is not as expected in Ps. 45.6, salvation does not arise from Zion to protect it, salvation comes in the person of the SM to save his disciples (a contrast further enriched with ideas of the activity of the divine warrior, for those who make the connection).[182] In this way, the phrase τότε ὄψονται (21.27) indicates that the coming occurs after the attack on Jerusalem in a logical sense rather than a purely chronological one: in other words, the contrast is between the two spheres of salvific action of YHWH – Jesus or Zion. The fall of the temple is met with salvation revealed in the SM: salvation is found in Jesus, not in the temple. The subsequent narrative of Luke–Acts, especially Acts 7, adds more detail to these implicatures.

---

179. That vindication is seen primarily in the resurrection and exaltation of Jesus (Acts 2.24-33).

180. This reading can help describe how the coming of the SM came to be associated with the parousia. The parousia is the final appearing of the SM, the final overcoming of chaos, and it is the ultimate example of his coming to bring salvation (it is possible that this was part of the interpretation of Lk. 21.27 as a secondary or weaker implicature). As time passed from the immediacy of 70 CE, the coming of the SM became increasingly associated with the eschatological consummation, and less with the reading proposed here. This would be encouraged by the use of Dan. 7.13 for the parousia elsewhere in Christian communities (e.g., 1 Thess. 4.15-17), such that the parousia would eventually become the context where relevance would be found, but this does not mean that it was the primary meaning of the text for Luke.

181. Angel, *Chaos*, 139.

182. Salvation is the primary image here, but God's salvation as divine warrior fighting for his people is always associated with judgement on the oppressors of the righteous.

Conclusion

Jesus continues to act as a prophet in Lk. 21.20-28, speaking about the fate of Jerusalem and its temple. The language of this oracle is drawn from the OT, especially the prophets, and 21.20-24 evokes imagery of the previous exile. It also makes textual links back to Luke 19, building on its discussion of the destruction of Jerusalem. In this way it adds a series of implicatures about the coming disaster, incorporating ideas of judgement, the defilement from the Gentiles, and weaker implicatures associated with personal feelings of fear. In addition, the evocation of Deut. 28.58-68 adds the implicature that the city will be destroyed because of unfaithfulness to the covenant. At this stage in the narrative this is an implicature, and the reader is left to explore possible causes for this unfaithfulness while anticipating that later parts of the narrative will make it plain.

The second part of the oracle (21.25-27) has distinctive language of cosmic disturbance that is commonly thought to refer to the parousia. Building on the work of Andrew Angel, this chapter has shown that this language repeats themes from *Chaoskampf* imagery in the OT prophets, and would most naturally be understood as describing the fall of the city. In doing so, it engages with the contexts of specific texts (notably Ps. 45 and Dan. 7.13) adding that the fall of Jerusalem is an event of great significance, and a judgement of God. Its language suggests rising chaos and the undoing of creation, imagery that adds to the impressions of the exile, and draws attention to the displacement of the city as the centre of the world. The most specific contribution of the chapter is in the idea that Zion is no longer a place of safety through the presence of YHWH. Enemies are coming against the city, and they are the judgement of the Lord against Zion; he will not rise up from the city to defend it (as Ps. 45 and Joel 3.5; 4.16); instead, the SM comes to save the faithful as the divine warrior. Jesus, not the temple, has become the locus of salvation.

Chapter 6

LUKE 23.26-31, 44-45:
THE DEATH OF THE SAVIOUR AND THE FATE
OF THE CITY

Jesus' final utterance about Jerusalem's fate (Lk. 23.28-31) is spoken on the way to his death;[1] he addresses Jerusalem on his exit from the city, as he did on his entrance.[2] The speech brings together the fate of Jesus and the fate of the city, and although these subjects are intertwined it is convenient to discuss them separately. This chapter will begin with these aspects of the speech, then assess the contribution of Jesus' death and the tearing of the temple veil (23.44-45) to its meaning because the oracle needs to be interpreted in the light of its significant setting.

Jesus as the Rejected Saviour

The focus on Jesus is predominantly in the saying at the climax of the oracle in 23.31. This looks like a proverb, but it is not anything well-known; instead, its cryptic nature signals that its interpretation requires increased processing effort and the search for contexts will include OT texts because they form a likely context for such sayings.

1. Significant works describing this event include: Jerome H. Neyrey, 'Jesus' Address to the Women of Jerusalem (Lk. 23. 27–31) – A Prophetic Judgment Oracle', *NTS* 29, no. 1 (1983); Giblin, *Jerusalem*, 93–104; Marion L. Soards, 'Tradition, Composition, and Theology in Jesus' Speech to the "Daughters of Jerusalem" (Luke 23,26–32)', *Bib* 68 (1987); Gregory E. Sterling, 'Mors Philosophi: The Death of Jesus in Luke', *HTR* 94, no. 4 (2001); Franz Georg Untergassmair, 'Der Spruch vom "grünen und dürren Holz" (Lk 23,31)', *SNTSU* 16 (1991); Michael Patella, *The Death of Jesus: The Diabolical Force and the Ministering Angel: Luke 23,44–49*, CahRB (Paris: Gabalda, 1999); Brant J. Pitre, 'Blessing the Barren and Warning the Fecund: Jesus' Message for Women Concerning Pregnancy and Childbirth', *JSNT* 81, no. 1 (2001).
2. Conzelmann, *Theology*, 134, 99.

OT Contexts
The language in Lk. 23.31 is distinctive:

ὅτι εἰ ἐν τῷ ὑγρῷ ξύλῳ ταῦτα ποιοῦσιν, ἐν τῷ ξηρῷ τί γένηται;

For if they do this when the wood is green, what will happen when it is dry?

Ὑγρός is a NT *hapax legomenon* and ξηρός occurs only eight times, but no text shares this language. Several texts do share some words and have conceptual similarity. Ezekiel 17.24 and 21.3 (20.47 ET) both refer to young and mature wood:[3]

Ezek. 17.24:

καὶ γνώσονται πάντα τὰ ξύλα τοῦ πεδίου διότι ἐγὼ κύριος ὁ ταπεινῶν ξύλον ὑψηλὸν καὶ ὑψῶν ξύλον ταπεινὸν καὶ ξηραίνων ξύλον χλωρὸν καὶ ἀναθάλλων ξύλον ξηρόν· ἐγὼ κύριος λελάληκα καὶ ποιήσω.

And all the trees of the plain shall know that I am the Lord, he who brings low a high tree and exalts a low tree and withers a green tree and makes a dry tree flourish. I, the Lord, have spoken, and I will do it.

Ezek. 21.3:

καὶ ἐρεῖς τῷ δρυμῷ Ναγεβ Ἄκουε λόγον κυρίου Τάδε λέγει κύριος κύριος Ἰδοὺ ἐγὼ ἀνάπτω ἐν σοὶ πῦρ, καὶ καταφάγεται ἐν σοὶ πᾶν ξύλον χλωρὸν καὶ πᾶν ξύλον ξηρόν, οὐ σβεσθήσεται ἡ φλὸξ ἡ ἐξαφθεῖσα, καὶ κατακαυθήσεται ἐν αὐτῇ πᾶν πρόσωπον ἀπὸ ἀπηλιώτου ἕως βορρᾶ·

And you shall say to the forest of the Nageb: Hear a word of the Lord, This is what the Lord says: Behold, I am kindling a fire in you, and it shall devour every green tree in you and every dry tree; the kindled flame shall not be quenched, and by it every face shall be burned up from east wind to north.

Both have some lexical similarity, using ξηρός for dry wood, but they use χλωρός (not Luke's ὑγρός) for green wood. In Ezek. 17.24 the trees have different fates; in Luke their fate is the same. Ezekiel 21.3 is closer conceptually because it compares green and dry wood, and they both suffer the same fate, but it identifies the wood with πᾶν ξύλον (not ἐν and a dative), and it does not have the sense of temporal separation between the two events that Luke's present and future verbs convey. More significantly, there is strong imagery of fire, and one would expect a more explicit

---

3. Fitzmyer, *Luke*, 2:1498–99; Alfred F. Loisy, *L'Évangile selon Luc* (Paris: Émile Nourry, 1924), 555; Caird, *Language*, 249.

reference to fire in Lk. 23.31 if Luke was evoking Ezek. 21.3. Both texts should therefore be rejected as strong intertexts.[4]

Several other verses mention fire devouring wood (e.g., Isa. 10.16-19; Ezek. 24.9-10, Jer. 5.14; 7.20; 21.14; Joel 1.19),[5] but they have little lexical similarity to Luke, apart from ξύλον in some cases. Their principal claim to association is a conceptual link through fire as judgement, but this is not the focus of Lk. 23.31 (although Luke's dry wood is at risk of fire, his focus is principally a comparison between green and dry, which these OT texts do not have). As such, fire cannot be enough to link with any specific verse in the absence of more particular links.

Even if the proverb does not point to a single verse, elements of it point to OT motifs. First, the apodosis of Lk. 23.31 suggests the wood is burned by fire, and is likely to be interpreted in the context of the motif of the destruction of wood as a judgement of God (typically by fire), something expressed in most of the texts above. Second, the distinctive language of 'green' and 'dry' is likely to point to other motifs. Israel is described as a fruitful green vine or olive tree (Isa. 5.1; Jer. 11.16; Hos. 10.1); this contrasts with the unfaithful who are dry or unfruitful (Isa. 37.27; Hos. 9.16; Joel 1.12; Nah. 1.10).[6] When these motifs are put together, it becomes apparent that their themes are present together in another text, Lk. 13.6-9, a parable about a fruitless fig tree which is given a temporary reprieve from destruction to see if it becomes fruitful. A reader searching for the meaning of the text is likely to make this connection because it is close at hand in the Lukan narrative and it is told in the context of punishment coming on the inhabitants of Jerusalem (13.5).[7]

The Events in the Green and the Dry

This saying plays an important role in explaining the reasons for the preceding descriptions of calamity,[8] but its specific reference is debated. The common interpretations are:[9] (1) if the Romans execute Jesus (who is innocent of revolution) then how will they treat a revolutionary

---

4. Giblin, *Jerusalem*, 102, rejects both Ezekiel texts.

5. For Isa. 10.16-19 see Caird, *Language*, 249. Pitre makes an association with Hos. 9.16 as part of an attempt to reconcile all of this logion to Hos. 9–10; Pitre, 'Barren', 71.

6. See Pao and Schnabel, 'Luke', 394.

7. The idea of a tree being expected to behave according to season is also expressed in Lk. 21.29-31.

8. Plummer, *Luke*, 529; Neyrey, 'Address', 79.

9. See the summaries in Bock, *Luke*, 2:1847–48; Plummer, *Luke*, 529; Fitzmyer, *Luke*, 2:1498–99; Bovon, *Luc*, 366–67.

Jerusalem?[10] (2) If the Jews treat Jesus (who has come to save them) in this way, then what treatment will they receive?[11] (3) If people behave in this way before wickedness is complete, what will happen when it is full? (4) If Jesus has not been spared by God, then how much more will the nation not be spared if it is unrepentant?[12] (5) It is a general statement about coming judgement which does not have specific referents.[13]

There are two principal issues in deciding between these options. First, the people in both clauses require identification. No one is named, but it seems logical that if the saying is about the rejection of Jesus, then the subjects of the protasis will be to be the people who led Jesus away in 23.26. This group is described with a personal pronoun, and 'they' are either the Jews who appealed for the death of Jesus (the chief priests, the leaders, and the people identified in 23.13),[14] the Romans,[15] or both.[16] A good case can be made for the Romans because they are the only ones with the authority to crucify, and the people crucifying the other criminals are also identified as 'they' (23.33) – and 'they' were unlikely to be Jews. But despite this, the narrative effect of the personal pronoun in 23.26 is to keep attention focused on the Jewish leadership as those killing Jesus: the Jews are the subject of 'they' in 23.25; they cried for crucifixion twice (23.21, 23); and Pilate handed Jesus over to them for death (23.25).[17] The saying of 23.31 would then refer to the same people as 23.26, the

---

10. Gaston, *Stone*, 365; Walker, *Jesus*, 77–78; Wright, *Victory*, 332, 567–70.

11. David L. Tiede, *Luke*, ACNT (Minneapolis: Augsburg, 1988), 415; Raymond Brown, *The Death of the Messiah: From Gethsemane to the Grave: A Commentary on the Passion Narratives in the Four Gospels*, ABRL, 2 vols. (New York: Doubleday; London: Geoffrey Chapman, 1994), 2:926–27; Neyrey, 'Address', 78–79. Darrell Bock argues this is a close second to view 4; see Bock, *Luke*, 2:1848.

12. With slight differences in emphasis, this is the most favoured scholarly view: Bock, *Luke*, 2:1847–48; Creed, *Luke*, 286; Danker, *Luke*, 236; Manson, *Sayings*, 343; Schneider, *Lukas*, 481; Fitzmyer, *Luke*, 2:1498–99; Marshall, *Gospel*, 865.

13. Nolland, *Luke*, 3:1138.

14. Fitzmyer, *Luke*, 2:1496; Lieu, *Luke*, 193; Danker, *Luke*, 236; Edwards, *Luke*, 680–81.

15. Marie-Joseph Lagrange, *Évangile Selon Saint Luc* (Paris: J. Gabalda, 1921), 584; Brown, *Death*, 1:856–59; George B. Caird, *The Gospel of St Luke*, (London: Penguin, 1963), 249; Marshall, *Gospel*, 863; Patella, *Death*, 36; Nolland, *Luke*, 3:1136.

16. Green, *Gospel*, 814; Carroll, *Luke*, 462–63.

17. For Marion Soards, 'they' are assumed to be the Jewish leadership in 23.26, but it becomes apparent later that it was the Romans; see Soards, 'Tradition', 226; see also Anton Büchele, *Der Tod Jesu im Lukasevangelium: Eine redaktionsgeschichtliche Untersuchung zu Lk 23*, FTS 26 (Frankfurt: Knecht, 1978), 42.

Jerusalem Jewish leadership,[18] because there is no indication that attention has shifted from the Jews to the Romans.[19] Alternatively, the subject of both clauses could be God, but this is unlikely because that would require 'they' in the protasis to be an indirect reference to God, and it makes God the subject of the crucifixion of Jesus – something Luke does not state elsewhere.[20] Finally, it is also unlikely to be the general reference to people of option 3 (above) because that is too general a reference,[21] and this option requires the green tree to refer to wickedness.

If the Jews are the subject of the protasis they cannot be the subject of the apodosis because they are its object.[22] Although some argue that the subjects of both clauses are the same, this is not necessary because the syntax of the proverb is not symmetrical: it has a plural (ποιοῦσιν) in the protasis, but the more indirect τί γένηται in the apodosis, and this is consistent with different actors in each section. So the Jerusalem leadership are the primary subject of the protasis, and the wider group of city inhabitants the object of the apodosis (i.e., 'because the leadership do this, then what will happen to their city?').

The second issue is whether the contrast in the proverb created by the two uses of ἐν has the force of 'in the case of' or 'in the time of'. Those interpreting it as the former typically note the OT texts with a comparison of destruction of green and dead trees by fire (representing the judgement on the righteous and unrighteous), creating a contrast in Luke between the death of Jesus, and the fall of Jerusalem.[23] A similar contrast is present in the later Rabbinic text *S. Eli. Rab.* 14 (F.65) ('When the fire consumes the green, what will the dry do?'), and John Nolland argues that this may reflect a common proverbial pattern.[24] But while later Rabbinic texts might demonstrate a lesser to greater contrast (as does Luke), they do not require Luke to be understood in a particular way.[25] Rather, because of the

---

18. Brown, *Death*, 2:926–27; Neyrey, 'Address', 79; Tiede, *Luke*, 415.
19. As argued by Fitzmyer, *Luke*, 2:1498; Bock, *Luke*, 2:1847.
20. See Green, *Gospel*, 816 n. 15; Brown, *Death*, 2:926.
21. Brown, *Death*, 926.
22. Walker, *Jesus*, 77 n. 78.
23. See, especially, the reference to Ezekiel texts in Caird, *Luke*, 249–50; and the discussion in Nolland, *Luke*, 3:1138.
24. Nolland, *Luke*, 3:1138; see also Str-B 2:263, and the comments in Giblin, *Jerusalem*, 103. Edwards notes that the saying in Luke may pick up on Jewish maxims; see Edwards, *Luke*, 684.
25. Evans, *Luke*, 863–64; Brown, *Death*, 2:925–26. Note that *S. Eli. Rab.* 14 (F.65) does not specifically mention wood, and it is a late text of uncertain contribution to the debate.

OT motif of faithfulness and unfaithfulness in Luke, it is more likely that ἐν has a temporal basis with a contrast between the time of the green of the tree and the time of the dry.²⁶ This is also suggested by the different tenses of the verbs (the protasis is a current event, and the apodosis still future) and it parallels the contrast of the times of the women weeping for the fate of Jesus (in the present) and the city (in the future).

So the proverb, like the contrast of 23.28, makes an association between the rejection of Jesus and the fate of the city, but its proverbial form shows that optimal relevance is beyond this. Several implicatures are created through Lk. 13.6-9 and through the OT motifs which both form its interpretive context. The season of the 'green' should have been a time of fruitfulness, but the actions of the Jerusalem leaders were inconsistent with such a time. Their rejection of Jesus was not the action of fruitful Israel, the fruitful vine of Hos. 10.1: the implied appropriate action for such a green time was to embrace Jesus as saviour, but their rejection of Jesus demonstrated that they were not fruitful. As a dry tree, their judgement was inevitable. It is interesting to note that this is a very similar idea and imagery to the cursing of the fig tree in Mark's account of the temple action.²⁷ The destruction of the city is therefore both inevitable and the consequence of their present actions.

The Fall of Jerusalem

The description of the fall of the city in Lk. 23.27-30 also draws on OT texts and motifs.

The OT Contexts
(i) The Mourning and Weeping (Lk. 23.27-29)

²⁷Ἠκολούθει δὲ αὐτῷ πολὺ πλῆθος τοῦ λαοῦ καὶ γυναικῶν αἳ ἐκόπτοντο καὶ ἐθρήνουν αὐτόν. ²⁸στραφεὶς δὲ πρὸς αὐτὰς [ὁ] Ἰησοῦς εἶπεν· θυγατέρες Ἰερουσαλήμ, μὴ κλαίετε ἐπ' ἐμέ· πλὴν ἐφ' ἑαυτὰς κλαίετε καὶ ἐπὶ τὰ τέκνα ὑμῶν, ²⁹ὅτι ἰδοὺ ἔρχονται ἡμέραι ἐν αἷς ἐροῦσιν· μακάριαι αἱ στεῖραι καὶ αἱ κοιλίαι αἳ οὐκ ἐγέννησαν καὶ μαστοὶ οἳ οὐκ ἔθρεψαν.

²⁷A great number of the people followed him, and among them were women who were beating their breasts and wailing for him. ²⁸But Jesus turned to them and said, 'Daughters of Jerusalem, do not weep for me, but weep for yourselves and for your children. ²⁹For the days are surely coming when

---

26. Pitre, 'Barren', 71 n. 28; Brown, *Death*, 2:926; Evans, *Luke*, 864; Soards, 'Tradition', 243; Neyrey, 'Address', 79.

27. Hooker, 'Traditions', 13–14, makes this observation.

they will say, "Blessed are the barren, and the wombs that never bore, and the breasts that never nursed". ³⁰Then they will begin to say to the mountains, "Fall on us"; and to the hills, "Cover us".'

The most likely intertext for Lk. 23.27-29 is Jeremiah 9; although normally noted as 9.18 (9.19 ET), the allusion is more obvious when the wider context is noted:[28]

¹⁷καὶ λαβέτωσαν ἐφ' ὑμᾶς θρῆνον, καὶ καταγαγέτωσαν οἱ ὀφθαλμοὶ ὑμῶν δάκρυα, καὶ τὰ βλέφαρα ὑμῶν ῥείτω ὕδωρ. ¹⁸ὅτι φωνὴ οἴκτου ἠκούσθη ἐν Σιων Πῶς ἐταλαιπωρήσαμεν κατῃσχύνθημεν σφόδρα, ὅτι ἐγκατελίπομεν τὴν γῆν καὶ ἀπερρίψαμεν τὰ σκηνώματα ἡμῶν. ¹⁹ἀκούσατε δή, γυναῖκες, λόγον θεοῦ, καὶ δεξάσθω τὰ ὦτα ὑμῶν λόγους στόματος αὐτοῦ, καὶ διδάξατε τὰς θυγατέρας ὑμῶν οἶκτον καὶ γυνὴ τὴν πλησίον αὐτῆς θρῆνον. ²⁰ὅτι ἀνέβη θάνατος διὰ τῶν θυρίδων ὑμῶν, εἰσῆλθεν εἰς τὴν γῆν ὑμῶν τοῦ ἐκτρῖψαι νήπια ἔξωθεν καὶ νεανίσκους ἀπὸ τῶν πλατειῶν.

¹⁸and let them raise a lament over us, and let our eyes bring down tears, and let our eyelids flow with water, ¹⁹because a sound of pity was heard in Sion: 'How we have suffered hardship! We were utterly shamed, because we have abandoned the land and we have cast down our quarters.' ²⁰Do hear, O women, a divine word, and let your ears accept words of his mouth, and teach to your daughters a dirge, and a woman to her companion a lament ²¹'because death has come up through our windows, has entered into our land, to destroy infants outside and young men from the squares'.

There are several reasons why this should be regarded as an intertext: (1) it concerns mourning in Zion, and Luke has lamenting 'daughters of Jerusalem' (Zion is rare in the NT);[29] (2) it describes weeping over the city – although it does not have Luke's κλαίω, it has θρῆνος (a cognate of Luke's θρηνέω), and the emotion of a lament is just as strongly expressed; (3) women and daughters are prominent in the mourning (9.19); (4) the disaster comes upon infants (Jer. 9.20), as it does in Lk. 23.29. Cumulatively these arguments make this the strongest intertextual link to 23.27-29.

The weeping women who follow Jesus (23.27-28) have been seen as a parallel to Zech. 12.10-14.[30]

---

28. As noted by NA[28]; Pao and Schnabel, 'Luke', 393; Rusam, *Lukas*, 234; Neyrey, 'Address', 77; Walker, *Jesus*, 77.

29. Seven occurrences in the NT, and none in Luke–Acts.

30. NA[28]; Green, *Gospel*, 815; Danker, *Luke*, 236; Fitzmyer, *Luke*, 2:1497 (as a literary motif); Bovon, *Luc*, 362; Bock, *Luke*, 1.1845; Edwards, *Luke*, 682. Nolland, *Luke*, 3:1137, is cautious, and thinks a link is 'possible but uncertain'. Most of these scholars restrict their observation to Zech. 12.10.

And I will pour out a spirit of grace and compassion on the house of Dauid and on the inhabitants of Ierousalem, and they shall look to me because they have danced triumphantly [ἐπιβλέψονται πρός με ἀνθ' ὧν κατωρχήσαντο], and they shall mourn [κόψονται] for him with a mourning as for a loved one, and they shall be pained with pain as for a firstborn. On that day the mourning in Ierousalem will be great like the mourning for a pomegranate orchard cut down in the plain. The land shall mourn, each family by itself; the family of the house of David by itself, and their wives [γυναῖκες] by themselves; the family of the house of Nathan by itself, and their wives by themselves; the family of the house of Levi by itself, and their wives by themselves; the family of the Shimeites by itself, and their wives by themselves; and all the families that are left, each by itself, and their wives by themselves.

Both Luke and Zechariah concern Jerusalem and mourning (using κόπτω), but the similarities are not that clear cut. Although Zech. 12.12 mentions mourning wives, it does not emphasise women. The relationship would be clearer with the MT, which refers to the people looking on one who they pierced, but the LXX has replaced this with ἐπιβλέψονται πρός με ἀνθ' ὧν κατωρχήσαντο. It is not a persuasive intertext.[31]

Other than this, some of the phrases in Lk. 23.27-29 resemble specific OT texts and motifs. The words κόπτω and θρηνέω occur together in Mic. 1.8 and Josephus, *Ant.* 6.377 (about the mourning for Saul from 1 Kgdms 31.11-13), but neither has other similarity to Luke 23.

Θυγατέρες 'Ιερουσαλήμ occurs relatively commonly in the OT, either as a vocative plural (as Lk. 23.28) in Song 1.5; 2.7; 3.5; 5.8, 16; 8.4;[32] or as a singular in Zeph. 3.14; Zech. 9.9; Lam. 2.13 (vocative) and 4 Kgdms 19.21; Mic. 4.8; Isa. 37.22; Lam. 2.15 (in other cases).[33] None of them shares other conceptual similarity with Luke, but the phrase in the Song of Songs is closest grammatically. Luke uses it to refer to the inhabitants of the city, and it echoes the similar use in the LXX, without pointing to a specific verse.[34]

In the same way ἰδοὺ ἔρχονται ἡμέραι is a LXX motif used in prophetic texts about exile and restoration. It is present (in the form ἰδοὺ ἡμέραι ἔρχονται) in Jer. 7.32; 9.24 (9.25 ET); 16.14; 19.6; 23.5, 7; 38.27, 31

---

31. See the dismissal of this verse in Lagrange, *Évangile*, 585; Douglas J. Moo, *The Old Testament in the Gospel Passion Narratives* (Sheffield: Almond, 1983), 221.

32. NA[28] (but not NA[27]) lists Song 2.7; 3.5, 10.

33. See the lists in Green, *Gospel*, 815; Fitzmyer, *Luke*, 2:1498; Pao and Schnabel, 'Luke', 393; Bovon, *Luc*, 364.

34. Green, *Gospel*, 815. The references to daughters of other nations noted by Soards contribute little. Soards, 'Tradition', 222 n. 6.

(31.27, 31 ET),[35] but none of them has sufficient similarity to be evoked on its own, and it is likely that the term evokes the prophetic genre, especially those dealing with judgement surrounding the exile. However, the reader might make a connection to the phrase ἥξουσιν ἡμέραι ἐπὶ σέ in Lk. 19.43 because of the common concern with Jerusalem and weeping.[36]

The beatitude of Lk. 23.29 has some similarity with Isa. 54.1:[37]

Εὐφράνθητι, στεῖρα ἡ οὐ τίκτουσα, ῥῆξον καὶ βόησον, ἡ οὐκ ὠδίνουσα, ὅτι πολλὰ τὰ τέκνα τῆς ἐρήμου μᾶλλον ἢ τῆς ἐχούσης τὸν ἄνδρα, εἶπεν γὰρ κύριος.

Rejoice, O barren one who does not bear; break forth, and shout, you who are not in labor! Because more are the children of the desolate woman than of her that has a husband,

While they share the distinctive word στεῖρα, it is singular in Isaiah and plural in Luke; Isaiah lacks Luke's distinctive reference to female anatomy;[38] and Isaiah does not have Luke's beatitude formula.[39] Finally, as John Nolland notes, where Isaiah refers to a 'bright future against a dark present', Luke has a 'dark future' which turns the values of the present world on its head.[40] All of this makes a textual link unlikely.[41]

---

35. Tiede, *Luke*, 414–15; Bovon, *Luc*, 364; Fitzmyer, *Luke*, 2:1498; Nolland, *Luke*, 3:1137; Pao and Schnabel, 'Luke', 394. Similar language can also be found in 4 Kgdms 20.17; Amos 4.2; 8.11; 9.13; Zech. 14.1; Jer. 28.52 (51.52 ET); 30.18 (49.2 ET); 31.12 (48.12 ET); 37.3 (30.3 ET); 38.38 (31.38 ET). The same word order as the LXX is present in a minority of NT MSS (ℵ C).

36. Luke 5.35; 17.22; 21.6, 22-23 have similar language (Pao and Schnabel, 'Luke', 394), but are not as close as 19.43.

37. NA[28]; Pao and Schnabel, 'Luke', 394; Fitzmyer, *Luke*, 2:1498; Tannehill, *Narrative Unity*, 1:166; Rusam, *Lukas*, 234; Tiede, *Luke*, 415; Walter Käser, 'Exegetische und theologische Erwägungen zur Seligpreisung der Kinderlosen Lc 23 29b', *ZNW* 54, no. 3-4 (1963): 246.

38. The reference to μήτρα and μαστός is not enough to make Hos. 9.11-14 an intertext, against Pitre, 'Barren', 69–70.

39. Wisdom 3.1 has μακαρία στεῖρα ἡ ἀμίαντος. This is a closer parallel in words but not in concept.

40. Nolland, *Luke*, 1137, who rejects this intertext, as does Brown, *Death*, 2:923; Bovon, *Luc*, 364 n. 89. Alternatively, Käser argues that the reference to mountains and hills in Lk. 23.30 echoes Isa. 54.10, turning up the volume; but it is several verses remote from 54.1, and Lk. 23.30 is clearly a quote from Hos. 10.8. Käser, 'Seligpreisung', 246–47, 52.

41. Especially because Lk. 23.39 supposedly subverts Isa. 54.1, but such textual relationships require close verbal echoing to create the link.

A better case can be made for a link to the woe pronounced on pregnant and nursing women in Lk. 21.23,[42] and to Jeremiah 9.

(ii) The Quotation in Luke 23.30
Luke 23.30 quotes from Hos. 10.8 closely:[43]

Hos. 10.8	Lk. 23.30
...	...
καὶ ἐροῦσιν τοῖς ὄρεσιν	ἄρξονται λέγειν τοῖς ὄρεσιν·
Καλύψατε ἡμᾶς,	πέσετε ἐφ' ἡμᾶς,
καὶ τοῖς βουνοῖς	καὶ τοῖς βουνοῖς·
Πέσατε ἐφ' ἡμᾶς.	καλύψατε ἡμᾶς·

There are some changes from the LXX: Luke prefers ἄρξονται λέγειν to ἐροῦσιν, he uses the second aorist πέσετε, and he inverts the order of the verbs in the LXX.[44] It is likely that the early Christian community had a version of Hosea closer to that in Luke 23 because variant A 106 of Hos. 10.8 has the same order for the verbs as Luke, and πέσετε.[45]

The Meaning of Luke 23.28-31
The women that follow Jesus are clearly distinct from those who lead him to death.[46] It is likely that they had at least some sympathy with him because they are mourning for him, even if the mourning is part of cultural expectation;[47] their presence thereby reinforces that not all rejected Jesus.[48] In addressing these women, Jesus speaks to them as representatives of the city, as θυγατέρες Ἰερουσαλήμ suggests through

---

42. Lieu, *Luke*, 153.
43. NA[28]; France, *Jesus*, 71; Fitzmyer, *Luke*, 2:1498; Nolland, *Luke*, 3:1137; Marshall, *Gospel*, 864; Brown, *Death*, 2:924; Tiede, *Luke*, 415.
44. Several texts read πέσατε, including ℵ^c L N W Δ Ψ.
45. It could be Christianised OT text: see the discussion in Traugott Holtz, *Untersuchungen über die alttestamentlichen Zitate bei Lukas* (Berlin: Akademie-Verlag, 1968), 28, and also Nolland, *Luke*, 3:1137. The quotation of Hos. 10.8 in Rev. 6.16 also has πέσετε and the same verb order as Lk. 23.30.
46. Fitzmyer, *Luke*, 2:1497; Lieu, *Luke*, 193. Jerome Neyrey is wrong to regard them as 'the element of Israel who continually rejected God's messengers' (Neyrey, 'Address', 75) because they do not express hostility to Jesus. See also the discussion in Bock, *Luke*, 2:1844–45.
47. Soards, 'Tradition', 229. For their role as mourners, see Marshall, *Gospel*, 863–64; for mourning as cultural rather than sympathetic, see Ellis, *Luke*, 266.
48. Bock, *Luke*, 2:1845.

its OT connotations;[49] their lamentation was misplaced because they did not understand the significance of his death or its consequences for the city,[50] and Jesus shows why their tears should be for Jerusalem. It focuses on city inhabitants at the time of the siege through two sayings: a beatitude which describes the hopelessness of those who witness the dreadful fate of children in war, by subverting the usual expectations of blessing through procreation;[51] and a quotation emphasising the terror of the catastrophe. It adds to these a proverb which links the coming catastrophe with the rejection of Jesus.

This combination of beatitude, quotation and proverbial saying suggests that optimal relevance is beyond a simple statement that the city will be destroyed. A full interpretation requires more processing effort exploring the sayings in their OT settings and this will lead to a series of implicatures.

First, the oracle continues the focus on the Jerusalem Jewish leadership as those who reject Jesus. They should have welcomed him (as Lk. 19.28-46 showed) but they reject him to his death. This is not the action of fruitful Israel (23.31), and their rejection of the saviour has direct consequences for the city. This rejection is thrown into sharp relief by the more positive responses of other people around Jesus: women mourn, a criminal expresses faith, a centurion has insight, and people beat their breasts at his death (23.40-43, 47-48);[52] some even embrace the salvation Jesus offers and act as the leaders should have 'in the green wood'. This difference of response becomes an important theme in Acts.

Second, Jesus was killed because of a rejection of his claim to bring salvation: this claim was the subject of his trial (22.67–23.2; 23.14, 38),[53]

---

49. Giblin, *Jerusalem*, 99; Brown, *Death*, 2:920–21; Pao and Schnabel, 'Luke', 393. For Jesus addressing the whole city, see Green, *Gospel*, 815.

50. See the discussion in Soards, 'Tradition'; Green, *Gospel*, 813.

51. Against Pitre, 'Barren', who reads it as a renouncement of procreation. For children as blessing, see Ps. 112.9, and the blessed barren women in the OT (Gen. 11.30; 16.1–21.7; 25.21; 29.31–30.24; Judg. 13.2-24; 1 Kgdms 1.1–2.11) (see ibid., 64). For Barrenness in classical literature, see Fitzmyer, *Luke*, 2:1498.

52. See Green, *Gospel*, 824; for the centurion, see Matthew C. Easter, '"Certainly This Man Was Righteous": Highlighting a Messianic Reading of the Centurion's Confession in Luke 23:47', *TynBul* 63, no. 1 (2012); Peter Doble, *The Paradox of Salvation: Luke's Theology of the Cross*, SNTSMS 87 (Cambridge: Cambridge University Press, 1996), 157. For a thorough treatment of δίκαιος in Luke–Acts, see ibid., 93–126.

53. The trial does not focus on his prophetic ministry, unlike Mt. 26.61; Mk 14.58. See Taylor, 'Temple', 476–77.

and the subject of the jeers around the cross (23.35, 37, 39).[54] However, Luke 23 illustrates this salvation by showing Jesus meeting the needs of those outside usual concern, in addressing the concerns of the women (23.28-31), and in bringing salvation to a condemned man (23.39-43).

Third, Lk. 23.28-30 evokes the exile, especially through the contexts of two prophetic texts. Jeremiah 9 called for public lamentation because the fall of Jerusalem was certain;[55] Hos. 10.8 describes the horrors of the fate falling upon unrepentant Israel.[56] In this way, the oracle builds on previous ideas of the fall of the city as a divine judgement, a catastrophic event, and a result of the sins of the people (specifically covenant unfaithfulness).[57] What is more, the call for lamentation, in concert with Jeremiah 9, emphasises the certainty of this destruction.[58] Luke 23 adds to this a range of weaker implicatures about personal tragedy, and the appropriateness of despair, weeping and hopelessness.

Fourth, it is also possible that a reader would associate the sin of idolatry in Hosea 10 with the situation in Jerusalem in Luke 23.[59] Hosea 10 emphasises Israel's cultic sin and God's refusal to ignore the altars and worship sites that they had made (Hos 10.1, 2, 5-6, 8); these sanctuaries were the places that would be destroyed in the coming judgement, and they are mentioned in the verse which Luke quotes. Whether such contextual information from Hosea would be appropriated as an implicature is difficult to say: there is no cultic imagery in 23.27-31 to make it particularly manifest, nor does Jeremiah 9 introduce the topic. Added to that, Luke uses the quotation to emphasise the desire of the people for death in the face of judgement, and it is likely that this is how the verse was used by the Christian community, as evidenced by its use in Rev. 6.16 (again, without a cultic emphasis). But a cultic context is strongly present in Hosea, and likely to be part of the encyclopaedic information available for a reader willing to expend further effort in the search for relevance.

---

54. Links made back to Lk. 19 here mean that the implicatures derived in that chapter are activated for the reader interpreting Lk. 23.

55. McKane, *Jeremiah*, 1:209; Rusam, *Lukas*, 234.

56. Stuart, *Hosea*, 159–64; A.A. Macintosh, *A Critical and Exegetical Commentary on Hosea*, ICC (Edinburgh: T&T Clark, 1997), 409–10; France, *Jesus*, 71; although Pao and Schnabel, 'Luke', 395, go too far in claiming the Lukan Jesus sees his oracle as the fulfilment of Hosea's prophecy.

57. For covenant unfaithfulness in Hos. 10, see Stuart, *Hosea*, 164.

58. For certainty in Jer. 9, see McKane, *Jeremiah*, 209.

59. Rusam, *Lukas*, 234–35. Wright argues that the context of Hos. 10 is important, including the judgement on the sanctuaries, but he does not note the idolatry; see Wright, *Victory*, 568–69.

However strongly evoked, such ideas are (at the very least) latent in the Hosea quotation, and their full significance must wait for a discussion in Acts 7.

Fifth, Jesus' prophetic role is emphasised. Although his prophetic ministry is not discussed at his trial, he is mocked as a prophet (22.63-64),[60] and the current oracle has Jesus acting like Jeremiah in encouraging lamentation for the city.[61]

The Temple Veil (Luke 23.44-45)

All three Synoptic Gospels report the temple veil as torn at the death of Jesus,[62] but only Luke places it before his death.[63] It is clearly a significant event, and has been interpreted in different ways. The most significant are:[64] (1) the destruction of the temple,[65] whether as a prophecy, or a symbolic

---

60. Patella, *Death*, 45.
61. Fisk, 'Tears', 164.
62. There is a large literature on this event, much of it on Matthew or Mark's account. Important works include: Daniel M. Gurtner, 'The Rending of the Veil (Matt. 27:51a Par): A Look Back and a Way Forward', *Them* 29, no. 3 (2004); idem, *The Torn Veil: Matthew's Exposition of the Death of Jesus*, SNTSMS 139 (Cambridge: Cambridge University Press, 2007); Stephen Motyer, 'The Rending of the Veil: A Markan Pentecost?', *NTS* 33, no. 1 (1987); J. Bradley Chance, 'The Cursing of the Temple and the Tearing of the Veil in the Gospel of Mark', *BibInt* 15, no. 3 (2007); Robert L. Plummer, 'Something Awry in the Temple? The Rending of the Temple Veil and Early Jewish Sources that Report Unusual Phenomena in the Temple around AD 30', *JETS* 48, no. 2 (2005); Brown, *Death*, 2:1098–134. For Luke, see Joel B. Green, 'The Demise of the Temple as "Culture Center" in Luke–Acts: An Exploration of the Rending of the Temple Veil', *RB* 101 (1994). For its historicity, see Bock, *Luke*, 2:1859–60; Nolland, *Luke*, 3:1156. See also the Jewish literature which describes possible historical events consistent with the torn veil in Plummer, 'Awry'; Daniel M. Gurtner, 'The Veil of the Temple in History and Legend', *JETS* 49, no. 1 (2006).
63. Though Bezae places it after his death. Luke also omits Mark's language paralleling Jesus' baptism (Mk 1.10; 15.38).
64. See the thorough list of options in Nolland, *Luke*, 3:1157, who includes divine displeasure at Jesus' fate, or representing Jesus as destroyed in death. See also the bibliography in Dennis D. Sylva, 'The Temple Curtain and Jesus' Death in the Gospel of Luke', *JBL* 105, no. 2 (1986): 241 n. 7 (who includes cessation of the cult as an option); and the recent list (predominantly on Matthew) in Gurtner, *Torn Veil*, 2–24.
65. Büchele, *Tod*, 52; Marshall, *Gospel*, 875; Goulder, *Luke*, 769; Joseph B. Tyson, *The Death of Jesus in Luke–Acts* (Columbia: University of South Carolina, 1986), 108; Danker, *Luke*, 240; Chance, *Jerusalem*, 118–20. For Beale, it is the destruction of the temple as the beginning of the destruction of the cosmos, with its

beginning to the destruction (Joel Green argues that the emphasis is not so much on destruction but the end of the temple's role as the organising centre of life[66]); (2) open access to God;[67] (3) an apocalyptic sign showing the importance of the event, or as a symbol of the death of Jesus;[68] or (4) a combination of the other views.[69] Deciding between them requires attention to two features of the Lukan narrative, and the contextual information associated with the veil itself.

The Period of Darkness

> Lk. 23.44-45:
>
> ⁴⁴Καὶ ἦν ἤδη ὡσεὶ ὥρα ἕκτη καὶ σκότος ἐγένετο ἐφ' ὅλην τὴν γῆν ἕως ὥρας ἐνάτης ⁴⁵τοῦ ἡλίου ἐκλιπόντος, ἐσχίσθη δὲ τὸ καταπέτασμα τοῦ ναοῦ μέσον.
>
> ⁴⁴It was now about noon, and darkness came over the whole land until three in the afternoon, ⁴⁵while the sun's light failed; and the curtain of the temple was torn in two.

The period of darkness occurring before the tearing of the veil in Lk. 23.44-45 is critically important in showing why the veil tore.[70] It is more than the common motif at the death of a significant figure in Graeco-Roman literature because it is too powerful a biblical image for that.[71] In identifying OT contexts, the most significant features in 23.44 are the temporal references and the unusual phrase τοῦ ἡλίου ἐκλιπόντος in 23.45,[72]

---

replacement with a new creation (beginning with Christ's resurrection). Gregory K. Beale, *The Temple and the Church's Mission: A Biblical Theology of the Dwelling Place of God*, NSBT 17 (Leicester: Apollos; Downers Grove: Inter Varsity Press, 2004), 189–90.

66. Green, 'Temple'.

67. Most significantly in Sylva, 'Curtain'. Also Caird, *Luke*, 253; Leon Morris, *The Gospel According to St. Luke: An Introduction and Commentary*, TNTC (London: Inter-Varsity Press, 1974), 330.

68. See the discussion in Nolland, *Luke*, 3.1157.

69. E.g., open access to God and the end of the cult for Geldenhuys, *Luke*, 611. Ellis, *Luke*, 269, adds impending destruction to these. See also the discussion in Bock, *Luke*, 2:1860–61.

70. Green, *Gospel*, 823.

71. For references, see Brown, *Death*, 2:1043.

72. Some MSS (A C³ K Q W ΓΔ Θ Ψ $f^{1.13}$) have καὶ ἐσκοτίσθη ὁ ἥλιος, but the best MSS ($\mathfrak{P}^{75}$ ℵ C*vid etc.) have τοῦ ἡλίου ἐκλιπόντος, and this is the harder reading (Metzger, *Commentary*, 155).

but there are no OT texts which echo them exactly. The closest text is Amos 8.9:[73]

> καὶ ἔσται ἐν ἐκείνῃ τῇ ἡμέρᾳ, λέγει κύριος ὁ θεός, καὶ δύσεται ὁ ἥλιος μεσημβρίας, καὶ συσκοτάσει ἐπὶ τῆς γῆς ἐν ἡμέρᾳ τὸ φῶς·
>
> And it will come to pass on that day, says the Lord, and the sun will go down at noon, and the light will become dark upon the earth in the daytime.

It has a reference to the sun, a parallel clause referring to darkness on the earth (using συσκοτάζω, a verb related to σκότος), and it refers to noon (μεσημβρίας, not ὥρα ἕκτη). This is probably enough to make a textual link, though the correspondence is not exact: it uses different terms for the temporal reference, and it has a setting sun, not the distinctive Lukan τοῦ ἡλίου ἐκλιπόντος.[74] No other LXX text is closer overall. Isaiah 13.10 shares some similarity:[75]

> οἱ γὰρ ἀστέρες τοῦ οὐρανοῦ καὶ ὁ Ὠρίων καὶ πᾶς ὁ κόσμος τοῦ οὐρανοῦ τὸ φῶς οὐ δώσουσιν, καὶ σκοτισθήσεται τοῦ ἡλίου ἀνατέλλοντος, καὶ ἡ σελήνη οὐ δώσει τὸ φῶς αὐτῆς.
>
> For the stars of heaven and Orion and all the ornament of heaven will not give light, and it will be dark when the sun rises, and the moon will not give its light.

Yet it is not that close conceptually, since its darkness is a failure of dawn. Other texts share the motif of darkness, but do not have sufficient lexical or conceptual similarity with Lk. 23.44-45 (e.g., Joel 2.10; 3.4 [2.31 ET]; 3.15 [4.15 ET]).[76] Zephaniah 1.15 describes a day of wrath and darkness, but it does not share language of sun or time with Luke.[77]

---

73. Noted by NA[28]; Bock, *Luke*, 2:1858; Pao and Schnabel, 'Luke', 398; Patella, *Death*, 97, though most do not see this as the sole text.

74. Amos does not have a reference to *all* the earth. See the rejection of this intertext in Dominic Rudman, 'The Crucifixion as *Chaoskampf*: A New Reading of the Passion Narrative in the Synoptic Gospels', *Bib* 84, no. 1 (2003): 104.

75. Patella, *Death*, 97.

76. Frank J. Matera, 'The Death of Jesus According to Luke: A Question of Sources', *CBQ* 47, no. 3 (1985): 473. For the imagery coming from these texts, see Nolland, *Luke*, 3:1156; Bock, *Luke*, 2:1858; Fitzmyer, *Luke*, 2:1517; Pao and Schnabel, 'Luke', 398. Anton Büchele regards the darkness and torn veil as the apocalyptic signs on heaven and earth of Joel 3.4; see Büchele, *Tod*, 52.

77. Green, *Gospel*, 825.

So while Amos 8.9 is the closest text, the lack of similarity in the significant phrasing will ensure that it is not examined too closely by the reader. Relevance is likely to be found in the general concept of darkness as part of the eschatological motif of the judgement of God, a motif common across several texts.[78] But darkness is a rich metaphor, and its presence twice in Lk. 23.44-45 points to its importance, encouraging greater effort in the search for relevance. As such, the distinct Lukan phrasing will modify the understanding from the OT by allowing other thoughts to be added to its *ad hoc* concept; these are likely to be from the use of darkness elsewhere in the Gospel. At his arrest, Jesus proclaims αὕτη ἐστὶν ὑμῶν ἡ ὥρα καὶ ἡ ἐξουσία τοῦ σκότους (Lk. 22.53); elsewhere in the passion narrative there are references to the activity of Satan (22.3, 31), and darkness functions as a metaphor representing the opposite of the salvation (e.g., Lk. 1.78-79; Acts 26.18). So while the darkness will be seen as an important eschatological event (as the OT imagery implies),[79] the Lukan language will point away from it being the activity of God, and towards it referring to the reign of darkness which surrounds the rejection and death of Jesus.[80]

Narrative Contrasts

The tearing of the veil is most naturally understood as an action of God because of the divine passive. So, if the darkness is opposition against Jesus, then the δὲ in 23.45 introduces a contrasting action of God as the veil is torn.[81] This makes it an act of God in response to the opposition against Jesus,[82] something consistent with the contrasts throughout the narrative of Lk. 23.26-49. There are several contrasts: the people who lead

---

78. Caird, *Language*, 253; Fitzmyer, *Luke*, 2:1517; Bock, *Luke*, 2:1858; Pao and Schnabel, 'Luke', 398. Despite its proximity, Lk. 21.25-26 is not likely to be evoked because of its reference to shaking.

79. For the signs of the torn veil and darkness as signs of the 'last days', see Matera, 'Death', 475.

80. Green, 'Temple', 505; Patella, *Death*, 148–50; Chance, *Jerusalem*, 119–20; Nolland, *Luke*, 3:1156. Rudman argues that the darkness refers to the forces of chaos gaining the upper hand, but despite the use of chaos language in Lk. 21 it is not likely here because the darkness is of limited duration and not defeated by a warrior god. See Rudman, 'Crucifixion', 105. For darkness as divine judgement, see Brown, *Death*, 2:1038, for whom the darkness and torn veil are both negative signs before the death of Jesus.

81. For the relationship between the clauses see the discussion in Brown, *Death*, 2:1103–106, though he regards the darkness as an action of God.

82. Green, *Gospel*, 824.

Jesus to death contrast with Simon who follows (23.26); the ridicule of one of the crucified criminals contrasts with the faith of the other (23.39-43); the derision of the soldiers (23.36) contrasts with the response of the centurion (23.47); and the rejection of most leaders (23.35-37) contrasts with another leader, Joseph (23.50-53). There are further contrasts in Jesus' oracle in 23.28-31: the women should cry for the city, not for Jesus (23.28), and the actions of the leaders 'in the green' contrast with the fall of the city 'in the dry' (23.31). These contrasts prepare the way for seeing the torn veil as a sign of judgement on the city as a result of the opposition to Jesus (symbolised in the darkness).[83]

The Imagery of the Veil

Τὸ καταπέτασμα τοῦ ναοῦ (23.45) is usually thought to refer either to the veil at the entrance of the holy of holies, or the veil at the entry to the holy place.[84] In favour of the latter is its greater visibility, but the former has more theological significance. Readers would be aware of both veils, so it is hard to imagine that visibility would decide the issue;[85] more likely a reader would think of the theologically significant inner veil because Luke's veil has theological significance, and Luke uses the specific term καταπέτασμα with ναός (the word he uses for the sanctuary).[86]

The significance of the tearing of this veil is not immediately illuminated by reference to the OT because there are no OT references to torn veils,[87] and no texts with sufficient parallel language to be intertexts.

---

83. Chance, *Jerusalem*, 119.

84. This over-simplifies the veil arrangements in the temple, but for theological purposes it is a useful distinction. For the inner veil, see Plummer, *Luke*, 537; Ellis, *Luke*, 269; Caird, *Luke*, 254; Lieu, *Luke*, 196; Evans, *Luke*, 876; Nolland, *Luke*, 1157; Head, 'Temple', 117. For the outer veil, see Marshall, *Gospel*, 875; Bock, *Luke*, 2:1860; Fitzmyer, *Luke*, 2:1514; Pierre Benoit, *The Passion and Resurrection of Jesus Christ*, trans. Benet Weatherhead (New York: Herder & Herder; London: Darton, Longman & Todd, 1969); Edwards, *Luke*, 695.

85. Visibility of the event is irrelevant because converted priests could have related the incident.

86. While καταπέτασμα can be used for the outer veil (Exod. 26.37; 38.18; Num. 3.26) so can κάλυμμα; καταπέτασμα is more usually used for the veil before the holy of holies (Exod. 26.31-35; Lev. 21.23; 24.3; Sir. 50.5) and it refers to this veil in the only text where both terms are used (1 Macc. 1.22); it is also used in later literature (Philo, *Moses* 2.86; Josephus, *Ant.* 8.75). See Head, 'Temple', 107–17. See the persuasive argument from the LXX in Daniel M. Gurtner, 'LXX Syntax and the Identity of the NT Veil', *NovT* 47, no. 4 (2005).

87. See the excellent discussion in Gurtner, *Torn Veil*, 29–46.

The reader's encyclopaedic knowledge about the veil would contain the common Jewish conceptions about the veils: many of the furnishings of the temple were highly symbolic (typically representing parts of the universe) and the veil symbolised the heavenly firmament.[88] In addition, the inner veil's role was also to separate the holy of holies from lesser holy spaces.[89] This means that the tearing of the veil was a removal of the distinction between these spaces.

The Significance of the Torn Veil
So, as the torn veil represents an opening of the division between the Holy of Holies and the rest of the temple, then what is the significance of this event? Several explanations can be offered. (1) Despite the symbolism of the heavenly firmament, it is not the beginning of the undoing of creation (emphasised in the failure of the sun) and its replacement with the new creation (with access through Jesus' death) because Luke does not emphasise creation themes.[90] (2) Nor is it about open access to God,[91] as Dennis Sylva proposes. Sylva does not interpret the torn veil in association with the episode of darkness that precedes it, but with Jesus' prayer after it: just as Stephen's parallel prayer was uttered after seeing into the opened heavens (Acts 7.55-56, 59), so Jesus prayed after heaven opened. But there are problems with this: it divorces the torn veil from the episode of darkness with which it belongs (because of the pattern of contrasts); it really requires all the veils to be torn; the other prayer of Jesus, which Stephen also prays, happens before the veil tears (23.34); and it emphasises only part of the Stephen and Jesus parallels.[92]

(3) It is also more than Joel Green's cessation of the temple's function as 'sacred symbol of socio-religious power'.[93] For Green, the torn veil prepares for the response of the centurion and the people in the narrative. It does not symbolise the destruction of the temple because that would be inconsistent with Luke's positive view of the temple in the early chapters of Acts;

---

88. Ibid., 95–96; Beale, *Temple*, 46, and the references to Philo and Josephus there.

89. Gurtner, *Torn Veil*, 70–71.

90. Against Beale, *Temple*, 189–90; though he is not specifically looking at Luke. Similarly, for Rudman, 'Crucifixion', it is a disruption of creation, a victory of chaos, but there is no other suggestion of creational disturbance in Lk. 23. The tearing before the death of Jesus also goes against this thesis.

91. Against Sylva, 'Curtain', who finds support from Nolland, *Luke*, 3:1157.

92. For Jesus and Stephen parallels see Chapter 7 of this book. See the rebuttals of Sylva in Green, 'Temple', 502–503; Brown, *Death*, 1104–106. Also note that Luke does not use σχίζω as a term to describe a tearing through which one passes (ibid., 1105).

93. Green, 'Temple', 495. See also idem, *Gospel*, 825–26.

rather, it represents the spread of the gospel to those outside the boundaries set by the temple, a breaking of the 'power of the temple to regulate socio-religious boundaries of purity and holiness'.[94] This observation about salvation for everyone is correct, but it does not explain the significance of the temple event. Green's case would be stronger if the outer veil had been torn because that veil is more associated with community boundaries,[95] and his emphasis on the significance of the centurion would be more persuasive if the crucified criminal (who is clearly outside acceptable boundaries) had not been saved before any temple event in 23.42-43. In any case, it must be rejected because the place of the temple in Acts cannot govern the meaning of an event in the Gospel; and most significantly, his view does not give sufficient emphasis to two things which would have been part of the interpretive encyclopaedic information of the reader: the imagery of the heavens associated with the veil, and the relationship of the torn veil with the words of Jesus in 23.28-31.

(4) Instead, the tearing of the inner veil represents the end of the separation between the holy of holies and the rest of the sanctuary, not as an open way to the divine, but as a negation of the special place of the holy of holies, much as Raymond Brown described for Mark's Gospel.[96] The temple was regarded as the meeting point of heaven and earth,[97] and the symbolism of the torn heavenly firmament indicates that this is no longer the case, suggesting that the inner sanctuary no longer represents the heavens (the dwelling place of God). In this way, the torn veil is a fulfilment of the words of Jesus in Lk. 13.35, ἰδοὺ ἀφίεται ὑμῖν ὁ οἶκος ὑμῶν, and represents divine abandonment of the temple, signalling its impending destruction. Like the words of 13.35, Jesus' words in 23.28-31 serve to illuminate this event: just as Jesus makes a connection between the fall of Jerusalem and his death in 23.28-31, God's departure from the temple (leading to its destruction) connects to the opposition against Jesus (which led to his death). Because the temple is no longer the meeting point of heaven and earth, it does not define the boundaries between Jew and Gentile (in this Green is correct); rather, Jesus is the place of salvation for all (this is demonstrated in the conversation with the thief and the statement of the centurion, 23.39–43, 47).[98]

---

94. Green, 'Temple', 506.
95. For Jew–Gentile relations and the veil, see the helpful discussion in Benoit, *Passion*, 201.
96. Brown, *Death*, 2:1101. The sanctuary is now empty; see Taylor, 'Temple', 477.
97. Beale, *Temple*, 29–50.
98. Easter, 'Righteous'.

Raymond Brown argues that Luke's tearing of the veil functions at the level of a sign, showing that the continuing rejection of Jesus will bring about the destruction of the temple, and this continued rejection happens in Acts as the disciples are persecuted. The temple is not desacralized at Jesus' death, it happens in Acts 7.[99] But this makes the death of Stephen more important than the death of Jesus, and it ignores the relationships demonstrated in the oracle of Jesus to the women of the city.[100] Divine abandonment of the temple in Luke 23 does not have to negate a positive outlook on the temple in the first chapters of Acts, but the reasons for this must await discussion in the next chapter, as must the question of whether the temple is abandoned in Acts 7.

Conclusion

In common with the other laments, the final words of Jesus about the fall of Jerusalem present Jesus as a prophet. The allusion to Jeremiah 9, quotation of Hos. 10.8, and the phrase ἰδοὺ ἔρχονται ἡμέραι, all evoke the language of the past exile to show the fate awaiting the city; this builds on the themes of judgement and catastrophe in the previous laments (Lk. 19.43 is specifically evoked) but it also shows how it affects people, evoking a sense of despair and personal tragedy to demonstrate the extent of the calamity.

The most significant contribution of Lk. 23.28-31 is its clear focus on the guilt of the Jerusalem leadership for their rejection of Jesus. Although this theme is present in Lk. 13.34-35 and 19.28-46, in Luke 23 they reject Jesus to his death. This rejection is linked to consequences for the city: the rejection of Jesus in the time of the green will inevitably result in the destruction of the city in the time of the dry; in this way, it is implied that the rejection of Jesus is not what faithful Israel would do. The rejection of Jesus is the rejection of the saviour; this chapter does not discuss the rejection of Jesus as a prophet, nor does it develop the ideas contained within Luke 19 or Luke 21 about attitudes to the temple. Such thoughts must wait for further development in Acts 7, though there is a hint that idolatry might be involved through the quotation of Hos. 10.8.

---

99. Brown, *Death*, 2:1104. Mark had to demonstrate the abandonment of the temple in his Gospel in order to vindicate the words of Jesus about the temple at his trial. Luke is not bound by this.

100. It contradicts all that the sayings of Jesus about the temple have prepared for.

Finally, when Jesus dies with the climactic opposition against him demonstrated in the heavenly darkness, the temple veil tears; this is understood as a symbol of the divine abandonment of the temple. This is the event referred to in Lk. 13.35 and, together with the language of 23.28-31, it speaks clearly of the inevitability of the city's fate. However, what this means for Luke's attitude toward the temple must again await discussion in Acts.

Chapter 7

ACTS 7:
STEPHEN AND THE TEMPLE

Stephen's speech has a critical role in the unfolding narrative of Luke–Acts. It has a clear focus on the temple (the narrative is set in the temple complex, and the trial addresses a disagreement over the temple),[1] and it is important in the discussion of the parting of the ways of the early church and Judaism.[2]

The vast scholarly literature on this speech contains substantial disagreement;[3] for the purposes here the most important discussion concerns

1. Dunn, *Parting*, 63.
2. For its importance in Luke–Acts see Johnson, *Acts*, 137; Moessner, *Lord*, 299–307. The parallels between Acts 7 and the structure of Luke–Acts are too exaggerated in Delbert Wiens, *Stephen's Sermon and the Structure of Luke–Acts* (Richland Hills: Bibal, 1995).
3. A. F. J. Klijn, 'Stephen's Speech–Acts VII. 2–53', *NTS* 4, no. 1 (1957); Leonard Ramaroson, 'Contre les "temples faits de main d'homme" (Actes 7,48, 17,24)', *RPh* 43 (1969); John J. Kilgallen, *The Stephen Speech: A Literary and Redactional Study of Acts 7, 2–53*, AnBib 67 (Rome: Biblical Institute Press, 1976); Earl Richard, *Acts 6.1–8.4: The Author's Method of Composition*, SBLDS 41 (Missoula: Scholars Press, 1978); M. É. Boismard, 'Le Martyre d'Etienne: Acts 6, 8–8, 2', *RSR* 69, no. 1 (1981); Peter Doble, 'The Son of Man Saying in Stephen's Witnessing', *NTS* 31, no. 1 (1985); Jacques Dupont, 'La Structure Oratoire du Discours d'Etienne (Actes 7)', *Bib* 66 (1985); C. K. Barrett, 'Old Testament History According to Stephen and Paul', in *Studien zum Text und zur Ethik des Neuen Testaments: Festschrift zum 80. Geburtstag von Heinrich Greeven*, ed. Wolfgang Schrage (Berlin: de Gruyter, 1986); F. F. Bruce, 'Stephen's Apologia', in *Scripture: Meaning and Method: Essays Presented to Anthony Tyrrell Hanson for His Seventieth Birthday*, ed. Barry P. Thompson (Hull: Hull University Press, 1987); Dennis D. Sylva, 'The Meaning and Function of Acts 7:46–50', *JBL* 106, no. 2 (1987); Weinert, 'Luke'; Sasagu Arai, 'Zum "Tempelwort" Jesu in Apostelgeschichte 6:14', *NTS* 34, no. 3 (1988); Peter Dschulnigg, 'Die Rede des Stephanus im Rahmen des Berichtes über Sein Martyrium (Apg 6,8–8,3)', *Jud* 44 (1988); David A. deSilva, 'The Stoning of Stephen: Purging and Consolidating an Endangered Institution', *StudBT* 17 (1989); John J. Kilgallen, 'The Function of

its criticism of the temple: some think that Luke is against the temple itself, regarding its construction as an act of disobedience;[4] others regard the speech as expressing a Lukan criticism of an aspect of the temple. This might be criticism against the leadership,[5] about assumptions of the dwelling place of YHWH,[6] that it has become an idol,[7] or to express that

---

Stephen's Speech (Acts 7,2–53)', *Bib* 70 (1989); Edvin Larsson, 'Temple-Criticism and the Jewish Heritage: Some Reflections on Acts 6–7', *NTS* 39, no. 3 (1993); Wiens, *Sermon*; Alan Watson, *The Trial of Stephen: The First Christian Martyr* (Athens: University of Georgia Press, 1996); H. Alan Brehm, 'Vindicating the Rejected One: Stephen's Speech as a Critique of the Jewish Leaders', in *Early Christian Interpretation of the Scriptures of Israel: Investigations and Proposals*, ed. Craig A. Evans and James A. Sanders, JSNTSup 148 (Sheffield: Sheffield Academic, 1997); Heinz-Werner Neudorfer, 'The Speech of Stephen', in *Witness to the Gospel: The Theology of Acts*, ed. I. Howard Marshall and David Peterson (Grand Rapids: Eerdmans, 1998); Michael Bachmann, 'Die Stephanusepisode (Apg 6,1–8,3): Ihre Bedeutung für die Lukanische Sicht des jerusalemischen Tempels und des Judentums', in Verheyden, ed., *The Unity of Luke–Acts*; Peter Doble, 'Something Greater than Solomon: An Approach to Stephen's Speech', in *The Old Testament in the New: Essays in Honour of J. L. North*, ed. Steve Moyise, JSNTSup 189 (Sheffield: Sheffield Academic, 2000); Alexandru Neagoe, *The Trial of the Gospel: An Apologetic Reading of Luke's Trial Narratives*, SNTSMS 116 (Cambridge: Cambridge University Press, 2002), 152–74; James P. Sweeney, 'Stephen's Speech (Acts 7:2–53): Is it as "Anti-Temple" as Is Frequently Alleged?', *TJ* 23, no. 2 (2002); Taylor, 'Stephen'; Todd C. Penner, *In Praise of Christian Origins: Stephen and the Hellenists in Lukan Apologetic Historiography*, Emory Studies in Early Christianity (New York: T&T Clark, 2004); Huub Van De Sandt, 'The Presence and Transcendence of God: An Investigation of Acts 7,44-50 in the Light of the LXX', *ETL* 80, no. 1 (2004); Matthew Sleeman, *Geography and the Ascension Narrative in Acts*, SNTSMS 146 (Cambridge: Cambridge University Press, 2009), 139–73; Shelly Matthews, *Perfect Martyr: The Stoning of Stephen and the Construction of Christian Identity* (Oxford: Oxford University Press, 2010); Peter Doble, '"Are These Things So?" (Acts 7:1): A Narrative-Intertextual Approach to Reading Stephen's Speech', in *The Scriptures of Israel in Jewish and Christian Tradition: Essays in Honour of Maarten J. J. Menken*, ed. Bart J. Koet, Steve Moyise, and Joseph Verheyden, NovTSup 148 (Leiden: Brill, 2013).

4. Jack T. Sanders, *The Jews in Luke–Acts* (London: SCM, 1987), 248; Kilgallen, *Speech*, 89–90; F. F. Bruce, *The Book of the Acts*, NICNT (Grand Rapids: Eerdmans, 1954), 159–61; Haenchen, *Acts*, 290; Jürgen Roloff, *Die Apostelgeschichte* (Gottingen: Vandenhoeck & Ruprecht, 1981), 125; I. Howard Marshall, *The Acts of the Apostles: An Introduction and Commentary*, TNTC (Leicester: Inter-Varsity, 1980), 146.

5. E.g., Brehm, 'Rejected One', 288–96.

6. E.g., Chance, *Jerusalem*, 40–41; Marshall, 'Acts', 568, thereby revising his earlier opinion (above).

7. E.g., Walker, *Jesus*, 66–67; Witherington, *Acts*, 273; Pao, *Acts*, 207.

the gospel has gone to the Gentiles.[8] Related to this, there is a debate whether the views expressed in the speech are those of Luke or Stephen; if Stephen, then the speech is typically thought to be a Hellenistic criticism of the Jerusalem temple,[9] a view Luke does not necessarily share.

In order to interpret the speech it is important to pay attention to its narrative setting, and its use of the OT. To pre-empt the conclusions of this chapter, it argues that Stephen's speech should be read within its trial setting, addressing the charges which are brought against him; it should also be read in continuity with the words of Jesus about the temple in the Gospel, because Stephen does not speak for himself, but represents Jesus and the views of the wider Christian community. The speech's history of Israel focuses on the fulfilment of promises made to Abraham – especially of deliverance and worship (Acts 7.7) – and describes two streams of Israel: those obedient to God's will, and those disobedient. Its allusions to the OT serve to draw the hearer (and reader) of the speech into the narrative of shared history, passing judgement on the disobedient Israelites. The argument finally pivots about the two quotations from the prophets in Acts 7.42-43, 49-50: these are especially marked quotations that serve as commentary on the history, and subvert expectations by accusing Stephen's hearers of belonging to the disobedient stream of Israel. These accusations are continued in the counter-charges of Acts 7.51-53, and maintain that Stephen's audience are descendants of those who rejected God's chosen deliverers (by rejecting Jesus), and participated in false worship; these charges effectively accuse them of their own charges against Stephen.

In order to demonstrate this, the present chapter will proceed in the following way. First, the narrative setting will be defined, with attention given to reasons for viewing Stephen in continuity with Jesus and the apostles.

Second, the use of the OT will be described. This involves: (1) the evaluation of quotations, demonstrating that the two prophetic quotations are especially marked; (2) the assessment of how the history is re-told through the use of OT allusions.

Third, a case will be made for reading the speech in the way described above, focusing on how it subverts the perspective of Stephen's hearers on the history of Israel, effectively charging them with two counter-charges.

---

8. Larsson, 'Temple-Criticism'.
9. Martin Hengel, *Acts and the History of Earliest Christianity* (London: SCM, 1979), 72–75.

Finally, the details of Stephen's argument over the temple will be evaluated, focusing on its development of the themes in the laments in Luke's Gospel.

The Narrative Setting

Stephen was initially accused of blasphemy against Moses and God (Acts 6.11);[10] when he arrived before the Sanhedrin the charges were twofold – speaking against both τοῦ τόπου τοῦ ἁγίου [τούτου] and τοῦ νόμου (6.13) – with an explanatory expansion that Stephen said, Ἰησοῦς ὁ Ναζωραῖος οὗτος καταλύσει τὸν τόπον τοῦτον καὶ ἀλλάξει τὰ ἔθη ἃ παρέδωκεν ἡμῖν Μωϋσῆς (6.14).[11] These charges form the basis for the trial, even though they are from false witnesses (6.11-13) and cannot be taken at face value.

Although the outcome of the speech in 7.57 seems more characteristic of a mob lynching than a considered verdict,[12] this does not invalidate the preceding scene as a trial. The executioners' stopped ears suggest that blasphemy was the reason for the stoning, and it is entirely possible for this to be a mob reaction to Stephen's final words at the end of a formal trial.[13] In that case, the speech should answer to the charges, but some commentators argue that it is not the defence one would expect.[14] However, it has judicial characteristics, and the narrative portrays it as a reply to the charges, even if its argument is unexpected.[15] It is effectively

---

10. For Stephen's opponents see Darrell L. Bock, *Acts*, BECNT (Grand Rapids: Baker Academic, 2007), 270 n. 2.

11. For two charges, see Witherington, *Acts*, 258; Sylva, 'Meaning', 268–69; Kilgallen, *Speech*, 31–32. Earl Richard argues that there are two charges in 6.11 and two in 6.13-14; see Richard, *Acts*, 317, 24–25.

12. See the discussion in John B. Polhill, *Acts*, NAC 26 (Nashville: Broadman, 1992), 208–209. Stoning is typical for the crime; see *m. Sanh.* 6.1; 7.4.

13. This is a better explanation than Luke stitching together a mob-lynching account with a trial narrative, as argued by Hans Conzelmann, *Acts of the Apostles: A Commentary on the Acts of the Apostles*, trans. James Limburg, A. Thomas Kraabel, and Donald H. Juel, Hermeneia (Philadelphia: Fortress, 1987), 48; see also the reconstruction of Boismard, 'Etienne'. Discussions about whether the Sanhedrin had authority for execution are irrelevant if it was a mob execution; see Witherington, *Acts*, 276. For blasphemy, see Bock, *Acts*, 313–14.

14. Haenchen, *Acts*, 286–89; Conzelmann, *Acts*, 57.

15. See the discussion in Penner, *Origins*, 92, and the references in n. 106; Brehm, 'Rejected One'. For judicial characteristics, see Marion L. Soards, *The Speeches in Acts: Their Content, Context, and Concerns* (Louisville: Westminster John Knox, 1994), 58; George A. Kennedy, *New Testament Interpretation through Rhetorical Criticism* (Chapel Hill: University of North Carolina Press, 1984), 121–22.

a defence that goes on the offensive, making counter-accusations;[16] in this way, the false accusations against Stephen prepare for an expression of what Stephen does believe.

It might seem logical to use rhetorical analysis to show how the speech addresses the charges, but approaches which evaluate the speech as judicial rhetoric typically give undue weight to Acts 7.35, and create a division between 7.50 and 7.51, which is not clear in the text (see the argument from the OT below).[17] An alternative division which avoids these problems is:[18] establishment of the charges (6.8–7.1);[19] introduction to the history, setting out its goals, especially the promises made to Abraham of slavery, deliverance, and worship 'in this place' (7.2-7);[20] the speech detailing the fulfilment of these promises, building to a climax accusing the hearers of obstructing them (7.8-53).[21]

The Trials of Stephen and Jesus

The parallels between Acts 6–7 and the account of Jesus' passion in Luke 22–23 are commonly observed.[22] Several of these parallels are

16. Parsons, *Acts*, 89–90.

17. Most widely accepted is Dupont, 'Structure', who proposes: *exordium*, 7.2a; *narratio*, 7.2b-34; *propositio*, 7.35; *argumentatio*, 7.36-50; *peroratio*, 7.51-53. Witherington, *Acts*, 260–61, agrees. See also the rhetorical analysis in Robert F. Wolfe, 'Rhetorical Elements in the Speeches of Acts 7 and 17', *JOTT* 6, no. 3 (1993).

18. These divisions agree with Todd Penner, who interprets the speech in close relationship with the surrounding narrative but as epideictic rhetoric; the speech is not 'a formal response to the charges but uses the accusations as a foil to energize a speech of praise and blame' (Penner, 'Narrative', 355).

19. *Exordium* in ibid., 358–60.

20. *Narratio / partitio* in ibid., 360–63.

21. Penner's *probatio*, which he follows with a *peroration* (7.54-60); see ibid., 363–66.

22. Johnson, *Acts*, 112, 42–43; Richard I. Pervo, *The Acts of the Apostles*, Hermeneia (Philadelphia: Fortress, 2008), 195–96; M. Sabbe, 'The Son of Man Saying in Acts 7, 56', in *Les Actes des Apôtres: Traditions, rédaction, théologie*, ed. J. Kremer, Bibliotheca Ephemeridum Theologicarum Loveniensium 48 (Leuven: Leuven University Press, 1978), 251–55; Tannehill, *Narrative Unity*, 2:97–99; Joseph A. Fitzmyer, *The Acts of the Apostles: A New Translation with Introduction and Commentary*, AB 31 (New York: Doubleday, 1998), 390; Bock, *Acts*, 315; Richard, *Acts*, 281; Parsons, *Acts*, 87; Witherington, *Acts*, 253; David P. Moessner, '"The Christ Must Suffer": New Light on the Jesus, Stephen, Paul Parallels in Luke–Acts', *NovT* 28, no. 3 (1986): 234. The list of parallels below is drawn from these works. Others note parallels between Stephen and Zechariah son of Jehoiada; see Isaac Kalimi, 'The Murders of the Messengers: Stephen Versus Zechariah and the Ethical Values of "New" versus "Old" Testament', *AusBR* 56 (2008); Matthews, *Martyr*, 72–73. They

quite general and could be true of any martyr's trial: both accounts have (1) a trial before the Sanhedrin (Acts 6.12; Lk. 22.66); (2) disapproving listeners (Acts 7.54, 57; Lk. 22.63); and (3) no formal sentence (Lk. 22.71–23.1; Acts 7.57). More significantly, at their death:[23] (4) both refer to the Son of Man (Acts 7.56; Lk. 22.69); (5) both men pray loudly (Acts 7.60; Lk. 23.46); (6) both pray for forgiveness for their executioners (Lk. 23.34; Acts 7.60);[24] and (7) both commend their spirit to God (Lk. 23.46; Acts 7.59).

This link between the trials of Stephen and Jesus makes Stephen represent Jesus, such that this is effectively a trial of Jesus and his words about the temple, placed in a setting which permits fuller exploration.[25] This idea is confirmed by the inclusion in Stephen's trial of several elements of the trial of Jesus which are *not* reported in Luke's Gospel, but which Matthew and Mark *do* report:[26] (1) both are charged with blasphemy (Acts 6.11; Mk 14.64); (2) false witnesses present the accusations (Act 6.13; Mk 14.56);[27] (3) the charge of Jesus claiming to destroy the temple (Acts 6.14) is similar to a charge in Mk 14.58, with both using καταλύω; (4) both Acts 7.48 and Mk 14.58 refer to the temple as made with hands (χειροποίητος); and (5) both Stephen and Jesus are interrogated by the High Priest (Acts 7.1; Mk 14.60-61).[28]

---

are not as close as the Jesus parallels, but a reader might make a connection because of references to Zechariah in Lk. 13. Thomas Brodie's parallels to Naboth (as part of a larger scheme of mimesis) are unconvincing; see Brodie, 'Internalization'.

23. Other suggested parallels are less persuasive: both are executed outside the city (Lk. 23.33; Acts 7.58), but by different methods; both mention garments (Acts 7.58; Lk. 23.34), but Jesus' are divided, and Stephen's executioners lay theirs down; both were buried by the devout (Acts 8.2; Lk. 23.50-53).

24. This prayer seems to interrupt the flow of the narrative in Lk. 23.34, and several early and important MSS omit it ($\mathfrak{P}^{75}$ B D* W Θ etc), leading some commentators to reject it (Fitzmyer, *Luke*, 2:1503–504; Metzger, *Commentary*, 154). But it should be retained because it is consistent with the Lukan narrative, and its omission can be explained by later anti-Semitic feeling; see the discussion in Marshall, *Gospel*, 867–68; Johnson, *Luke*, 876; see also the detailed discussion in Nathan Eubank, 'A Disconcerting Prayer: On the Originality of Luke 23:34a', *JBL* 129, no. 3 (2010).

25. Tannehill, *Narrative Unity*, 2:94; Walker, *Jesus*, 65. Bruce notes that it is postponed for discussion in the setting of the early church; see Bruce, *Acts*, 189.

26. Camille Focant, 'Du Fils de l'homme assis (Lc 22,69) au Fils de l'homme debout (Ac 7,56)', in Verheyden, ed., *The Unity of Luke–Acts*, 570–72. Of course, it is not necessary for Luke's readers to note these.

27. Luke only has a remnant of this saying in Lk. 22.71.

28. For this list, see Witherington, *Acts*, 253.

The relationship between Stephen's and Jesus' death allows all the laments of Luke's Gospel to become a manifest context for the interpretation of Stephen's speech.

Stephen and the Christian Community

The case for Stephen expressing Jesus' views would be weakened if Stephen represented the views of the Hellenist Christians alone (as in Acts 6.1-6) and not the whole Christian community, and many scholars do think that Stephen was exclusively Hellenist. This view builds on the assumption that the Hellenists and the Hebrews were two Jewish Christian communities, separated by different language and theology, with the more liberal Hellenists denying a place for the temple in the post-Easter era.[29] In criticising the temple, Stephen represents their views,[30] and as a result the Hellenists were scattered in Acts 8.1 and undertook a Gentile mission which made way for Pauline Christianity.[31]

However, Steve Walton argues persuasively that Stephen represented the entire Christian community, not just the Hellenists.[32] He observes that although the Hellenists came from the diaspora, they were not as separate from the Hebrews as commonly asserted:[33] the Hellenists would speak

---

29. Hengel, *Judaism*, 1:313–14; idem, *Acts*, 72–73. Others taking this view include: Philip F. Esler, *Community and Gospel in Luke–Acts: The Social and Political Motivations of Lucan Theology* (Cambridge: Cambridge University Press, 1987), 136–39; Conzelmann, *Acts*, 44–45; Haenchen, *Acts*, 264–68; Bruce, 'Apologia', 38. For further bibliography, see Craig C. Hill, *Hellenists and Hebrews: Reappraising Division within the Earliest Church* (Minneapolis: Fortress, 1992), 12–16; for detailed discussion, see Penner, *Origins*, 23–29; Steve Walton, 'How Mighty a Minority Were the Hellenists?', in *Earliest Christian History: History, Literature, and Theology. Essays from the Tyndale Fellowship in Honor of Martin Hengel*, ed. Michael F. Bird and Jason Maston, WUNT 2/320 (Tübingen: Mohr Siebeck, 2012), 306–308.

30. Whether the criticism concerns building the temple, or contemporary attitudes to a divinely appointed temple; the latter is closer to Martin Hengel, *Between Jesus and Paul: Studies in the Earliest History of Christianity* (London: SCM, 1983), 22–24; see Walton, 'Hellenists', 306–307.

31. James Dunn argues that Acts 7 is not Lukan theology but comes from a source and shows Stephen's use of Jesus traditions in arguing with Hellenistic synagogues, showing the temple was an idol. James D. G. Dunn, *Beginning from Jerusalem*, Christianity in the Making 2 (Grand Rapids: Eerdmans, 2009), 259, 62, 64, 66–67, 72–73.

32. Walton, 'Hellenists'.

33. Against Dunn, *Jerusalem*, 246–51, who regards Hellenists as returned diaspora Jews, still committed to temple and torah, but less conservative than Hebraic Jews.

some Aramaic;[34] Acts 6.1 suggests both groups were in regular contact,[35] with the persecution of the Jerusalem Christians in Acts 3–7 surely bringing the two groups together; and if the Hellenists returned to Jerusalem for religious reasons (which seems likely), then their view of the temple would have been more positive than usually claimed.[36] There is insufficient evidence to maintain that Hebrew Christians and Hellenists had significant theological differences (a difference cannot be extrapolated from the false charges against Stephen, or his response).[37] As such, it is likely that Stephen represented the entire early Christian community,[38] and that the charges were also against this whole community,[39] whose preaching was likely to have included the temple and Jesus' preaching about it.

Quotations in Acts 6–7

Old Testament quotations and allusions are significant to Acts 6–7 because of their sheer number,[40] and their role in directing the reader's interpretation of the history of Israel. The quotations are crucial, and they need to be described before the allusions. There are thirteen quotations: two are from the prophets, the others are all from the Pentateuch. In most cases the Pentateuch quotations are of spoken words, either by God (Acts 7.3, 5, 6-7, 32, 33, 34) or others (Acts 7.27-28, 35, 37, 40). They will be described in turn with an emphasis on their size and introductory formulae.[41]

Quotations of God Speaking
(i) Acts 7.3 (Twenty Words from Genesis 12.1).
The differences in wording are minor, and the first words of the quotation (referring to God speaking) function as introduction.[42]

---

34. Walton, 'Hellenists', 314–15, and references there.
35. The Christian community is described as unified in Acts 5.12; see ibid., 316.
36. Ibid.
37. Ibid., 317–20; Hill, *Hellenists*, 32–40, 49–50.
38. Witherington, *Acts*, 258–59.
39. Larsson, 'Temple-Criticism', 384.
40. All the quotations are from the LXX; see Richard, *Acts*, 354–55.
41. They are all noted by NA[28], and discussed in the commentaries. See especially Richard, *Acts*, 41–135; Fitzmyer, *Acts*, 370–84; Marshall, 'Acts', 557–68; Bock, *Acts*, 282–304; Johnson, *Acts*, 115–33. For quotations from Genesis, see Peter Mallen, 'Genesis in Luke–Acts', in *Genesis in the New Testament*, ed. Maarten J. J. Menken and Steve Moyise, LNTS 466 (London: Bloomsbury T&T Clark, 2012), 75–77.
42. There is an equivalent to δεῦρο in the Pseudo-Jonathan Targum which may mean it is a variant reading rather than a Lukan adaptation (C. K. Barrett, *A Critical*

Gen. 12.1	Acts 7.3
Καὶ εἶπεν κύριος τῷ Αβραμ	καὶ εἶπεν πρὸς αὐτόν·
Ἔξελθε ἐκ τῆς γῆς σου	ἔξελθε ἐκ τῆς γῆς σου
καὶ ἐκ τῆς συγγενείας σου	καὶ [ἐκ] τῆς συγγενείας σου,
καὶ ἐκ τοῦ οἴκου τοῦ πατρός σου	καὶ δεῦρο
εἰς τὴν γῆν, ἣν ἄν σοι δείξω·	εἰς τὴν γῆν ἣν ἄν σοι δείξω.

(ii) Acts 7.5 (Ten Words from Genesis 17.8 or 48.4).
This quotation of indirect speech has no introductory formula, and while clearly a quotation, it is difficult to be sure which text it refers to, Gen. 12.7; 13.15; 17.8; 48.4 are all possible. Acts 7.5 differs from them all by using the infinitive δοῦναι (not δώσω), and third-person phrases. While Gen. 12.7 could be favoured because of its proximity to other verses alluded to in this section of the speech, it does not contain μετὰ σὲ or εἰς κατάσχεσιν; Gen. 13.15 must be rejected for the same reason.

Gen. 17.8	Gen. 48.4	Acts 7.5
...	...	...
δώσω σοι	δώσω σοι	δοῦναι αὐτῷ
		εἰς κατάσχεσιν
	τὴν γῆν ταύτην	αὐτήν
καὶ τῷ σπέρματί	καὶ τῷ σπέρματί	καὶ τῷ σπέρματι
σου	σου	αὐτοῦ
μετὰ σὲ	μετὰ σὲ	μετ' αὐτόν,
τὴν γῆν,		...
...		
εἰς κατάσχεσιν	εἰς κατάσχεσιν	
αἰώνιον ...	αἰώνιον.	

Genesis 17.8 or 48.4 are more likely because they have ten words in common;[43] the word order is closer to Gen. 48.4 (which contains τὴν γῆν ταύτην, a phrase in Acts 7.4 represented by αὐτήν in 7.5), but this verse is addressed to Jacob, not Abraham. Overall Gen. 17.8 is closest, but a reader might regard it as a quotation to the promises in general because sufficient relevance would be achieved in this more immediate context.[44]

and Exegetical Commentary on the Acts of the Apostles, ICC, 2 vols., [Edinburgh: T&T Clark, 1994–98], 1:342). B and D omit ἐκ from ἐκ τῆς συγγενείας σου: this is significant as these MSS often disagree, and it is the more difficult reading, but the weight of manuscript evidence suggests ἐκ is retained.

43. Ignoring grammatical alterations, eleven words if αὐτήν = τὴν γῆν.
44. Richard, *Acts*, 45–48, notes all these texts. NA[28]; Mallen, 'Genesis', 75, note 17.8; 48.4. NA[27] adds 13.15. Johnson, *Acts*, 115, notes all but 12.7 and prefers

(iii) Acts 7.6-7 (Twenty-four Words from Genesis 15.13-14)
The changes to the Genesis text are relatively minor, and the section using indirect speech requires that the second person references become third person; it is introduced by a reference to God speaking.

Gen. 15.13	Acts 7.6
...πάροικον ἔσται τὸ σπέρμα σου ἐν γῇ οὐκ ἰδίᾳ, καὶ δουλώσουσιν αὐτοὺς καὶ κακώσουσιν αὐτοὺς καὶ ταπεινώσουσιν αὐτοὺς τετρακόσια ἔτη.	...ἔσται τὸ σπέρμα αὐτοῦ πάροικον ἐν γῇ ἀλλοτρίᾳ καὶ δουλώσουσιν αὐτὸ καὶ κακώσουσιν ἔτη τετρακόσια·
Gen. 15.14	Acts 7.7
τὸ δὲ ἔθνος, ᾧ ἐὰν δουλεύσωσιν, κρινῶ ἐγώ· μετὰ δὲ ταῦτα ἐξελεύσονται ...	καὶ τὸ ἔθνος ᾧ ἐὰν δουλεύσουσιν κρινῶ ἐγώ, ὁ θεὸς εἶπεν, καὶ μετὰ ταῦτα ἐξελεύσονται ...

(iv) Acts 7.32 (Twelve Words from Exodus 3.6)
The alterations from the LXX are minor, and ἐγένετο φωνὴ κυρίου in 7.31 acts as an introductory formula.[45]

Exod. 3.6	Acts 7.32
... Ἐγώ εἰμι ὁ θεὸς τοῦ πατρός σου, θεὸς Ἀβρααμ καὶ θεὸς Ισαακ καὶ θεὸς Ιακωβ ...	ἐγὼ ὁ θεὸς τῶν πατέρων σου, ὁ θεὸς Ἀβραάμ καὶ Ἰσαάκ καὶ Ἰακώβ ...

Gen. 48.4. Soards, *Speeches*, 62; Fitzmyer, *Acts*, 371; Keener, *Acts*, 2:1358, prefer Gen. 17.8; Conzelmann, *Acts*, 52 thinks it is a free quotation. Barrett, *Acts*, 1:344, argues that Luke is giving the sense of them all.

45. The variations from LXX are discussed in Richard, *Acts*, 91–96. Max Wilcox appeals to the Samaritan Pentateuch for the plural τῶν πατέρων (Max Wilcox, *The Semitisms of Acts* [Oxford: Clarendon, 1965], 29–30), but the plural form is a favourite phrase of Luke's (Richard, *Acts*, 93), and Samaritan influence should be rejected (Barrett, *Acts*, 1:360–61). For a discussion and rejection of Samaritan influence in Acts 7, see Barrett, 'History', 61–64.

(v) Acts 7.33 (Fourteen Words from Exodus 3.5)
The alterations from the LXX are minor, and εἶπεν...ὁ κύριος functions as an introductory formula.[46]

Exod. 3.5	Acts 7.33
...	εἶπεν δὲ αὐτῷ ὁ κύριος·
λῦσαι τὸ ὑπόδημα	λῦσον τὸ ὑπόδημα
ἐκ τῶν ποδῶν σου·	τῶν ποδῶν σου,
ὁ γὰρ τόπος,	ὁ γὰρ τόπος
ἐν ᾧ σὺ ἕστηκας,	ἐφ' ᾧ ἕστηκας
γῆ ἁγία ἐστίν.	γῆ ἁγία ἐστίν.

(vi) Acts 7.34 (Seventeen Words from Exodus 3.7-8 and Six Words from Exodus 3.10)
This is a highly edited quotation with significant omissions (including the reference to Pharaoh, and to YHWH's knowledge of the Israelites' distress); it has some minor changes to the LXX.[47] The Introductory formula is that of Acts 7.33.

Exod. 3.7	Acts 7.34
...	
Ἰδὼν εἶδον τὴν κάκωσιν τοῦ λαοῦ	ἰδὼν εἶδον τὴν κάκωσιν τοῦ λαοῦ
μου τοῦ ἐν Αἰγύπτῳ καὶ	μου τοῦ ἐν Αἰγύπτῳ καὶ
τῆς κραυγῆς αὐτῶν ἀκήκοα	τοῦ στεναγμοῦ αὐτῶν ἤκουσα,
...	
Exod. 3.8	
καὶ κατέβην ἐξελέσθαι αὐτοὺς	καὶ κατέβην ἐξελέσθαι αὐτούς·
...	
Exod. 3.10	
καὶ νῦν δεῦρο ἀποστείλω σε	καὶ νῦν δεῦρο ἀποστείλω σε
πρὸς Φαραω βασιλέα Αἰγύπτου,	εἰς Αἴγυπτον.
...	

Quotations of Israelites Speaking
(i) Acts 7.27-28 (Nineteen Words from Exodus 2.14)
This is an exact quotation; a reference to direct speech acts as an introductory formula.

---

46. For the differences to LXX, see Barrett, *Acts*, 1:361; Richard, *Acts*, 97–98.
47. Richard, *Acts*, 99; Barrett, *Acts*, 1:362.

Exod. 2.14	Acts 7.27-28
ὁ δὲ εἶπεν	ὁ δὲ ἀδικῶν τὸν πλησίον ἀπώσατο αὐτὸν εἰπών·
<u>Τίς σε κατέστησεν ἄρχοντα</u> <u>καὶ δικαστὴν ἐφ' ἡμῶν;</u> <u>μὴ ἀνελεῖν με σὺ θέλεις,</u> <u>ὃν τρόπον ἀνεῖλες ἐχθὲς</u> <u>τὸν Αἰγύπτιον;</u> ...	<u>τίς σε κατέστησεν ἄρχοντα</u> <u>καὶ δικαστὴν ἐφ' ἡμῶν;</u> <u>μὴ ἀνελεῖν με σὺ θέλεις</u> <u>ὃν τρόπον ἀνεῖλες ἐχθὲς</u> <u>τὸν Αἰγύπτιον;</u>

(ii) Acts 7.35 (Six Words from Exodus 2.14)
These are the same words as Acts 7.27 with a preceding reference to direct speech.

Exod. 2.14	Acts 7.35
...	...
<u>Τίς σε κατέστησεν ἄρχοντα</u> <u>καὶ δικαστὴν</u> ἐφ' ἡμῶν; ...	<u>τίς σε κατέστησεν ἄρχοντα</u> <u>καὶ δικαστήν;</u> ...

(iii) Acts 7.37 (Eleven Words from Deuteronomy 18.15)
This is not as close to the LXX as the quotation of Deut. 18.15 in Acts 3.22 but it is still clearly recognisable. It is introduced with a reference to Moses speaking.[48]

Deut. 18.15	Acts 7.37
	...
<u>προφήτην</u> <u>ἐκ τῶν ἀδελφῶν σου ὡς ἐμὲ</u> <u>ἀναστήσει σοι</u> κύριος ὁ θεός σου, αὐτοῦ ἀκούσεσθε	<u>προφήτην</u> ὑμῖν <u>ἀναστήσει ὁ θεὸς</u> <u>ἐκ τῶν ἀδελφῶν</u> ὑμῶν <u>ὡς ἐμέ.</u>

---

48. Max Wilcox argues some of the word order is closer Deut. 18.18, but there is no reason to favour this verse; see Wilcox, *Semitisms*, 33. The call to hear the prophet is present in some texts (C D E and many miniscules) but it looks like a scribal addition from the LXX; see Metzger, *Commentary*, 307.

(iv) Acts 7.40 (Twenty Words from Exodus 32.1 or 32.23)
The quotation has some differences to the LXX of both of these verses and it is not possible to decide between them;[49] the only introductory formula is εἰπόντες τῷ Ἀαρών.[50]

Exod. 32.1	Exod. 32.23	Acts 7.40
...λέγουσιν αὐτῷ...	λέγουσιν γάρ μοι	εἰπόντες τῷ Ἀαρών·
ποίησον ἡμῖν θεούς,	Ποίησον ἡμῖν θεούς,	ποίησον ἡμῖν θεούς
οἳ προπορεύσονται	οἳ προπορεύσονται	οἳ προπορεύσονται
ἡμῶν·	ἡμῶν·	ἡμῶν·
ὁ γὰρ Μωυσῆς οὗτος	ὁ γὰρ Μωυσῆς οὗτος	ὁ γὰρ Μωϋσῆς οὗτος,
ὁ ἄνθρωπος,	ὁ ἄνθρωπος,	
ὃς ἐξήγαγεν ἡμᾶς	ὃς ἐξήγαγεν ἡμᾶς	ὃς ἐξήγαγεν ἡμᾶς
ἐξ Αἰγύπτου,	ἐξ Αἰγύπτου,	ἐκ γῆς Αἰγύπτου,
οὐκ οἴδαμεν,	οὐκ οἴδαμεν,	οὐκ οἴδαμεν
τί γέγονεν αὐτῷ.	τί γέγονεν αὐτῷ.	τί ἐγένετο αὐτῷ.

Narrative Quotations without Speech
(i) Acts 7.18 (Ten Words from Exodus 1.8)
There are ten words in common if ἐπ' Αἴγυπτον is included in Acts 7.18;[51] there is no introductory marker.

Exod. 1.8	Acts 7.18
	ἄχρι οὗ
Ἀνέστη δὲ βασιλεὺς ἕτερος	ἀνέστη βασιλεὺς ἕτερος
ἐπ' Αἴγυπτον,	[ἐπ' Αἴγυπτον]
ὃς οὐκ ᾔδει τὸν Ιωσηφ.	ὃς οὐκ ᾔδει τὸν Ἰωσήφ.

49. D E Ψ and other texts have γέγονεν in Acts 7.40, but this is likely to be an emendation to bring it into line with the LXX; see Barrett, *Acts*, 1:367. Twenty words includes grammatical alterations.
50. Marshall ('Acts', 564) and Van De Sandt ('Presence', 3) both note Exod. 32.1 only.
51. It is absent in some texts (including 𝔓[45vid] D E 𝔐), notably those of Western origin, but present in Western and Alexandrian texts, including 𝔓[33vid, 74] ℵ A B C Ψ. Barrett (*Acts*, 1:352) thinks that its omission in the Western text is likely to be original because of the influence of the LXX on later copyists but Metzger (*Commentary*, 302–303) is less sure.

Quotations from the Prophets

(i) Acts 7.42-43 (Thirty-Five Words from Amos 5.25-27)

Despite the well-described differences to the MT, this is very close to the LXX.[52] There are differences (which are worth detailing because of the importance of the quotation): (1) the inversion of the phrases ἐν τῇ ἐρήμῳ and τεσσαράκοντα ἔτη;[53] (2) the omission of αὐτῶν after τοὺς τύπους; (3) οὓς ἐποιήσατε ἑαυτοῖς becomes οὓς ἐποιήσατε προσκυνεῖν αὐτοῖς, but this clarifies the sense; (4) the change of Δαμασκοῦ into Βαβυλῶνος.[54] Only the last is important. The quotation is introduced with the strong formula γέγραπται ἐν βίβλῳ τῶν προφητῶν.

Amos 5.25-26	Acts 7.42-43
	...
μὴ σφάγια καὶ θυσίας	μὴ σφάγια καὶ θυσίας
προσηνέγκατέ μοι	προσηνέγκατέ μοι
ἐν τῇ ἐρήμῳ	ἔτη τεσσεράκοντα
τεσσαράκοντα ἔτη,	ἐν τῇ ἐρήμῳ,
οἶκος Ἰσραηλ;	οἶκος Ἰσραήλ;
²⁶καὶ ἀνελάβετε τὴν σκηνὴν τοῦ Μολοχ	⁴³καὶ ἀνελάβετε τὴν σκηνὴν τοῦ Μόλοχ
καὶ τὸ ἄστρον τοῦ θεοῦ ὑμῶν Ραιφαν,	καὶ τὸ ἄστρον τοῦ θεοῦ [ὑμῶν] Ῥαιφάν,
τοὺς τύπους αὐτῶν,	τοὺς τύπους
οὓς ἐποιήσατε ἑαυτοῖς.	οὓς ἐποιήσατε προσκυνεῖν αὐτοῖς,
²⁷καὶ μετοικιῶ ὑμᾶς ἐπέκεινα Δαμασκοῦ,	καὶ μετοικιῶ ὑμᾶς ἐπέκεινα Βαβυλῶνος.
...	

(ii) Acts 7.49-50 (Twenty-Eight Words from Isaiah 66.1-2)

There are several changes: (1) λέγει κύριος is moved later in the quotation; (2) the replacement of ποῖος with τίς;[55] (3) the replacement of γάρ with οὐχί to create a question (the only significant change); and (4) the change

---

52. The principal changes to MT are in the names for the gods. For comparison of Acts, LXX and MT, see Marshall, 'Acts', 565; Barrett, *Acts*, 1:369–71. For Acts and LXX, see Richard, *Acts*, 124–26.

53. Though some Greek MSS have Luke's order rather than the order preserved in the LXX: see Richard, *Acts*, 125.

54. In addition there are MSS with the omission of ὑμῶν after τὸ ἄστρον τοῦ θεοῦ (e.g., B D), and with variant spellings of Ῥαιφάν (e.g., ℵ* B), but there is enough evidence to accept the reading as given above. See Barrett, *Acts*, 1:369.

55. D h have ποῖος to fit in with the LXX.

of the order and position of ταῦτα and πάντα. This quotation is also introduced by a strong formula, καθὼς ὁ προφήτης λέγει.

Isa. 66.1-2	Acts 7.49-50
¹Οὕτως λέγει κύριος	
Ὁ οὐρανός μοι θρόνος,	⁴⁹ὁ οὐρανός μοι θρόνος,
ἡ δὲ γῆ ὑποπόδιον	ἡ δὲ γῆ ὑποπόδιον
τῶν ποδῶν μου·	τῶν ποδῶν μου·
ποῖον οἶκον οἰκοδομήσετέ μοι;	ποῖον οἶκον οἰκοδομήσετέ μοι,
	λέγει κύριος,
ἢ ποῖος τόπος	ἢ τίς τόπος
τῆς καταπαύσεώς μου;	τῆς καταπαύσεώς μου;
²πάντα γὰρ	
ταῦτα ἐποίησεν	⁵⁰οὐχὶ
ἡ χείρ μου,	ἡ χείρ μου
...	ἐποίησεν ταῦτα πάντα;

Summary
All eleven quotations before Acts 7.42 are from the Pentateuch narrative, and they are used to tell the story of Israel; none of them have a strong introductory formula, and they typically repeat speech. In comparison, the two final quotations stand out: they are among the longest (only the combined quotations of Exod. 3.5-10 are longer, but this is not a continuous quotation); they are the only two from the prophets; they are introduced by the strongest introductory formulae; and they critique the surrounding historical narrative rather than tell its story.[56]

Allusions and the History of Israel

In addition to the quotations, Stephen's history is told through frequent references to the OT story, and a handful of allusions to other specific OT texts. It is helpful to examine the whole speech to identify which texts a reader would access in seeking relevance, even though this is a lengthy process.

The Charges Against Stephen (Acts 6.11–7.1)
There are few allusions: μάρτυρας ψευδεῖς (6.13) would remind a reader of the criticised practice in the LXX, because there are not enough lexical

---

56. The quotation of Deut. 18.15 in Acts 7.37 is also a form of commentary on the narrative, but it still sits within the narrative flow.

or conceptual links to any specific text;[57] Stephen's face appearing like an angel (6.15) could evoke Moses' transformation in Exod. 34.29-35 because of the reference to Moses in 6.14 and the familiarity of the account;[58] the inability of Stephen's enemies to stand against Stephen's wisdom and Spirit would probably recall the similar language in Lk. 21.15.

Abraham (Acts 7.2-8)

The distinctive phrase, Ὁ θεὸς τῆς δόξης (Acts 7.2) only occurs elsewhere in Ps. 28.3; despite God thundering in the psalm (ὁ θεὸς τῆς δόξης ἐβρόντησεν) but appearing in Acts (Ὁ θεὸς τῆς δόξης ὤφθη), the phrase is enough to point to the psalm.[59]

Stephen's description of Abraham leaving Mesopotamia (7.2-4) has well-known historical inconsistencies to the Genesis account, meaning it is difficult to press allusions too tightly.[60] David Peterson is probably right that the account refers to the whole story of Gen. 11.31–12.5:[61] it is likely that God's appearance in Acts 7.2 refers to Gen. 12.1 (not 12.7) because Acts 7.3 quotes Gen. 12.1 (not 12.7),[62] and Acts 7.4 is focused on the events of Gen. 11.31-32; 12.5.[63]

In Acts 7.5, the reference to childlessness evokes Gen. 16.1;[64] the lack of land possession in 7.5 is likely to evoke a motif of promises that remain unfulfilled beyond the Abraham story because its distinctive κληρονομία occurs frequently in Numbers (its only Genesis occurrence is 31.14,

---

57. E.g., Exod. 20.16; Prov. 14.5; 24.28. For LXX verses, see NA[28]; Barrett, *Acts*, 1:327 (who adds Pss. 26.12; 34.11).

58. There are other transformations in the LXX (e.g., Gen. 33.10; 1 Kgdms 29.9; 2 Kgdms 14.17; Est. 5.2 and Exod. 34.29-35). See the discussion in Barrett, *Acts*, 1:329–30.

59. E.g., NA[28]; Richard, *Acts*, 39–40; Marshall, 'Acts', 556; Bock, *Acts*, 281–82. For Kilgallen, *Speech*, 122, it is Lukan with some influence from the psalm, and it is rejected by Barrett, *Acts*, 1:341. Other possible texts do not have the article twice (e.g., Est. 13.14; *Pss. Sol.* 11.6; Bar. 5.1; Ezek. 10.22).

60. For differences, see Fitzmyer, *Acts*, 369–70. Some Jewish texts state Terah died before Abraham left (Bock, *Acts*, 284) and Luke might have followed them (Fitzmyer, *Acts*, 369–70). But such differences would not have concerned the ancient reader, as Parsons, *Acts*, 90 notes.

61. David G. Peterson, *The Acts of the Apostles*, PNTC (Nottingham: Apollos; Grand Rapids Eerdmans, 2009), 247.

62. Against Marshall, 'Acts', 556; Conzelmann, *Acts*, 51–52; Mallen, 'Genesis', 75.

63. NA[28]; Marshall, 'Acts', 557. Genesis 15.7 is a possible parallel (as Bock, *Acts*, 283), but this is not as obvious as references to Gen. 11–12.

64. NA[28]. Mallen, 'Genesis', 75, prefers Gen. 15.2, which is also possible.

but that shares little with Acts 7.5).⁶⁵ This on-going lack of fulfilment is emphasised by the use of the distinctive οὐδὲ βῆμα ποδός from Deut. 2.5,⁶⁶ which continues to pull attention away from the Abraham story.

Acts 7.6-7 quotes Genesis 15, and also refers to Exod. 2.22 (ἐν γῇ ἀλλοτρίᾳ)⁶⁷ and Exod. 3.12, where Luke's καὶ λατρεύσουσίν μοι ἐν τῷ τόπῳ τούτῳ adapts λατρεύσετε τῷ θεῷ ἐν τῷ ὄρει τούτῳ.⁶⁸ By changing the final phrase to τῷ τόπῳ τούτῳ, a link is created with τοῦ τόπου τοῦ ἁγίου [τούτου] in Acts 6.13.⁶⁹ Acts 7.8 probably refers to the covenant and circumcision in Gen. 17.10, 13,⁷⁰ and the birth of the patriarchs described in Gen. 21.1-5; 25.19-26; 29.31–30.24; 35.16-18;⁷¹ but it is unlikely that a reader would engage with specific texts, sufficient relevance would be obtained through the stories themselves.

Joseph (Acts 7.9-16)
Acts 7.9-10 re-tells the story from several Genesis verses, adapting details: it has patriarchs jealous of Joseph (not the brothers, as Gen. 37.11), and Joseph sold to Egypt (not to Ishmaelites, as Gen. 37.28). It also echoes ὃν ἀπέδοσθε εἰς Αἴγυπτον from Gen. 45.4, and ἦν κύριος μετά Ιωσηφ from Gen. 39.21 (which is more likely than Gen. 39.2-3 because it contains ἔδωκεν αὐτῷ χάριν).⁷² While other phrases may also find echoes (κατέστησεν αὐτὸν ἐφ' ὅλης γῆς Αἰγύπτου in Gen. 41.43; ἐναντίον Φαραω βασιλέως Αἰγύπτου in Gen. 41.46),⁷³ the verses are located together and relevance would likely be sought in the wider context of the story of

---

65. Its cognates occur more widely, see Marshall, 'Acts', 557.
66. NA²⁸; Richard, *Acts*, 46–47; Marshall, 'Acts', 557. It is possibly an unconscious allusion for Barrett, *Acts*, 1:343.
67. NA²⁸; Richard, *Acts*, 49–51.
68. NA²⁷; Marshall, 'Acts', 558.
69. Τούτου is omitted by significant texts in Acts 6.13 but its presence is not essential for the link.
70. Richard, *Acts*, 54. Διαθήκην περιτομῆς does not occur in the LXX.
71. Marshall, 'Acts', 558; NA²⁷ (NA²⁸ omits Gen. 29.31–30.24; 35.16-18). Mallen, 'Genesis', 76, notes Gen. 17.10-14; 21.2-4; 25.26; 35.23-26.
72. See NA²⁸; Richard, *Acts*, 61; Fitzmyer, *Acts*, 373, though Fitzmyer prefers Gen. 39.2 to 39.21. Haenchen, *Acts*, 279, notes references to Gen. 37; Mallen, 'Genesis', 76, has 37.2-3, 21, 23.
73. Genesis 45.8 has verbal parallels to Joseph as ruler over Egypt and all of Pharaoh's house but it is a less likely candidate because it is from later in Genesis. NA²⁸ notes all of these, as does Richard, *Acts*, 62–63. Mallen, 'Genesis', 76, records Gen. 41.33-44. Against Barrett, *Acts*, 1:347, Ps. 104.21 is not closer lexically, and lacks the volume of Genesis.

Gen. 41.38-45.[74] The famine in Egypt and Canaan (Acts 7.11) refers to the story of Gen. 41.54; 42.5 without remarkable lexical parallels.[75] Acts 7.12 adapts ἀκήκοα ὅτι ἔστιν σῖτος ἐν Αἰγύπτῳ from Gen. 42.2,[76] though effectively referring to the story in the wider context (e.g., Gen. 42.1-4).[77]

The rest of the Joseph Story passes quickly through the events of Genesis 45–46, and effectively evokes the whole narrative rather than specific texts, though several verses are closely associated: ἀνεγνωρίζετο τοῖς ἀδελφοῖς αὐτοῦ in Gen. 45.1;[78] the events of Gen. 45.2, 16;[79] the events of Gen. 45.9-11; 46.27 in Acts 7.14;[80] Gen. 46.3-4, 6 and Jacob's journey in Acts 7.15;[81] and the report of Jacob's death in Exod. 1.6.[82] The burial of the patriarchs in Acts 7.16 refers to the story in Gen. 33.19; 50.13,[83] and echoes the details of the purchase of the tomb and transport of bodies in Gen. 23.16 and Josh. 24.32,[84] but there are some historical changes to the OT text here, notably in the reference to Shechem.[85]

---

74. Barrett, *Acts*, 1:347. However, Fitzmyer, *Acts*, 373 argues that Ps. 104.16-22 is closer lexically, but a reader is more likely to focus on Genesis. It is possible that a well-established tradition of Joseph stories was used; there are examples of Jewish literature having motifs drawn from Joseph's life; see Brehm, 'Rejected One', 278–82.

75. NA[28]; Richard, *Acts*, 64–65; Marshall, 'Acts', 559. Psalm 36.19 does not have sufficient parallels to draw attention away from Genesis (against Conzelmann, *Acts*, 52; Bock, *Acts*, 287); Ps. 104.16-22 is unlikely because its distinctive vocabulary is absent; the supposed reference to this psalm in Acts 7.10 does not increase volume because the order of events is reversed in the psalm.

76. NA[28]; Marshall, 'Acts', 559; Barrett, *Acts*, 1:348–49.

77. Richard, *Acts*, 68; Fitzmyer, *Acts*, 373 (Gen. 42.3-5); Mallen, 'Genesis', 76 (Gen. 42.1-2).

78. NA[28]; Richard, *Acts*, 69. Its ἀναγνωρίζομαι is related to ἀναγνωρίζω and both are *hapax legomena*; ἀναγνωρίζω is preferred by most MSS in Acts 7.13 and is the better reading (against Barrett, *Acts*, 1:349).

79. NA[28] (Gen. 45.16 only); Richard, *Acts*, 70.

80. For both references: NA[28]; Richard, *Acts*, 70–73. For Gen. 45.9-11: Barrett, *Acts*, 1:350. For Gen. 46.27: Bock, *Acts*, 288. Note that the LXX has 75 people coming to Egypt but the MT has 70; see Marshall, 'Acts', 559. Exodus 1.5 also refers to the number of people coming but has less volume.

81. For Gen. 46.3-4: NA[28]. For Gen. 46.6: Richard, *Acts*, 72. For Gen. 46.1-7: Marshall, 'Acts', 559.

82. Exodus 1.6 refers to other ancestors and is closer than Gen. 49.33, Marshall, 'Acts', 559.

83. NA[28]; Richard, *Acts*, 73; Bock, *Acts*, 288.

84. NA[28] (including Gen. 23.3ff.); Richard, *Acts*, 73. Mallen prefers Gen. 50.12, 13 with Luke adapting the location to Shechem; see Mallen, 'Genesis', 77.

85. For historical differences, see Sterling, 'Scriptures', 211; Marshall, 'Acts', 559–60; Luke is probably following other Jewish tradition; see the discussion in

Moses Story (Acts 7.17-43)

Acts 7.17-19 abbreviates the story of Exodus 1, omitting the forced labour, power of the Israelites, and Egyptian fear. Certain phrases point to specific texts: the verbs αὐξάνω and πληθύνω in Acts 7.17 point to Exod. 1.7;[86] and Acts 7.18 quotes Exod. 1.8. The lexical similarity of Acts 7.19 to specific verses (κατασοφίζομαι in Exod. 1.10;[87] ζωογονέω in Exod. 1.22)[88] serves to anchor 7.19 to the whole story of Exod. 1.9-22.

Acts 7.20-29 tells the story of Exodus 2. Moses' beauty (ἀστεῖος) and the three months shelter (7.20) come from Exod. 2.2; his discovery and adoption (7.21) come from Exod. 2.5, 10; and Acts 7.20-21 effectively alludes to the whole story of the abandonment and discovery of Moses.[89] Acts 7.23-24 paraphrases the intervention of Moses in the fight between an Egyptian and an Israelite (Exod. 2.11-12), using the phrases τοὺς ἀδελφοὺς αὐτοῦ τοὺς υἱούς Ισραηλ and πατάξας τὸν Αἰγύπτιον.[90] Acts 7.26 evokes the sense of Exod. 2.13, although Moses speaks to both men in Acts, not the wrongdoer alone.[91] After the quotation from Exod. 2.14 (Acts 7.27-28), Acts 7.29 refers to Moses' flight to Midian (Exod. 2.15), and to his two sons (Exod. 2.20).[92]

Acts 7.30-34 tells the story of Exodus 3. Acts 7.30 places events at a mountain in the wilderness (albeit Sinai, not Horeb), like Exod. 3.1,[93] and it also repeats much of the description of the angel from Exod. 3.2.[94] Acts 7.31 summarises the narrative of Exod. 3.3-4, but adds Moses' amazement at the sight,[95] and the following three verses quote from Exod. 3.5-10.[96]

François Bovon, *Luke the Theologian: Fifty-Five Years of Research (1950-2005)*, 2nd ed. (Waco: Baylor University Press, 2006), 109–11.

86. NA[28]; Johnson, *Acts*, 124; Fitzmyer, *Acts*, 374; Keener, *Acts*, 2:1375. NA[28] adds Gen. 47.27 and Ps. 104.24, but despite similarities, relevance would be found in the immediate context of Exod. 1 without these texts being considered.

87. NA[28]; Fitzmyer, *Acts*, 375; Richard, *Acts*, 79–80; Keener, *Acts*, 2:1381. This verb only occurs in these two places and Jdt. 5.11; 10.19 in LXX and NT

88. Richard, *Acts*, 79–80, notes four lexical similarities to Exod. 1.9-22. NA[27]; Marshall, 'Acts', 561 note Exod. 1.17-18, 22. NA[28] prefers Exod. 1.9-11, 16, 22.

89. NA[28]; Marshall, 'Acts', 561; see also the discussion in Richard, *Acts*, 80–81.

90. Richard, *Acts*, 82; NA[28]. Exod. 2.11: Johnson, *Acts*, 126. There are no clear allusions in Acts 2.22 (NA[28] lists 3 Kgdms 5.10 but this is about Solomon).

91. NA[28]; Richard, *Acts*, 83–84; Fitzmyer, *Acts*, 377.

92. NA[28]; Richard, *Acts*, 86 (2.15 only); Marshall, 'Acts', 562.

93. Marshall, 'Acts', 562.

94. NA[28]; Marshall, 'Acts', 562; Fitzmyer, *Acts*, 377.

95. NA[28]; Richard, *Acts*, 89; Marshall, 'Acts', 562.

96. NA[28] adds Exod. 3.13, 15f to the texts alluded to in Acts 7.32, but despite lexical similarities the story is focused on the events of Exod. 3.1-6.

The speech now stops following particular chapters of Genesis and Exodus. After the quotation in Acts 7.35,⁹⁷ Acts 7.36 refers to the miracles performed in the exodus, specifically recounted in Exod. 7.3; 15.4, and the forty years of Num. 14.33-34; but these are well-known events, and the overall story is probably closer at hand for the reader than any single verse.⁹⁸ After the quotation in Acts 7.37, Stephen describes the giving of the law on Sinai (7.38), and many intertexts are suggested as potential sources for Luke's account.⁹⁹ Yet a reader is likely to find sufficient relevance in the most immediate context, the well-known story of the giving of the law on Sinai, perhaps with Exod. 31.18 as the most obvious context because of the reference to Exodus 32 in the coming verses.¹⁰⁰ Certain additional features of Acts 7.38 might also point the reader to specific verses: ἐν τῇ ἐκκλησίᾳ, together with the recent quotation of Deut. 18.15, could draw attention to Deut. 18.16;¹⁰¹ the reference to angels might create a link to Acts 7.35, but more likely (because of their association with giving the law) to Deut. 33.2.¹⁰² The description of the rejection of Moses in Acts 7.39 is likely to refer to the narrative of Num. 14.3.¹⁰³ After Acts 7.40 quotes Exod. 32.1, 23, Acts 7.41 continues the focus on Exodus 32 by referring to the making of a calf in Exod. 32.4, though it uses μοσχοποιέω (a novel word), and Israel is the subject (not Aaron);¹⁰⁴ it continues with

---

97. NA²⁸ notes Pss. 18.15; 77.35, which feature λυτρωτής, but neither is a close parallel.

98. NA²⁸ adds *As. Mos.* 3.11 and Neh. 9.12-21, but omits Pss. 104.27, which NA²⁷ has (and Bock, *Acts*, 296; Marshall, 'Acts', 563), but these verses are not close enough. Earl Richard's reconstruction (Richard, *Acts*, 104–108) is too complex for a reader to find relevance in it. It is possible that Deut. 34.11 would be noted, with its reference to τοῖς σημείοις καὶ τέρασιν (Johnson, *Acts*, 129); also note the use of τέρατα καί σημεῖα with reference to Stephen in Acts 6.8.

99. NA²⁷ lists Deut. 4.10; 9.10; 32.47; 33.3; Exod. 31.18. See the discussion in Richard, *Acts*, 111–14.

100. NA²⁸.

101. NA²⁸; Marshall, 'Acts', 563; however, this verse refers to Horeb, not Sinai. Deut. 4.10 also mentions ἐκκλησίᾳ but is not as close.

102. Bock, *Acts*, 297. Angels are mentioned in Exod. 23.20-21; 32.34; 33.2 (Richard, *Acts*, 112), but a law theme is strong here.

103. NA²⁸; Marshall, 'Acts', 564. Richard, *Acts*, 114–16 thinks there is also an influence of Deut. 18.21. Fitzmyer, *Acts*, 380, adds Exod. 16.3.

104. NA²⁸; Johnson, *Acts*, 131. Richard, *Acts*, 118, thinks this phrase comes from four verses in Exod. 32, but this is overly complex. NA²⁸ has Exod. 32.8 but it is less likely because it has God describing the event to Moses, and it occurs after the sacrifice and revelling of 32.6.

an abbreviated description of revelry from Exod. 32.6.[105] Luke's emphasis on idolatry – and the distinctive ἐν τοῖς ἔργοις τῶν χειρῶν αὐτῶν – is not explicitly stated in Exodus 32; the closest OT parallel with similar vocabulary is Deut. 4.28, but Exodus 32 is the more accessible context where sufficient relevance would be found.[106]

The introductory explanation to the quotation from Amos 5.25-27 in Acts 7.42-43 could allude to several OT texts. God turning away (ἔστρεψεν) may have resonances with God turning away his face in Deut. 31.18; 32.20;[107] and λατρεύειν τῇ στρατιᾷ τοῦ οὐρανοῦ has several potential OT referents, but only Deut. 4.19; 17.3 have the verb λατρεύω (with κόσμος τοῦ οὐρανοῦ not στρατιᾷ).[108] In any case, it is most likely that the term refers primarily to a motif which is quickly interpreted by the quotation from Amos – this will be its interpretive context for the reader.

From Tabernacle to Temple (Acts 7.44-48)

Σκηνὴ τοῦ μαρτυρίου (Acts 7.44) occurs several times in the OT, but a reader is likely to find relevance in the general concept and not seek a specific verse.[109] Acts 7.44 is likely to be seen in the context of the whole of Exodus 25 with its description of the tabernacle as divinely instructed: although it has specific links with the instructions of Exod. 25.1, 9 and Exod. 25.40 (referring to the contents of the tabernacle, not the tent itself), such textual specificity is not necessary for optimal relevance.[110]

For similar reasons the whole narrative of the conquest of Canaan is likely to be evoked by Acts 7.45, which places the tabernacle centrally in the story.[111] Acts 7.46 uses septuagintal language to describe David finding

105. NA[28]; εὐφραίνοντο is likely to be based on this verse; see Marshall, 'Acts', 564; see also Richard, *Acts*, 119. Fitzmyer, *Acts*, 380, has 32.4-6.

106. Psalm 113.12 (NA[27], not NA[28]); Ps. 105.19; Neh. 9.18 are not distinctive enough to attract attention away from the Pentateuch.

107. Richard, *Acts*, 122.

108. Aquila has στρατιᾷ, and this might be a textual tradition that Luke knew; see ibid., 123. Other texts include Jer. 7.18; 8.2; 19.13; Zeph. 1.5; Hos. 13.4; 2 Chron. 33.3, 5; 4 Kgdms 23.5. See NA[28] (Jeremiah and Hosea references only); Richard, *Acts*, 122–23; Marshall, 'Acts', 565; Fitzmyer, *Acts*, 381.

109. Several verses are possible; e.g., Exod. 27.21; 28.43; 33.7; Num. 1.50; 12.4; Deut. 31.14. See Fitzmyer, *Acts*, 382.

110. NA[28] has these three verses. See the discussion in Marshall, 'Acts', 566–67; Richard, *Acts*, 126–28.

111. NA[28] notes Josh. 3.14; 18.1 (the tabernacle artefacts), and Josh. 23.9; 24.18 (casting out the Canaanites), but they have insufficient lexical similarity to be specific intertexts; NA[27] has Gen. 17.8; 48.4; Deut. 32.49 (which are more distant). See Marshall, 'Acts', 567; and see the complex reconstruction in Richard, *Acts*, 128–29.

favour,[112] and then quotes Ps. 131.5 with εὑρεῖν σκήνωμα τῷ οἴκῳ 'Ιακώβ.[113] Second Kingdoms 7.1-13 is the most likely context for the narrative of David's request to build a temple and God's implied refusal together with Solomon's temple construction (Acts 7.46-47); 3 Kgdms 8.20 is also evoked because of the references to transcendence that follow.[114]

The unusual terms ὕψιστος and χειροποίητος in Acts 7.48 do not occur together in the LXX, and no text where they individually appear is distinctive enough to be an intertext.[115] The former is likely to emphasise the contrast with χειροποίητος, as typified in the dedication prayer of Solomon in 3 Kgdms 8.27, and this is the most likely intertext.[116] More importantly, χειροποίητος evokes the idea of idolatry (a context where it is often used) and it is highly likely that a reader will link it primarily to τοῖς ἔργοις τῶν χειρῶν αὐτῶν in Acts 7.41.

Other Charges and Vision (Acts 7.51-56)
Acts 7.51 contains some distinctive phrases with clear OT associations: σκληροτράχηλος is associated with the rebellious people during the Exodus;[117] ἀπερίτμητοι καρδίαις is a similar theme and found in Lev. 26.41;[118] and uncircumcised ears are present in Jer. 6.10.[119] Even if specific verses are apparent for the reader, optimal relevance is likely to be found in the context of the biblical theme of disobedience and unwillingness to listen. Isaiah 63.10 is sometimes cited as an intertext because it contains a

---

112. Not matching a specific text: Marshall, 'Acts', 567; for options, see Fitzmyer, *Acts*, 383.

113. This is widely accepted: e.g., NA[28]; Sylva, 'Meaning', 264; Van De Sandt, 'Presence', 47–53; Marshall, 'Acts', 567. Some texts (including ℵ² A C E Ψ) have θεῷ rather than οἴκῳ (present in 𝔓⁷⁴ ℵ* B D etc.), but the latter is preferred as the harder reading (Barrett, *Acts*, 1:372; Marshall, 'Acts', 567); against Richard, *Acts*, 131–32.

114. There is no reason to favour other texts about Solomon building (e.g., 3 Kgdms 6.2; 1 Chron. 22.6). For these four texts, see NA[28]; Marshall, 'Acts', 568. Further possibilities are given in Fitzmyer, *Acts*, 383.

115. NA[28] notes Isa. 16.12 which is about a temple, but a link is not persuasive; ὕψιστος occurs in Lk. 1.32, 35, 76; 2.14; 6.35; 8.28; 19.38; Acts 7.48; 16.17.

116. Fitzmyer, *Acts*, 384, notices its similarities.

117. Exodus 33.3, 5; 34.9; Deut. 9.6, 13. NA[28]; Bock, *Acts*, 304; Richard, *Acts*, 138; Fitzmyer, *Acts*, 384. This is a more obvious intertext than Neh. 9.16-17, 29-30, suggested by Vincent K. H. Ooi, *Scripture and Its Readers: Readings of Israel's Story in Nehemiah 9, Ezekiel 20, and Acts 7*, JTISup 10 (Winona Lake: Eisenbrauns, 2015), 175.

118. NA[28]; Marshall, 'Acts', 569 (who has other texts); Barrett, *Acts*, 1:376.

119. NA[28]; Barrett, *Acts*, 1:376. It is also used elsewhere; see Fitzmyer, *Acts*, 384–85.

rare LXX reference to the 'Holy' Spirit in the context of disobedience,[120] but the verb in Acts is different to Isaiah; instead, the reference to disobeying the Holy Spirit would probably be understood with the more immediate motif of Luke's concern with the Spirit.[121] The killing of the prophets in Acts 7.52 does not have an obvious OT parallel, but it brings to mind Jesus' similar words in Lk. 13.33-34. Acts 7.53 might evoke Deut. 33.2, with its reference to the angels and the law, but Acts 6.15 (Stephen's appearance as an angel) and Acts 7.38 are more immediately at hand for the reader.[122]

Gnashing teeth (7.54) is a motif well-represented in the LXX, but it may also be a contemporary idiom.[123] Although Stephen's vision of God's glory has a precedent in Ps. 62.3 and Isa. 6.1, there is no other conceptual link to these as texts, and both are set in the temple, not heaven.[124] Several texts are evoked, however: δόξα and θεός recall Acts 7.2; ἐκ δεξιῶν τοῦ θεοῦ might evoke Ps. 109.1;[125] τὸν υἱὸν τοῦ ἀνθρώπου could suggest Dan. 7.13-14.[126] But the most manifest context for interpretation of this text would be in the use of SM imagery in the Gospel accounts.[127]

Summary

There are three principal types of allusion in the narrative. First, allusions to the general story: here optimal relevance would be found in the recall of the story from the OT without any specific verse being accessed. This is more common with well-known stories, but much of the speech functions in this way. Second, allusions to specific texts within the story, where the reader would spend further processing effort in identifying and engaging with a text. This occurs where there is greater correspondence with a text, or where the narrative pace slows and extra detail is given. Third, allusions to texts outside the immediate story: in these cases the strong similarity with an OT text outside the story signals that optimal relevance requires engagement with it.

---

120. NA[28]; Marshall, 'Acts', 569; Johnson, *Acts*, 134. Numbers 27.14 has ἀντιπίπτω in the context of rebellion but nothing else to favour it; see NA[28]; Marshall, 'Acts', 569.

121. Richard, *Acts*, 138.

122. Deut. 33.6 (NA[28]) is more remote. For angels and the law, see Fitzmyer, *Acts*, 385–86.

123. E.g., Pss. 34.16; 36.12; 111.10; Lam. 2.16. See NA[28]; Marshall, 'Acts', 571; Peterson, *Acts*, 266.

124. NA[28]; Marshall, 'Acts', 571, note both.

125. Johnson, *Acts*, 139–40; Marshall, 'Acts', 571.

126. Johnson, *Acts*, 139–40; Marshall, 'Acts', 571.

127. See the fuller discussion below on pp. 181–87.

In narrative terms, the first two types serve to draw the reader into the world of the OT narrative, sometimes through recall of the story, at other times by engagement with specific details of the story. Where Stephen has used quotations from the words spoken in the OT narrative, these serve to make the specifics of the OT narrative more immediately apparent to the reader, inviting further analysis of the OT context in order to gain optimal relevance.

Finally, in engaging with clear allusions to texts outside the narrative, the reader is temporarily drawn outside the history being re-told. In exploring the context of these texts the reader will gain cognitive effects which either add colour to Stephen's re-telling of history, or provide Stephen's commentary on the history of Israel.

Reading the History of Israel

Stephen's history is highly selective – as any brief history of Israel must be – and compared with other Jewish histories his choice of focus is unusual.[128] Although he begins with Abraham, like many other histories,[129] he does not focus on other commonly discussed events (e.g., the Exodus from Egypt and the plagues, the wilderness wanderings, and the conquest of Canaan). His focus is on a small number of OT chapters, which are examined in detail (principally Gen. 11.31–12.5; 41–42; Exod. 1–3; 31–32) and he addresses events that others omit: the call of Abraham, Joseph in Egypt, the Golden calf incident, and Solomon's temple building.[130] The purpose of his historical survey is much discussed:[131] famously, for Martin Dibelius, it is largely irrelevant to the speech: 'From 7.2-34 the point of the speech is not obvious at all; we are simply given an account of the history of Israel';[132] but this does not give attention to its narrative effect. Nor is it enough to say that the history describes Joseph and Moses

---

128. There are histories in Deut. 6.20-24; 26.5-9; Josh. 24.2-15; Neh. 9.6-37; Pss. 77; 104; 105; 135; Ezek. 20; 1 Macc. 2.52-60; *3 Macc.* 2.2-12; Wis. 10–19; Sir. 44–50; Jdt. 5.6-21; CD 2.14–3.19; *4 Ezra* 14.19-31; Josephus, *Ant.* 3.84-88; 4.40-49: a list from Brehm, 'Rejected One', 274–75. See also Parsons, *Acts*, 106. For history-writing among Greek-speaking Jews and Samaritans, see Sterling, 'Scriptures', 202–208.

129. Creation is an alternative starting point.

130. For comparison between Stephen and other texts, see Brehm, 'Rejected One', 274–76.

131. See Richard, *Acts*, 38–155.

132. Martin Dibelius, *Studies in the Acts of the Apostles* (London: SCM, 1956), 167.

as types of Christ in their rejection,[133] or that it concerns the fulfilment of prophecy,[134] because these ideas do not account for the detail in the speech. Instead, the speech needs to be seen as part of Stephen's defence within Luke's narrative.[135] In this way, Stephen's re-telling of history has several important effects.

(1) It builds bridges between Stephen and his hearers because it is a story of common origins.[136] The OT allusions increase the sense of shared community because they depend on the reader noticing the allusion to have their required effect; they connote a shared textual history between writer and reader.[137] The audience is therefore drawn into the narrative as their history.[138]

(2) It discusses the charges within the wider story of God's dealings with Israel. God is introduced as Ὁ θεὸς τῆς δόξης, a phrase from Ps. 28.3 where he is lord of history,[139] and this plays out in the speech: God calls Abraham and gives him promises (of slavery, deliverance, and worship ἐν τῷ τόπῳ τούτῳ, Acts 7.6-7) which he then fulfils sequentially.[140] The speech is also full of the actions of God: he rescues Joseph (7.9-10), commissions Moses (7.30-38), judges idolatry (7.42), reveals plans (7.44), and drives out the nations (7.45). In many cases, quotations of God's words are used to emphasise his promises and his calling of people to accomplish his will; as such, the reader expects God to fulfil his promises.

(3) The history also concerns the Israelites' response to God's actions, often quoting their words. Some characters are obedient, but others resist God: the patriarchs sell Joseph (Acts 7.9), some reject Moses (7.27-28, 35), and reject God in idolatry (7.39-41). In this way, Israel is divided into two camps: those who are obedient and faithful, and those who reject God and engage in idolatry.[141]

---

133. E.g., Peterson, *Acts*, 246. Acts 7.37 invites the reader to see Moses as a type of Jesus, but the case for Joseph is weaker. See Bock, *Proclamation*, 217–18. See also the discussion in Marshall, 'Acts', 571.

134. Dahl, 'Story', 144–47.

135. Marshall, 'Acts', 570–71, gets close to this; Peterson, *Acts*, 270–75, also notes the counter-accusation but thinks the focus is more theological in the OT texts.

136. Tannehill, *Narrative Unity*, 2:88–91. Stephen does not distinguish himself from his audience until Acts 7.51 when they become '*your* ancestors'.

137. As noted in other texts by Brawley, *Text*, 95.

138. Something similar happens with the reader.

139. Craigie, *Psalms 1–50*, 249.

140. Penner, 'Narrative', 360–63; Parsons, *Acts*, 92; Mallen, 'Genesis', 77.

141. Parsons, *Acts*, 107. For disobedience, see Tannehill, *Narrative Unity*, 2:89. Such polarity is also present in Jewish writings (Jer. 2.2-5; Hos. 9.10). See Hilary Le

(4) The speech shows the divine disapproval of those who disobey, and encourages the audience to take sides against those who are portrayed as rebellious by Stephen.

Stephen's discussion of obedient and disobedient Israel is not made in general terms, it focuses on two principal themes, both introduced in the promises made to Abraham: God's deliverance, and worship. These themes also answer the two charges against Stephen of speaking against both the Law of Moses (because Moses is the principal agent of deliverance), and the temple. That is not to say that attention does not turn to Jesus at the climax of the speech: it does, but christology is not the theme of the history of Israel itself.[142] These themes of deliverance and temple need to be taken in turn.

Theme of Deliverance

God acts to deliver Israel, but some members of Israel oppose God. The pattern is established with Joseph, who is sold into Egypt (Acts 7.9), leading to God's vindication of him (7.10);[143] and it is developed in the lengthy Moses story. Moses is rejected after he struck an Egyptian (7.24), and 7.25 interprets this rejection in terms of his role as a divinely appointed deliverer of the people. Subsequently, one of the two Israelites who Moses attempted to reconcile rejects him with words quoted from the Exodus account (Acts 7.27-28); these same words are quoted as the words of many in Acts 7.35. Significantly, despite their rejection of Moses the ruler and judge (ἄρχοντα καὶ δικαστήν), God commissioned him as ruler and liberator (ἄρχοντα καὶ λυτρωτήν, 7.35). Acts 7.35 also begins the climax of the Moses story, a section with a rhetorical flourish consisting of a sequence of five statements about Moses all using οὗτος: the repeated statements highlight Moses' role as a divinely appointed deliverer,[144] contrasting it with his rejection by the people of God, climaxing in the rejection of Moses (and God) in the golden calf incident.[145] In the middle

---

Cornu and Joseph Shulam, *A Commentary on the Jewish Roots of Acts* (Jerusalem: Academon, 2003), 358–59; Penner, *Origins*, 324–25.

142. Peter Doble argues that the speech is essentially about christology, but this emphasises certain aspects of the speech at the expense of the whole history; see Doble, 'Son of Man'; idem, 'These Things'. Kilgallen, 'Function', 185–89, has Jesus as a third theme together with the themes from the charges.

143. Brehm, 'Rejected One', 283–84.

144. Bock, *Acts*, 296.

145. Rejection references flank the five statements; see Tannehill, *Narrative Unity*, 2:91.

of this, Stephen draws a strong implicit parallel between Moses and Jesus by quoting Deut. 18.15 and its reference to a future Mosaic prophet (Acts 7.37), this quotation was used to refer to Jesus in Acts 3.22.[146]

Surprisingly, having made the link between a rejected Moses and Jesus, the comparison is not pressed; instead, the argument turns to the second theme.

Theme of Worship

The promise to Abraham of λατρεύσουσίν μοι ἐν τῷ τόπῳ τούτῳ (7.7) gives the history a well-defined goal of worship. In Abraham's context, τόπος would refer to worship in the land;[147] but it is unlikely that readers would understand the phrase this way in Acts 7.7, they would be more likely to associate it with the temple because of the similar language in 6.13 and 7.49.[148] However, Stephen's history is not explicit that the temple is the goal, and it utilises this ambiguity by developing the implication that it refers to the temple before challenging it.[149] Having identified the temple as the goal, the reader would progress through Stephen's history where God's plans for true worship contrast with disobedient Israelites who engage in idolatry. Moses was an obedient worshipper who spoke with God and trembled on holy ground (7.32-33). In contrast, some Israelites worshipped a golden calf: their revelry is described in detail, and identified as idolatry, with sacrifice to the idol referred to as τοῖς ἔργοις τῶν χειρῶν αὐτῶν – terms not in Exodus 32. After the quotation from Amos in Acts 7.42-43 (which criticises such practices) Acts 7.44-47 focuses on the tabernacle and the construction of the temple, both positive things in Stephen's account.

---

146. For conceptual parallels between Acts 7.35 and Acts 3.13-15, see Johnson, *Acts*, 129. The Jesus and Moses parallel is widely recognized; see, e.g., Kilgallen, *Speech*, 66–67, 79–80; Haenchen, *Acts*, 288–89. Against Ooi, who thinks the allusion is not used to refer to Jesus; see Ooi, *Scripture*, 163.

147. Dahl, 'Story', 144–45; Sleeman, *Geography*, 145–46. As such, it is fulfilled when Israel enters the land in 7.45; see Peterson, *Acts*, 261–62.

148. It would be understood as the temple or Jerusalem; see Barrett, *Acts*, 1:345; Conzelmann, *Acts*, 52; Tannehill, *Narrative Unity*, 2:93.

149. For τόπος and temple, see Penner, *Origins*, 308–309. While he notices a dual meaning (temple and land), regarding it as deliberate (ibid., 96 n. 120), he argues that ideas of temple are made secondary to land; similarly, Parsons (*Acts*, 93) thinks it refers to the land but that the temple would not have been missed.

The Role of Amos and Isaiah

The two quotations of the prophets act as commentary on this behaviour of the Israelites. The first quotation (Amos 5.25-27 in Acts 7.42-43) concerns the divine rejection of Israelite idolatry; its strong introductory formula draws attention to it and indicates that optimal relevance goes beyond this simple statement. A reader is likely to note three further implicatures. First, by linking the idolatry of Amos' day with the Exodus, an association is made that there has always been idolatry in Israel, even when it did not seem obvious.[150] This association is made clear in its opening question, which expects a negative reply: in the Acts setting, sacrifices were not made to YHWH because they were made to other gods, even though this meaning is not obvious in Amos.[151] Second, the final phrase (μετοικιῶ ὑμᾶς ἐπέκεινα Βαβυλῶνος) replaces the Damascus of the original, and effectively extends the events beyond the deportation of the northern tribes.[152] If Stephen was only using Amos to demonstrate idolatry at the time of the exodus then his argument would not require this phrase at all.[153] Third, some of the language of the quotation is repeated in Acts 7.44 to describe a more positive approach to worship (σκηνή, ἔρημος, ποιέω, τύπος).[154] This repetition emphasises the contrast between the idolatry of Amos, and the implied fulfilment of the promise to Abraham in Acts 7.44-47.

The second quotation criticises the practice of Stephen's contemporaries by associating them with the disobedient worshippers. The introduction gives the meaning of the quotation: God is transcendent and is not housed in a temple.[155] This is not a criticism of building a house for God (and preferring the tabernacle) because neither is mentioned in

---

150. Sylva, 'Meaning', 266; Taylor, 'Stephen', 77; Bruce, 'Apologia', 45.

151. Bruce, *Acts*, 154–55. In Amos it probably refers to a lack of sufficient materials to sacrifice; see Stuart, *Hosea*, 355. For alternative meanings in Acts see Marshall, 'Acts', 565–56. For Acts to be taken in the same manner as Amos would demand a more idealised view of the exodus wanderings than Stephen has presented; see Barrett, 'Luke/Acts', 1:368–70.

152. Bock, *Acts*, 300.

153. Earl Richard, 'The Creative Use of Amos by the Author of Acts', *NovT* 24, no. 1 (1982): 41–42.

154. Van De Sandt, 'Presence', 35, argues that there is a fuller parallelism between 7.38-43 and 7.44-50, naming these lexical parallels among his evidence.

155. This point is also emphasised by truncating the quotation before it turns to ethical matters; see ibid., 55–56.

Acts 7.48; instead, it is a criticism of attitudes towards the temple.[156] Nor is it claiming that God cannot be met in a temple, it is saying that a temple cannot have exclusive claim to deity;[157] in other words, God cannot be domesticated.[158] This is hardly a novel insight: Jewish theology referred to God's glory or name (and not God) as resident in the temple;[159] and Solomon's dedicatory prayer for the temple (3 Kgdms 8.15-53) describes the inadequacy of the temple as a dwelling for God.[160] It is therefore unlikely that Stephen is giving a correction to inadequate theology of transcendence among his hearers; rather, it is written to show that their attitudes and practice have ended up treating the temple as if it were God's dwelling – which it is not, as they know. The end of the quotation is phrased as a rhetorical question, not a summary statement like the original, and this directs the accusation at Stephen's opponents.[161] They were not using the temple as God intended; instead they belonged in the disobedient line of Jewish history, and were part of the people they had judged during Stephen's re-telling of history.[162]

As a result of this, the speech must be reinterpreted, and the stinging critique contained in the Amos quotation is seen to apply to Stephen's accusers. The idolatry Amos describes is extrapolated beyond his own day, right to the time of Stephen's speech, and the second person verbs used in that quotation speak directly to his audience and inform them of their exile beyond Babylon (7.43).[163] In this way, the first charge against Stephen is redirected against his accusers, and its significance is explored by implicature in the relationship between the two quotations. The second charge is then addressed through the continued accusation in Acts 7.51-53, with an explicit association of the audience as heirs of those who rejected God's deliverers, making them those who reject the law (7.53). This makes the quotation of Isaiah the beginning of the climax of the speech.

---

156. Beverly R. Gaventa, *Acts*, ANTC (Nashville: Abingdon, 2003), 129; Witherington, *Acts*, 263; Peterson, *Acts*, 262–63. It is not an argument against Solomon's temple-building project, see Sylva, 'Meaning'; Walton, 'Tale', 138–43.

157. Koet, 'Isaiah', 90.

158. Witherington, *Acts*, 273–74.

159. Gregory Stevenson, *Power and Place: Temple and Identity in the Book of Revelation*, BZNW 107 (Berlin: de Gruyter, 2001), 122–23.

160. Sylva, 'Meaning', 265.

161. Van De Sandt, 'Presence', 55, notes the change from Isaiah but thinks it 'sets the tone' for 7.51.

162. Parsons, *Acts*, 88, 107.

163. There is a theme of reversal here, Tannehill, *Narrative Unity*, 2:90.

Alternative Views

Two commonly held views of the climax of the speech disagree with the proposal above, and they both need to be examined.

(i) A Criticism of Solomon's Temple

For many scholars, the language in Acts 7.46-48 confirms Stephen's overall negative attitude to the Jerusalem temple. Solomon was wrong in attempting to localise God:[164] he built a permanent structure (οἶκος) that God did not command, rather than a tent (σκήνωμα);[165] and it is most natural to read the adversatives δέ and ἀλλά in 7.47, 48 as a contrast between Solomon's error and David.[166] But this is not necessarily the case, as Dennis Sylva has persuasively shown.[167]

First, σκήνωμα in Acts 7.46 does not clearly refer to a tent rather than a temple. It is used for both in the LXX,[168] and Acts 7.46 does not echo any text where it clearly means 'tent'. It does allude to Ps. 131.5, but it is unclear whether this verse refers to the temple or tabernacle; if anything, the use of Ps. 131.8-10 at the dedication of the temple in 2 Chron. 6.41-42 suggests the temple.[169] Therefore, it is not possible to insist that Acts 7.46 refers to David seeking a place for the tent in Jerusalem, rather than a temple.[170] Secondly, δέ does not always take such a strongly

---

164. This criticism is directed against either Solomon, the temple, or both. See, e.g., Bruce, *Acts*, 159–60; Marcel Simon, *Verus Israel: A Study of the Relations between Christians and Jews in the Roman Empire (135–425)*, trans. H. McKeating (Oxford: Oxford University Press, 1985 [first published 1948]), 86; Haenchen, *Acts*, 285; Roloff, *Apostelgeschichte*, 125; Klijn, 'Speech'; Dunn, *Parting*, 63–67; Gaston, *Stone*, 156–61; Richard, *Acts*, 329; Matthews, *Martyr*, 70; Taylor, 'Stephen', 76–77; Ooi, *Scripture*, 172–75. Or it does not criticise the temple – rather it criticizes Solomon for the disobedience which made him not act as David's true son; see Doble, 'Intertextuality', 196; Sleeman, *Geography*, 161–63. For a bibliography of older works and views, see Sylva, 'Meaning', 261–62; Taylor, 'Stephen', 76 n. 64.

165. See the discussion in Van De Sandt, 'Presence', 32–33.

166. Barrett, 'Attitudes', 352 n. 21, states that an alternative reading is that Solomon built a house, *but* this had to be seen according to the ideas of 7.48-50.

167. Sylva, 'Meaning'. Others take a similar view; see Witherington, *Acts*, 263; Walton, 'Tale', 139–43; Neagoe, *Gospel*, 166–68; Hill, *Hellenists*, 69–80; Larsson, 'Temple-Criticism', 388–92.

168. Tent in 3 Kgdms 2.28; 8.4; and temple in Pss. 14.1; 73.7.

169. Walton, 'Tale', 139. This verse functions to focus the reader on David's plans in the narrative. They suggest the temple. See the discussion of the psalm in Witherington, *Acts*, 272–73; Goldingay, *Psalms*, 3:547–48.

170. Sylva, 'Meaning', 264; and the discussion in Van De Sandt, 'Presence', 49–51.

adversative meaning, it commonly means 'and';[171] in addition, ἀλλα can have a concessive meaning such as 'yet'.[172] This means Acts 7.47-48 can be translated: '...*and* it was Solomon who built a house for him. *Yet* the Most High does not dwell in houses made with human hands' (7.47-48). Third, it is notable that 3 Kingdoms 8 is alluded to in Stephen's narrative of Solomon's temple-building, and in 3 Kgdms 8.27 Solomon makes a similar point to Isa. 66.1-2 about the transcendence of YHWH: it would be strange to allude to this text while criticising Solomon for building the temple.[173] Fourth, it is unlikely that Stephen uses Isa. 66.1-2 to denounce the temple itself because Isa. 66.6 refers to those who observe the voice of YHWH coming from the temple, and it is likely that this context is activated in the mind of the reader.[174]

Therefore, the speech does not criticise the temple or Solomon for building it,[175] and Acts 7.47 is not the turning point of the history of the temple.

(ii) Acts 7.51 as the Climax
Acts 7.51-53 is often regarded as the climax of the speech, as a sudden invective or the beginning of the peroration,[176] but this separates it from the quotation in Acts 7.49-50, and there are several reasons why it must be kept in relationship with it.

First, Acts 7.51-53 undoubtedly contains strong language aimed at Stephen's accusers, it makes a clear charge (the murder of Jesus), and an explicit identification of the audience as disobedient Israelites; but the quotation from Isaiah also criticises and charges the audience, and implies

171. BDAG, 213; Sylva, 'Meaning', 264–65; see the discussion in Kilgallen, *Speech*, 89; Sweeney, 'Speech', 198 n. 53.

172. Witherington, *Acts*, 273.

173. Sylva, 'Meaning', 265–66. Some think Luke quotes Isa. 66, rather than 3 Kgdms 8 because he opposed Solomon (see the discussion in Sweeney, 'Speech', 200–201), but this does not follow: Isa. 66 probably suited his purposes better.

174. It is a strongly marked quotation which invites wider exploration of its context for optimal relevance.

175. Witherington, *Acts*, 263; Marshall, 'Acts', 568. The quotation of Isaiah is not critical of the temple itself; see Beale, *Temple*, 224–25; Witherington, *Acts*, 273–74; Mallen, *Transformation*, 114.

176. It is a change of 'subject' and 'posture' (Pervo, *Acts*, 192); a shift in emphasis, or beginning of invective or accusation (Dschulnigg, 'Rede', 196; Van De Sandt, 'Presence', 30; Marshall, 'Acts', 569; Peterson, *Acts*, 264; Kilgallen, 'Function', 174–75); the beginning of peroration (Polhill, *Acts*, 205; Parsons, *Acts*, 102–103; Witherington, *Acts*, 260–61). Others are not as quick to divide it off so strongly (Johnson, *Acts*, 133–35; Bock, *Acts*, 304).

that they are disobedient Israelites. The former relates principally to the theme of deliverance, the quotation to worship, and together they address the charges against Stephen (in the same order that they are presented in Acts 6.13). These themes relate together in the speech – in the promises to Abraham,[177] and the golden calf incident – and it is logical that they are addressed together at the climax. Second, the question at the end of Acts 7.50 creates a parallel with the question of Acts 7.52: both are aimed at the leadership, questioning the two principal themes of the speech. Third, both Acts 7.48-50 and 7.51-53 refer back to the golden calf incident; the former through χειροποίητος (7.48); the latter through σκληροτράχηλοι and ἀπερίτμητοι καρδίαις (Acts 7.51).[178] This suggests that they both explore contemporary applications of this story. Fourth, the refusal of the people to listen in Acts 7.51 is similar to the people not listening to the Lord in the wider context of the Isaiah quotation (Isa. 66.4-6), a context likely to be apparent to the reader. Therefore, it is important not to separate Acts 7.48-49 from 7.51-53, and the Isaiah quotation functions as the turning point of the speech.

The Interpretation of the Speech

The speech is therefore structured so that the history of Israel prepares the reader for the counter-charge beginning in the two quotations of the prophets. But this is not all it communicates. There are many signals that it is appropriate to expend further processing effort in order to gain extra cognitive effects in the form of implicatures. These signals include the complex historical re-telling with multiple OT references, the evocation of other OT texts which serve as commentary on the history, the repeated examination of certain themes so that they are addressed from more than one angle, and the evocation of the laments of the Gospel (especially through the reference to Jesus' claims over the fate of the temple). Because Stephen represents Jesus in his trial, the reader can expect the speech to expand upon the themes present in the laments of Jesus; this is where many of the further cognitive effects of the speech lie.

These themes in the speech are the subject of the remainder of the chapter. In order to emphasise the continuity with the sayings of Jesus in the Gospel, they are categorised and discussed in connection with themes that have been found in the Gospel, beginning with the two most explicit themes in the speech.

177. Penner, *Origins*, 95–96.
178. Boismard, 'Etienne', 186; Tannehill, *Narrative Unity*, 2:87 n. 17. Σκληροτράχηλοι occurs immediately after the golden calf incident in Exod. 33.3, 5.

Jesus as Rejected Saviour

The accusation of murdering Jesus (Acts 7.52) was also made earlier in Acts (2.22-23, 36; 3.12-15a; 4.8b-10; 5.30);[179] the contribution of Stephen is in the implicatures that arise from the indirect language used to describe Jesus (ὁ δίκαιος), and the parallels between Jesus and Moses.

The implicatures associated with ὁ δίκαιος go beyond its messianic use in the prophets,[180] and arise in association with the two Lukan texts which it evokes. First, Peter uses it in Acts 3.14, where it conveys the innocence of Jesus and infers the guilt of the audience;[181] second, it is spoken by the centurion in Lk. 23.47, showing that even outsiders recognise Jesus as righteous while the Jewish leaders reject him.

The parallels between Moses and Jesus encourage other associations to be made: Moses' mission was defined in terms of σωτηρία (7.25), a term used (together with its cognates) to describe Jesus and his work (e.g., Lk. 1.69; 6.9; 19.9; Acts 2.21; 4.9, 12);[182] Moses was also a bringer of peace (Acts 7.26), like Jesus (Lk. 19.42); and both are described in a time of visitation (Acts 7.23; Lk. 19.44).[183] Jesus is also a rejected saviour, like Moses, and this builds on the rejection of salvation theme in Lk. 19.29-44. These parallels encourage Jesus to be seen as a prophet-like-Moses, a deliverer or saviour who has led his people in a New Exodus,[184] adding the provision of salvation to the restoration from exile theme from Lk. 13.34.

---

179. Matthews, *Martyr*, 58.

180. E.g., Isa. 32.11; 53.11; Jer. 23.5; Zech. 9.9. See Peterson, *Acts*, 175.

181. Witherington, *Acts*, 274. See also the discussion of ὁ δίκαιος in J. Julius Scott Jr., 'Stephen's Defense and the World Mission of the People of God', *JETS* 21, no. 2 (1978): 135–36. For the Lukan use of the term, see Doble, *Paradox*, 93–126, 139–45; he identifies Wis. 2–5 as especially significant, and the vindication of Jesus as an important theme in Acts 7.

182. Gaventa, *Acts*, 125–26; Joel B. Green, 'Salvation to the End of the Earth: God as the Saviour in the Acts of the Apostles', in Marshall and Peterson, eds., *Witness to the Gospel*.

183. Some argue for two visitations in the Joseph and Moses stories, with apostolic preaching the equivalent second visitation of Jesus (Pervo, *Acts*, 179, 81; Johnson, *Acts*, 137). But Joseph's brothers' visits are not about salvation, and Luke is clear about the consequences of rejecting Jesus at the first visitation (Lk. 19.44) even if further opportunities are offered for repentance in Acts; see Gaventa, *Acts*, 123; Barrett, *Acts*, 1:349.

184. For Jesus and Moses parallels as rejected saviour see Keener, *Acts*, 2:1392–93. For Jesus as a Mosaic prophet, see Julie E. Robb, 'A Prophet Like Moses: Its Jewish Context and Use in the Early Christian Tradition' (Ph.D. diss., King's College, London, 2003).

Weaker associations might also be made; for example, the exodus involved a saved community gathered around Moses, and salvation through Christ involves a community of people gathered around Jesus in a life of openness to the Holy Spirit (not closed to the Spirit as Acts 7.51).[185]

Idolatry

In Acts 7.48, the introduction to the quotation from Isaiah directs the reader to the primary context where it will achieve relevance, and two of its distinctive words have associations with idolatry. Ὕψιστος is typically used to speak of the supreme God, and it contrasts God with competing deities such as Moloch and Rephan, who are idols of the Israelites in Acts 7.43.[186] More significantly, χειροποίητος is generally associated with idols in the LXX (e.g., Deut. 4.8; 31.29),[187] but it is likely that it would make the golden calf incident the context where a reader would find relevance because of the phrase τοῖς ἔργοις τῶν χειρῶν αὐτῶν in 7.41.[188] This would encourage the development of implicatures associated with this notorious event,[189] including divine judgement, shame, and worshipping what the people have created themselves.[190] With this context in mind, a reader could think of the discussion of wrong worship in the wider context of Isa. 66.3-4,[191] where cultic activity is offensive to God. In this way, the attitudes of Stephen's opponents to the temple are shown to be as offensive to God as the golden calf.

This confirms the suggestion in the Gospel that Jesus' criticism of the temple included idolatry; the quotation of Hos. 10.8 in Lk. 23.30 implied

---

185. For salvation and openness to the Spirit, see Green, 'Salvation', 95.

186. The heavenly bodies are likely to be linked to idols (like the golden calf) through Deut. 4.27-28; see Van De Sandt, 'Presence', 36–37. For ὕψιστος, see Fitzmyer, *Acts*, 384.

187. Leviticus 26.1, 30; Isa. 2.18; 10.11; 19.1; 21.9; 31.7; 46.6; Dan. 5.4, 23; 6.28; Jdt. 8.18; Wis. 14.8 (Beale, *Temple*, 224 n. 45). See also, Penner, *Origins*, 317; Van De Sandt, 'Presence', 54; Taylor, 'Stephen', 79. Χειροποίητος is sometimes taken as evidence for the temple being an idol (Penner, *Origins*, 310–18; F. Scott Spencer, *Acts*, Readings: A New Biblical Commentary [Sheffield: Sheffield Academic, 1997], 78; Dunn, *Parting*, 66–67), but this is not the case.

188. Keener, *Acts*, 2:1405.

189. For its notoriety, see Brevard S. Childs, *Exodus: A Commentary* (London: SCM, 1974), 573–81; Keener, *Acts*, 2:1407.

190. For the calf event, see Joel H. Hunt, 'Idols, Idolatry, Teraphim, Household Gods', in *Dictionary of the Old Testament: Pentateuch*, ed. T. Desmond Alexander and David W. Baker (Leicester: Inter-Varsity, 2003), 439.

191. Brevard S. Childs, *Isaiah*, OTL (Louisville: Westminster John Knox, 2001), 540.

this, as did Jeremiah 7 in Lk. 19.46. It is notable that Luke records quotations to Isaiah 66, Amos 5, Hosea 10 and Jeremiah 7 in the temple material, all of which deal with idolatry in Israel; the citation of two of them in Acts 7 is likely to evoke the use of the other two in Luke's Gospel, encouraging a re-reading of the laments where they are quoted.

Acts 7 makes the association between idolatry and the rejection of Jesus. The two major themes of the chapter are the actions of Israel in rejecting the deliverer and idolatry; these themes are associated throughout the speech, most clearly in the golden calf incident. In Acts 7.39-41, instead of receiving Moses, the people rejected him and followed other Gods. Because this story is clearly alluded to at the climax of the speech (Acts 7.48, 51), the reader is also likely to associate the rejection of Jesus with temple idolatry.

It is sometimes assumed that the rejection of Jesus leads to idolatry, but it does not necessarily happen this way round.[192] The rejection of Moses does not lead to idolatry in Acts 7.39-40 – the people reject both Moses and God together.[193] Similarly, the relationship between Acts 7.49-50 and 7.51-52 does not require that the rejection of Jesus comes first; rather, the idolatry is mentioned before the rejection of Jesus, perhaps suggesting an alternative sequence of events.

Luke's Gospel supports the idea that idolatry was present before Jesus was rejected because Lk. 13.33-35 suggests that Jesus' criticism of temple practices as idolatry led to his rejection as a prophet. Similarly, the allusion to idolatry in Lk. 23.30 implies it came first. In Luke 19, the welcome of Ps. 117.26 should have come from the temple, embracing the eschatological life that Jesus brought, but it did not. Instead the temple had become a den for those who rejected Jesus and engaged in idolatrous practice. This suggests again that the rejection of Jesus arose as a fruit of the attitudes that Luke–Acts describes as idolatrous. The wider context of Isaiah 66 supports this, because it rebukes those who with wrongful worship practices refused to listen to God.[194] So, the temple leaders had built their activity in the

---

192. Kilgallen, 'Function', 188, states, 'what leads to false worship now...is the willingness to contradict the word of God's Spirit through the prophet'. See also Robb, 'Prophet', 121.

193. Luke's account omits the Israelites noting Moses' absence before rebelling (Kilgallen, *Speech*, 84); it is far from clear that Acts has the rejection of Moses leading to idolatry (Kilgallen, 'Function', 176).

194. Like Jer. 7, it refers to those who do not listen to God because of their wrongful dependence on the temple; see Brehm, 'Rejected One', 290, though his interpretation of Lk. 19 is focused on the use of the temple as a marketplace (p. 295).

temple after their own construction, not what God required,[195] and in Acts, the temple continued to be a focus for the rejection of the disciples and their eschatological life of prayer, healing, meeting and revelatory teaching in Jesus' name (Acts 3.1, 11-26; 5.12, 20-21).[196]

The Manipulation and Localisation of God
It is likely that a reader would develop other implicatures about idolatry. First, God is not restricted to Zion or the land.[197] He appeared to Abraham in Mesopotamia (7.2), was with Joseph in Egypt (7.9), and, when he appeared to Moses (7.30-34), Luke emphasises the holiness of the place by inverting the order of events from the Exodus account.[198] The holy place is not the temple, but the place where God is present,[199] and God can be present in the remotest of places.[200]

This idea of locality would contribute to a weaker implicature about mission because salvation cannot be limited to the temple.[201] The reader expects the gospel to go to the nations (Acts 1.8), but this will not happen by the Gentiles coming to Jerusalem; instead, the gospel goes to them, and after Acts 7 the mission leaves the temple courts. This adds confirmation to the idea in Lk. 21.27 that Jerusalem is no longer the centre of the earth.[202]

Second, their idolatry involves wrong assumptions about the cult. Any reference to temple worship would include the cult as part of its encyclopaedic information because the temple and cult cannot be separated. This means that the challenge of Isa. 66.3-4 would be in the reader's mind on reading the quotation of Isa. 66.1-2: God requires humility and obedience

---

195. As suggested by the use of χειροποίητος.
196. Holmås, 'House', 402.
197. Neagoe, *Gospel*, 163–64; Marshall, *Acts*, 135; Sterling, 'Scriptures', 212–14; Bruce, 'Apologia', 40–41.
198. It is likely that this incident would be understood in the context it has in the Exodus story (revelation and calling from God), and not in the context of Jesus' words about resurrection in Lk. 20.37-39 (as Doble, 'These Things', 105–10). Stephen's use of the story might begin with the same words Jesus quotes (in modified form) but it quickly passes on to the point of the narrative – the calling of Moses.
199. Johnson, *Acts*, 128; Witherington, *Acts*, 270. It is possible that τόπος in Acts 4.31 reflects similar ideas as the place where the disciples prayed was shaken, (Holmås, 'House', 411).
200. The rabbis noted the significance of the burning bush: 'to teach men that there is no place, however desolate, not even a thornbush, without the shekinah' (Str-B 2:680, as cited in Haenchen, *Acts*, 282 n. 2).
201. For the emphasis on place in Stephen's day, see Scott, 'Defense', 133–34.
202. Walton, 'Tale', 144–49.

to his word, not just sacrifice.²⁰³ This leads to the implicature that the cult does not excuse their disobedience. A similar accusation was levelled through the quotation of Jer. 7.11 in Lk. 19.46, and the presence of the same implicature in two settings does much to reinforce that this is a significant criticism of current practice in the temple.

Such cultic activity and restrictive localisation of God had become a way of manipulating God; as the temple leadership in Isaiah 66 decided what God could and could not do, so did Stephen's accusers.²⁰⁴ Ben Witherington puts the point well:

> God's presence can't be confined there, nor can God be controlled or manipulated by the building of a temple and by the rituals of the temple cultus or the power moves of the temple hierarchy. What is being opposed is a God-in-a-box theology that has magical overtones, suggesting that if God can be located and confined, God can be magically manipulated and used to human ends. Such an approach is idolatry – the attempt to fashion or control God with human hands and according to human devices.²⁰⁵

Covenant Unfaithfulness
Stephen's hearers are accused of being ἀπερίτμητοι καρδίαις καὶ τοῖς ὠσίν (7.51), effectively undoing the covenant of circumcision mentioned in Acts 7.8;²⁰⁶ they also received the law, but did not keep it (7.53). While this language primarily concerns Jesus' death, it also evokes the exodus generation and the golden calf episode (7.39-40), when the law was received, but not kept through idolatry.²⁰⁷ In this way, the covenant unfaithfulness of Stephen's hearers is associated with idolatry.

The reader is aware of covenant unfaithfulness and its association with idolatry in Lk. 23.28-31, through its quotation of Hos. 10.8 and Stephen's clearer statement confirms it. However, Lk. 21.20-24 makes a clearer association between such covenant unfaithfulness and the destruction of the city.

---

203. Childs, *Isaiah*, 540; John D. W. Watts, *Isaiah 34–66*, WBC 25 (Waco: Word, 1987), 356.
204. For Isaiah, see Watts, *Isaiah 34–66*, 356; for Acts, see Witherington, *Acts*, 274 n. 313.
205. Witherington, *Acts*, 273.
206. Tannehill, *Narrative Unity*, 2:90–91.
207. Huub Van De Sandt, 'The Minor Prophets in Luke–Acts', in *The Minor Prophets in the New Testament*, ed. Steve Moyise and Maarten J. J. Menken (London: T&T Clark, 2009), 65–69.

Exile

Although Stephen does not have the same OT language of siege as Jesus' laments, his quotation from Amos 5.25-27 threatens exile by adapting Damascus to Babylon, and using the distinctive verb μετοικίζω (which was also used in 7.4: the disobedient will be relocated from the land, just as obedient Abraham was relocated into it).[208]

This exilic imagery will bring to mind the language used by Jesus, allowing a refinement of implicatures. First, Jesus used the imagery for the totality of the destruction of the city and the temple; this information makes the inevitability of destruction apparent in Stephen's use of exile language. This is important because Stephen does not otherwise make this point. Second, Stephen is clear that temple-associated sin is the cause of the exile, and this adds specificity to the picture from the Gospel.

The Abandonment of the Temple

The glory of God was closely associated with the temple and tabernacle in OT theology: it described the presence of God (Exod. 40.34-35; Lev. 9.6, 23; 3 Kgdms 8.11); it was used to express prophetic desire for YHWH's return to Zion (Isa. 24.23; 35.2; 40.5; 59.19; 60.1-2; 66.11, 18-19); and the glory of YHWH was present in the sanctuary (Pss. 25.8; 62.3; Ezek. 10.4; 43.5; 44.4; Hag. 2.7).[209] Stephen's vision of δόξα θεοῦ in Acts 7.55 would be seen against this background, and make the point: the glory of God is in heaven, *not* the temple.[210]

This goes beyond the statements about transcendence in 7.48-50, adding the implicature that the glory has departed the temple, because it would be interpreted in the light of the laments, especially the saying of Lk. 13.35 about the abandonment of the temple. It also confirms that the torn temple veil in Lk. 23.45 represented the abandonment of the temple. The continued use of the temple by the disciples in the early chapters of Acts is not evidence that they thought otherwise: it shows that they regarded it as an appropriate place for prayer and revelatory teaching; the eschatological life they experienced in the temple was a life they brought with them through Jesus by the power of the Spirit, not something in the temple itself.[211]

---

208. Penner, 'Narrative', 362; Tannehill, *Narrative Unity*, 2:90–91.

209. See the discussion in C. John Collins, 'כבד', in *New International Dictionary of Old Testament Theology and Exegesis*, ed. Willem A. VanGemeren, 5 vols. (Carlisle: Paternoster, 1996), 2:581–83.

210. Gaventa, *Acts*, 131. God's glory is a marked phrase in the speech, also occurring in Acts 7.2. See the comments in Soards, *Speeches*, 61; Johnson, *Acts*, 114.

211. Against Le Donne, 'Offering'. He argues that 'the Lord is present within the Jerusalem temple, as mediated by the *Ekklesia*' through the Holy Spirit in Acts

The Alternative to the Temple

The vision in 7.55-56 has a vital role in the speech, developing its christological themes, and it ultimately leads to Stephen's mob execution;[212] but the vision has not been discussed yet, so it requires attention before noting how it contributes to the theology of the temple.

As a vision, it can be expected to function as other visions in Luke–Acts and reveal a true (or heavenly) state of affairs,[213] but there is considerable debate over what it reveals. The imagery of the vision is familiar enough – Jesus as Son of Man (SM), and God's right hand – but the

---

1–7; this is the eschatological return of the Lord to the temple within the church (ibid., 349). He regards this as significant for understanding the Ananias and Sapphira narrative (ibid., 359–64), where their location in the temple is important, but this is likely to be a side issue: the central point is that the church is the eschatological community of the Spirit, they just happen to be in the temple (they also meet in houses, Acts 2.46). There is no fulfilment of the return of the Lord to the temple in Acts, although Le Donne suggests this in two ways: first, he notes that the wider context of the Joel quotation in Acts 2 refers to the Lord dwelling in Zion (Joel 4.17, 21 LXX). But Luke does not refer to the temple in Acts 2 so it is unlikely that Zion references in the wider context are evoked; even if they are, Luke uses the quotation to refer to the eschatological gift of the Spirit in the Christian community away from the temple, so the reader would assume that the meaning of Joel in the wider context is transformed to refer to this (like Isaiah is elsewhere; see Mallen, *Transformation*). Luke does allude to Joel in regard to the temple in Lk. 21, where the meaning is the opposite of that suggested by Le Donne. Secondly, he notes that Lk. 13.35 expects the temple to be abandoned until the words of Ps. 118.26 (ET) are spoken, seeing the answer to this in the words from the same psalm in Acts 4.10-11; but this is not the utterance of the psalm's blessing that Lk. 13.35 anticipates. Le Donne downplays the early church as a replacement for the temple itself but this is the focus that Luke has, rather than a focus on the temple itself. This all means that that Stephen's speech is not a transition point, showing that the presence of the Lord (which has been in the temple until this point) now goes beyond it, as Le Donne claims (pp. 348–59).

212. For the vision, see Edith M. Humphrey, *And I Turned to See the Voice: The Rhetoric of Vision in the New Testament*, Studies in Theological Interpretation (Grand Rapids: Baker Academic, 2007), 48–54. It is not primarily about Stephen (against Penner, *Origins*, 292), rather, it is 'a charisma specifically related to the content of the preaching' (Max Turner, 'The Spirit of Prophecy and the Power of Authoritative Preaching in Luke–Acts: A Question of Origins', *NTS* 38, no. 1 [1992]: 69). It has a focus on christology (Sleeman, *Geography*, 166); however, the content of that christology differs from Sleeman; see below.

213. Doble, 'Son of Man', 74.

standing posture is unique and it has been interpreted in a number of ways.[214]

1. There is little christological significance in the posture; it functions to describe Jesus as transcendent.[215]
2. It describes Jesus as one of the angels who stands before God in service.[216]
3. Jesus stands with a priestly function, ministering in the heavenly temple;[217] or Jesus at the right hand of God represents the way to God, replacing the temple.[218]
4. Jesus stands with a judicial function: either as a judge accepting Stephen's testimony and judging in his favour;[219] or judging against Stephen's accusers, finding them guilty.[220] Alternatively, Jesus is an advocate for Stephen, witnessing about the one who bore him witness (fulfilling Lk. 12.8);[221] or he is both judge and advocate.[222] For others, the emphasis is on Jesus as intercessor within in a judicial context.[223]

---

214. See the list of interpretations in Barrett, *Acts*, 1:384–85; and also in Bock, *Acts*, 311–12; Focant, 'Fils', 564–70; Sabbe, 'Son of Man', 267–68; David M. Crump, *Jesus the Intercessor: Prayer and Christology in Luke–Acts* (Grand Rapids: Baker, 1999), 178–203.

215. Sabbe, 'Son of Man'; Richard, *Acts*, 294–96; Dodd, *Scriptures*, 35; William J. Larkin Jr., *Acts*, IVPNTC 5 (Leicester: InterVarsity, 1995), 121–22.

216. Heinz Eduard Tödt, *The Son of Man in the Synoptic Tradition*, trans. Dorothea M. Barton, NTL (London: SCM, 1965), 303–305.

217. Alan Richardson, *An Introduction to the Theology of the New Testament* (London: SCM, 1958), 200; Eberhard Nestle, 'The Vision of Stephen', *ExpTim* 22 (1911). Beale notes that this occurs in the heavenly temple but does not state Jesus is a priest; see Beale, *Temple*, 219–20.

218. Bruce, *Acts*, 166. For Peterson, the posture adds the idea of judgement; see Peterson, *Acts*, 266–67.

219. Rudolf Pesch, *Die Vision des Stephanus: Apg 7, 55-56 im Rahmen der Apostelgeschichte*, SBS 12 (Stuttgart: Katholisches Bibelwerk, 1966), 54–58; Polhill, *Acts*, 208.

220. Conzelmann, *Acts*, 60; Polhill, *Acts*, 208; Peterson, *Acts*, 267; Gerhard Schneider, *Die Apostelgeschichte*, HTKNT, 2 vols. (Freiburg: Herder, 1980), 1:475.

221. Witherington, *Acts*, 275; Tannehill, *Narrative Unity*, 2:98–99. Marshall argues it is this together with a welcome (Marshall, *Acts*, 149).

222. Bock, *Acts*, 312 argues that they cannot be distinguished here; see also Humphrey, *Voice*, 52–53. Parsons regards it as partly juridical and welcoming; see Parsons, *Acts*, 103–104.

223. Crump, *Jesus*, 197–99.

5. Jesus stands for Stephen, to welcome the persecuted disciple.[224]
6. Jesus is coming to Stephen's aid,[225] or it is a form of personal parousia, where the standing Jesus is coming to aid Stephen in the way that he will for all believers at the end.[226]
7. Finally, Jesus stands in anticipation of his parousia.[227]

The text signals that optimal relevance requires the expenditure of extra processing effort: it contains repetition (of heaven[s], and standing), suggesting the importance of the vision; it refers to Jesus as SM,[228] a term of indirect reference; and it is a vision, and visions frequently have highly symbolic meanings. This means that option 1 must be rejected because optimal relevance goes beyond that.

Two of the other interpretations can also be quickly dismissed. It is unlikely to be welcoming a martyr because there was no developed theology of martyrdom in Luke's time for it to form a context for interpretation.[229] Nor is it likely to be a priestly context: the SM is not a priestly figure, ἵστημι is too general a verb to evoke priestly activity, and Stephen has not directly addressed priestly functions in the speech.[230] The key to the interpretation of the vision lies in its repetition in Acts 7.55-56:

---

224. Johnson, *Acts*, 139. This might be combined with a judicial setting; see Parsons, *Acts*, 103–104; Marshall, *Acts*, 149.

225. T. E. Page and A. S. Walpole, *The Acts of the Apostles: With Introduction and Notes* (London: Macmillan, 1895), 59; William K. L. Clarke, *Divine Humanity; Doctrinal Essays on New Testament Problems* (London: SPCK, 1936), 30.

226. Barrett, *Acts*, 384–85; idem, 'Stephen and the Son of Man', in *Apophoreta: Festschrift für Ernst Haenchen*, ed. W. Eltester and F. H. Kettler, BZNW 30 (Berlin: de Gruyter, 1964); David J. Williams, *Acts*, NIBCNT 5 (Peabody, MA: Hendrickson, 1990), 146; Stephen G. Wilson, *The Gentiles and the Gentile Mission in Luke–Acts* (Cambridge: Cambridge University Press, 1973), 77–78.

227. H. P. Owen, 'Stephen's Vision in Acts VII.55–6', *NTS* 1, no. 3 (1955), argues that Luke marks Jesus career in six words which show movement from the cross to parousia: the death as ἔξοδος (Lk. 9.31); going into glory as εἰσέρχομαι (Lk. 24.26); receipt into heaven as ἀναλαμβάνω (Acts 1.2, 11, 22); sitting at the right hand as κάθημαι (Lk. 20.42; 22.69; Acts 2.34); standing as ἵστημι (Acts 7.55-56); and as judge with ἔρχομαι (Lk. 9.26; 12.36-38; 18.8; 19.23; 21.27; Acts 1.11).

228. A few texts (e.g., $\mathfrak{P}^{74}$ 614) have τὸν υἱόν τοῦ θεοῦ, which Kilpatrick argued was original, but the case is not compelling. See George D. Kilpatrick, 'Acts vii.56: Son of Man?', *TZ* 21 (1965).

229. Crump, *Jesus*, 185.

230. Seeing it as priestly effectively imports concerns from Hebrews into Acts.

⁵⁵ὑπάρχων δὲ πλήρης πνεύματος ἁγίου ἀτενίσας εἰς τὸν οὐρανὸν εἶδεν δόξαν θεοῦ καὶ Ἰησοῦν ἑστῶτα ἐκ δεξιῶν τοῦ θεοῦ ⁵⁶καὶ εἶπεν· ἰδοὺ θεωρῶ τοὺς οὐρανοὺς διηνοιγμένους καὶ τὸν υἱὸν τοῦ ἀνθρώπου ἐκ δεξιῶν ἑστῶτα τοῦ θεοῦ.

⁵⁵But filled with the Holy Spirit, he gazed into heaven and saw the glory of God and Jesus standing at the right hand of God. ⁵⁶"Look," he said, "I see the heavens opened and the Son of Man standing at the right hand of God!"

Acts 7.55 reports that Jesus stands at the right hand of God, evoking Ps. 109.1 and referring to Jesus' exaltation; this psalm was also alluded to in Acts 2.34, where it was said to have been fulfilled at Pentecost.[231] However, this psalm does not explain the significance of the standing posture, and a reader is likely to begin creating a range of weak implicatures about the meaning of this posture pending further information; this information is given in 7.56, which repeats the vision, adding that it is the SM who stands at the right hand. Because of the rarity of this title in Acts, it suggests that the significance of the vision goes beyond Jesus' exaltation, and the reader will therefore focus interpretive effort on understanding the posture in the light of Jesus as SM.[232]

In understanding the SM reference, the closest and most obvious intertext is Lk. 22.69 (ἀπὸ τοῦ νῦν δὲ ἔσται ὁ υἱὸς τοῦ ἀνθρώπου καθήμενος ἐκ δεξιῶν τῆς δυνάμεως τοῦ θεοῦ). There are three reasons for this: first, it has significant lexical parallel through the reference to the SM and the right hand of God. Second, it is a part of the parallelism between Stephen's trial and Jesus trial. Third, like Stephen, Jesus utters this saying before the Sanhedrin (Lk. 22.66; Acts 6.12). Because it is the closest context, the reader will begin the search for relevance here, leading to two important cognitive effects: Acts 7.55-56 would be understood as referring to the exaltation and vindication of Jesus because these are the central concerns of Lk. 22.69;[233] similarly, the vision also implies the vindication of Stephen and his message because he sees the exalted Jesus.[234]

---

231. Green, *Gospel*, 795–96.

232. Peter Doble argues that the standing is interpreted by looking back to δίκαιος in Acts 7.52, and δίκαιος standing before oppressors in Wis. 4.20–5.2; see Doble, 'These Things', 103. But δίκαιος is not mentioned in either report of the vision, whereas SM is.

233. Nolland, *Luke*, 3:1110; Johnson, *Luke*, 359–60; Bock, *Luke*, 2:1796–97.

234. Crump, *Jesus*, 190; Kilgallen, 'Function', 185–86. It is less likely to refer to Lk. 12.8 because there is no reference angels in Stephen's vision. For arguments in favour of Lk. 22.69, see Sabbe, 'Son of Man', 260–62. It is noted in NA[28]; and many commentaries including Fitzmyer, *Acts*, 392; Johnson, *Acts*, 140; Bock, *Acts*, 313.

In this way, Acts 7.56 builds on the message of Acts 7.55 and develops the relationship of Stephen with Jesus' trial.

Although some readers would stop searching for relevance at this point, the majority would continue their search. Despite the ease of their processing, the cognitive effects from Lk. 22.69 are not enough to satisfy expectations of optimal relevance created by the repetition of the vision and the SM title because they do not go sufficiently beyond those attained through Acts 7.55; more significantly, they do not explain the repeated reference to Jesus' posture because in Lk. 22.69 the SM is sitting, not standing. If Luke had intended the reader to find interpretation through Lk. 22.69 alone then he would have been better served to repeat its imagery more closely with a reference to sitting and ἐκ δεξιῶν τῆς δυνάμεως τοῦ θεοῦ. So, a reader would hold on to the ideas of vindication raised by Lk. 22.69, and continue to search to interpret ἵστημι because it implies something additional to enthronement. This process of continuing to search beyond Lk. 22.69 is also seen in modern scholars' readings of the text: despite recognising the importance of Lk. 22.69, most are not content to interpret the saying in this context alone and proceed to others (as evidenced by the range of interpretations above).[235]

For many, the search for meaning is best understood in a judicial setting. Several OT texts relate standing to judgement (Gen. 18.22; Exod. 8.20; 9.13; Isa. 3.13; Jer. 18.20; Zech. 3.1-8),[236] but only Zech. 3.1 refers to standing at the right hand (where Satan the accuser stands), and this text is not similar enough to the Acts vision to control its interpretation. Despite arguments that standing at the right hand *can* have a judicial sense,[237] this does not require that it is the meaning in Acts 7. Imagery of God's right hand is primarily about power and authority, but the session at the right hand itself is not associated with any particular activity, regardless of posture.[238] Ignoring the reference to the right hand, standing

---

235. Modern scholars are not proof of the various ways that a first-century reader would approach the text (because their available interpretive contexts are different), but their range of opinion bears witness to a dissatisfaction with interpreting the text in the light of Lk. 22.69 alone.

236. Johnson, *Acts*, 139, though he does also note standing as cultic or prophetic. See also Parsons, *Acts*, 103–104.

237. E.g., Crump, *Jesus*, 191–93, whose case is built on the possibility of the language having this meaning, together with the setting in the trial, and the parallel advocate function of the SM in Lk. 12.8.

238. David M. Hay, *Glory at the Right Hand: Psalm 110 in Early Christianity*, SBLMS 18 (New York: Abingdon, 1973), 52–59.

in heaven could have a judicial meaning, and for many scholars this is where the meaning is found, tying in with the theme of vindication.[239] But standing can also represent other things.[240] Particularly significant is Ps. 81.8 (82.8 ET), which has God standing in the presence of the divine heavenly assembly, but not simply to judge (despite the common translation). John Goldingay argues that the verse is the supplication of a worshipper asking for God to act, because the previous verses implied that other council members have as much right to divinity as God if he does not act. Goldingay translates it, 'Arise, God, *exercise authority* for the earth because you yourself own all the nations'.[241] The issue is whether God is able to rule the world in the way required: to rescue the poor and needy (81.4). Similar thoughts are present in Pss. 43.27; 75.10 (44.26; 76.9 ET), and it is possible that the standing in Stephen's vision also refers to such preparation for action.

So, the important question is whether a judicial setting sufficiently explains the imagery. It does not, because despite its links to the vindication theme of Lk. 22.69, it does not make a clear association with the SM. Elsewhere, when the SM is said to be involved in judgement he is not explicitly standing (he is seated for judgement in *1 En.* 62.1-12),[242] and the language of Acts 7.55-56 is very different to the places where a judicial role for Jesus is present (Acts 10.42; 17.31), suggesting that this is not Luke's meaning in Acts 7.55-56.[243] Such an interpretation seems to be an assumption in scholarship that one should not search contexts to do with the SM further than Lk. 22.69, but this is a questionable assumption.

---

239. E.g., Keener, *Acts*, 2:1441–42.

240. E.g., standing in a prophetic setting (Ezek. 1.21; 2.12); see Johnson, *Acts*, 139.

241. Goldingay, *Psalms*, 2:568–69, the quotation is from 568, italics added. Such standing of God in the assembly is unusual. The standing in v. 1 might well be in anticipation of the taking action in v. 8; see ibid., 2:562.

242. For this reference, see Darrell D. Hannah, 'The Elect Son of Man in the *Parables of Enoch*', in *'Who Is This Son of Man?': The Latest Scholarship on a Puzzling Expression of the Historical Jesus*, ed. Larry W. Hurtado and Paul Owen, LNTS 390 (London: T&T Clark, 2011), 146. This is not presupposing that Luke knew Enochic literature, only that it represents the sort of contextual information present within a Jewish environment.

243. Sabbe, 'Son of Man', 275.

In order to explain the imagery, a reader would expend extra processing effort within Luke's description of other activities of the SM and find a series of satisfying contextual assumptions which fulfil the expectations of relevance about the standing SM. This can occur in Lk. 21.27. It might not have a lexical relationship with Acts 7.56 beyond τὸν υἱὸν τοῦ ἀνθρώπου,[244] and its SM is not explicitly standing,[245] but it develops a conceptual link with Stephen's vision because it supplements Lk. 22.69 by describing a scenario which explains the standing posture of the SM. For Stephen's hearers, 21.27 describes a still-future action of the SM (coming on the clouds to bring salvation), an activity of the SM beyond enthronement.[246] As such, Lk. 21.27 describes the next event in the sequence of activities of the SM, an event before the parousia.[247] This gives sufficient cognitive effects for optimal relevance: Stephen's SM is standing in preparation for action (like Ps. 81.8), in order to come on the clouds. In other words, the vision of Stephen is about the coming of the SM as well as about the exalted SM.[248]

But is Lk. 21.27 a readily accessible context for interpretation? There are several reasons to think that it is. First, for the reader searching for an explanation of the standing SM, 21.27 details a well-known future action of the SM for which he would have to stand from his throne; therefore it is closer at hand than a judicial context, which bears no direct relation to the SM imagery. Second, as argued earlier in the chapter, the accusations that Stephen claimed Jesus would destroy the temple (Acts 6.14) brings Jesus' temple-critical material to mind, including Luke 21. Third, this reading of the text is encouraged by the introductory phrase ἰδοὺ θεωρῶ τοὺς οὐρανοὺς διηνοιγμένους in Acts 7.56. This language is evocative of apocalyptic and might draw Lk. 21.27 to mind; more than that, οὐρανός and ἀνοίγω (to

---

244. It also contains δόξα, like Acts 7.55.

245. Though the cloud chariot is best understood as a war chariot and as such the SM would be standing, not sitting. See the imagery of ancient Near Eastern war chariots in Othmar Keel and Timothy J. Hallett, *The Symbolism of the Biblical World: Ancient Near Eastern Iconography and the Book of Psalms* (London: SPCK, 1978), 238, and fig. 321 on p. 235, and the gods riding to war in figs 294–95 (p. 216).

246. Barrett, 'Stephen', 36. Although Owen's full argument of about the progression of verbs in Luke–Acts is questionable, he is surely right that standing comes between sitting and coming on clouds; see Owen, 'Vision'.

247. Luke 21 describes a coming associated with the fall of Jerusalem, a coming separate to the parousia described (in different language) in Acts 1.9-11.

248. E.g., David E. Aune, *The Cultic Setting of Realized Eschatology in Early Christianity* (Leiden: Brill, 1972), 93, who sees it as the incorporation of 'a very old cultic vision-form of the exalted and coming Son of man into a new context'.

which διανοίγω is related) are typically used in Luke–Acts (and the rest of the NT) where there is some connection being made between heaven and earth, usually opening the way for travel between the two.[249] As such, a reader of Acts 7.56 would be looking for a context where such a connection happens, and the coming SM in Lk. 21.27 meets this expectation.[250] Fourth, in Acts 7.59 Stephen commits his spirit to Jesus (κύριε Ἰησοῦ, δέξαι τὸ πνεῦμά μου). This parallels the saying of Jesus in Lk. 23.46 drawn from Ps. 30.6, but it is Jesus who is identified as the saviour by Stephen. Jesus has been identified as a divinely appointed deliverer during Acts 7, and the prayer of Acts 7.59 serves to reinforce a meaning for the vision in Acts 7.55–56 that has Jesus as saviour. Fifth, Lk. 21.27 refers to people seeing the SM (ὄψονται τὸν υἱὸν τοῦ ἀνθρώπου), and Lk. 21.28 has people lifting their heads to see their coming salvation (ἐπάρατε τὰς κεφαλὰς ὑμῶν). Neither statement is lexically close to Acts 7.55-56, but conceptually they bear a relationship to its repeated reference to Stephen looking into heaven, turning up the volume on the textual relationship formed by the other points above.

Finally, there is some corroborating evidence that Acts 7.56 refers to both the enthronement of the SM and his impending coming on clouds in the association of these two concepts elsewhere in early Christian literature. Although a Lukan reader would not be expected to notice it, the parallels to Lk. 22.69 in Mt. 26.64 and Mk 14.62 refer to both enthronement and coming; if these two events were closely associated in the encyclopaedic knowledge of the Christian community, then this increases the chance that this is where a reader would find relevance in Acts 7.55-56. The enthronement and coming of the SM are also combined in Hegesippus' much later report of the death of James the Just (as preserved by Eusebius).[251] This parallels Stephen's death in Acts 7: both men die because of conflict over the temple; they are stoned by a violent mob; and both pray for forgiveness for their executioners.[252] Notably, both utter a saying about the SM before their death: James answers his accusers '...τί με ἐπερωτᾶτε περὶ τοῦ υἱοῦ τοῦ ἀνθρώπου, καὶ αὐτὸς κάθηται ἐν τῷ οὐρανῷ ἐκ δεξιῶν τῆς μεγάλης δυνάμεως, καὶ μέλλει ἔρχεσθαι ἐπὶ τῶν

---

249. See the use in Mt. 3.16; Lk. 3.21; Jn 1.51; Acts 10.11; Rev. 4.1; 19.11. For this observation in Jn 1.51, see Benjamin E. Reynolds, 'The Use of the Son of Man Idiom in the Gospel of John', in Hurtado and Owen, eds., *'Who Is this Son of Man?'*, 114.

250. Ἰδού θεωρῶ is typical language of a seer. See Humphrey, *Voice*, 53.

251. Eusebius, *Hist. eccl.* 2.23.4-18.

252. Matthews, *Martyr*, 85–89.

νεφελῶν τοῦ οὐρανοῦ;'.²⁵³ This demonstrates that in later Christian martyr tradition, the enthronement and the future coming of the SM belong together, increasing the likelihood that this is how early readers of Acts 7.55-56 would have found relevance. What is notable is that Hegesippus clarifies Acts 7.56, with μέλλει ἔρχεσθαι ἐπί τῶν νεφελῶν τοῦ οὐρανοῦ – the SM is *about to come*. While it is likely that this saying was modelled on Acts 7.55-56,²⁵⁴ it is impossible to claim this with any certainty: if it was borrowed from Acts 7, then it repeats how Stephen's vision was understood; otherwise, at the very least, it shows that the combination of the enthroned and coming SM was regarded as an appropriate saying for a dying martyr.

Stephen's vision therefore incorporates both the exaltation and the anticipation of the coming of the SM.²⁵⁵ If the coming motif is present in Acts 7.55-56, then why is it absent from Lk. 22.69, especially when there is a coming motif in Mk 14.62?²⁵⁶ It seems a reasonable proposal that, like the omission of accusations of blasphemy,²⁵⁷ it is omitted because Luke transferred its discussion from Jesus' trial to the trial of Stephen in Acts 7. If this is the case, then the exclusion of the saying in Lk. 22.69 focuses its discussion around the vindication of Jesus through enthronement, something explaining other Lukan redactional changes including the more

---

253. Eusebius, *Hist. eccl.* 2.23.13.

254. It could have come taken directly from the Jesus tradition (as Matthews, *Martyr*, 173 n. 24; see also the discussion in Aune, *Cultic Setting*, 93 n. 1). However, there are good reasons for challenging this judgement. Although Hegesippus' account repeats the phrases ...κάθηται ἐν τῷ οὐρανῷ ἐκ δεξιῶν τῆς...δυνάμεως, καὶ μέλλει ἔρχεσθαι ἐπί τῶν νεφελῶν τοῦ οὐρανοῦ from Mt. 26.64 almost verbatim, it has significant differences in κάθηται ἐν τῷ οὐρανῷ, τῆς μεγάλης δυνάμεως, and μέλλει ἔρχεσθαι. This deviation is noticeable because James' prayer of forgiveness is exactly the same as that in Lk. 23.34 (Eusebius, *Hist. eccl.* 2.23.16). It seems likely that Hegesippus was aware of the Acts saying because of the other parallels to the Stephen account, and because the intrusion ἐν τῷ οὐρανῷ in Hegesippus' account might be a trace of ἀτενίσας εἰς τὸν οὐρανόν...θεωρῶ τοὺς οὐρανοὺς διηνοιγμένους in Acts 7.55-56.

255. Acts 7.56 probably reflects both the seated and coming SM in Mk 14.62, as argued by, Aune, *Cultic Setting*, 92; Norman Perrin, *Rediscovering the Teaching of Jesus* (London: SCM, 1967), 177–78.

256. See the discussion about the omission of a vision form of the parousia in Lk. 22.67 in Aune, *Cultic Setting*, 93–94 and 93 n. 2. For a recent discussion on the SM saying in Jesus' trial, see Darrell L. Bock, 'The Use of Daniel 7 in Jesus' Trial, with Implications for His Self-Understanding', in Hurtado and Paul Owen, eds., *'Who Is This Son of Man?'*.

257. See Mk 15.64, its omission in Lk. 22.71, and the implicit presence of blasphemy in Acts 7.57.

explicit reference to Ps. 109.1. The SM coming on clouds motif is then referred to in implicit form in Acts 7.56 because if it was explicitly stated then it might direct a reader to the theme of Acts 1.9-11 rather than the SM saying in Lk. 21.27.

The vision of Acts 7.55-56 will be interpreted as referring to the vindication of Jesus and Stephen, but it is also about Jesus standing in preparation to come, bringing salvation (and judgement).[258] This is not standing in preparation for the parousia,[259] or its visionary foreshadowing,[260] although it can embrace its anticipation as the ultimate coming of salvation. There are three main implicatures that will arise from seeing the vision this way. First, Jesus saves as the Danielic SM figure; this is emphasised by Stephen's entrustment of his Spirit to Jesus (Acts 7.59). Second, Jesus is the locus of God's salvific action, and has taken this function from the temple: salvation is found in Jesus alone throughout Acts (e.g., 4.23-31, and the many conversion stories). As such, Greg Beale is wrong to understand the descent of the Spirit at Pentecost as the replacement of the temple; it is Jesus.[261] Third, it raises awareness of the fall of the temple, because the coming of Jesus is associated with it in Lk. 21.27.

Jesus the Prophet
Stephen, a man full of the Spirit (Acts 6.5, 10; 7.55), with a face like an angel (6.15), is a true spokesman for God,[262] but his words are violently rejected by those who oppose the Spirit. This rejection places Stephen among the prophets killed by rebellious people. The parallels between Stephen and Jesus have shown that Stephen represents Jesus as prophet, and his death represents the rejection of Jesus for what he said over the temple. Despite the lack of mention of the temple in the trial of Jesus,

---

258. The SM comes to bring judgement as well as salvation; both themes are present in Lk. 21 and Acts 7, but the salvation theme has greater prominence in both texts.

259. Against Owen, 'Vision'.

260. Against John Nolland, 'Salvation-History and Eschatology', in Marshall and Peterson, eds., *Witness to the Gospel*, 76.

261. Gregory K. Beale, 'The Descent of the Eschatological Temple in the Form of the Spirit at Pentecost: Part 1: The Clearest Evidence', *TynBul* 56, no. 1 (2005); idem, 'The Descent of the Eschatological Temple in the Form of the Spirit at Pentecost: Part 2: The Corroborating Evidence', *TynBul* 56, no. 2 (2005). Though he does also refer to Jesus' role in Beale, *Temple*, Chapter 6. For Jesus as the replacement of the temple in Acts see, Walton, 'Tale', 144–48.

262. For the significance of Stephen's appearance, see Crispin H. T. Fletcher-Louis, *Luke–Acts: Angels, Christology and Soteriology*, WUNT 2/94 (Tübingen: Mohr Siebeck, 1997), 96–98.

the words of Jesus in Lk. 13.33-34 are therefore fulfilled: he is killed as a prophet speaking about the temple, speaking about the temple in similar terms to the OT prophets; but he also offered a way to avoid the destruction that was not accepted (Lk. 13.34).

Conclusion

Acts 7 is reported as a trial with two principal themes of deliverance and worship: these themes are introduced in the promises made to Abraham, and they are used to answer the charges brought against Stephen, leading to his counter-charges. Stephen's rich use of the OT draws the reader into the re-told history of Israel, showing that there were obedient Israelites who followed God, and disobedient Israelites who rejected God. The reader is encouraged to judge the disobedient during the speech, before the quotations from the prophets show that the Jerusalem temple leadership are heirs of the disobedient stream of Judaism in their idolatry and their rejection of God's deliverer.

The speech implies far more than this. Luke transfers the charge of speaking against the temple from the trial of Jesus to the trial of Stephen, where it can receive greater attention. Because of this, Stephen's speech needs to be understood in continuity with Jesus' sayings about Jerusalem and its temple from the Gospel. This is not to say that Acts 7 or the laments cannot be read separately but, as the final section of this chapter has shown, Acts 7 examines the same themes as Luke's Gospel with respect to judgement on Jerusalem and the temple.

Stephen is a prophetic figure who represents Jesus the prophet, and the language of exile continues to be used to show the significance of destruction. The rejection of Jesus, which is related to the fall of Jerusalem in the Gospel, is also the chief sin in Acts 7; but it adds that the Jerusalem leadership's rejection of God's deliverer and their idolatry go together, just as with the wilderness generation who worshipped a calf. Stephen's vision also shows that Jesus is the locus of salvation, not the temple.

In some places, Stephen clarifies things that are tentatively present in the Gospel: (1) that the Jerusalem leadership are involved in idolatry in their attitude to the temple, and this leads to them rejecting Jesus; (2) that the tearing of the temple curtain is the time of God's abandonment of the temple; (3) that the salvific activity which Jesus brings is the focus of God's eschatological action, not the temple; (4) that the temple is not the focus of blessing the nations – the Gentiles will be blessed without coming to the temple; (5) that Jesus was critical of the temple as a prophet.

But the Gospel accounts are also important to illuminate Acts 7. Viewing the speech in this way is not new – most commentators interpret difficulties in Acts through similar material in Luke's Gospel – but a preferred reading of Acts 7 against the laments does allow them to enrich the message of Stephen in several important ways: (1) it confirms that the temple and city will fall; without the link to the laments, the fate of the temple is less clear in Acts 7; (2) Lk. 21.27 is a helpful context for bringing clarity to the disputed vision of the SM; and (3) the offer of saving action in Lk. 13.34 makes it clear that it is not Jesus who destroys the temple.

Chapter 8

CONCLUSION

This study focused on texts of apparent temple-criticism in Luke–Acts, and noted a series of themes established throughout Jesus' laments over Jerusalem that are developed in Acts 7. In some cases, Acts 7 makes explicit something that is implicit in the Gospels, thereby enriching understanding of the Gospel accounts; in other places, the Gospel is a vital interpretive background for Acts 7. Throughout, it is noted that Jesus is rejected by the Jerusalem leaders as both a prophet and a saviour.

Jesus the Prophet and Saviour

The theme of Jesus as the prophet rejected to death is introduced in Lk. 13.33-34, where he is associated with Zechariah son of Jehoiada through allusion to 2 Chron. 24.20-21. Zechariah was killed for his message about wrongful worship in the temple (including idolatry), and associating Jesus with him suggests that Jesus was also killed for his message about the temple. The theme of Jesus' rejection as a prophet does not reappear until Acts 7 (Lk. 19.47 refers to rejection of his teaching, not prophecy). Unlike Matthew and Mark, Luke does not have the charge that Jesus claimed to destroy the temple during his trial, but it does appear in Acts 6.14; it is likely that Luke deferred discussion of this charge against Jesus until Acts, where it could be explored more fully.

Jesus is portrayed as a prophet in the Gospel; his words in the laments focus on fate of Jerusalem, and in the temple action (19.45-46) he performs a prophetic enactment of the temple's fate. His prophetic statements echo the language of the prophets concerning the exile, beginning in Lk. 13.35 with a saying about the abandonment of the temple (fulfilled as the temple curtain is torn, Lk. 23.45), continuing through descriptions of the besieged city (19.42-44; 21.20-24), and the evocation of Jeremiah 9 and Hos. 10.8 in Lk. 23.23-31. This language is understood with several implicatures, including the immensity of the coming destruction, its inevitability, and the judgement of God. Acts 7.42-43 returns to this imagery through the quotation of Amos 5.25-27; in recalling this imagery the reader appreciates that Stephen is referring to the fall of the city, even without its explicit statement.

Exilic language in the laments also implicitly associates the destruction of the city with covenant unfaithfulness, especially in the evocation of Deut. 28.58-68 and Hos. 9.7 (Lk. 21.22-24), and Hos. 10.8 (Lk. 23.30). Covenant unfaithfulness is made explicit in Acts 7.51, 53, where it is associated with idolatry as well as Jesus' death. This description of idolatry is a significant development in Acts 7 through its focus on the golden calf incident as the rejection of God in favour of false deities of their own creation (Acts 7.39-41); Stephen makes a counter-accusation of idolatry against his opponents and this was an important trigger in his death. By implication, it was a significant aspect in the rejection of Jesus the prophet as well. It is notable that both quotations from the prophets in Acts come from chapters which concern idolatry, as do Jeremiah 7 and Hosea 10 in Lk. 19.46; 23.30. The association of these texts together in the mind of the reader causes a re-examination of Jesus' message, and a realisation that concerns about idolatry have formed a significant part of Jesus' criticism of temple-practice. Acts 7 explores this theme in more detail than the Gospel; it involves a false localisation of God to the temple, an assumption that the cult covers sin, and a manipulation of the deity from the temple. Such themes are implicit in the quotation of Jer. 7.11 in Lk. 19.46, and the temple action narrative can be re-read with benefit with this extra detail. In the same way, it adds detail to the ideas of false localisation of God to the temple in Lk. 21.25-27, where YHWH comes in the person of Jesus and not from Zion; as the temple is destroyed, it is seen to be the centre of the world no longer, and the Gospel goes to the nations rather then the nations coming to Jerusalem.

Luke 13.34-35 also introduces Jesus as a rejected saviour. Jesus' offer of protection from threat is rejected (13.34), but the quotation of Ps. 117.26 in Lk. 13.35 holds out hope that Jesus would be welcomed subsequently as Messiah and God's agent of eschatological salvation. When this psalm is repeated during the entry to Jerusalem (Lk. 19.28-40), it is only on the lips of Jesus' disciples, not the city leadership, making this a non-triumphal entry. The lament of 19.42-44 equates this rejection of Jesus' peace and saving visitation with inevitable disaster, and the subsequent quotation of Isa. 56.7 (19.45-46) criticises the leadership for failing to embrace the eschatological age which Jesus inaugurates. Luke 23.28-31 also makes an association between the leaders' rejection of Jesus, and the destruction of the city: they did not act as fruitful Israel, bearing fruit and welcoming the Messiah in the time of the green, and the consequences will be realised in the time of the dry (Lk. 23.31).

The rejection motif continues in Acts with the rejection of the apostles' teaching (3.1, 11-26; 5.12, 20-21), and in the strong counter-accusation made by Stephen (7.52). Finally, in Stephen's vision (7.55-56) Jesus is seen as the locus of salvation, taking the function of the temple.

The Fate of the Temple

Luke is clear that the temple (and city) will be destroyed; although he is not critical of the temple itself, he is critical of the attitudes of the Jerusalem leadership towards it. The laments imply that the destruction of the temple is a divine judgement, and it happens as a consequence of the leaders rejecting Jesus as saviour (Lk. 19.42, 44; 23.28-31, confirmed by the torn temple veil). While the rejection of Jesus is the most significant accusation made, Acts 7 also showed that the destruction of the city was the result of idolatry, an idolatry centred on the temple as a place of false localisation of God, and manipulation of God. These accusations of rejection of Jesus and idolatry are related together in Acts 7, like the rejection of Moses and idolatry in Acts 7.39-41. In part, this is because both actions provide evidence of the people's rejection of God, but also because their idolatry led to the rejection of Jesus. In limiting God to the temple, they refused to listen to God speaking outside their defined confines, and they refused to welcome his eschatological salvation (Lk. 19.46); rejecting Jesus was therefore the fruit of their idolatry, and in killing Jesus the judgement falls on their covenant unfaithfulness centred on temple practices.

At the same time, killing Jesus was also the final rejection of the only offer of salvation that could avert this coming disaster. Jesus had offered to protect the people from this threat in Lk. 13.34; and Lk. 19.30-40 portrayed Jesus as the coming king who brought peace, whose rejection (in 19.42) had the inevitable consequence of military action.[1]

General Observations

The study also permits observations to be made on four areas of debate within Lukan scholarship.

First, it confirms the conclusions of Chapter 2 that Luke's use of the OT is varied. The OT is used to create frameworks of expectancy, whether through a single verse (e.g., Zech. 9.9 in Lk. 19.30-37), or through allusion to texts and motifs in Stephen's history in Acts 7. Quotations can have a

---

1. The same point is made in 19:44.

literary function in subverting expectations (Amos 5.25-27; Isa. 66.1-2 in Acts 7.42-43, 49-50), and in linking texts (Ps. 117.26 in Lk. 13.35; 19.38), as well as evoking a prior context in order to add to the argument (e.g., Jer. 7.11 in 19.46). Texts are fulfilled (e.g., τοῦ πλησθῆναι πάντα τὰ γεγραμμένα, Lk. 21.22), and intertextual allusions made throughout the texts examined – sometimes the allusion is to a motif, a genre (e.g., prophetic threats and laments in Lk. 19.42-44), as well as specific texts. OT texts also develop a theological framework: though not as obvious as the Isaianic New Exodus, or Peter Doble's observations about the Psalms,[2] four chapters from the OT which refer to idolatry in a temple setting play a significant role (Jer. 7; Hos. 10; Amos 5; Isa. 66), and after Acts 7 it is likely that a reader would re-read the Jesus material with this linkage in mind.

Second, this study adds further evidence for the unity of Luke–Acts because of the relationship of Acts 7 to the laments in the Gospel. This is more than the observation that there is benefit in reading them together, it is a unity of intent that they should be read together, shown in the postponement of the discussion of Jesus' temple material to Stephen's trial.

Third, the majority of scholars date Luke and Acts between 70 CE and 90 CE; a significant part of the argument concerns the language of military siege in Lk. 19.41-44 and 21.20-24, and the emphasis on Jerusalem (rather than the temple) which suggest a date after 70 CE.[3] But this must be challenged. Luke's descriptions in 19.41-44 and 21.20-24 omit specific details found in Josephus' version of events, and 19.41-44 contains Semitisms suggestive of original Jesus material.[4] So, if Luke wrote after the event, it suggests that it was very soon after, and before alternative traditions were established.[5] While it is difficult to press matters too far, the omission of fire from the description would require remarkable restraint if he wrote after the event, and this suggests a date

---

2. Pao, *Acts*; Doble, 'Psalms'.

3. E.g., Johnson, *Luke*, 2–3; Spencer, *Acts*, 16; Witherington, *Acts*, 60–63. For a comprehensive review of the dating issues, see Colin J. Hemer, *The Book of Acts in the Setting of Hellenistic History*, WUNT 49 (Tübingen: J. C. B. Mohr [Paul Siebeck], 1989), 367–70; Fitzmyer, *Acts*, 51–55. For a much later date for Acts, see Joseph B. Tyson, *Marcion and Luke–Acts: A Defining Struggle* (Columbia: University of South Carolina Press, 2006); Richard I. Pervo, *Dating Acts: Between the Evangelists and the Apologists* (Santa Rosa: Polebridge, 2006)

4. See Dupont, 'Pierre', 312.

5. Bovon, *Luc*, 42.

in the late sixties. Acts is probably written after the event,[6] but nothing in Acts 7 decides matters one way or the other. Perhaps the omission of the description of the fall of the city from Acts 7 supports a date after 70 CE because description is redundant, with readers already aware of it. This raises the interesting possibility that the Gospel was written just before the event and Acts after, but this is conjecture.

Fourth, Luke's overall view of the temple cannot be stated here because the more positive material has not been examined, but certain statements can be made. Luke does not reject the temple at any point in this apparently critical material; the message is strongly critical of attitudes towards the temple, which amount to idolatry, but this criticism is made through allusion to the prophets, making Luke–Acts as critical as the OT prophets are. The foretold destruction of the temple occurred because of the idolatry of the people (like in the prophets); it was a consequence of refusing Jesus' offer of protection. But Luke is positive about the temple in many places: it should have been a place for prayer and preaching (as it was for many characters in his narrative); however, the Jerusalem leaders did not allow the temple to take this eschatological role that belonged to it (Lk. 19.46). Even after the divine abandonment of the temple (Lk. 23.45), the temple continued to have an important role, up until the martyrdom of Stephen. Yet it was not the locus of salvation – Jesus alone was saviour. For a more comprehensive statement, however, it is important to engage with the other material.

---

6. Though likely before the reign of Domitian (81–96 CE) because there is no clear reference to the persecution associated with that emperor in the narrative; see Fitzmyer, *Acts*, 54–55.

Bibliography

Abasciano, Brian J. 'Diamonds in the Rough: A Reply to Christopher Stanley Concerning the Reader Competency of Paul's Original Audiences'. *NovT* 49 (2007): 153–83.

Adams, Edward. *The Stars Will Fall from Heaven: Cosmic Catastrophe in the New Testament and Its World*. LNTS 347. London: T&T Clark, 2007.

Ådna, Jostein. *Jesu Stellung zum Tempel*. WUNT 2/119. Tübingen: Mohr Siebeck, 2000.

———. 'Jesus and the Temple'. Pages 2635–75 in vol. 3 of *Handbook for the Study of the Historical Jesus*. Edited by Tom Holmén and Stanley E. Porter. 4 vols. Leiden: Brill, 2011.

———. 'Jesus' Symbolic Act in the Temple (Mark 11:15–17): The Replacement of the Sacrificial Cult by His Atoning Death'. Pages 461–75 in *Gemeinde ohne Tempel / Community without temple: zur Substituierung und Transformation des Jerusalemer Tempels und seines Kults im Alten Testament, antiken Judentum und frühen Christentum*. Edited by Beate Ego, Armin Lange and Peter Pilhofer. WUNT 118. Tübingen: Mohr Siebeck, 1999.

Ahearne-Kroll, Stephen P. *The Psalms of Lament in Mark's Passion: Jesus' Davidic Suffering*. SNTSMS 142. Cambridge: Cambridge University Press, 2007.

Aland, Barbara, Kurt Aland, Johannes Karavidopoulos, Carlo M. Martini, and Bruce M. Metzger, eds. *Novum Testamentum Graece*. 27th ed. Stuttgart: Deutsche Bibelgesellschaft, 1996.

———, eds. *Novum Testamentum Graece*. 28th ed. Stuttgart: Deutsche Bibelgesellschaft, 2012.

Albl, Martin C. *And Scripture Cannot Be Broken: The Form and Function of the Early Christian Testimonia Collections*. NovTSup 96. Leiden: Brill, 1999.

Alexander, Joseph A. *The Gospel According to Mark*. GSC. Edinburgh: Banner of Truth Trust, 1960 (orig. 1858).

Alexander, Loveday C. A. 'The Preface to Acts and the Historians'. Pages 73–103 in *History, Literature and Society in the Book of Acts*. Edited by Ben Witherington. Cambridge: Cambridge University Press, 1996.

———. 'Reading Luke–Acts from Back to Front'. Pages 419–46 in *The Unity of Luke–Acts*. Edited by Jozef Verheyden. BETL 142. Leuven: Leuven University Press, 1999.

Allen, Leslie C. *The Books of Joel, Obadiah, Jonah and Micah*. NICOT. London: Hodder & Stoughton, 1976.

———. *Psalms 101–150*. WBC 21. Waco: World Books, 1983.

Allison, Dale C. *The Intertextual Jesus: Scripture in Q*. Harrisburg, PA: Trinity Press International, 2000.

———. 'Jesus and the Victory of Apocalyptic'. Pages 126–41 in *Jesus and the Restoration of Israel: A Critical Assessment of N. T. Wright's Jesus and the Victory of God*. Edited by C. C. Newman. Carlisle: Paternoster, 1999.

———. *Jesus of Nazareth: Millenarian Prophet*. Minneapolis: Fortress, 1998.

———. 'Matt. 23:39 = Luke 13:35b as Conditional Prophecy'. *JSNT* 18 (1983): 75–84.

Almazán García, Eva María. 'Dwelling in Marble Halls: A Relevance-Theoretic Approach to Intertextuality in Translation'. *RAEI* 14 (2001): 7–19.

Angel, Andrew R. *Chaos and the Son of Man: The Hebrew Chaoskampf Tradition in the Period 515 BCE to 200 CE*. LSTS 60. London: T&T Clark, 2006.

———. 'The Son of Man: Jesus, Eschatology and Mission'. *Anvil* 26, no. 3–4 (2009): 219–30.

Arai, Sasagu. 'Zum "Tempelwort" Jesu in Apostelgeschichte 6:14'. *NTS* 34, no. 3 (1988): 397–410.

Arndt, William, Frederick W. Danker, Walter Bauer, and Gringrich. F. W., eds. *A Greek–English Lexicon of the New Testament and Other Early Christian Literature*. 3rd ed. Chicago: University of Chicago Press, 2000.

Attridge, Harold W. *The Epistle to the Hebrews: A Commentary on the Epistle to the Hebrews*. Hermeneia. Philadelphia: Fortress, 1989.

Aune, David E. *The Cultic Setting of Realized Eschatology in Early Christianity*. Leiden: Brill, 1972.

Bachmann, Michael. 'Die Stephanusepisode (Apg 6,1-8,3): Ihre Bedeutung Für die Lukanische Sicht des jerusalemischen Tempels und des Judentums'. Pages 545–62 in *The Unity of Luke–Acts*. Edited by Jozef Verheyden. BETL 142. Leuven: Leuven University Press, 1999.

Baldwin, John T. 'Reimarus and the Return of Christ Revisited: Reflections on Luke 21:24b and Its Phrase "Times of the Gentiles" in Historicist Perspective'. *JATS* 11, no. 1–2 (2000): 295–306.

Ballard, H. Wayne Jr. *The Divine Warrior Motif in the Psalms*. BDS 6. North Richland Hills: Bibal, 1999.

Baltzer, Klaus. 'The Meaning of the Temple in the Lukan Writings'. *HTR* 58, no. 3 (1965): 263–77.

Barrett, C. K. 'Attitudes to the Temple in the Acts of the Apostles'. Pages 345–67 in *Templum Amicitiae: Essays on the Second Temple Presented to Ernst Bammel*. Edited by William Horbury. JSNTSup 48. Sheffield: JSOT, 1991.

———. *A Critical and Exegetical Commentary on the Acts of the Apostles*. ICC. 2 vols. Edinburgh: T&T Clark, 1994–98.

———. 'The House of Prayer and the Den of Thieves'. Pags 13–20 in *Jesus und Paulus: Festschrift Für Werner Georg Kümmel*. Edited by E. Earle Ellis and Erich Gräßer. Göttingen: Vandenhoeck und Ruprecht, 1975.

———. 'Luke/Acts'. Pages 231–44 in *It Is Written: Scripture Citing Scripture: Essays in Honour of Barnabas Lindars*. Edited by D. A. Carson and H. G. M. Williamson. Cambridge: Cambridge University Press, 1988.

———. 'Old Testament History According to Stephen and Paul'. Pages 57–69 in *Studien zum Text und zur Ethik des Neuen Testaments: Festschrift zum 80. Geburtstag von Heinrich Greeven*. Edited by Wolfgang Schrage. Berlin: de Gruyter, 1986.

———. 'Stephen and the Son of Man'. Pages 32–38 in *Apophoreta: Festschrift für Ernst Haenchen*. Edited by W. Eltester and F. H. Kettler. BZNW 30. Berlin: de Gruyter, 1964.

Bauckham, Richard, ed. *The Gospels for All Christians: Rethinking the Gospel Audiences*. Grand Rapids: Eerdmans, 1998.

———. 'Jesus' Demonstration in the Temple'. Pages 72–89 in *Law and Religion: Essays on the Place of the Law in Israel and Early Christianity*. Edited by Barnabas Lindars. Cambridge: James Clarke, 1988.

———. *Jude, 2 Peter*. WBC 50. Waco: Word Books, 1983.

———. 'The Restoration of Israel in Luke–Acts'. Pages 435–87 in *Restoration: Old Testament, Jewish, and Christian Perspectives*. Edited by M. Scott. JSPSup 7. Leiden: Brill, 2001.

Beale, Gregory K. 'The Descent of the Eschatological Temple in the Form of the Spirit at Pentecost: Part 1: The Clearest Evidence'. *TynBul* 56, no. 1 (2005): 73–102.

———. 'The Descent of the Eschatological Temple in the Form of the Spirit at Pentecost: Part 2: The Corroborating Evidence'. *TynBul* 56, no. 2 (2005): 63–90.

———. *The Temple and the Church's Mission: A Biblical Theology of the Dwelling Place of God*. NSBT 17. Leicester: Apollos; Downers Grove: InterVarsity Press, 2004.

Beasley-Murray, George R. *Jesus and the Kingdom of God*. Grand Rapids: Eerdmans; Exeter: Paternoster, 1986.

———. *Jesus and the Last Days: The Interpretation of the Olivet Discourse*. Peabody, MA: Hendrickson, 1993.

Benoit, Pierre. *The Passion and Resurrection of Jesus Christ*. Translated by Benet Weatherhead. New York: Herder and Herder; London: Darton, Longman & Todd, 1969.

Betz, Hans Dieter. 'Jesus and the Purity of the Temple (Mark 11:15-18): A Comparative Religion Approach'. *JBL* 116, no. 3 (1997): 455–72.

Bird, Michael F. 'The Unity of Luke–Acts in Recent Discussion'. *JSNT* 29, no. 4 (2007): 425–48.

Blass, Friedrich, Albert Debrunner, and Robert Walter Funk, eds. *A Greek Grammar of the New Testament and Other Early Christian Literature*. Chicago: University of Chicago Press, 1961.

Blenkinsopp, Joseph. 'The Oracle of Judah and the Messianic Entry'. *JBL* 80, no. 1 (1961): 55–64.

Bloom, Harold. *The Anxiety of Influence: A Theory of Poetry*. 2nd ed. New York; Oxford: Oxford University Press, 1997.

Bloomquist, L. Gregory. 'Rhetorical Argumentation and the Culture of Apocalyptic: A Socio-Rhetorical Analysis of Luke 21'. Pages 173–209 in *The Rhetorical Interpretation of Scripture: Essays from the 1996 Malibu Conference*. Edited by Stanley E. Porter and Dennis L. Stamps. JSNTSup 180. Sheffield: Sheffield Academic, 1999.

Bock, Darrell L. *Acts*. BECNT. Grand Rapids: Baker Academic, 2007.

———. *Luke*. BECNT. 2 vols. Grand Rapids: Baker Academic, 1994–96.

———. *Proclamation from Prophecy and Pattern: Lucan Old Testament Christology*. JSNTSup 12. Sheffield: JSOT, 1987.

———. *A Theology of Luke and Acts: Biblical Theology of the New Testament*. Grand Rapids: Zondervan, 2012.

———. 'The Use of Daniel 7 in Jesus' Trial, with Implications for His Self-Understanding'. Pages 78–100 in *'Who Is This Son of Man?': The Latest Scholarship on a Puzzling Expression of the Historical Jesus*. Edited by Larry W. Hurtado and Paul Owen. LNTS 390. London: T&T Clark, 2011.

Boismard, M. É. 'Le Martyre D' Etienne: Acts 6, 8-8, 2'. *RSR* 69, no. 2 (1981): 181–94.

Bolt, Peter G. *The Cross from a Distance: Atonement in Mark's Gospel*. NSBT 18. Leicester: Apollos, 2004.

Borg, Marcus J. *Conflict, Holiness, and Politics in the Teachings of Jesus*. Harrisburg, PA: Trinity Press International, 1998.

———. 'Luke 19:42–44 and Jesus as Prophet'. *Forum* 8, no. 1–2 (1992): 99–112.

Bovon, François. *L'Évangile Selon Saint Luc 19,28–24,53*. CNT Deuxième Série 3d. Genève: Labor et Fides, 2009.

———. *Luke the Theologian: Fifty-Five Years of Research (1950-2005)*. 2nd rev. ed. Waco: Baylor University Press, 2006.

Brandon, S. G. F. *Jesus and the Zealots: A Study of the Political Factor in Primitive Christianity*. Manchester: Manchester University Press, 1967.

Braumann, Georg. 'Die lukanische Interpretation der Zerstörung Jerusalems'. *NovT* 6, no. 2 (1963): 120–27.

Brawley, Robert L. *Luke–Acts and the Jews: Conflict, Apology, and Conciliation*. Atlanta: Scholars Press, 1987.

———. *Text to Text Pours Forth Speech: Voices of Scripture in Luke–Acts*. ISBL. Bloomington: Indiana University Press, 1995.

Brehm, H. Alan. 'Vindicating the Rejected One: Stephen's Speech as a Critique of the Jewish Leaders'. Pages 166–97 in *Early Christian Interpretation of the Scriptures of Israel: Investigations and Proposals*. Edited by Craig A. Evans and James A. Sanders. Sheffield: Sheffield Academic, 1997.

Bridge, Steven L. *'Where the Eagles Are Gathered': The Deliverance of the Elect in Lukan Eschatology*. JSNTSup 240. London: Sheffield Academic, 2003.

Bright, John. *Jeremiah*. AB 21. New York: Doubleday, 1965.

Brodie, Thomas L. *The Birthing of the New Testament. The Intertextual Development of the New Testament Writings*. Sheffield: Sheffield Phoenix, 2004.

———. 'Intertextuality and Its Use in Tracing Q and Proto-Luke'. Pages 469–77 in *The Scriptures in the Gospels*. Edited by C. M. Tuckett. Leuven: Leuven University Press/Uitgeverij Peeters, 1997.

———. 'Luke 7, 36–50 as an Internalization of 2 Kings 4, 1–37: A Study in Luke's Use of Rhetorical Imitation'. *Bib* 64, no. 4 (1983): 457–85.

———. 'Luke's Use of the Elijah–Elisha Narrative'. Pages 6–29 in *The Elijah–Elisha Narrative in the Composition of Luke*. Edited by John S. Kloppenborg and Jozef Verheyden. LNTS 493. London: Bloomsbury T&T Clark, 2014.

———. 'Towards Unraveling the Rhetorical Imitation of Sources in Acts: 2 Kings 5 as One Component of Acts 8, 9–40'. *Bib* 67, no. 1 (1986): 41–67.

Brown, Raymond. *The Death of the Messiah: From Gethsemane to the Grave: A Commentary on the Passion Narratives in the Four Gospels*. ABRL. 2 vols. New York: Doubleday; London: Geoffrey Chapman, 1994.

Bruce, F. F. *The Acts of the Apostles: The Greek Text and Introduction with Commentary*. 3rd ed. Leicester: Apollos, 1990.

———. *The Book of the Acts*. NICNT. Grand Rapids: Eerdmans, 1954.

———. 'Stephen's Apologia'. Pages 37–50 in *Scripture: Meaning and Method: Essays Presented to Anthony Tyrrell Hanson for His Seventieth Birthday*. Edited by Barry P. Thompson. Hull: Hull University Press, 1987.

Brueggemann, Walter. *A Commentary on Jeremiah: Exile and Homecoming*. Grand Rapids: Eerdmans, 1998.

———. 'Kingship and Chaos: A Study in Tenth Century Theology'. *CBQ* 33, no. 3 (1971): 317–32.

———. *Theology of the Old Testament: Testimony, Dispute, Advocacy*. Minneapolis: Fortress, 1997.

———. 'Weariness, Exile and Chaos: A Motif in Royal Theology'. *CBQ* 34, no. 1 (1972): 19–38.

Brunson, Andrew. *Psalm 118 in the Gospel of John: An Intertextual Study on the New Exodus Pattern in the Theology of John*. WUNT 2/158. Tübingen: Mohr Siebeck, 2003.

Bryan, Steven M. *Jesus and Israel's Traditions of Judgement and Restoration*. SNTSMS 117. Cambridge: Cambridge University Press, 2002.

Büchele, Anton. *Der Tod Jesu im Lukasevangelium: Eine redaktionsgeschichtliche Untersuchung zu Lk 23*. FTS 26. Frankfurt: Knecht, 1978.

Buckwalter, Douglas. *The Character and Purpose of Luke's Christology*. SNTSMS 89. Cambridge: Cambridge University Press, 1996.

Bultmann, Rudolf. *The History of the Synoptic Tradition*. Translated by John Marsh. Rev ed. Oxford: Blackwell, 1968.

Buzzard, Anthony F. 'Luke's Prelude to the Kingdom of God: The Fall of Jerusalem and the End of the Age — Luke 21:20-33'. *JRadRef* 4, no. 4 (1995): 32–43.

Cadbury, Henry J. *The Making of Luke–Acts*. London: SPCK, 1961; orig. pub., 1927.

Caird, George B. *The Gospel of St Luke*. London: Penguin, 1963.

———. *The Language and Imagery of the Bible*. London: Duckworth, 1980.

Caird, George B., and Lincoln D. Hurst. *New Testament Theology*. Oxford: Clarendon Press, 1994.

Carr, Dhyanchand. 'Jesus, the King of Zion: A Traditio-Historical Enquiry into the So-Called 'Triumphal' Entry of Jesus'. Ph.D. diss., Kings College, London, 1980.

Carrington, Philip. *According to Mark: A Running Commentary on the Oldest Gospel*. Cambridge: University Press, 1960.

Carroll, John T. *Luke: A Commentary*. NTL. Louisville: Westminster John Knox, 2012.

———. *Response to the End of History: Eschatology and Situation in Luke–Acts*. SBLDS 92. Atlanta: Scholars Press, 1988.

Casey, Maurice. 'Culture and Historicity: The Cleansing of the Temple'. *CBQ* 59, no. 2 (1997): 306–32.

———. *The Solution to the "Son of Man" Problem*. LNTS 343. London: T&T Clark, 2007.

Catchpole, David R. 'The "Triumphal" Entry'. Pages 319–34 in *Jesus and the Politics of His Day*. Edited by Ernst Bammel and C. F. D. Moule. Cambridge: Cambridge University Press, 1984.

Catto, Stephen K. *Reconstructing the First-Century Synagogue: A Critical Analysis of Current Research*. LNTS 363. London: T&T Clark, 2007.

Chance, J. Bradley. 'The Cursing of the Temple and the Tearing of the Veil in the Gospel of Mark'. *BibInt* 15, no. 3 (2007): 268–91.

———. *Jerusalem, the Temple, and the New Age in Luke–Acts*. Macon: Mercer University Press, 1988.

Childs, Brevard S. *Exodus: A Commentary*. London: SCM, 1974.

———. *Introduction to the Old Testament as Scripture*. Philadelphia: Fortress, 1979.

———. *Isaiah*. OTL. Louisville: Westminster John Knox, 2001.

Clark, Herbert H., and Richard J. Gerrig. 'Quotations as Demonstrations'. *Language* 66, no. 4 (1990): 764–805.

Clarke, William K. L. *Divine Humanity; Doctrinal Essays on New Testament Problems*. London: SPCK, 1936.

———. 'The Use of the Septuagint in Acts'. Pages 66–105 in vol. 2 of *The Beginnings of Christianity*. Edited by F. J. Foakes Jackson and Kirsopp Lake. 5 vols. London: Macmillan, 1920–33.

Clifford, Richard J. *The Cosmic Mountain in Canaan and the Old Testament*. Cambridge: Harvard University Press, 1972.

Collins, Adela Yarbro. 'Introduction: Early Christian Apocalypticism'. *Semeia* 36 (1986): 1–11.

Collins, C. John. 'כבד'. Pages 577–87 in vol. 2 of *NIDOTTE*.
Collins, John J. Review of Chaos and the Son of Man: The Hebrew Chaoskampf Tradition in the Period 515 BCE to 200 CE. *JJS* 58 (2007): 338–9.
———. *Daniel: A Commentary on the Book of Daniel*. Hermeneia. Minneapolis: Fortress, 1993.
———. 'Introduction: Towards the Morphology of a Genre'. *Semeia* 14 (1979): 1–19.
———. *The Scepter and the Star: The Messiahs of the Dead Sea Scrolls and Other Ancient Literature*. New York: Doubleday, 1995.
Conzelmann, Hans. *Acts of the Apostles: A Commentary on the Acts of the Apostles*. Translated by James Limburg, A. Thomas Kraabel and Donald H. Juel. Hermeneia. Philadelphia: Fortress, 1987.
———. *The Theology of St. Luke*. Translated by Geoffrey Buswell. London: Faber, 1960.
Cook, Stephen L. 'Cosmos, *Kabod*, and Cherub: Ontological and Epistemological Hierarchy in Ezekiel'. Pages 179–97 in *Ezekiel's Hierarchical World: Wrestling with a Tiered Reality*. Edited by Stephen L. Cook and Corrine L. Patton. Atlanta: Society of Biblical Literature, 2004.
Craigie, Peter C. *Psalms 1–50*. WBC 19. Waco: Word Books, 1983.
Craigie, Peter C., Page H. Kelley, and Joel F. Drinkard. *Jeremiah 1–25*. WBC 26. Dallas: Word Books, 1991.
Creed, John M. *The Gospel According to St. Luke: The Greek Text with Introduction, Notes, and Indices*. London: Macmillan, 1930.
Croatto, J. Severino. 'Jesus, Prophet Like Elijah, and Prophet-Teacher Like Moses in Luke–Acts'. *JBL* 124, no. 3 (2005): 451–65.
Crossan, John Dominic. *The Historical Jesus: The Life of a Mediterranean Jewish Peasant*. Edinburgh: T&T Clark, 1991.
Crump, David M. *Jesus the Intercessor: Prayer and Christology in Luke–Acts*. Grand Rapids: Baker, 1999.
Dahl, Nils A. 'The Story of Abraham in Luke–Acts'. Pages 139–58 in *Studies in Luke–Acts: Essays Presented in Honor of Paul Schubert*. Edited by Leander E. Keck and J. Louis Martyn. Nashville: Abingdon, 1966.
Dahood, Mitchell J. *Psalms*. AB 16–17a. 3 vols. Garden City: Doubleday, 1965–70.
Danker, Frederick W. *Jesus and the New Age: A Commentary on St. Luke's Gospel*. Philadelphia: Fortress, 1972.
Davies, W. D., and Dale Allison, C. *A Critical and Exegetical Commentary on the Gospel According to Saint Matthew*. ICC. 3 vols. Edinburgh: T&T Clark, 1988–97.
Day, John. *Yahweh and the Gods and Goddesses of Canaan*. Sheffield: Sheffield Academic, 2002.
Denova, Rebecca I. *The Things Accomplished among Us: Prophetic Tradition in the Structural Pattern of Luke–Acts*. JSNTSup 141. Sheffield: Sheffield Academic, 1997.
Derrett, J. Duncan M. 'Law in the New Testament: The Palm Sunday Colt'. *NovT* 13, no. 4 (1971): 241–58.
deSilva, David A. 'The Stoning of Stephen: Purging and Consolidating an Endangered Institution'. *StudBT* 17 (1989): 165–84.
Dibelius, Martin. *Studies in the Acts of the Apostles*. London: SCM, 1956.
Doble, Peter. '"Are These Things So?" (Acts 7:1): A Narrative-Intertextual Approach to Reading Stephen's Speech'. Pages 95–113 in *The Scriptures of Israel in Jewish and Christian Tradition: Essays in Honour of Maarten J. J. Menken*. Edited by Bart J. Koet, Steve Moyise and Joseph Verheyden. NovTSup 148. Leiden: Brill, 2013.

———. 'Luke 24.26, 44—Songs of God's Servant: David and His Psalms in Luke–Acts'. *JSNT* 28, no. 3 (2006): 267–83.
———. *The Paradox of Salvation: Luke's Theology of the Cross*. SNTSMS 87. Cambridge: Cambridge University Press, 1996.
———. 'The Psalms in Luke–Acts'. Pages 83–117 in *The Psalms in the New Testament*. Edited by Steve Moyise and Maarten J. J. Menken. London: T&T Clark, 2004.
———. 'Something Greater Than Solomon: An Approach to Stephen's Speech'. Pages 181–207 in *The Old Testament in the New: Essays in Honour of J. L. North*. Edited by Steve Moyise. JSNTSup 189. Sheffield: Sheffield Academic, 2000.
———. 'The Son of Man Saying in Stephen's Witnessing'. *NTS* 31, no. 1 (1985): 68–84.
Dodd, C. H. *According to the Scriptures: The Sub-Structure of New Testament Theology*. London: Fontana, 1952.
———. 'The Fall of Jerusalem and the "Abomination of Desolation"'. Pages 69–83 in *More New Testament Studies*. Edited by C. H. Dodd. Manchester: Manchester University Press, 1968.
———. *The Parables of the Kingdom*. Revised ed. London: Nisbet, 1935.
Drury, John. *Tradition and Design in Luke's Gospel: A Study in Early Christian Historiography*. Atlanta: John Knox, 1976.
Dschulnigg, Peter. 'Die Rede des Stephanus im Rahmen des Berichtes über Sein Martyrium (Apg 6,8-8,3)'. *Jud* 44 (1988): 195–213.
Duff, Paul B. 'The March of the Divine Warrior and the Advent of the Greco-Roman King: Mark's Account of Jesus' Entry into Jerusalem'. *JBL* 111, no. 1 (1992): 55–71.
Dunn, James D. G. *Beginning from Jerusalem*. Christianity in the Making 2. Grand Rapids: Eerdmans, 2009.
———. *Jesus Remembered*. Christianity in the Making 1. Grand Rapids: Eerdmans, 2003.
———. *The Partings of the Ways: Between Christianity and Judaism and Their Significance for the Character of Christianity*. London: SCM, 1991.
Dupont, Jacques. *Études sur Les Actes des Apôtres*. LD. Paris: Éditions du Cerf, 1967.
———. 'Il n'en sera pas laissé pierre sur pierre (Marc 13,2; Luc 19,44)'. *Bib* 52 (1971): 301–20.
———. 'La Structure Oratoire du Discours d'Etienne (Actes 7)'. *Bib* 66 (1985): 153–67.
Dyer, Keith D. *The Prophecy on the Mount: Mark 13 and the Gathering of the New Community*. ITS 2. Bern: Peter Lang, 1998.
Easter, Matthew C. '"Certainly This Man Was Righteous": Highlighting a Messianic Reading of the Centurion's Confession in Luke 23:47'. *TynBul* 63, no. 1 (2012): 35–51.
Edwards, James R. *The Gospel According to Luke*. PNTC. Nottingham: Apollos, 2015.
Ellis, E. Earle. *The Gospel of Luke*. NCB. London: Oliphants, 1966.
———. *The Old Testament in Early Christianity: Canon and Interpretation in the Light of Modern Research*. Tübingen: J. C. B. Mohr (Paul Siebeck), 1991.
Ernst, Josef. *Das Evangelium nach Lukas*. RNT. Regensburg: Friedrich Pustet, 1977.
Esler, Philip F. *Community and Gospel in Luke–Acts: The Social and Political Motivations of Lucan Theology*. Cambridge: Cambridge University Press, 1987.
Eubank, Nathan. 'A Disconcerting Prayer: On the Originality of Luke 23:34a'. *JBL* 129, no. 3 (2010): 521–36.
Evans, Christopher F. 'The Central Section of Luke's Gospel'. Pages 37–53 in *Studies in the Gospels: Essays in Memory of R. H. Lightfoot*. Edited by Dennis Eric Nineham. Oxford: Blackwell, 1955.
———. *Saint Luke*. TPINTC. London: SCM, 1990.

Evans, Craig A. 'Early Rabbinic Sources and Jesus Research'. *SBLSP* 34 (1995): 53–76.
———. 'God's Vineyard and Its Caretakers'. Pages 381–406 in *Jesus and His Contemporaries: Comparative Studies*. Edited by Craig A. Evans. AGJU 25. Leiden: Brill, 1995.
———. 'Jesus and the "Cave of Robbers": Towards a Jewish Context for the Temple Action'. Pages 345–65 in *Jesus and His Contemporaries: Comparative Studies*. Edited by Craig A. Evans. AGJU 25. Leiden: Brill, 1995.
———. 'Jesus' Action in the Temple and Evidence of Corruption in the First-Century Temple'. Pages 319–44 in *Jesus and His Contemporaries: Comparative Studies*. Edited by Craig A. Evans. AGJU 25. Leiden: Brill, 1995.
———. 'Jesus' Action in the Temple: Cleansing or Portent of Destruction?'. *CBQ* 51, no. 2 (1989): 237–70.
———. 'Luke and the Rewritten Bible: Aspects of Lukan Hagiography'. Pages 170–201 in *The Pseudepigrapha and Early Biblical Interpretation*. Edited by James H. Charlesworth and Craig A. Evans. JSPSup 14. Sheffield: JSOT, 1993.
———. *Mark 8:27–16:20*. WBC 34B. Nashville: Thomas Nelson, 2001.
———. 'Midrash'. Pages 544–48 in *DJG*.
———. 'Old Testament in the Gospels'. Pages 579–90 in *DJG*.
Evans, Craig A., and James A. Sanders. 'Gospels and Midrash: An Introduction to Luke and Scripture'. Pages 1–13 in *Luke and Scripture: The Function of Sacred Tradition in Luke–Acts*. Edited by Craig A. Evans and James A. Sanders. Minneapolis: Fortress, 1993.
Fantin, Joseph D. *The Lord of the Entire World: Lord Jesus, a Challenge to Lord Caesar?* Sheffield: Sheffield Phoenix, 2011.
Fay, Ron C. 'The Narrative Function of the Temple in Luke–Acts'. *TJ* 27, no. 2 (2006): 255–70.
Fisk, Bruce N. 'See My Tears: A Lament for Jerusalem (Luke 13:31–35; 19:41–44)'. Pages 147–78 in *The Word Leaps the Gap: Essays on Scripture and Theology in Honor of Richard B. Hays*. Edited by J. Ross Wagner, Christopher Kavin Rowe and A. Katherine Grieb. Grand Rapids: Eerdmans, 2008.
Fitzmyer, Joseph A. *The Acts of the Apostles: A New Translation with Introduction and Commentary*. AB 31. New York: Doubleday, 1998.
———. *Gospel According to Luke: A New Translation with Introduction and Commentary*. AB 28–28A. 2 vols. New York: Doubleday, 1981–85.
———. 'The Use of the Old Testament in Luke–Acts'. *SBLSP* 31 (1992): 524–38.
Fletcher-Louis, Crispin H. T. 'The Destruction of the Temple and the Relativization of the Old Covenant: Mark 13:31 and Matthew 5:18'. Pages 145–69 in *The Reader Must Understand: Eschatology in Bible and Theology*. Edited by Mark Elliott and Kent Brower. Nottingham: Apollos, 1998.
———. *Luke–Acts: Angels, Christology and Soteriology*. WUNT 2/94. Tübingen: Mohr Siebeck, 1997.
Flückiger, F. 'Luk 21.20-24 und die Zerstörung Jerusalems'. *TZ* 28 (1972): 385–90.
Focant, Camille. 'Du Fils de l'homme assis (Lc 22,69) au Fils de l'homme debout (Ac 7,56)'. Pages 563–76 in *The Unity of Luke–Acts*. Edited by Jozef Verheyden. BETL 142. Leuven: Leuven University Press, 1999.
Foerster, Werner. 'Ἐπισυναγωγή' (translated by Geoffrey William Bromiley). Pages 841–43 in vol. 7 of *TDNT*.

France, R. T. *The Gospel of Mark: A Commentary on the Greek Text*. NIGTC. Carlisle: Paternoster, 2002.

———. *Jesus and the Old Testament: His Application of Old Testament Passages to Himself and His Mission*. Vancouver: Regent College Publishing, 1998.

Fredriksen, Paula. *Jesus of Nazareth, King of the Jews: A Jewish Life and the Emergence of Christianity*. London: Macmillan, 1999.

Frein, Brigid C. 'Narrative Predictions, Old Testament Prophecies and Luke's Sense of Fulfilment'. *NTS* 40, no. 1 (1994): 22–37.

Furlong, Anne. 'Relevance Theory and Literary Interpretation'. Ph.D. diss., University College London, 1996.

Fusco, Vittorio. 'Problems of Structure in Luke's Eschatological Discourse (Luke 21:7–36)' (trans. Matthew J. O'Connell). Pages 72–92 in *Luke and Acts*. Edited by Gerald O'Collins and Gilberto Marconi. New York: Paulist Press, 1993.

Gaston, Lloyd. *No Stone on Another: Studies in the Significance of the Fall of Jerusalem in the Synoptic Gospels*. NovTSup 23. Leiden: Brill, 1970.

Gaventa, Beverly R. *Acts*. ANTC. Nashville: Abingdon, 2003.

Geiger, Ruthild. *Die Lukanischen Endzeitreden: Studien zur Eschatologie des Lukas-Evangeliums*. Bern: Herbert Lang; Frankfurt: Peter Lang, 1973.

Geldenhuys, Norval. *Commentary on the Gospel of Luke*. NLC. London: Marshall, Morgan & Scott, 1950.

Gibbs, Jeffrey A. *Jerusalem and Parousia: Jesus' Eschatological Discourse in Matthew's Gospel*. Saint Louis: Concordia Academic Press, 2000.

Giblin, Charles H. *The Destruction of Jerusalem According to Luke's Gospel: A Historical-Typological Moral*. Rome: Biblical Institute Press, 1985.

Goldingay, John. *Daniel*. WBC 30. Dallas: Word Books, 1989.

———. *Psalms*. 3 vols. BCOTWP. Grand Rapids: Baker Academic, 2006–2008.

Gombis, Timothy G. 'Ephesians 2 as a Narrative of Divine Warfare'. *JSNT* 26, no. 4 (2004): 403–18.

Gould, Ezra P. *A Critical and Exegetical Commentary on the Gospel According to St. Mark*. ICC. Edinburgh: T&T Clark, 1896.

Goulder, Michael D. *Luke: A New Paradigm*. JSNTSup 20. Sheffield: Sheffield Academic, 1994.

Gray, Timothy C. *The Temple in the Gospel of Mark: A Study of Its Narrative Role*. Grand Rapids: Baker Academic, 2008.

Green, Gene L. *The Letters to the Thessalonians*. PNTC. Leicester: Apollos, 2002.

———. 'Relevance Theory and Biblical Interpretation'. Pages 217–40 in *The Linguist as Pedagogue: Trends in the Teaching and Linguistic Analysis of the Greek New Testament*. Edited by Stanley E. Porter and Matthew Brook O'Donnell. Sheffield: Sheffield Phoenix, 2009.

———. 'Relevance Theory and Theological Interpretation: Thoughts on Metarepresentation'. *JTI* 4, no. 1 (2010): 75–90.

Green, Joel B. 'The Demise of the Temple as "Culture Center" in Luke–Acts: An Exploration of the Rending of the Temple Veil'. *RB* 101 (1994): 495–515.

———. *The Gospel of Luke*. NICNT. Grand Rapids: Eerdmans, 1997.

———. 'Learning Theological Interpretation from Luke'. Pages 55–78 in *Reading Luke: Interpretation, Reflection, Formation*. Edited by Craig G. Bartholomew, Joel B. Green and Anthony C. Thiselton. SHS 6. Grand Rapids: Zondervan, 2005.

———. 'The Problem of a Beginning: Israel's Scriptures in Luke 1–2'. *BBR* 4 (1994): 61–86.

———. 'Salvation to the End of the Earth: God as the Saviour in the Acts of the Apostles'. Pages 83–106 in *Witness to the Gospel: The Theology of Acts*. Edited by I. Howard Marshall and David Peterson. Grand Rapids: Eerdmans, 1998.

———. *The Theology of the Gospel of Luke*. NTT 3. Grand Rapids: Cambridge University Press, 1995.

Green, Keith. 'Relevance Theory and the Literary Text: Some Problems and Perspectives'. *JLS* 22, no. 3 (1993): 207–17.

Gregory, Andrew F. *The Reception of Luke and Acts in the Period before Irenaeus: Looking for Luke in the Second Century*. WUNT 2/169. Tübingen: Mohr Siebeck, 2003.

Gregory, Andrew F., and C. Kavin Rowe. *Rethinking the Unity and Reception of Luke and Acts*. Columbia: University of South Carolina Press, 2010.

Grogan, Geoffrey. *Psalms*. THOTC. Grand Rapids: Eerdmans, 2008.

Grundmann, Walter. *Das Evangelium nach Lukas*. THKNT 3. 2nd ed. Berlin: Evangelische Verlagsanstalt, 1961.

Gunkel, H. 'The Influence of Babylonian Mythology Upon the Biblical Creation Story'. Pages 25–52 in *Creation in the Old Testament*. Edited by Bernhard W. Anderson. Philadelphia: Fortress, 1984.

Gurtner, Daniel M. 'LXX Syntax and the Identity of the NT Veil'. *NovT* 47, no. 4 (2005): 344–53.

———. 'The Rending of the Veil (Matt. 27:51a Par): A Look Back and a Way Forward'. *Them* 29, no. 3 (2004): 4–14.

———. *The Torn Veil: Matthew's Exposition of the Death of Jesus*. SNTSMS 139. Cambridge: Cambridge University Press, 2007.

———. 'The Veil of the Temple in History and Legend'. *JETS* 49, no. 1 (2006): 97–114.

Gutt, Ernst-August. 'Approaches to Translation: Relevance Theory'. Pages 416–20 in *ELL*.

———. 'Unraveling Meaning: An Introduction to Relevance Theory'. *Notes* 112 (1986): 10–20.

Habel, Norman C., ed. *The Earth Story in the Psalms and the Prophets* Vol. 4. Sheffield: T&T Clark; Cleveland: The Pilgrim Press, 2001.

Haenchen, Ernst. *The Acts of the Apostles: A Commentary*. Translated by R. M. Wilson. Oxford: Blackwell, 1971.

Hannah, Darrell D. 'The Elect Son of Man in the *Parables of Enoch*'. Pages 130–58 in *'Who Is This Son of Man?': The Latest Scholarship on a Puzzling Expression of the Historical Jesus*. Edited by Larry W. Hurtado and Paul Owen. LNTS 390. London: T&T Clark, 2011.

Harris, J. Rendel. *Testimonies*. 2 vols. Cambridge: Cambridge University Press, 1916.

Hartman, Lars. *Prophecy Interpreted: The Formation of Some Jewish Apocalyptic Texts and of the Eschatological Discourse Mark 13*. ConBNT 1. Lund: Gleerup, 1966.

Hastings, Adrian. *Prophet and Witness in Jerusalem: A Study of the Teaching of St. Luke*. London: Longmans, 1958.

Hatina, Thomas R. 'The Focus of Mark 13:24-27—the Parousia, or the Destruction of the Temple?'. *BBR* 6 (1996): 43–66.

Hay, David M. *Glory at the Right Hand: Psalm 110 in Early Christianity*. SBLMS 18. New York: Abingdon Press, 1973.

Hayes, John H. 'The Tradition of Zion's Inviolability'. *JBL* 82, no. 4 (1963): 419–26.

Hays, Richard B. *Echoes of Scripture in the Letters of Paul*. New Haven; London: Yale University Press, 1989.

———. *Reading Backwards: Figural Christology and the Fourfold Gospel Witness*. Waco: Baylor University Press, 2014.

Hayward, Robert. *The Targum of Jeremiah: Translated, with a Critical Introduction, Apparatus, and Notes*. ArBib 12. Edinburgh: T&T Clark, 1987.

Head, Peter. 'The Temple in Luke's Gospel'. Pages 101–20 in *Heaven on Earth*. Edited by T. Desmond Alexander and Simon J. Gathercole. Carlisle: Paternoster, 2004.

Heil, John Paul. *The Rhetorical Role of Scripture in 1 Corinthians*. SBLStBL 15. Atlanta: Society of Biblical Literature, 2005.

Hemer, Colin J. *The Book of Acts in the Setting of Hellenistic History*. WUNT 49. Tübingen: J. C. B. Mohr (Paul Siebeck), 1989.

Hengel, Martin. *Acts and the History of Earliest Christianity*. London: SCM, 1979.

———. *Between Jesus and Paul: Studies in the Earliest History of Christianity*. London: SCM, 1983.

———. *Judaism and Hellenism: Studies in Their Encounter in Palestine During the Early Hellenistic Period*. Translated by John Bowden. 2 vols. London: SCM, 1974.

Hill, Craig C. *Hellenists and Hebrews: Reappraising Division within the Earliest Church*. Minneapolis: Fortress, 1992.

Hollander, John. *Figure of Echo: A Mode of Allusion in Milton and After*. Berkeley: University of California Press, 1981.

Holmås, Geir Otto. '"My House Shall Be a House of Prayer": Regarding the Temple as a Place of Prayer in Acts within the Context of Luke's Apologetical Objective'. *JSNT* 27, no. 4 (2005): 393–416.

Holmén, Tom. *Jesus and Jewish Covenant Thinking*. BIS 55. Leiden: Brill, 2001.

Holtz, Traugott. *Untersuchungen über die alttestamentlichen Zitate bei Lukas*. Berlin: Akademie-Verlag, 1968.

Hooker, Morna. 'Traditions About the Temple in the Sayings of Jesus'. *BJRL* 70 (1988): 7–19.

Hoppe, Leslie J. *The Holy City: Jerusalem in the Theology of the Old Testament*. Collegeville, MD: Liturgical Press, 2000.

Humphrey, Edith M. *And I Turned to See the Voice: The Rhetoric of Vision in the New Testament*. Studies in Theological Interpretation. Grand Rapids: Baker Academic, 2007.

Hunt, Joel H. 'Idols, Idolatry, Teraphim, Household Gods'. Page 439 in *DOTP*.

Hutcheon, Cyprian Robert. '"God Is with Us": The Temple in Luke–Acts'. *SVTQ* 44, no. 1 (2000): 3–33.

Instone Brewer, David. *Techniques and Assumptions in Jewish Exegesis before 70 CE*. Tübingen: Mohr, 1992.

Jeremias, Joachim. *The Eucharistic Words of Jesus*. Translated by Norman Perrin. London: SCM, 1966.

———. *Jesus' Promise to the Nations: The Franz Delitzsch Lectures for 1953*. SBT. London: SCM, 1958.

———. *The Parables of Jesus. Revised Edition*. Translated by S. H. Hooke. 3rd ed. London: SCM, 1963.

Jobes, Karen H. 'Relevance Theory and the Translation of Scripture'. *JETS* 50, no. 4 (2007): 773–97.

Johnson, Luke T. 'Literary Criticism of Luke–Acts: Is Reception-History Pertinent'. *JSNT* 28, no. 2 (2005): 159–62.

———. *The Acts of the Apostles*. SP 5. Collegeville, MD: Liturgical Press, 1992.

———. *The Gospel of Luke*. SP 3. Collegeville, MD: Liturgical Press, 1991.

———. *Prophetic Jesus, Prophetic Church: The Challenge of Luke–Acts to Contemporary Christians*. Grand Rapids: Eerdmans, 2011.

———. *Septuagintal Midrash in the Speeches of Acts (the Pere Marquette Lecture in Theology 2002)*. Milwaukee: Marquette University Press, 2002.

Juel, Donald H. *Messianic Exegesis: Christological Interpretation of the Old Testament in Early Christianity*. Philadelphia: Fortress, 1988.

Kalimi, Isaac. 'The Murders of the Messengers: Stephen Versus Zechariah and the Ethical Values of "New" versus "Old" Testament'. *AusBR* 56 (2008): 69–73.

Käser, Walter. 'Exegetische und theologische Erwägungen zur Seligpreisung der Kinderlosen Lc 23 29b'. *ZNW* 54, no. 3–4 (1963): 240–54.

Keel, Othmar, and Timothy J. Hallett. *The Symbolism of the Biblical World: Ancient near Eastern Iconography and the Book of Psalms*. London: SPCK, 1978.

Keener, Craig S. *Acts: An Exegetical Commentary*. 4 vols. Grand Rapids: Baker Academic, 2012–2015.

Kelle, Brad E. 'Warfare Imagery'. Pages 829–35 in *DOTWPW*.

Kennedy, George A. *New Testament Interpretation through Rhetorical Criticism*. Chapel Hill: University of North Carolina Press, 1984.

Kilgallen, John J. 'The Function of Stephen's Speech (Acts 7,2–53)'. *Bib* 70 (1989): 173–93.

———. *The Stephen Speech: A Literary and Redactional Study of Acts 7, 2–53*. AnBib 67. Rome: Biblical Institute Press, 1976.

Kilpatrick, George D. 'Acts vii.56: Son of Man?'. *TZ* 21 (1965): 209.

Kimball, Charles A. *Jesus' Exposition of the Old Testament in Luke's Gospel*. JSNTSup 94. Sheffield: JSOT, 1994.

Kinman, Brent. *Jesus' Entry into Jerusalem: In the Context of Lukan Theology and the Politics of His Day*. Leiden: Brill, 1995.

———. 'Lukan Eschatology and the Missing Fig Tree'. *JBL* 113, no. 4 (1994): 669–78.

———. 'Parousia, Jesus' "A-Triumphal" Entry, and the Fate of Jerusalem (Luke 19:28–44)'. *JBL* 118, no. 2 (1999): 279–94.

Klangwisan, Yael. *Earthing the Cosmic Queen: Relevance Theory and the Song of Songs*. Eugene: Pickwick, 2014.

Klijn, A. F. J. 'Stephen's Speech–Acts VII. 2–53'. *NTS* 4, no. 1 (1957): 25–31.

Kloppenborg, John S. *The Formation of Q: Trajectories in Ancient Wisdom Collections*. SAC. Philadelphia: Fortress, 1987.

Knowles, Michael. *Jeremiah in Matthew's Gospel: The Rejected Prophet Motif in Matthaean Redaction*. JSNTSup 68. Sheffield: JSOT, 1993.

Koet, Bart J. *Five Studies on Interpretation of Scripture in Luke–Acts*. SNTA. Leuven: Leuven University Press, 1989.

———. 'Isaiah in Luke–Acts'. Pages 79–100 in *Isaiah in the New Testament*. Edited by Steve Moyise and Maarten J. J. Menken. London: T&T Clark, 2005.

Kristeva, Julia. *Desire in Language: A Semiotic Approach to Literature and Art*. Translated by Leon S. Roudiez. Oxford: Blackwell, 1980.

Kümmel, Werner Georg. *Promise and Fulfilment: The Eschatological Message of Jesus*. Translated by Dorothea M. Barton. 2nd ed. London: SCM, 1961.

Kurz, William. 'Promise and Fulfilment in Hellenistic Jewish Narratives and in Luke and Acts'. Pages 147–70 in *Jesus and the Heritage of Israel*. Edited by David P. Moessner. Harrisburg, PA: Trinity Press International, 1999.

Lachs, Samuel Tobias. *A Rabbinic Commentary on the New Testament: The Gospels of Matthew, Mark, and Luke*. Hoboken: KTAV, 1987.

Lagrange, Marie-Joseph. Évangile Selon Saint Luc. Paris: J. Gabalda, 1921.
Lappenga, Benjamin J. *Paul's Language of Ζῆλος: Monosemy and the Rhetoric of Identity and Practice*. BIS 137. Leiden: Brill, 2015.
Larkin, William J. Jr. *Acts*. IVPNTC 5. Leicester: InterVarsity Press, 1995.
Larsson, Edvin. 'Temple-Criticism and the Jewish Heritage: Some Reflections on Acts 6–7'. *NTS* 39, no. 3 (1993): 379–95.
Le Cornu, Hilary, and Joseph Shulam. *A Commentary on the Jewish Roots of Acts*. Jerusalem: Academon, 2003.
Le Donne, Anthony. 'Diarchic Symbolism in Matthew's Procession Narrative: A Dead Sea Scrolls Perspective'. Pages 87–95 in *Early Christian Literature and Intertextuality*. Edited by Craig A. Evans and H. Daniel Zacharias. LNTS 391. London: T&T Clark, 2009.
———. 'The Improper Temple Offering of Ananias and Sapphira'. *NTS* 59, no. 3 (2013): 346-64.
Leaney, A. R. C. *A Commentary on the Gospel According to St Luke*. London: A. & C. Black, 1958.
Lieu, Judith. *The Gospel of Luke*. Epworth Commentaries. Peterborough: Epworth, 1997.
Lindars, Barnabas F. C. *New Testament Apologetic: The Doctrinal Significance of the Old Testament Quotations*. London: SCM, 1961.
Litwak, Kenneth D. *Echoes of Scripture in Luke–Acts: Telling the History of God's People Intertextually*. JSNTSup 282. London: T&T Clark International, 2005.
Loisy, Alfred F. *L'Évangile selon Luc*. Paris: Émile Nourry, 1924.
Longman, Tremper. 'The Divine Warrior: The New Testament Use of an Old Testament Motif'. *WTJ* 44, no. 2 (1982): 290–307.
Luckensmeyer, David. *The Eschatology of First Thessalonians*. Göttingen: Vandenhoeck & Ruprecht, 2009.
Mabie, Frederick J. 'Chaos and Death'. Pages 41–54 in *DOTWPW*.
Macintosh, A. A. *A Critical and Exegetical Commentary on Hosea*. ICC. Edinburgh: T&T Clark, 1997.
Maddox, Robert. *The Purpose of Luke–Acts*. Göttingen: Vandenhoeck & Ruprecht, 1982.
Malherbe, Abraham J. *The Letters to the Thessalonians: A New Translation with Introduction and Commentary*. AB 32B. New York: Doubleday, 2000.
Mallen, Peter. 'Genesis in Luke–Acts'. Pages 60–82 in *Genesis in the New Testament*. Edited by Maarten J. J. Menken and Steve Moyise. LNTS 466. London: Bloomsbury T&T Clark, 2012.
———. *The Reading and Transformation of Isaiah in Luke–Acts*. LNTS 367. London: T&T Clark, 2008.
Mann, C. S. *Mark: A New Translation with Introduction and Commentary*. AB 27. Garden City: Doubleday, 1986.
Manson, Thomas W. *The Sayings of Jesus as Recorded in the Gospels According to St. Matthew and St. Luke, Arranged with Introduction and Commentary*. London: SCM, 1949.
Marguerat, Daniel. 'Luc-Actes: une unité à construire'. Pages 57–81 in *The Unity of Luke–Acts*. Edited by Jozef Verheyden. BETL 142. Leuven: Leuven University Press, 1999.
Marshall, I. Howard. 'Acts'. Pages 513–606 in *Commentary on the New Testament Use of the Old Testament*. Edited by G. K. Beale and D. A. Carson. Grand Rapids: Baker Academic, 2007.
———. *The Acts of the Apostles: An Introduction and Commentary*. TNTC. Leicester: Inter-Varsity, 1980.

———. *The Gospel of Luke: A Commentary on the Greek Text*. NIGTC. Exeter: Paternoster, 1978.

Matera, Frank J. 'The Death of Jesus According to Luke: A Question of Sources'. *CBQ* 47, no. 3 (1985): 469–85.

Matthews, Shelly. *Perfect Martyr: The Stoning of Stephen and the Construction of Christian Identity*. Oxford: Oxford University Press, 2010.

Maxwell, Kathy R. *Hearing Between the Lines: The Audience as Fellow-Worker in Luke–Acts and Its Literary Milieu*. LNTS 425. London: T&T Clark, 2010.

McConville, J. Gordon. *Deuteronomy*. AOTC 5. Leicester: Apollos; Downers Grove: InterVarsity Press, 2002.

McKane, William. *A Critical and Exegetical Commentary on Jeremiah*. ICC. Edinburgh: T&T Clark, 1986, 1996.

McLay, Tim. *The Use of the Septuagint in New Testament Research*. Grand Rapids: Eerdmans, 2003.

McNicol, Allan J. *Jesus' Directions for the Future: A Source and Redaction-History Study of the Use of the Eschatological Traditions in Paul and in the Synoptic Accounts of Jesus' Last Eschatological Discourse*. NGS 9. Macon: Mercer, 1996.

Meadowcroft, Tim. 'Relevance as a Mediating Category in the Reading of Biblical Texts: Venturing Beyond the Hermeneutical Circle'. *JETS* 45, no. 4 (2002): 611–27.

Meek, James A. *The Gentile Mission in Old Testament Citations in Acts: Text, Hermeneutic, and Purpose*. LNTS 385. London: T&T Clark, 2008.

Meier, John P. *A Marginal Jew*. ABRL. 5 vols. New York: Doubleday, 1991–2015.

Metzger, Bruce M. *A Textual Commentary on the Greek New Testament*. 2nd ed. Stuttgart: United Bible Societies, 1994.

Miller, Robert J. 'The Rejection of the Prophets in Q'. *JBL* 107, no. 2 (1988): 225–40.

Moessner, David P. '"The Christ Must Suffer": New Light on the Jesus, Stephen, Paul Parallels in Luke–Acts'. *NovT* 28, no. 3 (1986): 220–56.

———, ed. *Jesus and the Heritage of Israel*. Harrisburg, PA: Trinity Press International, 1999.

———. *Lord of the Banquet: The Literary and Theological Significance of the Lukan Travel Narrative*. Minneapolis: Fortress, 1989.

Moessner, David P., and David L. Tiede. 'Conclusion: "And Some Were Persuaded…"'. Pages 358–68 in *Jesus and the Heritage of Israel*. Edited by David P. Moessner. Harrisburg, PA: Trinity Press International, 1999.

Moffitt, David M. 'Righteous Bloodshed, Matthew's Passion Narrative, and the Temple's Destruction: Lamentations as a Matthean Intertext'. *JBL* 125, no. 2 (2006): 299–320.

Moo, Douglas J. *The Old Testament in the Gospel Passion Narratives*. Sheffield: Almond, 1983.

Morgen, M. 'Lc 17.20-37 et Lc 21,8-11.20-24: "Arrière-Fond Scripturaire"'. Pages 307–26 in *The Scriptures in the Gospels*. Edited by C. M. Tuckett. Leuven: Leuven University Press/Uitgeverij Peeters, 1997.

Morris, Leon. *The Gospel According to St. Luke: An Introduction and Commentary*. TNTC. London: Inter-Varsity Press, 1974.

Motyer, Stephen. 'The Rending of the Veil: A Markan Pentecost?'. *NTS* 33, no. 1 (1987): 155–57.

Mowinckel, Sigmund. *The Psalms in Israel's Worship*. Translated by D. R. Ap-Thomas. 2 vols. Oxford: Blackwell, 1962.

Moyise, Steve. *Evoking Scripture: Seeing the Old Testament in the New*. London: T&T Clark, 2008.

———. 'Intertextuality and the Study of the Old Testament in the New'. Pages 14–41 in *The Old Testament in the New: Essays in Honour of J. L. North*. Sheffield: Sheffield Academic, 2000.

Myers, Jacob M. *I and II Esdras: Introduction, Translation and Commentary*. AB 42. New York: Doubleday, 1974.

Neagoe, Alexandru. *The Trial of the Gospel: An Apologetic Reading of Luke's Trial Narratives*. SNTSMS 116. Cambridge: Cambridge University Press, 2002.

Nelson, Richard D. *Deuteronomy: A Commentary*. OTL. Louisville: Westminster John Knox, 2002.

Nestle, Eberhard. 'The Vision of Stephen'. *ExpTim* 22 (1911): 423.

Neudorfer, Heinz-Werner. 'The Speech of Stephen'. Pages 255–94 in *Witness to the Gospel: The Theology of Acts*. Edited by I. Howard Marshall and David Peterson. Grand Rapids: Eerdmans, 1998.

Neusner, Jacob. 'Money-Changers in the Temple: The Mishnah's Explanation'. *NTS* 35, no. 2 (1989): 287–90.

Neyrey, Jerome H. 'Jesus' Address to the Women of Jerusalem (Lk. 23. 27–31) – A Prophetic Judgment Oracle'. *NTS* 29, no. 1 (1983): 74–86.

Noh, Eun-Ju. *Metarepresentation: A Relevance-Theory Approach*. Amsterdam: Benjamins, 2000.

Nolland, John. *Luke*. WBC 35A–C. 3 vols. Dallas: Word, 1989–93.

———. 'Salvation-History and Eschatology'. Pages 63–81 in *Witness to the Gospel: The Theology of Acts*. Edited by I. Howard Marshall and David Peterson. Grand Rapids: Eerdmans, 1998.

———. '"The Times of the Nations" and a Prophetic Pattern in Luke 21'. Pages 133–47 in *Biblical Interpretation in Early Christian Gospels*. Vol. 3, *The Gospel of Luke*. Edited by Thomas R Hatina. LNTS 376. London: T&T Clark, 2010.

Ollenburger, Ben C. *Zion, the City of the Great King: A Theological Symbol of the Jerusalem Cult*. Sheffield: JSOT, 1987.

Ooi, Vincent K. H. *Scripture and Its Readers: Readings of Israel's Story in Nehemiah 9, Ezekiel 20, and Acts 7*. JTISup 10. Winona Lake: Eisenbrauns, 2015.

Oswalt, John N. *The Book of Isaiah Chapters 1–39*. NICOT. Grand Rapids: Eerdmans, 1986.

Owen, H. P. 'Stephen's Vision in Acts VII.55–6'. *NTS* 1, no. 3 (1955): 224–26.

Paesler, Kurt. *Das Tempelwort Jesu: die Traditionen von Tempelzerstörung und Tempelerneuerung im Neuen Testament*. FRLANT 184. Göttingen: Vandenhoeck & Ruprecht, 1999.

Page, T. E., and A. S. Walpole. *The Acts of the Apostles: With Introduction and Notes*. London: Macmillan, 1895.

Pao, David W. *Acts and the Isaianic New Exodus*. Grand Rapids: Baker Academic, 2000.

Pao, David W., and Eckhard J. Schnabel. 'Luke'. Pages 251–414 in *Commentary on the New Testament Use of the Old Testament*. Edited by G. K. Beale and D. A. Carson. Grand Rapids: Baker Academic, 2007.

Parsons, Mikeal C. *Acts*. PCNT. Grand Rapids: Baker, 2008.

Parsons, Mikeal C., and Richard I. Pervo. *Rethinking the Unity of Luke and Acts*. Minneapolis: Fortress, 1993.

Patella, Michael. *The Death of Jesus: The Diabolical Force and the Ministering Angel: Luke 23,44–49*. CahRB. Paris: Gabalda, 1999.

Pattemore, Stephen W. *The People of God in the Apocalypse: Discourse, Structure and Exegesis*. SNTSMS 128. Cambridge: Cambridge University Press, 2004.

Pearson, Birger A. '1 Thessalonians 2:13–16: A Deutero-Pauline Interpolation'. *HTR* 64, no. 1 (1971): 79-94.
Penley, Paul T. *The Common Tradition Behind Synoptic Sayings of Judgment and John's Apocalypse: An Oral Interpretive Tradition of OT Prophetic Material*. LNTS 424. London: T&T Clark, 2010.
Penner, Todd C. *In Praise of Christian Origins: Stephen and the Hellenists in Lukan Apologetic Historiography*. Emory Studies in Early Christianity. New York: T&T Clark, 2004.
———. 'Narrative as Persuasion: Epideictic Rhetoric and Scribal Amplification in the Stephen Episode in Acts'. *SBLSP* 35 (1996): 352–67.
Perrin, Nicholas. *Jesus the Temple*. London: SPCK; Grand Rapids: Baker, 2010.
Perrin, Norman. *Rediscovering the Teaching of Jesus*. London: SCM, 1967.
Pervo, Richard I. *The Acts of the Apostles*. Hermeneia. Philadelphia: Fortress, 2008.
———. *Dating Acts: Between the Evangelists and the Apologists*. Santa Rosa: Polebridge, 2006.
Pesch, Rudolf. *Die Vision des Stephanus: Apg 7, 55-56 im Rahmen der Apostelgeschichte*. SBS 12. Stuttgart: Katholisches Bibelwerk, 1966.
Peterson, David G. *The Acts of the Apostles*. PNTC. Nottingham: Apollos; Grand Rapids Eerdmans, 2009.
Phillips, Thomas E. 'The Genre of Acts: Moving toward a Consensus?'. *CBR* 4, no. 3 (2006): 365–96.
Pilkington, Adrian. 'Introduction: Relevance Theory and Literary Style'. *LL* 5, no. 3 (1996): 157–62.
———. 'Metaphor Comprehension: Some Questions for Current Account in Relevance Theory'. Pages 156–72 in *Explicit Communication: Robyn Carston's Pragmatics*. Edited by Belén Soria and Esther Romero. Basingstoke: Palgrave Macmillan, 2010.
———. 'Poetic Effects'. *Lingua* 87, no. 1–2 (1992): 29–51.
———. *Poetic Effects: A Relevance Theory Perspective*. PBNS 75. Amsterdam: Benjamins, 2000.
Piper, Ronald A. *Wisdom in the Q-Tradition: The Aphoristic Teaching of Jesus*. SNTSMS. Cambridge: Cambridge University Press, 1989.
Pitre, Brant J. 'Blessing the Barren and Warning the Fecund: Jesus' Message for Women Concerning Pregnancy and Childbirth'. *JSNT* 81, no. 1 (2001): 59–80.
Plummer, Alfred. *A Critical and Exegetical Commentary on the Gospel According to S. Luke*. ICC. 5th ed. Edinburgh: T&T Clark, 1922.
Plummer, Robert L. 'Something Awry in the Temple? The Rending of the Temple Veil and Early Jewish Sources That Report Unusual Phenomena in the Temple around AD 30'. *JETS* 48, no. 2 (2005): 301–16.
Polhill, John B. *Acts*. NAC 26. Nashville: Broadman, 1992.
Porter, Stanley E. 'Scripture Justifies Mission: The Use of the Old Testament in Luke–Acts'. Pages 104–26 in *Hearing the Old Testament in the New Testament*. Edited by Stanley E. Porter. MNTS. Grand Rapids: Eerdmans, 2006.
Raabe, Paul R. 'The Particularizing of Universal Judgment in Prophetic Discourse'. *CBQ* 64, no. 4 (2002): 652–74.
Rackham, Richard B. *Acts of the Apostles*. 9th ed. London: Methuen, 1922.
Rad, Gerhard von. *Old Testament Theology*. Translated by D. M. G. Stalker. New York: Harper & Row, 1962, 1965.
Ramaroson, Leonard. 'Contre les "temples faits de main d'homme" (Actes 7,48, 17,24)'. *RPh* 43 (1969): 217–38.

Reitzel, Frank X. 'St. Luke's Use of the Temple Image'. *RfR* 38, no. 4 (1979): 520–39.
Rese, Martin. *Alttestamentliche Motive in der Christologie des Lukas*. SNT 1. Gütersloh: G. Mohn, 1969.
Reynolds, Benjamin E. 'The Use of the Son of Man Idiom in the Gospel of John'. Pages 101–29 in *'Who Is This Son of Man?': The Latest Scholarship on a Puzzling Expression of the Historical Jesus*. Edited by Larry W. Hurtado and Paul Owen. LNTS 390. London: T&T Clark, 2011.
Richard, Earl. *Acts 6.1-8.4: The Author's Method of Composition*. SBLDS 41. Missoula: Scholars Press, 1978.
———. 'The Creative Use of Amos by the Author of Acts'. *NovT* 24, no. 1 (1982): 37–53.
Richards, Christine. 'Inferential Pragmatics and the Literary Text'. *JPrag* 9, no. 2–3 (1985): 261–85.
Richardson, Alan. *An Introduction to the Theology of the New Testament*. London: SCM, 1958.
Richardson, Peter. 'Why Turn the Tables? Jesus' Protest in the Temple Precincts'. *SBLSP* 31 (1992): 507–23.
Ringgren, Helmer. 'Luke's Use of the Old Testament'. *HTR* 79 (1986): 227–35.
Robb, Julie E. 'A Prophet Like Moses: Its Jewish Context and Use in the Early Christian Tradition'. Ph.D. diss., King's College, London, 2003.
Robbins, Vernon K. 'The Claims of the Prologues and Graeco-Roman Rhetoric: The Prefaces to Luke and Acts in Light of Graeco-Roman Rhetorical Strategies'. Pages 63–83 in *Jesus and the Heritage of Israel*. Edited by David P. Moessner. Harrisburg, PA: Trinity Press International, 1999.
Roberts, J. J. M. 'Zion in the Theology of the Davidic-Solomonic Empire'. Pages 93–108 in *Studies in the Period of David and Solomon and Other Essays*. Edited by T Ishida. Tokyo: Yamakawa-Shuppausha, 1982.
Roloff, Jürgen. *Die Apostelgeschichte*. Gottingen: Vandenhoeck & Ruprecht, 1981.
Rosner, Brian S. 'Acts and Biblical History'. Pages 65–82 in *The Book of Acts in Its First Century Setting. Volume 1. The Book of Acts in Its Ancient Literary Setting*. Edited by Bruce W. Winter and Andrew D. Clark. Grand Rapids: Eerdmans, 1993.
Ross, J. M. 'Which Zechariah?'. *IBS* 9, no. 2 (1987): 70–73.
Rowe, C. Kavin. 'History, Hermeneutics and the Unity of Luke–Acts'. *JSNT* 28, no. 2 (2005): 131–57.
Rudman, Dominic. 'The Crucifixion as *Chaoskampf*: A New Reading of the Passion Narrative in the Synoptic Gospels'. *Bib* 84, no. 1 (2003): 102–07.
Rusam, Dietrich. *Das Alte Testament bei Lukas*. ZNW 112. Berlin; New York: de Gruyter, 2003.
Russell, James S. *The Parousia, a Critical Inquiry into the New Testament Doctrine of Our Lord's Second Coming*. Bradford.: Kingdom Publications, 1996 orig. 1877.
Sabbe, M. 'The Son of Man Saying in Acts 7, 56'. Pages 241–79 in *Les Actes des Apôtres: Traditions, rédaction, théologie*. Edited by J. Kremer. BETL 48. Leuven: Leuven University Press, 1978.
Sanders, E. P. *Jesus and Judaism*. London: SCM, 1985.
Sanders, Jack T. *The Jews in Luke–Acts*. London: SCM, 1987.
Sanders, James A. 'A Hermeneutic Fabric: Psalm 118 in Luke's Entrance Narrative'. Pages 140–53 in *Luke and Scripture: The Function of Sacred Tradition in Luke–Acts*. Edited by Craig A. Evans and James A. Sanders. Minneapolis: Fortress, 1993.
Schneider, Gerhard. *Das Evangelium nach Lukas*. ÖTK 3. Gütersloh: Mohn; Würzburg: Echter-Verlag, 1977.

———. *Die Apostelgeschichte*. HTKNT. 2 vols. Freiburg: Herder, 1980.
Schubert, Paul. 'The Structure and Significance of Luke 24'. Pages 165–86 in *Neutestamentliche Studien für Rudolf Bultmann*. Edited by Walther Eltester. BZNW 21. Berlin: Töpelmann, 1957.
Schulz, Siegfried. *Q: Die Spruchquelle der Evangelisten*. Zürich: Theologischer Verlag., 1972.
Schweizer, Eduard. *The Good News According to Luke*. London: SPCK, 1984.
Scott, J. Julius Jr. 'Stephen's Defense and the World Mission of the People of God'. *JETS* 21, no. 2 (1978): 131–41.
Simon, Marcel. *Verus Israel: A Study of the Relations between Christians and Jews in the Roman Empire (135-425)*. Translated by H. McKeating. Oxford: Oxford University Press, 1985, First Published 1948.
Slater, Thomas B. 'One Like a Son of Man in First-Century Judaism'. *NTS* 41, no. 2 (1995): 183–98.
Sleeman, Matthew. *Geography and the Ascension Narrative in Acts*. SNTSMS 146. Cambridge: Cambridge University Press, 2009.
Smith, Neil, and Deirdre Wilson. 'Introduction'. *Lingua* 87, no. 1 (1992): 1–10.
Soards, Marion L. *The Speeches in Acts: Their Content, Context, and Concerns*. Louisville: Westminster/John Knox Press, 1994.
———. 'Tradition, Composition, and Theology in Jesus' Speech to the "Daughters of Jerusalem" (Luke 23,26–32)'. *Bib* 68 (1987): 221–44.
Sommer, Benjamin D. *A Prophet Reads Scripture: Allusion in Isaiah 40-66*. Stanford: Stanford University Press, 1998.
Song, Nam Sun. 'Metaphor and Metonymy'. Pages 87–104 in *Relevance Theory: Applications and Implications*. Edited by Robyn Carston and Seiji Uchida. PBNS 37. Amsterdam: Benjamins, 1998.
Spencer, F. Scott. *Acts*. Readings: A New Biblical Commentary. Sheffield: Sheffield Academic, 1997.
Spencer, Patrick E. 'The Unity of Luke–Acts: A Four-Bolted Hermeneutical Hinge'. *CBR* 5, no. 3 (2007): 341–66.
Sperber, Dan, and Deirdre Wilson. 'A Deflationary Account of Metaphors'. Pages 97–122 in *Meaning and Relevance*. Edited by Deirdre Wilson and Dan Sperber. Cambridge: Cambridge University Press, 2012.
———. 'Introduction: Pragmatics'. Pages 1–27 in *Meaning and Relevance*. Edited by Deirdre Wilson and Dan Sperber. Cambridge: Cambridge University Press, 2012.
———. *Relevance: Communication and Cognition*. 2nd ed. Oxford: Blackwell, 1995.
Stamps, Dennis L. 'Rhetoric'. Pages 953–56 in *DNTB*.
———. 'The Use of the Old Testament in the New Testament as a Rhetorical Device: A Methodological Proposal'. Pages 9–37 in *Hearing the Old Testament in the New Testament*. Edited by Stanley E. Porter. MNTS. Grand Rapids: Eerdmans, 2006.
Stanley, Christopher D. *Arguing with Scripture: The Rhetoric of Quotations in the Letters of Paul*. New York; London: T&T Clark International, 2004.
———. 'Paul and Homer: Greco-Roman Citation Practice in the First Century CE'. *NovT* 32, no. 1 (1990): 48–78.
———. 'The Rhetoric of Quotations: An Essay on Method'. Pages 44–58 in *Early Christian Interpretation*. Edited by Craig A. Evans and James A. Sanders. JSNTSup 148. Sheffield: Sheffield Academic, 1997.

Steck, Odil Hannes. *Israel und das gewaltsame Geschick der Propheten: Untersuchungen zur Überlieferung des deuteronomistischen Geschichtsbildes im Alten Testament, Spätjudentum und Urchristentum*. WMANT 23. Neukirchen-Vluyn: Neukirchener Verlag, 1967.

Stenschke, Christoph W. *Luke's Portrait of Gentiles Prior to Their Coming to Faith*. WUNT 2/108. Tübingen: Mohr Siebeck, 1999.

Sterling, Gregory E. 'Mors Philosophi: The Death of Jesus in Luke'. *HTR* 94, no. 4 (2001): 383–402.

———. '"Opening the Scriptures": The Legitimation of the Jewish Diaspora and the Early Christian Mission'. Pages 199–225 in *Jesus and the Heritage of Israel*. Edited by David P. Moessner. Harrisburg, PA: Trinity Press International, 1999.

Stevens, Bruce A. 'Divine Warrior in the Gospel of Mark'. *BZ* 31 (1987): 101–10.

Stevenson, Gregory. *Power and Place: Temple and Identity in the Book of Revelation*. BZNW 107. Berlin: de Gruyter, 2001.

Steyn, Gert J. 'Luke's Use of ΜΙΜΗΣΙΣ'. Pages 551–57 in *The Scriptures in the Gospels*. Edited by C. M. Tuckett. Leuven: Leuven University Press/Uitgeverij Peeters, 1997.

———. *Septuagint Quotations in the Context of the Petrine and Pauline Speeches of the Acta Apostolorum*. CBET. Kampen: Kok Pharos, 1995.

Strauss, Mark L. *The Davidic Messiah in Luke–Acts: The Promise and Its Fulfillment in Lukan Christology*. JSNTSup 110. Sheffield: Sheffield Academic, 1995.

Stuart, Douglas. *Hosea-Jonah*. WBC 31. Waco: Word Books, 1987.

Sweeney, James P. 'Stephen's Speech (Acts 7:2–53): Is It as "Anti-Temple" as Is Frequently Alleged?'. *TJ* 23, no. 2 (2002): 185–210.

Sylva, Dennis D. 'The Meaning and Function of Acts 7:46–50'. *JBL* 106, no. 2 (1987): 261–75.

———. 'The Temple Curtain and Jesus' Death in the Gospel of Luke'. *JBL* 105, no. 2 (1986): 239–50.

Talbert, Charles H. 'Promise and Fulfilment in Lucan Theology'. Pages 91–103 in *Luke–Acts: New Perspectives from the Society of Biblical Literature Seminar*. Edited by Charles H. Talbert. New York: Crossroad, 1984.

Talbert, Charles H., and P. Stepp. 'Succession in Mediterranean Antiquity: Luke–Acts'. *SBLSP* 37 (1998): 169–79.

———. 'Succession in Mediterranean Antiquity: The Lukan Milieu'. *SBLSP* 37 (1998): 148–68.

Tan, Kim Huat. *The Zion Traditions and the Aims of Jesus*. SNTSMS 91. New York: Cambridge University Press, 1997.

Tannehill, Robert C. *The Narrative Unity of Luke–Acts*. 2 vols. Minneapolis: Fortress, 1986–90.

Tannen, Deborah. 'What Is a Frame? Surface Evidence for Underlying Expectations'. Pages 15–56 in *Framing in Discourse*. Edited by Deborah Tannen. Oxford: Oxford University Press, 1993.

Tasker, R. V. G. *The Gospel According to St. Matthew: An Introduction and Commentary*. TNTC. Leicester: Inter-Varsity Press, 1961.

Taylor, N. H. 'The Destruction of Jerusalem and the Transmission of the Synoptic Eschatological Discourse'. *HvTSt* 59, no. 2 (2003): 283–311.

———. 'The Jerusalem Temple in Luke–Acts'. *HvTSt* 60, no. 1/2 (2004): 459–85.

———. 'Luke–Acts and the Temple'. Pages 709–21 in *The Unity of Luke–Acts*. Edited by Jozef Verheyden. BETL 142. Leuven: Leuven University Press, 1999.

———. 'Stephen, the Temple, and Early Christian Eschatology'. *RB* 110, no. 1 (2003): 62–85.
Tendahl, Markus, and Raymond W. Gibbs Jr. 'Complementary Perspectives on Metaphor: Cognitive Linguistics and Relevance Theory'. *JPrag* 40, no. 11 (2008): 1823–64.
Tiede, David L. *Luke*. ACNT. Minneapolis: Augsburg, 1988.
———. *Prophecy and History in Luke–Acts*. Philadelphia: Fortress, 1980.
Tiemeyer, Lena-Sofia. 'The Priests and the Temple Cult in the Book of Jeremiah'. Pages 233–64 in *Prophecy in the Book of Jeremiah*. Edited by Hans M. Barstad and Reinhard Gregor Kratz. BZAW 388. Berlin: de Gruyter, 2009.
Todorov, Tzvetan. *Genres in Discourse*. Translated by Catherine Porter. Cambridge: Cambridge University Press, 1990.
Tödt, Heinz Eduard. *The Son of Man in the Synoptic Tradition*. Translated by Dorothea M. Barton. NTL. London: SCM, 1965.
Trocmé, Étienne. 'L'expulsion des marchands du Temple'. *NTS* 15, no. 1 (1968): 1–22.
Trotter, David. 'Analysing Literary Prose: The Relevance of Relevance Theory'. *Lingua* 87, no. 1–2 (1992): 11–27.
Tsumura, David. *Creation and Destruction: A Reappraisal of the Chaoskampf Theory of the Old Testament*. Winona Lake: Eisenbrauns, 2005.
Tuckett, Christopher M. 'The Christology of Luke–Acts'. Pages 133–64 in *The Unity of Luke–Acts*. Edited by Jozef Verheyden. BETL 142. Leuven: Leuven University Press, 1999.
Tull Willey, Patricia. *Remember the Former Things: The Recollection of Previous Texts in Second Isaiah*. SBLDS 161. Atlanta: Scholars Press, 1997.
Turner, Max. *Power from on High: The Spirit in Israel's Restoration and Witness in Luke–Acts*. JPTSS 9. Sheffield: Sheffield Academic, 1996.
———. 'The Spirit of Prophecy and the Power of Authoritative Preaching in Luke–Acts: A Question of Origins'. *NTS* 38, no. 1 (1992): 66–88.
Tyson, Joseph B. *The Death of Jesus in Luke–Acts*. Columbia: University of South Carolina, 1986.
———. *Images of Judaism in Luke–Acts*. Columbia: University of South Carolina Press, 1992.
———. *Marcion and Luke–Acts: A Defining Struggle*. Columbia: University of South Carolina Press, 2006.
Uchida, Seiji. 'Text and Relevance'. Pages 161–78 in *Relevance Theory: Applications and Implications*. Edited by Robyn Carston and Seiji Uchida. PBNS 37. Amsterdam: Benjamins, 1998.
Untergassmair, Franz Georg. 'Der Spruch vom "grünen und dürren Holz" (Lk 23,31)'. *SNTSU* 16 (1991): 55–87.
Van De Sandt, Huub. 'The Minor Prophets in Luke–Acts'. Pages 57–77 in *The Minor Prophets in the New Testament*. Edited by Steve Moyise and Maarten J. J. Menken. London: T&T Clark, 2009.
———. 'The Presence and Transcendence of God: An Investigation of Acts 7,44-50 in the Light of the LXX'. *ETL* 80, no. 1 (2004): 30–59.
Van der Henst, Jean-Baptiste, and Dan Sperber. 'Testing the Cognitive and Communicative Principles of Relevance'. Pages 279–306 in *Meaning and Relevance*. Edited by Deirdre Wilson and Dan Sperber. Cambridge: Cambridge University Press, 2012.
Van der Waal, C. 'The Temple in the Gospel According to Luke'. *Neot* 7 (1973): 49–59.
Van Iersel, Bas. 'The Sun, Moon and Stars of Mark 13, 24–25 in a Greco-Roman Reading'. *Bib* 77 (1996): 84–92.

Verheyden, Joseph. 'Describing the Parousia: The Cosmic Phenomena in Mk 13,24–25'. Pages 525–50 in *The Scriptures in the Gospels*. Edited by C. M. Tuckett. Leuven: Leuven University Press/Uitgeverij Peeters, 1997.

———, ed. *The Unity of Luke–Acts*. BETL 142. Leuven: Leuven University Press, 1999.

———. 'The Unity of Luke–Acts: What Are We Up To?'. Pages 3–56 in *The Unity of Luke–Acts*. Edited by Jozef Verheyden. BETL 142. Leuven: Leuven University Press, 1999.

Wagner, J. Ross. 'Psalm 118 in Luke–Acts: Tracing a Narrative Thread'. Pages 154–78 in *Early Christian Interpretation of the Scriptures of Israel: Investigations and Proposals*. Edited by Craig A. Evans and James A. Sanders. JSNTSup 148. Sheffield: Sheffield Academic, 1997.

Walker, Peter W. L. *Jesus and the Holy City: New Testament Perspectives on Jerusalem*. Grand Rapids: Eerdmans, 1996.

Walton, Steve. 'How Mighty a Minority Were the Hellenists?'. Pages 305–28 in *Earliest Christian History: History, Literature, and Theology. Essays from the Tyndale Fellowship in Honor of Martin Hengel*. Edited by Michael F. Bird and Jason Maston. WUNT 2/320. Tübingen: Mohr Siebeck, 2012.

———. *Leadership and Lifestyle: The Portrait of Paul in the Miletus Speech and 1 Thessalonians*. SNTSMS 108. Cambridge: Cambridge University Press, 2000.

———. 'A Tale of Two Perspectives? The Place of the Temple in Acts'. Pages 135–50 in *Heaven on Earth*. Edited by T. Desmond Alexander and Simon J. Gathercole. Carlisle: Paternoster, 2004.

Wanamaker, Charles A. *The Epistles to the Thessalonians: A Commentary on the Greek Text*. NIGTC. Grand Rapids: Eerdmans, 1990.

Watson, Alan. *The Trial of Stephen: The First Christian Martyr*. Athens: University of Georgia Press, 1996.

Watson, Rebecca S. *Chaos Uncreated: A Reassessment of the Theme of "Chaos" in the Hebrew Bible*. BZAW 341. Berlin: de Gruyter, 2005.

Watts, John D. W. *Isaiah 34–66*. WBC 25. Waco: Word Books, 1987.

Weinert, Francis D. 'Luke, Stephen, and the Temple in Luke–Acts'. *BTB* 17, no. 3 (1987): 88–90.

———. 'Luke, the Temple, and Jesus' Saying About Jerusalem's Abandoned House'. *CBQ* 44 (1982): 68–76.

———. 'The Meaning of the Temple in Luke–Acts'. *BTB* 11 (1981): 85–89.

Weinfeld, Moshe. 'Zion and Jerusalem as Religious and Political Capital: Ideology and Utopia'. Pages 75–115 in *The Poet and the Historian: Essays in Literary and Historical Biblical Criticism*. Edited by Richard E. Friedman. Chico: Scholars Press, 1983.

Wenham, David. *The Rediscovery of Jesus Eschatological Discourse*. Gospel Perspectives 4. Sheffield: JSOT, 1984.

Wiens, Delbert. *Stephen's Sermon and the Structure of Luke–Acts*. Richland Hills: Bibal, 1995.

Wilcox, Max. 'The Old Testament in Acts 1–15'. *AusBR* 4 (1956): 1–41.

———. *The Semitisms of Acts*. Oxford: Clarendon, 1965.

Williams, David J. *Acts*. NIBCNT 5. Peabody, MA: Hendrickson, 1990.

Wilson, Alistair I. *When Will These Things Happen? A Study of Jesus as Judge in Matthew 21–25*. PBM. Carlisle: Paternoster, 2004.

Wilson, Deirdre. 'Metarepresentation in Linguistic Communication'. Pages 230–58 in *Meaning and Relevance*. Edited by Deirdre Wilson and Dan Sperber. Cambridge: Cambridge University Press, 2012.

———. 'Relevance and Understanding'. Pages 37–58 in *Language and Understanding*. Edited by Gillian Brown. Oxford: Oxford University Press, 1994.

Wilson, Deirdre, and Dan Sperber, eds. *Meaning and Relevance*. Cambridge: Cambridge University Press, 2012.

———. 'Relevance Theory'. Pages 607–32 in *Handbook of Pragmatics*. Edited by Laurence Horn and Gregory Ward. Oxford: Blackwell, 2003.

Wilson, Stephen G. *The Gentiles and the Gentile Mission in Luke–Acts*. Cambridge: Cambridge University Press, 1973.

Witherington, Ben. *The Acts of the Apostles: A Socio-Rhetorical Commentary*. Grand Rapids: Eerdmans; Carlisle: Paternoster, 1998.

———. *The Christology of Jesus*. Minneapolis: Fortress, 1990.

Wolfe, Robert F. 'Rhetorical Elements in the Speeches of Acts 7 and 17'. *JOTT* 6, no. 3 (1993): 274–83.

Wright, N. T. *Jesus and the Victory of God*. Christian Origins and the Question of God 2. London: SPCK, 1996.

———. *The New Testament and the People of God*. Christian Origins and the Question of God 1. London: SPCK, 1992.

Yoder Neufeld, Thomas R. *Put on the Armour of God: The Divine Warrior from Isaiah to Ephesians*. JSNTSup 140. Sheffield: Sheffield Academic, 1997.

Zeitlin, Solomon. 'The Hallel: A Historical Study of the Canonization of the Hebrew Liturgy'. *JQR* 53, no. 1 (1962): 22–29.

Zmijewski, Josef. *Die Eschatologiereden des Lukas-Evangeliums. Eine traditions- und redaktionsgeschichtliche Untersuchung zu Lk 21, 5-36 und Lk 17, 20-37*. BBB 40. Bonn: Hanstein, 1972.

Index of References

Old Testament/Hebrew Bible

Genesis

Ref	Page	Ref	Page	Ref	Page
4.1-12	37	35.16-18	156	*Exodus*	
4.10	37	35.23-26	156	1–3	163
11–12	155	37	156	1	158
11.30	22, 129	37.2-3	156	1.5	157
11.31–12.5	155, 163	37.11	156	1.6	157
11.31-32	155	37.21	156	1.7	158
12.1	147, 148, 155	37.23	156	1.8	152, 158
		37.28	156	1.9-22	158
12.5	155	39.2-3	156	1.9-11	158
12.7	148, 155	39.2	156	1.10	158
13.15	148	39.21	156	1.16	158
15	156	41–42	163	1.17-18	158
15.2	155	41.33-44	156	1.22	158
15.7	155	41.38-45	157	2	158
15.13-14	149	41.43	156	2.2	158
15.13	149	41.46	156	2.5	158
15.14	149	41.54	157	2.10	158
16.1–21.7	129	42.1-4	157	2.11-12	158
16.1	155	42.1-2	157	2.11	158
17.8	148, 149, 160	42.2	157	2.13	158
		42.3-5	157	2.14	150, 151, 158
		42.5	157		
17.10-14	156	43.3-4	157	2.15	158
17.10	156	45–46	157	2.20	158
17.13	156	45.1	157	2.22	156
18.11	22	45.2	157	3	158
18.22	182	45.4	156	3.1-6	158
19.17	85	45.8	156	3.1	158
19.19	85	45.9-11	157	3.2	158
21.1-5	156	45.16	157	3.3-4	158
21.2-4	156	46.1-7	157	3.5-10	154, 158
23.16	157	46.3-4	157	3.5	150
25.19-26	156	46.6	157	3.6	149
25.21	129	46.27	157	3.7-8	150
25.26	156	47.27	158	3.7	150
29.31–30.24	129, 156	48.4	148, 149, 160	3.8	150
31.14	155			3.10	150
33.10	155	49.33	157	3.12	156
33.19	157	49.11	56	3.13	158
34.26	88	50.12	157	3.16	61
		50.13	157	7.3	159
		50.24-25	61	7.4	86

Index of References

Exodus (cont.)		Numbers		Joshua	
8.20	182	1.50	160	3.14	160
9.13	182	3.26	135	7.9	65
12.12	86	12.4	160	18.1	160
15.4	159	14.3	159	19.48	88
16.3	159	14.33-34	159	23.9	160
20.16	155	27.14	162	24.2-15	163
23.20-21	159	33.4	86	24.18	160
25	160			24.32	157
25.1	160	Deuteronomy			
25.9	160	2.5	156	Judges	
25.40	160	4.8	173	1.34	85
26.31-35	135	4.10	159	6.2	85
26.37	135	4.19	160	13.2-24	129
27.21	160	4.27-28	173	13.2	22
28.43	160	4.28	160		
31–32	163	6.20-24	163	Ruth	
31.18	159	9.6	161	2.12	41
32	159, 160,	9.10	159		
	166	9.13	161	1 Samuel/1 Kingdoms	
32.1	152, 159	17.3	160	1.1–2.11	129
32.4-6	160	18.15	151, 154,	2.31	39
			159, 166	23.8	65
32.4	159	18.16	159	23.19	85
32.6	159, 160	18.18	151	26.1	85
32.8	159	18.21	159	29.9	155
32.23	152, 159	26.5-9	163	31.11-13	126
32.34	159	28	86		
33.2	159	28.41	89	2 Samuel/2 Kingdoms	
33.3	161, 171	28.49-57	92	7.1-13	161
33.5	161, 171	28.58-68	86, 89,	12.11	39
33.7	160		91, 92,	14.17	155
34.9	161		118, 191	15.14	88
34.29-35	155	28.64	86, 89	17.13	66
38.18	135	31.14	160	18.33	43
40.34-35	177	31.18	160		
		31.29	173	1 Kings/3 Kingdoms	
Leviticus		32.11	41	1	56, 78
9.6	177	32.20	160	1.3-12	22
9.23	177	32.35	85, 92	1.28-53	56
21.23	135	32.47	159	2.28	169
24.3	135	32.49	160	5.10	158
26.1	173	33.2	159, 162	6.2	161
26.30	173	33.3	159	8	7, 170
26.31-33	92	33.6	162	8.4	169
26.41	161	33.26	97	8.11	177
		34.11	159	8.15-53	168

8.20	161	9.16-17	161	68.26 LXX	46
8.27	161, 170	9.18	160	68.34	97
9.1-9	44	9.26	36	72.19 LXX	84
9.6-9	92	9.29-30	161	73.7 LXX	169
9.6-9	86			73.12-17 LXX	97
11.31	39	*Esther*		74.12-17	97
17.19	14	5.2	155	75.10 LXX	183
18.4	36	13.14	155	76.9	183
18.13	36			76.18-21 LXX	97
19.10	36	*Job*		77 LXX	163
19.14	36	10.12	61	77.17-21	97
22.17	85			77.35 LXX	159
		Psalms		77.68-69 LXX	67
2 Kings/4 Kingdoms		14.1 LXX	169	78.1 LXX	90
6.14	64	16.8 LXX	40	81.1 LXX	183
8.11	59	17.6-19 LXX	97	81.4	183
8.12	66	17.8	40	81.8 LXX	183, 184
15.16	66	17.12 LXX	97	82.8	183
19.21	126	18.5-18	97	88.10 LXX	107
20.17	127	18.11	97	90.4 LXX	41
21.16	36	18.15 LXX	159	103.3 LXX	97
23.5	160	19.3 LXX	67	104 LXX	163
24.14	89	25.8 LXX	67, 177	104.3	97
		26.12 LXX	155	104.16-22 LXX	157
1 Chronicles		28.3 LXX	155, 164	104.21 LXX	156
22.6	161	30.6 LXX	185	104.24 LXX	158
		34.11 LXX	155	104.27 LXX	159
2 Chronicles		34.16 LXX	162	105 LXX	163
6.41-42	169	35.8 LXX	39-41	105.19 LXX	160
7.19-22	44	36.12 LXX	162	105.47 LXX	43
23.2	83	36.19 LXX	157	106.23-32 LXX	107
24.20-22	37	43.27 LXX	183	109.1 LXX	162, 181, 187
24.20-21	36, 37, 54, 190	44.26	183		
		45 LXX	108, 112, 113, 118	110	20
24.21	45			111.10 LXX	162
24.22	37	45.1-4 LXX	112	112.9 LXX	129
33.3	160	45.3 LXX	108	113.12 LXX	160
33.5	160	45.4 LXX	107	115.1 MT	49
36.21	84	45.5-8 LXX	112	117 LXX	49-51
		45.6 LXX	112, 117	117.19-27 LXX	51
Ezra		45.7 LXX	108	117.26 LXX	45, 48, 51, 53-55, 57, 58, 67, 71, 79, 174, 191, 193
9.7	87	56.2 LXX	40		
		60.5 LXX	40		
Nehemiah		62.3 LXX	162, 177		
1.4	59	62.8 LXX	40		
9.6-37	163	64.8 LXX	107		
9.12-21	159	67.35 LXX	97		

Psalms (cont.)		10.3	61, 92	49.6	4, 20		
118 LXX	20	10.11	173	51.15	107		
118 MT	49	10.16-19	121	52.12	43		
118.1 MT	49	13	94, 100	53.11	172		
118.15 MT	49	13.7-8	106	53.12	4, 13		
118.26	178	13.9-13	96	54.1	127		
118.27 MT	49	13.10	95, 98,	54.10	127		
118.27-28 MT	49		101, 105,	56.1	71		
127.5 LXX	67		111, 133	56.4-5	71		
131.5 LXX	161, 169	13.15	88	56.6-7	71		
131.6-10 LXX	76	15.5	85	56.7	69-72,		
131.8-10 LXX	169	16.12	161		77, 79,		
131.13-14 LXX	67	17.12-14	97		191		
133.3 LXX	67	17.12	107	56.8	71		
134.21 LXX	67	19.1	97, 173	59.19	177		
135 LXX	163	21.9	173	60.1-2	177		
136.1 LXX	59	24–27	99	61	20		
136.9 LXX	66	24	99	61.1-2	13		
137.1	59	24.18	107	61.2	92		
146.2 LXX	43	24.19	106, 107	63.4	92		
		24.23	177	63.10	161		
Proverbs		25.10	89	63.18	90		
14.5	155	26.6	89	64.10-11	45		
24.28	155	27.12	43	65.12	88		
		29.3	63, 64,	66	170, 174,		
Song of Songs			83		176, 193		
1.5	126	30.7	97	66.1-2	20, 153,		
2.7	126	31.5	42		154, 170,		
3.5	126	31.7	173		175, 193		
3.10	126	32.11	172	66.3-4	173, 175		
5.8	126	34	100	66.4-6	171		
5.16	126	34.4	95, 96,	66.6	170		
8.4	126		106, 108,	66.11	177		
			113	66.15	97		
Isaiah		34.8	92	66.18-19	177		
2.18	173	34.13	95				
3.13	182	35.2	177	*Jeremiah*			
3.25	88	36.2	116	2.2-5	164		
5.1-7	16	37.22	126	2.30	36		
5.1	121	37.27	121	4.7	84		
5.13	89	37.33-35	76	4.23-28	96		
5.30	107	37.33	63, 64	5.14	121		
6.1	67, 162	40–55	19	5.22	97, 107		
6.9-10	4	40.3-5	19	5.26-29	47		
8.5-8	97	40.5	177	5.29	92		
8.22	106, 107	46.2	89	6	61		
10	87	46.6	173	6.1-8	92		

6.6	61	18.20	182	34.1	83
6.8	61	19.6	126	34.21	85
6.10	161	19.13	160	37.3 LXX	127
6.11	61	19.46	193	38.4-6	36
6.13	47	20.4-6	87	38.6	67
6.14	61	21.7	88	38.27 LXX	126
6.15	61	21.8-10	85	38.31 LXX	126
7	75, 76, 174, 191, 193	21.14	121	38.35-37 LXX	109
		22.1-8	44	38.36 LXX	97, 107, 109
		22.1-2	44		
7.4	76	22.5	44, 45, 47	38.38 LXX	127
7.5-6	47			39.1-10 MT	87
7.6	76	22.7	47	41.1 LXX	83
7.8-15	92	22.9	47	41.21 LXX	85
7.9	75, 76	22.10	46	44.6	84
7.10-14	44	22.22	89	44.22	84
7.11	69, 70, 73, 75, 76, 79, 176, 191, 193	22.29	43	45.4-6 LXX	36
		23.5	126, 172	46.1-3 LXX	87
		23.7	126	46.10	85, 92
		25.29	90	48.12	127
		26.4-6	44	49.2	127
7.18	160	26.10 LXX	85, 92	49.8	85
7.20	121	26.19	92	50–52	87
7.26	78	26.20-23	36	50.6	85
7.32	126	27.6 LXX	85	50.27	92
8.2	160	27.21 LXX	86	50.31	86
8.23 LXX	59	27.27 LXX	92	51.6 LXX	84
9	125, 128, 130, 138, 190	27.29	64	51.6	85, 86, 92
		28.6 LXX	85, 86, 92		
				51.22 LXX	84
9.1	59	28.42	107	51.52	127
9.18 LXX	125	28.52 LXX	127	52.5	64
9.19 LXX	125	30.2 LXX	85	52.7	85
9.19	125	30.3	127		
9.20 LXX	125	30.18 LXX	127	*Lamentations*	
9.24 LXX	126	31	112	2.13	126
9.25	126	31.12 LXX	127	2.15	126
10.15	61	31.27	127	2.16	162
11.16	121	31.31	127	4.19	85
12.7	45	31.35 LXX	107		
13.17	59	31.35	97	*Ezekiel*	
14.12-18	88	31.35-37	109	1.21	183
14.17	59	31.38	127	2.12	183
15.2	89	32.15 LXX	90	4.2	63, 66, 79
16.4	88	33.4-6 LXX	44		
16.14	126	33.19 LXX	92	5.8	39
16.16	85	33.20-23 LXX	36	7.16	85

Ezekiel (cont.)

8.6	46			4.16 LXX	106, 109, 113, 118
9.1	86, 92			4.17 LXX	178
10	46, 47			4.21 LXX	178
10.1-22	46				
10.4	177				
10.18-19	46, 47				
10.18	44				
10.22-25	46				
10.22	155				
11.23	46, 47				
12.3	89				
17.24	120				
20	163				
20.47	120				
21.3 LXX	120, 121				
21.22	64				
21.27 LXX	64				
24.9-10	121				
32.7	95, 98, 105				
32.9	89				
39.23	88				
43.5	177				
44.4	177				

Hosea

9–10	121
9.7	85, 91, 92, 191
9.10	164
9.11-14	127
9.16	121
10	130, 174, 191, 193
10.1	121, 124, 130
10.2	130
10.5-6	130
10.8	127, 128, 130, 138, 173, 176, 190, 191
10.14	65-67, 79
13.4	160
13.16	65
14.1 LXX	65

Daniel

5.4	173
5.23	173
6.28	173
7	115, 116
7.13-14	162
7.13	110, 115-18
7.14	116
8.13-14	90
8.13	10
9.26	86, 92
11.31 LXX	84
12.7	90
12.11	84
12.11 LXX	84
12.11 Th.	84

Joel

1.1–2.27	96
1.12	121
1.19	121
2.10	101, 106, 109, 111, 133
2.28-32 ET	102
2.30-31 ET	105
2.31 ET	101, 133
2.32 ET	113
3–4 LXX	95
3.1-5 LXX	102
3.3-4 LXX	105
3.4 LXX	101, 133
3.5 LXX	105, 113, 118
3.15 ET	99, 106, 133
3.16 ET	109, 113
4.15 LXX	98, 99, 106, 111, 133

Amos

1.2	67
1.13	66
4.2	127
5	174, 193
5.19-20	85
5.25-27	153, 160, 167, 177, 191, 193
5.25-26	153
8.9	95, 133, 134
8.11	127
9.3	97
9.4	89
9.11-12	10
9.13	127

Micah

1	99
1.3-4	96
1.8	126
1.16	89
3.1	101
3.12	66, 78, 86, 92
4.8	126

Nahum

1.2-8	96
1.3-5	97
1.10	121
3.10	66
3.18	85

Habakkuk

2.11	58
3.1-15	97
3.10-11	98

Zephaniah		Judith		2 Maccabees	
1.2-3	96	5.6-21	163	1.27	43
1.5	160	5.11	158	2.7	78
1.15	133	8.18	173	2.18	43
3.14	126	10.19	158	5.27	85
				8.2	90
Haggai		Wisdom of Solomon		8.12	83
2	109	2–5	172	9.2	65
2.6-7	108	3.1	127	9.9	83
2.7	177	3.7	61		
		3.13	61	New Testament	
Zechariah		4.20–5.2	181	Matthew	
1.1	37	5.17-23	112	3.16	185
2.10	43	10–19	163	8.23-27	98, 101
3.1-8	182	12.8	83	14.22.23	98
3.1	182	14.8	173	21.5	55
6	78	41.12	83	21.8-9	58
8.1-8	92	48.12 LXX	83	21.9	56, 78
9.9	55-57, 78, 79, 126, 172, 192			21.13	70
		Sirach		23.34-36	35
		5.7	86, 92	23.35	37
		28.18	88	23.37-39	35
10.5	89	44–50	163	23.38	46
11.6	92	50.5	135	24	3
12.3	90			24.3	81
12.3 LXX	10	Baruch		24.29	106
12.10-14	125	5.1	155	24.31	43
12.10	125			26.61	78, 129
12.12	126	1 Maccabees		26.64	185, 186
14	50	1.22	135		
14.1	127	1.54	84	Mark	
14.2	89	2.28	85	1.10	131
14.5	85	2.52-60	163	1.15	103
14.10	83	3.45	90	1.33	43
		3.51	90	4.35-41	98, 101
Malachi		4.60	90	6.45-52	98
3.1-4	78	6.7	83	6.47-52	101
		7.10-11	116	7.1-23	4
Apocrypha/Deutero-Canonical Works		9.60	116	11.8-9	58
		10.33	89	11.10	56, 78
2 Esdras		11.63	116	11.12-14	55
1.30	42, 43	12.24	116	11.15-17	69
		12.42	116	11.17	70, 72
Tobit		13.12	116	11.20-24	55
1.4	67	15.13-14	64	13	3, 93, 98, 116
1.10	89				
14.5	78, 90			13.1-2	81

Mark (cont.)

13.3	81	2.41-49	73	13.33		36, 38
13.10	103	2.41-42	73	13.34-35		2, 3, 7, 8,
13.14	82, 84	2.46-49	1			35, 38,
13.16	82	3.4-6	19			53, 54,
13.17	82	3.21	185			138, 191
13.24-25	94, 100	4.9-12	1	13.34		36-39,
13.25	106	4.16-30	14, 19,			42, 43,
13.26	94, 116		73			45, 51,
13.27	43, 116	4.18-21	13			52, 54,
14.26	50	4.24	38			72, 172,
14.56	145	4.25-27	20			188, 189,
14.58	78, 129,	5.35	127			191, 192
	145	6.4	44	13.35		7, 38, 39,
14.60-61	145	6.9	172			44-46,
14.62	185, 186	6.35	161			48-53,
14.64	145	7.16	38			57, 58,
15.38	131	7.27	10			67, 79,
15.64	186	7.39	38			137, 139,
		8.10	4, 10			177, 178,
		8.22-25	98, 101			190, 191,
Luke		8.28	161			193
1–2	71	9.22	13, 36	14.1-24		73
1.5-38	22	9.26	180	14.32		60
1.5-6	73	9.31	180	17.20-37		3
1.8-22	1	9.44	13	17.22		127
1.10	73	9.51–19.44	18	17.37		2
1.11	73	9.51–19.27	1	18.8		180
1.13-17	13	10.21-24	73	18.38-39		57
1.13	73	11.47-48	38	19		6, 53, 77,
1.26-37	13	11.49-51	35-37,			78, 80,
1.27	20		54			91, 92,
1.32	161	11.49	37			118, 138,
1.35	161	11.51	37, 44			174
1.67-79	13	12.1	43	19.9		57, 172
1.69	172	12.8	179, 181,	19.11-27		57, 67
1.76	161		182	19.14		75
1.78-79	134	12.36-38	180	19.23		180
2.11	20	13	51, 145	19.27		75
2.14	61, 161	13.5	121	19.28-46		129, 138
2.22-38	1	13.6-9	121, 124	19.28-44		72
2.22-24	73	13.31-35	3, 35, 67,	19.28-40		191
2.23	10		70	19.28-39		79
2.24	73	13.31-33	35, 36	19.29-46		55
2.25-38	73	13.33-35	79, 174	19.29-44		71, 172
2.28-32	4, 73	13.33-34	36, 59,	19.29-40		55
2.37	73		162, 188,	19.30-40		192
2.39	73		190	19.30-37		192

19.30	56	20.6	88	21.20	82-84, 92, 102, 104
19.33	56	20.9-19	16, 75		
19.35	56	20.9-18	16, 67, 82	21.21	82, 84, 102
19.36	58				
19.37	56, 58	20.17	20, 78		
19.38-47	73	20.21-25	77	21.22-24	191
19.38	53, 54, 57, 60, 61, 71, 161, 193	20.37-39	175	21.22-23	127
		20.38	10	21.22	85, 91, 92, 193
		20.41-44	20		
		20.42	180	21.23-24	104
19.39	58	20.45	82	21.23	86, 89, 91, 104, 128
19.40-44	84	20.46–21.4	82		
19.40	58	20.46-47	75		
19.41-46	61	20.47–21.2	74	21.24-25	108
19.41-44	2, 6, 8, 55, 59, 67, 76, 79, 91, 105, 193	21	1, 3, 10, 81, 82, 85, 91, 98, 100, 101-103, 134, 138, 178, 184, 187	21.24	10, 87, 88, 103, 104, 115
				21.25-28	82, 93
				21.25-27	94, 98-102, 113, 116, 118, 191
19.41	46				
19.42-44	91, 190, 191, 193				
19.42	59-62, 65, 67, 71, 172, 192	21.5-36	18	21.25-26	104, 105, 109, 111-13, 115, 134
		21.5-7	6, 81, 102		
		21.5	74, 82		
19.43-44	59, 63, 66	21.6	91, 93, 127	21.25	102-109, 111, 114
19.43	63, 84, 127, 138	21.7	104, 116	21.26	106, 108, 113, 115, 116
		21.8-9	82		
19.44	59-62, 65, 67, 71, 79, 86, 91, 172, 192	21.8	82, 102		
		21.9-11	104	21.27-28	116, 117
		21.9	82, 102	21.27	102, 103, 110, 114-17, 175, 180, 184, 185, 187, 189
		21.12-19	82, 92, 102		
19.45-46	6, 68, 79, 190, 191	21.12	92, 104		
		21.15	155		
19.45	73	21.20-28	10, 81, 118		
19.46	44, 70, 73, 77, 174, 176, 191-94			21.28	102, 104, 105, 114, 116, 185
		21.20-26	114		
		21.20-24	2, 6, 8, 19, 82, 91, 102-105, 111, 118, 176, 190, 193	21.29-31	121
19.47	1, 2, 70, 73, 76, 190			21.31	104
				21.32	104
				22–23	144
20.1-47	2			22.3	134
20.4	88			22.31	134

Luke (cont.)		23.34	136, 145,	2	21, 178
22.37	4, 13		186	2.14-36	20
22.53	134	23.35-37	135	2.15	158
22.63-64	131	23.35	130	2.17-21	13, 102
22.63	145	23.36	135	2.19	105
22.66-71	3	23.37	130	2.21	172
22.66	145, 181	23.38	65, 129	2.22-23	172
22.67–23.2	129	23.39-43	130, 135,	2.22	158
22.67	186		137	2.24-33	117
22.69	145,	23.39	127, 130	2.32-36	20
	180-86	23.40-43	129	2.34	180, 181
22.71–23.1	145	23.42-43	137	2.36	172
22.71	145, 186	23.44-45	119, 131-	2.46	178
23	126, 130,		34	3–7	147
	136, 138	23.44	132	3.1	175, 192
23.13	122	23.45	132, 134,	3.11–4.2	1
23.14	129		135, 177,	3.11-26	2, 175,
23.21	122		190, 194		192
23.23-31	190	23.46	145, 185	3.12-15	172
23.23	122	23.47-48	129	3.13-15	166
23.25	122	23.47	135, 137,	3.14	172
23.26-49	134		172	3.22-23	38
23.26-31	119	23.50-53	135, 145	3.22	151, 166
23.26	122, 135	24	13	4	21
23.27-31	130	24.19	38	4.1-31	20
23.27-30	124	24.26	180	4.1-22	2
23.27-29	124-26	24.44-49	19	4.8-10	172
23.27-28	125	24.44	20	4.9	172
23.28-31	2, 8, 119,	24.47	19	4.10-11	178
	128, 130,	24.48-49	13	4.11	10, 20
	135,	24.53	1	4.12	172
	137-39,			4.23-31	187
	176, 191,	*John*		4.31	175
	192	1.51	185	5.12	2, 147,
23.28-30	130	6.16-21	98, 101		175, 192
23.28-29	46	10.24	83	5.17-42	2
23.28	124, 126,	12.15	55	5.20-26	1
	135			5.20-21	2, 175,
23.29	125, 127	*Acts*			192
23.30	127, 128,	1–7	1	5.30	172
	173, 174,	1.2	180	5.42	1
	191	1.6-8	19	6–7	7, 144,
23.31	119-22,	1.8	19, 175		147
	129, 135,	1.9-11	101, 184,	6.1-6	146
	191		187	6.1	147
23.33	122, 145	1.11	180	6.5	187
		1.22	180	6.8–7.1	144

6.8	159	7.9	164, 165,	7.38	159, 162
6.10	187		175	7.39-41	164, 174,
6.11–7.1	154	7.10	157, 165		191, 192
6.11-13	143	7.11	157	7.39-40	174, 176
6.11	143, 145	7.12	157	7.39	159
6.12	145, 181	7.13	157	7.40	147, 152,
6.13-14	1, 143	7.14	157		159
6.13	143, 145,	7.15	157	7.41	159, 161,
	154, 156,	7.16	157		173
	166, 171	7.17-43	158	7.42-43	142, 153,
6.14	3, 143,	7.17-19	158		160, 166,
	145, 155,	7.17	158		167, 190,
	184, 190	7.18	152, 158		193
6.15	155, 162,	7.19	158	7.42	154, 164
	187	7.20-29	158	7.43	168, 173
7	2, 3, 5-8,	7.20-21	158	7.44-50	167
	54, 77,	7.20	158	7.44-48	160
	80, 117,	7.21	158	7.44-47	166, 167
	131, 138,	7.23-24	158	7.44	160, 164,
	140, 146,	7.23	172		167
	149, 172,	7.24	165	7.45	160, 164
	174, 175,	7.25	165, 172	7.46-48	169
	182, 185-	7.26	158, 172	7.46-47	161
	94	7.27-28	147, 150,	7.46	160, 169,
7.1	145		151, 158,		178
7.2-34	144, 163		164, 165	7.47-48	170
7.2-8	155	7.27	151	7.47	169, 170
7.2-7	144	7.29	158	7.48-50	169, 171,
7.2-4	155	7.30-38	164		177
7.2	144, 155,	7.30-34	158, 175	7.48-49	171
	162, 175,	7.30	158	7.48	145, 161,
	177	7.31	149, 158		168, 169,
7.3	147, 148,	7.32-33	166		171, 173,
	155	7.32	147, 149,		174
7.4	148, 155,		158	7.49-50	20, 142,
	177	7.33	147, 150		153, 154,
7.5	147, 148,	7.34	147, 150		170, 174,
	155, 156	7.35	144, 147,		193
7.6-7	147, 149,		151, 159,	7.49	166
	156, 164		164-66	7.50	144, 171
7.6	149	7.36-50	144	7.51-56	161
7.7	10, 142,	7.36	159	7.51-53	142, 144,
	149, 166	7.37	38, 147,		168, 170,
7.8-53	144		151, 154,		171
7.8	156, 176		159, 164,	7.51-52	174
7.9-16	156		166		
7.9-10	156, 164	7.38-43	167		

Acts (cont.)

Ref	Pages
7.51	144, 161, 164, 170, 171, 173, 174, 176, 191
7.52	162, 171, 172, 181, 192
7.53	162, 168, 176, 191
7.54-60	144
7.54	145, 162
7.55-56	136, 178, 180, 181, 183, 185-87, 192
7.55	177, 181, 182, 184, 187
7.56	145, 181, 182, 184-87
7.57	143, 145, 186
7.58	145
7.59	136, 145, 185, 187
7.60	145
8.1	146
8.2	145
8.32-33	4, 21
9.2	19
10	4
10.11	185
10.42	183
11.27-28	13
13	21
13.16-31	20
13.46-47	19
13.47	4, 20
14.20	83
15	1
15.13-18	20
15.16-18	10
16.17	161
17	2
17.24	1
17.31	183
19.9	19
19.23	19
21	2
21.15–23.22	1
21.30	2
22.4	19
24.14	19
24.22	19
26.18	134
28	4
28.23-28	4
28.25-28	19

1 Corinthians

| 15 | 101 |

2 Corinthians

| 2.4 | 106 |

Ephesians

| 6.11-17 | 101 |

1 Thessalonians

2.14-16	48
4.13-18	101
4.15-17	117
5.8	101

2 Thessalonians

| 2.1 | 43 |

Hebrews

10.25	43
11.30	83
12.25-29	101

2 Peter

| 3.5-13 | 101 |

Revelation

4.1	185
4.3	64
4.4	64
4.8	64
6.16	128, 130
11.2	10, 103
12.1-17	101
13.1-18	101
19.11	185

Pseudepigrapha

1 Enoch

1.3-9	101
1.5	95, 101
6.2-8	95
12.3-6	95
14.3-6	95
15.4-16	95
24–25	78
39.7	42
48.10	115
52.4	115
60	50
62.1-12	183
80.4-7	95
89–90	78

2 Enoch

| 7.18 | 95 |

2 Baruch

| 1–8 | 78 |
| 36.1–37.1 | 95 |

3 Maccabees

| 2.2-12 | 163 |
| 6.17 | 83 |

4 Baruch

| 1–4 | 78 |

4 Ezra

| 13 | 115 |
| 14.19-31 | 163 |

4 Maccabees

| 3.13 | 83 |

Index of References

Apocalypose of Abraham
12.3-10	95
27	78

Assumption of Moses
3.11	159
7.6-10	74

Ezekiel the Tragedian
188-92	51

Jubilees
1.12	36
1.15-17	78
1.28	67
4.15	95
4.26	78
5.1	95
16	50

Liber Antiquitatum Biblicarum
11.5	98
23.10	98
32.7-8	98

Lives of the Prophets
23.1	38

Martyrdom of Isaiah
5.1-14	36

Psalms of Solomon
11.6	155
17	78
17.22	90
17.25	90
17.30	78

Sibylline Oracles
3.265-81	78
3.796	95
4.115-18	78

Testament of Judah
9.7	60

Testament of Levi
4.1-5	95

Testament of Moses
10.4-6	99-101
10.7	99
10.9-10	99
10.9	99

Testament of Naphthali
3.5	95

Testament of Reuben
5.6-7	95

QUMRAN
1QH
10.12-16	112
11.6-18	112
11.19-36	99, 100
11.19-28	99
11.29-36	99

1QM
2.5-6	78
7.10	78

1QpHab
8.8-12	74
8.12	74
9.4-5	74
9.5	74
10.1	74
12.8-9	74
12.10	74

4QpPs
37 3.11	78

11QTemple
29.8-10	78

CD
2.14–3.19	163

MISHNAH
Pesaḥim
5.7	50
10.5-7	50

Sanhedrin
6.1	143
7.4	143

Sukkah
3.9	50
4.1	50
4.5	50
4.8	50

TALMUD
b. Abodah Zarah
13b	42

b. Giṭṭin
57b	38

b. Ketubot
26a	74

b. Pesaḥim
118a	49
118b	49
57	74

b. Šabbat
31a	42

b. Sanhedrin
96b	38

b. Soṭah
13b	42

b. Yebamot
86a-b	74

y. Berakot
4b (2.4)	49

y. Ma'aserot
5.15	74

t. Mena'ot
13.22B-D   74

t. Zebaḥim
11.16-17   74

OTHER RABBINIC WORKS
Abot deRabbi Nathan
12a   42

Ecclesiastes Rabbah
3.16   38
10.4   38

Genesis Rabbah
47.10   42

Midrash Psalms
36 §6   49

Pesiqta deRab Kahana
16.1   42
17.7   49

Pesiqta Rabbati
14.2   42

Seder Eliyahu Rabbah
14 (F.65)   123

Sipra Qedoshim Pereq
8.205   42

Sipre Deuteronomy
32.2   42
296.3   42
306.4   42
314.1   42

Sipre Numbers
80.1   42

TARGUMS
Targum Jeremiah
7.9   75
7.11   75
8.10   75
23.11   75

PHILO
De vita Mosis
2.86   135

JOSEPHUS
Antiquities
3.80   98
3.84-88   163
4.40-49   163
5.60   98
5.205   98
6.24-28   63
6.27   98
6.377   126
8.75   135
10.38   36
14.105   74

14.110   74
14.415   76
15.345-48   76
18.4.1   78
20.180-81   74

War
5.466   62, 63
5.502-11   62
6.5.2   78
6.24-28   63
6.93   63
6.228   63
7.1-4   62, 63
7.375-77   62, 63

GREEK, ROMAN, CLASSICAL
Aristotle
Rhetoric
1.15.3   24
1.15.13-17   24

Eusebius
Historia ecclesiastica
2.23.4-18   185
2.23.13   186
2.23.16   186

Quintilian
Institutio oratoria
2.7.4   24

Index of Authors

Abasciano, B. J. 25
Adams, E. 81, 93, 95, 96, 97, 99-101, 111, 112
Ådna, J. 68, 69, 71, 72, 76, 77
Ahearne-Kroll, S. P. 26
Albl, M. C. 10
Alexander, J. A. 94
Alexander, L. C. A. 4
Allen, L. C. 49, 50, 113
Allison, D. C. 37, 38, 45, 49, 52, 71, 96
Almazán García, E. M. 30
Angel, A. R. 81, 94, 97-99, 101, 107, 109-14, 116, 117
Arai, S. 140
Attridge, H. W. 101
Aune, D. E. 184, 186

Bachmann, M. 141
Baldwin, J. T. 81, 103
Ballard, H. W. Jr. 112, 114, 116
Baltzer, K. 6, 7
Barrett, C. K. 8, 12, 73, 76, 140, 147, 149, 150, 152, 153, 155-57, 161, 166, 167, 169, 172, 179, 180, 184
Bauckham, R. 26, 43, 68, 69, 72, 78, 101
Beale, G. K. 131, 132, 136, 137, 170, 173, 179, 187
Beasley-Murray, G. R. 35, 46, 82, 93, 111
Benoit, P. 135, 137
Betz, H. D. 68
Bird, M. F. 3
Blenkinsopp, J. 56
Bloom, H. 15
Bloomquist, L. G. 18, 24, 81
Bock, D. L. 9-14, 21, 35, 37, 39, 41-46, 52, 56, 58, 59, 61-63, 65, 66, 68, 71, 73, 78, 81, 83-86, 88-90, 92, 93, 103, 105-108, 121-23, 125, 128, 131-35, 143, 144, 147, 155, 157, 159, 161, 164, 165, 167, 170, 179, 181, 186
Boismard, M. É. 140, 143, 171
Bolt, P. G. 94
Borg, M. J. 44, 46, 59, 63, 67-69, 76
Bovon, F. 63, 64, 73, 93, 113, 121, 125-27, 158, 193

Brandon, S. G. F. 68
Braumann, G. 93
Brawley, R. L. 5, 13, 15, 16, 33, 164
Brehm, H. A. 141, 143, 157, 163, 165, 174
Bridge, S. L. 3, 43, 81
Bright, J. 76
Brodie, T. L. 17, 18, 145
Brown, R. 122-24, 127-29, 131, 132, 134, 136-38, 187
Bruce, F. F. 2, 140, 141, 145, 146, 167, 169, 175, 179
Brueggemann, W. 76, 98, 112-14
Brunson, A. 49-51, 53, 57
Bryan, S. M. 62, 68, 71-73
Büchele, A. 122, 131, 133
Buckwater, D. 21
Bultmann, R. 39, 62
Buzzard, A. F. 81, 93

Cadbury, H. J. 3, 12
Caird, G. B. 95, 97, 112, 115, 120-23, 132, 134, 135
Carr, D. 61
Carrington, P. 94
Carroll, J. T. 53, 57, 93, 122
Casey, M. 68, 110
Catchpole, D. R. 57
Catto, S. K. 25
Chance, J. B. 2, 6, 73, 81, 90, 131, 134, 135, 141
Childs, B. S. 50, 173, 176
Clark, H. H. 24
Clarke, W. K. L. 9, 180
Clifford, R. J. 112
Collins, A. Y. 102
Collins, C. J. 177
Collins, J. J. 98-100, 102, 115, 116
Conzelmann, H. 5-7, 12, 69, 73, 93, 119, 143, 146, 149, 155, 157, 166, 179
Cook, S. L. 47
Craigie, P. C. 76, 112, 164
Creed, J. M. 61, 122
Croatto, J. S. 38

Crossan, J. D. 68
Crump, D. M. 179-82

Dahl, N. A. 12, 164, 166
Dahood, M. J. 49
Danker, F. W. 2, 58, 83, 93, 122, 125, 131
Davies, W. D. 37, 38
Day, J. 112
Denova, R. I. 14
deSilva, D. A. 140
Derrett, J. D. M. 57
Dibelius, M. 163
Doble, P. 20, 21, 129, 140, 141, 165, 169, 172, 175, 178, 181, 193
Dodd, C. H. 7, 10, 44, 63-65, 67, 83, 179
Drinkard, J. F. 76
Drury, J. 11
Dschulnigg, P. 140, 170
Duff, P. B. 116
Dunn, J. D. G. 68, 69, 78, 115, 140, 146, 169, 173
Dupont, J. 12, 62, 63, 140, 144, 193
Dyer, K. D. 94

Easter, M. C. 129, 137
Edwards, J. R. 41, 122, 123, 125, 135
Ellis, E. E. 5, 11, 44, 81, 82, 93, 103, 128, 132, 135
Ernst, J. 46, 52, 58
Esler, P. F. 146
Eubank, N. 145
Evans, C. A. 11, 14, 50, 68, 74-76, 78, 82, 116
Evans, C. F. 18, 43, 60, 68, 75, 93, 103, 123, 124, 135

Fantin, J. D. 28
Fay, R. C. 6
Fisk, B. N. 1, 36, 38, 44-47, 52, 53, 59, 60, 131
Fitzmyer, J. A. 5, 10, 12, 23, 35, 44-46, 56, 58, 61, 63, 65, 66, 81, 83, 85, 88-90, 93, 103-108, 113, 114, 120-23, 125, 126-29, 133-35, 144, 145, 147, 149, 155-62, 173, 181, 193, 194
Fletcher-Louis, C. H. T. 114, 187
Flükiger, F. 63
Focant, C. 145, 179
Foerster, W. 43

France, R. T. 56, 84, 94, 95, 100, 115, 128, 130
Fredriksen, P. 68
Frein, B. C. 12
Furlong, A. 28, 31, 32
Fusco, V. 81, 93, 102, 103, 114

Gaston, L. 2, 52, 58, 59, 89, 122, 169
Gaventa, B. R. 168, 172, 177
Geiger, R. 93
Geldenhuys, N. 44, 52, 83, 93, 132
Gerrig, R. J. 24
Gibbs, J. A. 94
Gibbs, R. W. Jr. 31, 33
Giblin, C. H. 7, 39, 44, 63, 66, 81, 82, 86, 102-104, 119, 121, 123, 129
Goldingay, J. 112, 115, 169, 183
Gombis, T. G. 116
Gould, E. P. 94
Goulder, M. D. 93, 131
Gray, T. C. 69, 77
Green, G. L. 28, 30, 48
Green, J. B. 5, 15, 17, 44, 53, 56, 52, 58, 60, 62-64, 67, 68, 73, 75, 82, 85, 88, 90, 92, 93, 103, 106, 114, 122, 123, 125, 126, 129-34, 136, 137, 172, 173, 181
Green, K. 28
Gregory, A. F. 3
Grogan, G. 112
Grundmann, W. 93
Gunkel, H. 97
Gurtner, D. M. 131, 135, 136
Gutt, E.-A. 28

Habel, N. C. 98
Haenchen, E. 5, 141, 143, 146, 156, 166, 169, 175
Hallett, T. J. 184
Hannah, D. D. 183
Harris, J. R. 10
Hartman, L. 10, 83, 89, 91, 92, 111
Hastings, A. 61
Hatina, T. R. 93-95, 98, 99, 101, 102, 115
Hay, D. M. 182
Hayes, J. H. 112
Hays, R. B. 13, 15-17, 34
Hayward, R. 75
Head, P. 1, 2, 6, 8, 44-46, 135
Heil, J. P. 24

Index of Authors

Hemer, C. J. 193
Hengel, M. 23, 142, 146
Hill, C. G. 146, 147, 169
Hollander, J. 15, 16
Holmås, G. O. 2, 73, 175
Holmén, T. 74
Holtz, T. 128
Hooker, M. 68, 70, 124
Hoppe, L. J. 112, 114
Humphrey, E. M. 178, 179, 185
Hunt, J. H. 173
Hurst, L. D. 115
Hutcheon, C. R. 6

Instone Brewer, D. 11

Jeremias, J. 44, 49, 69
Jobes, K. H. 28
Johnson, L. T. 3, 4, 10, 21, 38, 41, 59, 61, 69, 88, 89, 92, 93, 140, 144, 145, 147, 148, 158, 159, 162, 166, 170, 172, 175, 177, 180-83, 193
Juel, D. H. 13

Käser, W. 127
Kalimi, I. 144
Keel, O. 184
Keener, C. S. 26, 149, 158, 172, 173, 183
Kelle, B. E. 114
Kelley, P. H. 76
Kennedy, G. A. 143
Kilgallen, J. J. 140, 141, 143, 155, 165, 166, 170, 174, 181
Kilpatrick, G. D. 180
Kimball, C. A. 11, 12, 23, 81
Kinman, B. 49, 55-60
Klangwisan, Y. 28
Klijn, A. F. J. 140, 169
Kloppenborg, J. S. 39
Knowles, M. 59
Koet, B. J. 4, 5, 70, 168
Kristeva, J. 15
Kümmel, W. G. 44
Kurz, W. 12

Lachs, S. T. 106
Lagrange, M.-J. 122, 126
Lappenga, B. J. 27, 28
Larkin, W. J. Jr. 179

Larsson, E. 141, 142, 147, 169
Le Cornu, H. 164, 165
Le Donne, A. 51, 78, 177, 178
Leaney, A. R. C. 93
Lieu, J. 93, 122, 128, 135
Lindars, B. F. C. 49, 53
Litwak, K. D. 11, 13, 15, 22, 23, 56
Loisy, A. F. 120
Longman, T. 116
Luckensmeyer, D. 48

Mabie, F. J. 97, 100, 112
Macintosh, A. A. 130
Maddox, R. 93
Malherbe, A. J. 48
Mallen, P. 9, 11, 13, 19-21, 147, 148, 155-57, 164, 170
Mann, C. S. 94
Manson, T. W. 44, 52, 59, 122
Marguerat, D. 4
Marshall, I. H. 9, 37-39, 41, 42, 44, 45, 52, 53, 56, 61, 63, 65, 66, 81, 83, 85, 93, 103, 113, 114, 116, 122, 128, 131, 135, 141, 145, 147, 152, 153, 155-62, 164, 167, 170, 175, 179, 180
Matera, F. J. 133, 134
Matthews, S. 141, 144, 169, 172, 185, 186
Maxwell, K. R. 26
McConville, J. G. 86
McKane, W. 76, 130
McLay, T. 10
McNicol, A. J. 10
Meadowcroft, T. 28
Meek, J. A. 11-13
Meier, J. P. 14
Metzger, B. M. 35, 46, 132, 145, 151, 152
Miller, R. J. 39
Moessner, D. P. 3, 18, 22, 23, 44, 140, 144
Moffitt. D. M. 59
Moo, D. J. 126
Morgen, M. 81, 85, 88, 90
Morris, L. 132
Motyer, S. 131
Mowinckel, S. 49
Moyise, S. 14-17
Myers, J. M. 42

Neagoe, A. 141, 169, 175
Nelson, R. D. 41
Nestle, E. 179
Neudorfer, H.-W. 141
Neusner, J. 69, 77
Neyrey, J. H. 119, 121-25, 128
Noh, E.-J. 33
Nolland, J. 39, 41, 44, 45, 49, 61, 62, 64, 66, 78, 81, 83-85, 87-90, 93, 102-108, 111, 122, 123, 125, 127, 128, 131-36, 181, 187

Ollenburger, B. C. 112
Ooi, V. K. H. 161, 166, 169
Oswalt, J. N. 42, 95
Owen, H. P. 180, 184, 187

Paesler, K. 69, 77
Page, T. E. 180
Pao, D. W. 9, 19-21, 36, 38, 39, 41, 42, 44, 45, 56, 58, 59, 61-66, 83-88, 90, 92, 105-108, 121, 125-27, 129, 130, 133, 134, 141, 193
Parsons, M. C. 3, 26, 144, 155, 163, 164, 166, 168, 170, 179, 180, 182
Patella, M. 119, 122, 131, 133, 134
Pattemore, S. W. 28, 30
Pearson, B. A. 48
Penley, P. T. 10, 35
Penner, T. C. 23, 141, 143, 144, 146, 164-66, 171, 173, 177, 178
Perrin, Nicholas 68, 69, 71, 74, 75
Perrin, Norman 186
Pervo, R. I. 3, 144, 170, 172, 193
Pesch, R. 179
Peterson, D. G. 155, 162, 164, 166, 168, 170, 172, 179
Phillips, T. E. 3
Pilkington, A. 28, 29, 31-33
Piper, R. A. 39
Pitre, B. J. 119, 121, 124, 127, 129
Plummer, R. L. 39, 41, 42, 52, 58, 93, 103, 121, 131, 135
Polhill, J. B. 143, 170, 179
Porter, S. E. 12

Raabe, P. R. 96
Rackham, R. B. 4
Rad, G. von 111

Ramaroson, L. 140
Reitzel, F. X. 8
Rese, M. 13
Reynolds, B. E. 185
Richard, E. 140, 143, 144, 147-50, 153, 155-63, 167, 169, 179
Richards, C. 28
Richardson, A. 179
Richardson, P. 77
Ringgren, H. 10
Robb, J. E. 172, 174
Robbins, V. K. 4
Roberts, J. J. M. 112
Roloff, J. 141, 169
Rosner, B. S. 23
Ross, J. M. 37
Rowe, C. K. 3, 4
Rudman, D. 133, 134, 136
Rusam, D. 53, 125, 127, 130
Russell, J. S. 94

Sabbe, M. 144, 179, 181, 183
Sanders, E. P. 68, 75, 77, 78
Sanders, J. A. 11, 49, 56-58
Sanders, J. T. 141
Schnabel, E. J. 9, 36, 38, 39, 41, 42, 44, 45, 56, 58, 59, 61-66, 83-88, 90, 92, 105-108, 121, 125-27, 129, 130, 133, 134
Schneider, G. 58, 122, 179
Schubert, P. 12
Schulz, S. 37, 38
Schweizer, E. 53, 56, 69, 81, 93
Scott, J. J. Jr. 172, 175
Shulam, J. 165
Simon, M. 169
Slater, T. B. 115
Sleeman, M. 141, 166, 169, 178
Smith, N. 27
Soards, M. L. 119, 122, 124, 126, 128, 129, 143, 149, 177
Sommer, B. D. 33
Song, N. S. 28, 31
Spencer, F. S. 4, 173, 193
Spencer, P. E. 3
Sperber, D. 27-29, 31-33
Stamps, D. L. 9, 23, 24
Stanley, C. D. 23-26
Steck, O. H. 39, 44

Stenschke, C. W. 25
Stepp, P. 4
Sterling, G. E. 4, 119, 157, 163, 175
Stevens, B. A. 116
Stevenson, G. 168
Steyn, G. J. 12, 14, 18
Strauss, M. L. 21, 52
Stuart, D. 67, 105, 130, 167
Sweeney, J. P. 141, 170
Sylva, D. D. 131, 132, 136, 140, 143, 161, 167-70

Talbert, C. H. 4, 13, 14
Tan, K. H. 35, 36, 39, 43-45, 52, 55, 56, 68-70, 72, 73
Tannehill, R. C. 3, 4, 127, 144, 145, 164-66, 168, 171, 176, 177, 179
Tannen, D. 22, 23
Tasker, R. V. G. 94
Taylor, N. H. 1, 3, 7, 83, 129, 137, 141, 167, 169, 173
Tendahl, M. 31, 33
Tiede, D. L. 23, 57, 59, 60, 122, 123, 127, 128
Tiemeyer, L.-S. 47, 76
Tödt, H. E. 179
Todorov, T. 28
Trocmé, E. 73
Trotter, D. 28
Tsumura, D. 97, 112
Tuckett, C. M. 21
Tull Willey, P. 15, 33
Turner, M. 19, 21, 37, 178
Tyson, J. B. 26, 131, 193

Uchida, S. 28
Untergassmair, F. G. 119

Van De Sandt, H. 141, 152, 161, 167-70, 173, 176
Van Iersel, B. 94
Van der Henst, J.-B. 27
Van der Waal, C. 7
Verheyden, J. 3, 111, 113

Wagner, J. R. 49-51, 53, 56, 58
Walker, P. W. L. 6, 7, 92, 103, 104, 114, 122, 123, 125, 141, 145
Walpole, A. S. 180
Walton, S. 2, 4, 8, 146, 147, 168, 169, 175, 187
Wanamaker, C. A. 48
Watson, A. 141
Watson, R. S. 97, 98, 112
Watts, J. D. W. 176
Weinert, F. D. 6, 44, 140
Weinfeld, M. 112
Wenham, D. 10
Wiens, D. 140, 141
Wilcox, M. 10, 149, 151
Williams, D. J. 180
Wilson, A. I. 94-96, 100, 102, 115
Wilson, D. 27-33
Wilson, S. G. 180
Witherington, B. 5, 24, 69, 141, 143-45, 147, 168-70, 172, 175, 176, 179, 193
Wolfe, R. F. 144
Wright, N. T. 19, 43, 44, 46, 51, 63, 69, 71, 73, 76-78, 92, 94, 95, 99, 115, 122, 130

Yoder Neufeld, T. R. 116

Zeitlin, S. 50
Zmijewski, J. 82, 103